S0-AHG-835

THE QUEEN

John Parker has been a journalist all his working life and his varied career has taken him from local newspapers in Northamptonshire where he trained, to international assignments, including investigative work for *Life* magazine. Back in England, he spent almost twenty years in Fleet Street, latterly in senior editorial roles, before becoming a full-time author in 1987. His daily involvement in news and current affairs resulted in a series of successful books, published worldwide, including a quartet on members of the royal family: the bestselling *King of Fools*, a biography of the Duke of Windsor, *The Princess Royal*, *Prince Philip* and now, *The Queen*.

Also by John Parker

King of Fools
The Princess Royal
Five for Hollywood
The Trial of Rock Hudson
Prince Philip: A Biography
The Joker's Wild

The Queen
The New Biography

John Parker

HEADLINE

Copyright © 1991 John Parker

The right of John Parker to be identified as the Author of the Work has been asserted by him in accordance with the Copyright, Designs and Patents Act 1988.

First published in 1991
by HEADLINE BOOK PUBLISHING PLC

First published in paperback in 1992
by HEADLINE BOOK PUBLISHING PLC

10 9 8 7 6 5 4 3 2

All rights reserved. No part of this publication may be reproduced, stored in a retrieval system, or transmitted, in any form or by any means without the prior written permission of the publisher, nor be otherwise circulated in any form of binding or cover other than that in which it is published and without a similar condition being imposed on the subsequent purchaser.

ISBN 0 7472 3809 X

Picture research by Ivor Game

Typeset by Avocet Typesetters, Bicester, Oxon

Printed and bound in Great Britain by
HarperCollins Manufacturing, Glasgow

HEADLINE BOOK PUBLISHING PLC
Headline House
79 Great Titchfield Street
London W1P 7FN

Contents

List of Illustrations

Prologue

It was a filthy, chilly spring and the economy was as miserable as the climate. The miners were threatening a strike if their wages were cut again and the Trades Union Congress debated whether to bring the rest of the nation's industrial workers out in support. The army had been alerted by the government, ready to be called into action if there was a general strike, and thousands of troops were camped in readiness in Hyde Park. But in a house in West London, number 17 Bruton Street, which was three-quarters of a mile from Buckingham Palace, there was concern only for the health of the Duchess of York, expecting her first baby. Words were not minced; they spoke quietly of internal complications – a breechbirth. Doctors were in constant attendance, and in the evening of 20 April, three of the most eminent specialists in the land hurried to the house, and upstairs to the shaded room where the young mother to be lay in desperate pain on her canopied bed. They decided a Caesarian operation was necessary and the throng of people who waited outside, stood silent and anxious, well into the night. Some drifted away but there was still a crowd in the street when the healthy cry of a newborn baby was heard at precisely 2.40 a.m. on 21 April 1926. The Secretary of State for Home Affairs, Sir William Joynson-Hicks, was on hand to witness the birth, as was the custom until it was abrogated in 1948 when the baby had one of her own; a daughter to Elizabeth, Duchess of York. The child was wrapped in a white muslin blanket and shown to all concerned and the Secretary of State was able to do his duty and report to the Prime Minister that only one was born. A medical bulletin had been prepared to say that a 'certain line of treatment' had been used for the birth, indicating that it was by Caesarian section. The people of the nation had followed the pregnancy with avid interest; the Duke of York, or 'Bertie' as he was well known, and his 'Dainty Duchess' had become the most popular young couple in the country since their marriage in April 1923.

The King and Queen were informed of the birth immediately by telephone at Windsor Castle. Queen Mary was overjoyed, and hardly had any sleep for the rest of the night. It was one of those fatalistic coincidences that later in the day two guests were to arrive at Windsor for lunch with the Queen: Princess Andrew of Greece and the Dowager Marchioness of Milford Haven – the mother and grandmother of the newborn baby's future husband.

No one would have predicted then that the infant would, when she was ten, become heiress presumptive and when she was twenty-five become Queen of Great Britain, Northern Ireland, the Dominions and the Commonwealth, go on to rank among the longest-ruling British monarchs, be served by at least nine British prime ministers (probably more) and sit upon her throne for a reign packed with event upon event that would be comparable to that of her ancestor, the first Elizabeth who ruled for forty-five years.

There was no reason to suspect that the child, born at the London home of her maternal grandparents, Lord and Lady Strathmore, would come anywhere near eventual succession; only one newspaper, the *Daily Mail*, ventured the suggestion, 'The baby who was the chief topic of conversation throughout the kingdom yesterday could conceivably become Queen of England.' No one paid that suggestion much regard. At the time, the heir apparent to King George V was his eldest son Edward, Prince of Wales and Mrs Wallis Warfield Spencer was four thousand miles away, in the process of divorcing her first husband and about to cast an eye in the direction of her second, a married man named Ernest Simpson. True, the Prince of Wales was unmarried in 1926 and had already caused a few raised eyebrows over his friendships with other men's wives but he was the most eligible bachelor in England, and probably the world; there was no reason to believe that he might not shortly choose a bride who would become his queen and produce his own line of succession which would take precedence over all others. He would be encouraged by his entire family to do so, even to the point when his closest friend and cousin Lord Louis Mountbatten produced a list of suitable European princesses he might consider.

Yet, for those who cared to remember, and dare recall publicly, there was a remarkably accurate prediction to be found in the records of the House of Commons. It was uttered by Mr Keir Hardie, MP, a founder of the British Labour Party, who rose to comment on the birth of Prince Edward in June 1894. He was uncannily clairvoyant in his observations:

> The fierce white light that we are told beats upon the throne reveals things . . . which are better to keep covered. The assumption is that the newly born child will be called upon some day to reign over this Empire but up to the present we certainly have no means of knowing his qualifications or fitness for this position. From childhood, this boy will be surrounded by sycophants and flatterers and will be taught to believe himself to be of superior creation. In due course . . . he will be sent on a tour around the world and probably rumour of a morganatic marriage will follow and in the end it will be the country which is called upon to pay the bill.

The prediction was written down and possibly forgotten by 1926 when a new royal child came upon this earth and no one would have said as they gathered for the christening of the baby princess, Elizabeth Alexandra Mary, that the infant baptised in the blue and gold private chapel at Buckingham Palace was a future queen, least of all her father Bertie, Duke of York. He was a peaceable kind of man, simple in thought, deed and desire and roused to excitement only when his brother the Prince of Wales encouraged him to join him galloping through the Leicestershire countryside with the Belvoir or the Quorn to blow away the cares of state.

His wife Elizabeth looked demure but she had strength and enough, it turned out, for both of them; enough to launch her husband into a life he had not anticipated and to launch her daughter, prematurely, into one that she had.

They were called into royal duties, of course, since the Duke of York was then second in line to the throne. And so, as one of the top three, he had duties to perform. On 6 January 1927 he and the duchess sailed from Southampton aboard the battle cruiser *Renown* for a 6-month tour of the Antipodes, to visit the Dominions and open the Australian Parliament in the new capital of Canberra. The infant princess was left in the care of the nursery staff, and the grandparents – King George V and Queen Mary and Lord and Lady Strathmore. 'I quite felt it, leaving on Thursday,' the duchess wrote to Queen Mary, 'the baby was so sweet, playing with the buttons on Bertie's uniform, that it quite broke me up.' Little more than a quarter of a century later, the role would be reversed and 'the baby' would be starting an almost identical trip, lasting just as long – leaving her own two children with their grandmother.

On their return from their important and successful tour, the Duke and Duchess of York gave Princess Elizabeth her first starring role on the balcony at Buckingham Palace, when cheering crowds welcomed them home on 27 June 1927; the overseas journeys took so long in those days that a public welcome home was invariably arranged. Queen Mary held the baby under an umbrella on the typical drizzling English summer's day.

The Yorks' first home was ready upon their return and their baby daughter had already moved into 145 Piccadilly with its huge nursery at the top of the house, light and airy overlooking treetops, along with the nurse and servants. Her parents remained in constant demand and Elizabeth spent her early days alternating between Piccadilly and the homes of her grandparents. However, the duchess kept total charge of her daughter's upbringing and was unremitting in her wish to see that she was surrounded by every normal homely influence that was possible, given their enforced lifestyle. She wanted to ensure that her daughter would grow up neither spoiled nor spiteful, which were common traits in young gels of the upper classes.

She would also try to shield her daughter from the public glare and keep her life as quiet and simple as possible. Her grandfather King George V doted on the toddling princess and when he was taken seriously ill in the autumn of 1928 and went to Bognor for a long convalescence, his granddaughter kept him company there at his own request. He called her Lilibet, which was her own first spoken version of her name, and thus she remained to her family for the rest of her life, even to nieces and nephews who addressed her as Aunt Lilibet.

She was four when Margaret was born in August 1930. Eventually, they became the best of friends, more than just sisters. Partly because of their isolation during these early years, followed by their confinement within the walls of Windsor Castle during the war, Margaret was to be Elizabeth's closest companion until the day she married. When their elder daughter was six, the Duke and Duchess of York were given the Royal Lodge at Windsor Great Park by George V as their country home and it was here that, above all, the small family – 'just the four of us' as the duke recalled when he was George VI – spent some idyllic days, with all kinds of pets, dogs and ponies for the two sisters to enjoy. They also had their own little thatched 'house', a miniature one which they could walk into, presented to the princess by the people of Wales on her sixth birthday.

Education was rather relaxed and informal. Like all royal children up until Prince Charles and Princess Anne, neither Elizabeth nor Margaret went to school. Instead, the Duchess of York spent time with them and in 1933, when Elizabeth was seven a governess was appointed; Miss Marion Crawford came as a live-in tutor and general carer. In a room one floor below the nursery at the house in Piccadilly, a small schoolroom was set up. Elizabeth had the undivided attention of 'Crawfie' for lessons, which were conducted with discipline as near school-like as possible. Margaret joined her a year or so later.

The children were seldom seen by the public. They would be photographed with their parents going to church when they were holidaying at Sandringham, the royal estate in Norfolk, or their Scottish home of Balmoral; otherwise they continued to lead a fairly sheltered life. Public appearances tended to be only for family occasions, such as in 1934, when Princess Elizabeth was bridesmaid at the wedding of her uncle, George, Duke of Kent to Princess Marina of Greece, and again the following year when another uncle, Henry, Duke of Gloucester married Lady Alice Scott. She had also experienced one of the great royal celebrations of the age, with all the pomp and ceremonial that can be mustered by British royalty, for the Silver Jubilee of her grandfather King George V, at which Elizabeth and Margaret rode in the carriage with their parents in the procession to St Paul's Cathedral for a service of thanksgiving. This was her first real experience of the life that lay before her, riding past cheering crowds, one wave after another. That noise, the cheering, is all she would ever hear as she drove past on so many state occasions. And the sea of faces when she appeared on the balcony at Buckingham Place later with the King and Queen, the Prince of Wales and her mother and father, was a scene which she would preside over many, many times in the future.

The King looked happy, and healthy. Though his cheeks were tinged with blue, it was not a worrying sign because they always had been. Not many months had passed, however, before the King died. On Friday, 17 January, 1936, Elizabeth, then nine years old, was playing with her sister in the snow at Sandringham when she looked up and saw her grandmother, Queen Mary, crossing the lawn towards her. With her characteristic directness and sense of occasion, Queen Mary explained that the King was very ill. She allowed Elizabeth and Margaret to put the finishing touches to their snowman, then took them inside and later escorted Elizabeth to his bedside for what was to be her last farewell. Straightaway, Elizabeth and Margaret were put in a car and taken to Windsor. The public announcement merely said the King was suffering from a cold. He died at 11.55 p.m. on Monday, 20 January – eased to the other side, we learned later, by injections of three-fourths of a gram of morphia and one gram of cocaine thus hastening his anticipated demise so that the news would make the morning papers instead of the 'less appropriate' evening editions.

At that moment, Elizabeth became second in line to the throne by virtue of the fact that the new King, her Uncle

David, was still unmarried. His family had despaired that he would ever find a bride and his mother worried that his current infatuation with Mrs Wallis Simpson, the third and most public of his affairs with married women, would be the ruination of him. Perhaps she never really believed her son would betray the family and the nation, renounce his birthright, his duty and service to which he had been trained, simply for the fascination of 'that woman' but, of course, he did and on 10 December 1936 spoke over the radio the words 'You must believe me when I tell you that I have found it impossible to carry the heavy burden of responsibility and to discharge my duties as king as I would wish to do, without the help and support of the woman I love.' It was being billed as the greatest love story of the century; it had a darker side that no one, except a few in the inner circle, would discover until many years later. Only the royals and a few in government knew what Mrs Simpson was and had been, or of her dubious friendships at the German and Italian embassies or the hold she had over the King.

The Duke and Duchess of York reluctantly assumed the mantle they had never dreamed would come their way and Elizabeth became heiress presumptive. The reasons for it, and the implications, were perhaps too confusing for such a young mind. To her, Uncle David was a jolly little man who came to tea occasionally. But on the last occasion she saw him, she did not have tea with him. She remembered vaguely catching sight of Wallis Simpson when the King brought her to her parents' home at the Royal Lodge on that day and Elizabeth and her sister were ushered outside. 'Now you two, have tea in your own little house,' their mother said. And Crawfie hurried them away without either meeting the woman who got out of the car with her hand resting on Uncle David's arm. 'Who is that lady?' she asked Crawfie. No one of importance, she was informed, as she was shepherded quickly out of sight. No one of importance.

In the gloom of that December, with a mist of uncertainty and wondering that encircled them all, it was left to Crawfie to try eventually to explain to Elizabeth what was going on, and she had sufficient grasp of the situation to write a note about 'Abdication Day' – the major consequence of which, for her family, was that they would move immediately from the cosy, protective warmth of 145 Piccadilly into the vast and often cold Buckingham Palace. 'What, for always . . .?' she asked Crawfie. 'Yes,' said her governess. 'Uncle David is going away for a long time.' On the 12th, the little princess peeked through the banisters as she watched her father dressed as admiral of the fleet, nervously leaving for the Proclamation of his Accession.

'When he returns,' said Crawfie, 'he will be King and you will have to curtsy to him every day of your life.'

The coronation that was to have been her uncle's became her father's and Elizabeth and her sister walked in the great procession ahead of Queen Mary along the nave at Westminster Abbey. Later, back at the palace, there was another balcony appearance to placate the massive crowds outside, stretching as far as the eye could see down the Mall, and the two princesses were given a special cheer to themselves. The following day, in the schoolroom, Elizabeth wrote an essay on her father's Coronation, which is now preserved in the Royal Archives at Windsor. It was headed 'To Mummy and Papa, in memory of their Coronation' and began:

> At 5 o'clock in the morning I was woken up by the band of the Royal Marines striking up just outside my window. I leapt out of bed and so did Bobo (Margaret 'Bobo' Macdonald who joined the Yorks' staff as undermaid, and was destined to become Elizabeth's closest companion, apart from her sister, for the next four decades). We put on our dressing gowns and shoes and Bobo made me put on the eiderdown as it was so cold and we crouched in the window looking onto a cold, misty morning. There were already some people in the stands . . . Every now and then we were hopping in and out of bed looking at the bands and the soldiers.

An immediate effect of the abdication was that Elizabeth would have to be protected from the fierce white light which would now shine upon her as her father's successor. She had to be prepared for her abnormal position and Queen Elizabeth fought against any dramatic change. In fact, life went on for Princess Elizabeth pretty much as before. There were additional playmates being brought into the palace through the formation of a Girl Guide troop and when the family were at Windsor she took part in local dramatic productions and the annual pantomime. She was also a keen horsewoman and did well in the local gymkhanas.

Elizabeth was thirteen at the outbreak of war, and on holiday with her sister at Balmoral where they remained until Christmas. They came back south to the Royal Lodge at Windsor for the subdued festivities and by the time of her fourteenth birthday in April the 'phoney' war of inactivity was already drawing to its close. Belgium was invaded by the Germans on 10 May 1940 and the next day the two young princesses were moved into Windsor Castle which would be their home for the duration. The King and Queen had made the decision of not sending the children away to Canada, as had been suggested, though their whereabouts was kept secret. Their shelter was within the sturdy battlements of the castle, where the Crown Jewels were also stored, wrapped unceremoniously in newspaper and stacked in packing cases deep in the castle vaults. The Nazi propagandist Dr Goebbels announced several times over the radio that the King's children had been sent to America and everyone in Windsor laughed.

That October, with so many children being evacuated, Princess Elizabeth made her first broadcast. It was regarded as her official entry into public life. She sent the unhappy evacuees on their way with this message:

> I feel I am speaking to friends and companions who have shared with my sister and myself many a happy *Children's Hour*. Thousands of you in this country have had to leave your homes and be separated from your fathers and mothers. My sister Margaret Rose and I feel so much for you, as we know from experience what it means to be away from those we love most of all. To you living in new surroundings, we send a message of true sympathy and at the same time we would like to thank the kind people who have welcomed you into their homes.

In these early teenage years, her education was broadened by the addition of a further tutor to her study programme,

Sir Henry Marten, the Provost of nearby Eton. It entailed an expansion of her history lessons, for which Marten was renowned, and long discussions on current events and the development of the war. And so her schoolroom studies were based upon the background of the war, involving as it did reflections on the past animosity, involving her own German relations, from which Hitler's rise to power had stemmed. She also had specialist subjects for study, such as the British Constitution and Anglo-American relations.

As the threat of invasion lifted, Elizabeth was allowed to join activities which would broaden her contact with the outside world, which had been virtually nil during the first two years of the war, such as the Sea Rangers and in February 1942, as she approached her sixteenth birthday, she was given her first military rank as honorary colonel of the Grenadier Guards. Her first ceremonial came on the day of her birthday when she was given the official task of inspecting the regiment. She also went to Windsor Labour Exchange later that week in Girl Guide uniform to register under the youth registration scheme. It was really the start of her increasing involvement in what her father described as the family firm and very soon she would find herself plunged in at the deep end, with an increasing round of engagements. The royal family was thin on the ground by the middle of the war and Princess Elizabeth also found herself representing her father while he was away visiting troops in the Mediterranean. In July 1943, she acted as a Counsellor of State and during the same year she embarked on a range of appearances, largely connected with young people and charitable work. The words 'service' and 'duty' were not very often spoken, but she knew full well what they meant in terms of her immediate family's relationship with the public at large. She was brought into the social world of the King and Queen and on May Day 1944 she attended her first official dinner, placed between General Jan Smuts and Mackenzie King, two of the four Dominion prime ministers then in London. Next, she was installed as President of the National Society for the Prevention of Cruelty to Children and gave her presidential address at the Mansion House. The preparation was progressing steadily.

Her first solo full dress public engagement came in August

when, accompanied only by a lady in waiting and a detective, she went to Greenock to launch the battleship HMS *Vanguard*. In the midst of this activity, she was pestering her father to be allowed to join the ATS; the King was dubious because of all the other tasks she had become involved in, but finally relented. The age of call-up for all young people was eighteen and the princess did not want to be an exception. She was gazetted second subaltern in March 1945 and sent to No. 1 Mechanical Transport Training Centre at Aldershot where she learned to drive ambulances, buses and lorries and took a course in basic mechanics. She was, said her instructress's report, an extremely good and considerate driver.

As the war ended, a remarkable focus of celebration fell upon the royal family. Never before had the monarchy been at such a pinnacle of public affection or esteem, not necessarily for any great acts of heroism or bravery – but for being there, at the heart of it during bad and worrying times, never flinching in their calm and strength, unswerving in duty, never putting private and personal thoughts above the demands of sovereignty. On VE Day, 8 May 1945, Buckingham Palace became the centre, the magnet, for the celebrations and thousands packed themselves around the Victoria Memorial, singing and chanting the King's name and dancing in fine humour. Inside, the palace was a hive of activity, with courtiers and high-ranking officials of the household pacing through the red-carpeted corridors going about their business. Finally, in response to the chants 'We want the King', the family appeared on the balcony to tumultuous cheering. The royal family became the pivot for the expression of relief. It went on for hours, and time and again the King brought his family back on to the balcony. Soon after eleven in the evening, with the crowd still chanting, Princess Elizabeth had an idea; she asked her father if she and Margaret could go out into the crowds below. He gave his permission, provided they took escorts with them and that they put headscarves on to cover their faces. And so the two princesses left the palace through the tradesmen's gate and went off to mingle with the crowd. In the crush, they became separated from the escorts and pushed themselves into the crowd unrecognised until well after midnight.

It was against this background that Princess Elizabeth began in earnest the preparation for the role that would come her way all too quickly; even so the King and Queen made every effort to ensure that their daughter was not forced too quickly into the limelight. They had considered it carefully by studying what had gone before. Edward VII as Prince of Wales had been brought up too strictly and his mother Queen Victoria refused to allow him any part in national affairs, even well into mid-life, so that he grew up bored and in constant search of pleasure. His son and heir apparent Prince Eddy was similarly drawn by a social life that was flecked with scandal and a mad homosexual lover who ended his days locked away in an asylum in Northampton. It may well have been fortuitous that Eddy died in January 1892 before darker allegations became public. His brother Prince George assumed his place as next in line of succession, and in his younger days spent most of his time in the Royal Navy. He was not so heavily involved in public duties until much later in life and became a rather grey and distant character but as King George V, he was a successful monarch. Edward VIII, on the other hand, had been thrust under the public microscope while still in his teens; his personal insistence on going to France to serve in the First World War made him a hero and brought him huge popularity, consolidated by his 150,000 miles of world tours, when such travel was a massive undertaking. It left him tired, restless and discontented enough to declare privately that he was 'fed up with all this princing'.

George VI escaped most of the rigours of royal youth experienced by the number one son, and similarly his bride, Lady Elizabeth Bowes-Lyons, had a fairly sane and unexaggerated training. Based on their own experiences, and knowing how the royal life can quickly go sour, the King and Queen sought to strike the balance for Elizabeth so that she would end up neither with the same kind of priggishness that affected Queen Victoria in the early part of her reign through too much power and responsibility, nor with the conceit of Edward VII or the vanity of Edward VIII. And so it was laid down that the princess should get only limited exposure and those in the closest of court circles knew well that the one thing which angered George VI more than anything was a story in the newspapers about his daughters, or a photograph of the 'snatched' variety. 'The children are my private life,' he would say. 'Why can't they leave it alone?'

Slowly but surely, Princess Elizabeth emerged from the royal cocoon and it was no coincidence that her final 'coming out' on her twenty-first birthday was to be marked while she was touring the Union of South Africa with her parents and Princess Margaret. The 6,000 mile voyage was Elizabeth's first outside of her home country; in the succeeding four decades she travelled a million miles or more. It was also to be her first experience of stepping into a politically sensitive, highly charged atmosphere where the monarchy was being used by unctuous politicians in the cause of peace and unity against a growing nationalism of people who didn't want them there in the first place. The aim of the royal visit was twofold, first to pay tribute to South Africa's war effort and secondly to try to halt the surge of republicanism that threatened to take the Union out of the British Commonwealth, already in turmoil with violence in India, where Lord Louis Mountbatten had been sent to oversee partition with Pakistan and exit from the British Empire. In South Africa Jan Smuts's opponents refused to take part in the festivities which were aimed at strengthening the monarchy within the Union. There was a warm greeting in spite of the republicans. The King opened the South African Parliament and later in the tour repeated the formalities for the Parliament of Southern Rhodesia in Salisbury. It was the last time that a British monarch would set foot in either camp, but that was another of those eventualities that no one in the royal circle would contemplate, least of all the King.

It was no coincidence either that South Africa was to be the scene of Princess Elizabeth's final 'coming out' when she celebrated her twenty-first birthday in April 1947. The day was given added focus in the country when it was declared a national holiday and a suitable array of ceremonial was laid on to make the most of the occasion. In the afternoon, Prime Minister Jan Smuts turned out his entire Cabinet for a reception and then the princess inspected a parade of the

South Africa military in Cape Town and took the salute. In the evening, there were two grand balls, one a state occasion. But the most memorable, and perhaps most important, of all the day's events was Princess Elizabeth's broadcast to the entire Commonwealth over the radio. It was important because her speech was a declaration of intent for the future.

The fact that it was directed at millions of listeners was almost incidental. The princess had spent hours, with her father's help, preparing a speech which in the event was almost as correct in its prediction of her life to come as Keir Hardie's was about her Uncle David:

> On my twenty-first birthday, I welcome the opportunity to speak to all the peoples of the British Commonwealth and Empire wherever they live and whatever race they come from and whatever language they speak . . . We must not be daunted by the anxieties and hardships the war has left behind for every nation of the Commonwealth. We know that these things are the price we cheerfully undertook to pay for the high honour of standing alone seven years ago in defence of the liberty of the world . . .
>
> If we all go forward together with an unwavering faith, high courage and a quiet heart we shall be able to make this Commonwealth an even grander thing – more free, more prosperous, more happy and a more powerful influence for good in the world than it has been in the greatest days of our forefathers. To accomplish that we must give nothing less than the whole of ourselves.

It was here that the princess made her vow:

> There is a motto which has been borne by many of my ancestors, a noble motto, 'I serve'. These words were an inspiration to many bygone heirs to the throne when they made their knightly dedication as they came to manhood. I cannot do quite as they did . . . but I can make a solemn act of dedication with a whole Empire listening. I should like to make that dedication now. It is very simple:
>
> I declare before you that my whole life whether it be

long or short shall be devoted to your service and the service of our great imperial family to which we all belong but I shall not have strength to carry out this resolution alone unless you join in it with me, as I now invite you to do. God help me to make good my vow, and God bless all of you who are willing to share in it.

There was an earnest sincerity in her voice that is said to have brought tears into the eyes of Winston Churchill and must have made a lasting impression on her millions of listeners. Viewed from a distance of almost half a century, when it is difficult not to take a slightly cynical view, especially of political developments, and more especially those in her host country on that day, the speech may have sounded a little trite. But it was not; for Elizabeth it was her statement of intent to serve her people until she is no longer able to do so by some misfortune, illness, or death itself. It was made with such a firmness that it must remain the ideal even today, and one that must be taken into account as we consider, in the last chapter of this book, the prospect of Elizabeth II's retirement in favour of her heir apparent, Prince Charles.

Palace aide Brigadier Stanley Clark who was on the tour, recalled that this was the moment the King realised his daughter had truly moved into adulthood. 'The laughing girl with the lovely golden hair, wonderful pink and white complexion and beautiful eyes, had been a child to the King throughout the war years,' Clark observed. 'Now she was suggesting full entry into the world; he remained cautiously responsive . . . but had mixed feelings that his elder daughter was now ready to bear some of the burdens of one of the world's most difficult jobs.' The moment of her arrival at that point perhaps struck him most poignantly when they were visiting the grave of Cecil Rhodes in the Matopo Hills, outside Bulawayo. At the top of the hill after a steep climb, Princess Elizabeth stood alone gazing across the bush country below. Her father watched and turned to one of his aides and said prophetically, 'Poor Elizabeth. Already she is realising that she will be alone and lonely all her life; no matter who she has by her side, only she can make the final decision.'

The question of who she would have at her side for the rest

of her life was, in Elizabeth's eyes, already settled and had been for some time. Only the King and Queen were procrastinating, perhaps for good reason. They had nothing against Prince Philip of Greece personally, though the King had balked somewhat at the way Lord Mountbatten had been pushing his nephew's case; it had been fairly obvious since before the war that Mountbatten dreamed that his family name might yet encompass the greatest monarchy in the world and he had fired a goodly supply of arrows from his cupid's bow. Princess Elizabeth did not need much convincing, and those around her would always insist that she was sufficiently strong-willed to know her own mind, that she would not be pushed and that the only reason she was drawn to Philip was because she was in love with him. She knew perhaps that, as the future Queen, she could fall in love only once. There could be no trial and error selection of a husband and it was fortunate that she was in full agreement with what was, to all intents and purposes, an arranged marriage, arranged by Mountbatten. Philip was a lively, handsome young man who had been regularly on the periphery of British royalty since the mid-thirties. His background might well have been called into question by the King's ministers who would have to vet his daughter's choice in matrimony and in those sensitive postwar days, there were, as approved royal biographer Helen Cathcart put it, certain 'inconvenient German relations' attached to Philip's pedigree, not to mention the rather chequered life of the young man concerned who could bring nothing to the union but himself and a few meagre possessions. What Clement Attlee's Cabinet actually said about Philip when a file on him was presented to a meeting at No. 10 Downing Street, remains classified; the file is closed for 100 years. Philip did not even have a title, having renounced it in order to seek British citizenship. He was a product of the Greek royal house, the poorest monarchy in Europe, where once he was third in line to the throne, though in fact none of the family had a drop of Greek blood in their veins. The monarchy was imported from Denmark because the Greeks had no royal family of their own, and came from a long line of Danish-Germanic stock, steeped in ancestry running through the ruling houses of Denmark, Sweden, Russia, Germany and various other

European countries. Philip's father was Prince Andrew of Greece, one of the seven children of George I of the Hellenes who was Danish by birth and the brother of Edward VII's Queen Alexandra. Through this connection, the Greek royals were regular visitors to the British court. There in Britain too, was Philip's mother, Princess Alice of Battenberg whom Andrew married in 1903. She was the elder daughter of Prince Louis of Battenberg and Princess Victoria of Hesse (Queen Victoria's granddaughter) who lived permanently in England. Prince Louis was a career sailor in the British Royal Navy and rose to become First Lord of the Admiralty, a position he held until the First World War when he was forced to resign because too many politicians and military men felt it unacceptable that the British navy should have a 'German boss'. The younger of his two sons was Louis, who became Lord Mountbatten when the family name was anglicised along with all other British-held German titles and names in the royal family, on the direction of George V during the First World War (his own was changed from Saxe-Coburg-Gotha to Windsor).

Prince Andrew and Princess Alice had four daughters and a son, Philip. Their life, initially tranquil and happy, was soon upset by the uncertainties of the Greek royal court where they successively faced exile and hard times through intermittent changes in government which would alternately send them into exile and then invite them back with open arms and ceremony. During one of the periods when they were out of favour, Philip's father Andrew was arrested and charged with treason and desertion of duty following an unsuccessful campaign against the Turks in 1921. He was rescued from the firing squad only at the eleventh hour by the intervention of his cousin, King George V. He was freed to the custody of a British warship moored off the Greek coast, and after picking up his family in Corfu Andrew was taken into permanent banishment from Greece in 1922 to France where he remained for the rest of his days, indolent and bitter. Philip's mother, deeply affected by these traumas, was in and out of hospitals on the continent for twelve years and gradually she and her husband drifted apart. They more or less separated in 1929, when he moved to Monte Carlo and found the companionship of a mistress while Alice became obsessively devoted to helping the underprivileged. Philip's welfare and upbringing fell to the generosity of his mother's brothers in England, Lord Louis Mountbatten and George, Marquess of Milford Haven who financed his schooling at Cheam and Gordonstoun. Only once did his four sisters, who all married into the elite of German families, attempt what his cousin ex-Queen Alexandra of Yugoslavia described as a polite custody battle but they gave up, because Philip clearly did not care much for the heel-clicking regime of the Hitler Youth at a school in Salem run by one of his brothers-in-law, and he was returned to the care of his uncles in England.

So it was that he went to Dartmouth Naval College and then into the British Navy, following the course of his grandfather Prince Louis of Battenberg and his uncles. It was at the naval college that Princess Elizabeth first noticed Philip when she came for a visit with her mother and father in 1939; the meeting was engineered by Mountbatten who would be later accused of placing his nephew in front of the British royal family at every opportunity. Vice-Admiral Harry Baillie-Grohman, a friend of Mountbatten's, who took Philip on his first posting aboard HMS *Ramillies*, observed in his unpublished diaries, that Philip once told him, 'My uncle Dickie has plans for me; he thinks I should marry Princess Elizabeth.' Similar talk was rife among Philip's relatives though it became subdued during the war years when he and the rest of his family in England were split from the German faction. In the aftermath, one of the men in the German family was arrested by the Americans at the end of the war and in 1947 was still being held in a POW compound, accused of being a Nazi activist. He was eventually sentenced to a term of imprisonment and ordered to give up part of his estates and property. Notwithstanding Philip's own record in the British Navy, the German connections presented King George VI with an undoubtedly embarrassing problem as he witnessed his daughter's growing attachment to the young man in 1946, and more than once he had to quell Lord Mountbatten's own enthusiasm to set aside all hurdles and let love take its course. The King would not be hurried and the Queen was quietly still hoping that someone else would turn up and capture her daughter's heart.

In September that year, Buckingham Palace took the

unusual step of denying the mounting speculation that Elizabeth was about to become engaged and it has been said that by then the couple had already taken matters into their own hands by becoming unofficially engaged that summer. Was the King to allow his daughter to wed the man of her choice? In the austere and depressing postwar days when memories were still fresh, Nazi war crimes tribunals were being held and the concentration camp horror stories were emerging daily, it would have been a massive risk. This was only confirmed by an opinion poll in one of the newspapers which showed that 40 per cent of those questioned were deeply opposed to the princess being allowed to marry a foreigner. What would the percentages have been had the public known then that the man the princess might marry was not merely a foreigner by birth, but a stateless prince by virtue of his banishment, whose only inheritance when his father died penniless in 1942 was a couple of suits and a bone-handled shaving brush, and whose closest living kin were in Germany? Those were the stark facts that could have been presented at any moment in the newspapers.

At the time of Philip's naturalisation, Lord Mountbatten even went to some lengths to try to ensure he received a good press; as it turned out, it was not necessary. Time is a healer, of course, and the months dragged on, lengthened by the royal tour of South Africa, until the royal family nervously proceeded to the point of announcing the engagement on 10 July 1947. Then, according to the approved version of events recorded by the King's biographer Sir John Wheeler-Bennett, 'there could no longer be any question as to the wishes and affections of both parties and their pertinacity and patience were rewarded'. A veil was drawn across Philip's background and certain details were edited out of his biographical highlights and in the great celebrations that were to follow for the wedding of the world's most glamorous young princess in sight, everything went according to plan. Philip was, by and large, welcomed by all and sundry and even *The Times* adjudged it to be 'a suitable match in every way'.

Britain needed cheering up and a great royal spectacle was just the kind of tonic that the nation could do with; the fairytale princess and her handsome prince. On the morning of the wedding the King bestowed upon Philip a clutch of impressive titles befitting the husband of a future queen, and thereafter he would be known as the Duke of Edinburgh. The people's enthusiasm for the wedding was not wholeheartedly shared by Clement Attlee's Labour government, who bemoaned the extravagance of it all in the very week the Cabinet had been forced to cut the meat ration to a shilling's-worth (five new pence) a week per person. The King, through his aides, had formally inquired if the wedding day might be classed a public holiday.

'Certainly not,' Attlee retorted. 'The nation cannot afford it.' A school holiday was thought appropriate and through the return channels to Buckingham Palace, Attlee suggested the King might announce that it was his daughter who thought there should be no public holiday. 'Certainly not,' retorted the King. 'If there is criticism it will then lie upon Elizabeth's shoulders.' The King had a further brush with his government later in the year over the question of money, the amount to be paid from the Civil List to his daughter and her husband upon their marriage. The King took the unusual step of sending a message to the House of Commons on the issue and said he was relying on the liberality and affection of his faithful Commons. He did not get it; in fact, many in the Commons took quite the opposite view – that far from being liberal and affectionate, they should show restraint and economy by not granting any further money to the princess and none whatsoever to her husband. Attlee sent his Chancellor, Hugh Dalton – whom the King hated – to Buckingham Palace to discuss it. The King accepted the need for economies, but said he attached the greatest importance to the maintenance of traditional procedures. But why did the King's new son-in-law need financing to such a degree? The King rejoined that it was essential that the Duke of Edinburgh should be given an allowance so that he 'may enjoy a proper degree of independence in financial matters'. It was also pointed out that when Prince Albert married Queen Victoria, he was given £30,000 a year. 'If I can live on £1,000 a year including expenses,' shouted William Gallacher, MP, in the Commons, 'why is it necessary for this couple to have £1,000 a week?' It was a rhetorical question which could never be answered and it was the first time in more than a decade that there had been such a note of criticism. The King wasn't at all keen about the situation. Eventually, Princess Elizabeth was awarded an allowance of £40,000 a year while Philip was given £10,000. The King chipped in a further £100,000 out of his own Civil List savings to get them started.

More trouble arose over the costs of refurbishing Clarence House which was to be the couple's home in London. The cost was going to be £50,000, to be paid by the state, but reached a figure four times that amount before it was finished and the King had to stump up some of the money himself. Wasn't there enough space in Buckingham Palace, with its 600 rooms, some of the disenchanted were asking. And was it sabotage or accident that caused to burn to the ground a house at Sunninghill which the King had planned to give his daughter as a weekend retreat, thus thwarting plans of the local council who were going to turn it into flats? Never mind, a loyal financier, Philip Hall, offered Elizabeth a replacement which they could rent from him, a thirteen-roomed house near Windsor called Windlesham Moor. It was immaculately decorated and had a dazzling 50 foot drawing room, seven superb bedroom suites, 50 acres of parkland and a miniature golf course, and the princess was breathlessly impressed.

They were privileged, of course, in an age of deprivation and the Labour government was ever ready to rap knuckles. 'May I remind you,' MP Richard Cobden wrote to the King before the wedding, 'that any banqueting and display of wealth would be an insult to the British people at the present time', while Aneurin Bevan, Attlee's Minister of Health, bluntly refused to put on a 'monkey suit' for the pre-wedding party at Buckingham Palace.

What had gone wrong? This was supposed to be a happy day they were leading up to; now it was as if someone had turned the heads of the politicians towards the palace and said, 'Look . . . that's our money they're spending.' Well, it soon blew over after four or five months of pressure but not before the royals had been put through the mangle. Elizabeth had watched her father steer a firm but tactful course through a difficult period. It was an experience that neither the princess nor Philip would forget in a hurry, and one from which she learned that to listen to criticism and heed it where necessary was certainly a good deal safer than ignoring it.

What no one knew at the time, because she was doing it privately and without any publicity whatsoever, was that she was involved in a scheme whose motive became a feature of her eventual reign: she really did care and wanted to *serve*. Food parcels were flooding in from America and the Dominions at the time of the wedding, along with literally tons of canned food of every kind, sent as wedding presents from British communities overseas for the princess to distribute. Ignoring the advice that it should all be handed over to the Ministry of Food, she set up a team of helpers from the WVS and commandeered space at Buckingham Palace, and for months they worked dividing up the food and making it into smaller parcels. It took almost a year, and by the time her first child was due, Elizabeth's team had sent out thousands of food parcels to widows and pensioners, and inside each one she popped a hand-written note.

'Philip is entering the royal cage,' said Queen Wilhelmina of the Netherlands. Elizabeth was more used to the life by now but neither of them had anticipated the public reaction to the wedding. Thousands of presents poured in from all over the world, ranging from trousers for him to mink coats for her. They were fêted everywhere and Philip looked apprehensively at the diary entries that had already been pencilled in for him. Their first major visit was to France, at Whitsun 1948, and they were astounded by the reception they received from the French, who lined the streets of Paris to wave and cheer tumultuously. Not long afterwards, the princess announced that she was cancelling all immediate engagements; she was expecting her first child and the media went into a new round of raptures for the birth of Prince Charles on 14 November, when the news 'It's a boy' darted by word of mouth across London.

Prince Philip was anxious to get back to his naval duty. He yearned for the sea again, having been stuck behind a desk at the Admiralty prior to the marriage. King George gave him permission and Lord Mountbatten, now returned from giving India its independence, for which the right-wingers branded him a traitor, was running the show in the

Mediterranean and found Philip a ship. For the next eighteen months, Philip commuted between Malta and London, while Elizabeth did the reverse as they proceeded with their individual careers. They also took a villa in Malta and for a time they came as close as they ever would to a 'normal life'. Even so, they had to withstand criticism over the effect their lifestyle was having on their family, which was increased in August 1950 by the arrival of Princess Anne. In fact, the question was academic because their way of life was to be very quickly curtailed. The King was ill and increasingly Princess Elizabeth was being called upon to deputise for him. Towards the summer of 1951, it had reached such a degree that Philip was forced to take leave of absence from the navy. He would never return to duty; the door to the royal cage slammed shut. In June the King was too unwell to preside at a dinner to welcome King Haakon of Norway; the princess took her father's place and read his speech. She deputised for him at the King's Birthday Parade, taking the salute of the Household Cavalry and riding back to the palace at their head in a stunning scarlet tunic with blue ribbon Garter and plumed tricorn hat.

With the Duke of Edinburgh, the princess was to have left England on 25 September, for a tour of Canada. However, the King had an operation for the removal of his left lung and the tour departure was delayed until he was out of danger. Philip suggested that they might fly the Atlantic in a BOAC stratocruiser, instead of going by sea, as they normally did. The move was a great departure; no member of the royal family had previously flown across the Atlantic and Winston Churchill protested to Clement Attlee: 'It would be wrong in my opinion to allow it . . . this seems to be more important than any inconvenience which may be caused by changing the plans in Canada.' Attlee telephoned the chairman of British Overseas Airways who assured him of the aircraft's safety and then called a Cabinet meeting to discuss it on 27 September. The conclusion was that they should be allowed to fly, which merely added to Canada's excitement. They were met by vast crowds. Nothing quite like it had ever been witnessed before in terms of crowds and Philip often found himself stepping forward with a protective arm to ward off eager photographers and well-wishers. They travelled across the continent twice, and then went down to Washington to call on President Truman. While they were there, the results of the British general election came through. Labour had lost and Winston Churchill was restored to the premiership. 'I'm so glad your father's been re-elected,' said Mrs Truman.

King George made steady progress while they were away and over Christmas seemed to have recovered well from what was then a most severe operation. He told everyone not to worry and said he felt better and stronger than he had for many months. He was still not well enough to take on onerous tasks and Princess Elizabeth and Prince Philip once again found themselves deputising for him on the planned tour of Australia and New Zealand which the whole family had been studying with maps and routes spread out on the royal floors during the holidays. They were all together for the last time on 30 January 1952 when the King and Queen took Princess Margaret and Elizabeth and Philip to the Drury Lane Theatre to see *South Pacific*. At noon the next day, on the cold and bitter last day of the month, the King was standing on the tarmac at London Airport to kiss his daughter goodbye as she and Philip took off on the first leg of their journey to Nairobi.

That evening the King read a story to Prince Charles and Princess Anne, knelt down with them and prayed as he always did and kissed them goodnight . . .

Chapter One

Destiny (1952)

> We do now hereby with one Voice and Consent of Tongue and Heart publish and proclaim that the High and Mighty Princess Elizabeth Alexandra Mary is now, by the death of our late Sovereign of Happy Memory, become Queen Elizabeth the Second, by the Grace of God Queen of this Realm and of all her other Realms and Territories, Head of the Commonwealth. Defender of the Faith, to whom her lieges do acknowledge all Faith and Constant Obedience, with hearty and humble Affection, beseeching God, by whom Kings and Queens do reign, to bless the Royal Princess Elizabeth II, with long and happy years to reign over us. God Save the Queen.
>
> Proclamation of
> Queen Elizabeth II,
> 8 February 1952

At the time, the arrival of a new young queen, in terms of reaction from her noblemen, her ministers and her subjects at large, was something akin to the Second Coming. The moment has been described often enough but it remains one of the most touching scenes in modern history, as opposed to the high drama that surrounded her father's proclamation as king, and since it is the starting point of the reign of Elizabeth II, and thus this story, it is worthy of re-examination. At a time unknown but in the early hours of

6 February 1952, Princess Elizabeth succeeded her father King George VI to become the forty-second sovereign of England and her sixth sovereign queen, when the King passed peacefully from this life, as he slept, in his bedroom at Sandringham House, engulfed in the wintry, frosty shroud of the Norfolk countryside that he loved so much. She was twenty-five years old and became the titular head of Office, Law and Honour, to reign over her citizens and subjects throughout the Commonwealth, who at that time numbered 539 million people.

The great burden of office was placed upon her shoulders at an unexpectedly early age. Although he had been seriously ill, George VI's death had not been predicted as imminent and his daughter and her husband Prince Philip were already in tropical Africa. In terms of age, only Queen Victoria was a younger monarch in the past two centuries, aged seventeen on accession. George IV was fifty-seven, William IV was sixty-five, Edward VII was fifty-nine, George V was forty-four, Edward VIII was forty-one (though never crowned) and George VI forty-one. She also became the first sovereign whose moment of succession cannot be precisely known and the first sovereign to succeed to the throne while overseas since George I became king while in Hanover in 1714 and, previously, since King Edward I succeeded while on a crusade when his father Henry III died in 1272.

There was another fact which made her accession unique; none of the previous five sovereign queens had ruled in succession to a parent. Queen Mary I, daughter of Henry VIII and Catherine of Aragon, followed her half-brother Edward VI. She was succeeded in 1558 by Elizabeth I, daughter of Henry VIII and Anne Boleyn, who was also twenty-five when she became Queen and whose forty-five years would later be offered as an all too optimistic blueprint for the new Elizabethan age dawning on that wintry morning of 1952. Mary II was Queen Regnant in name only, when her husband William of Orange was invited to take the English throne in 1688 after James II had fled. The portly Queen Anne who succeeded her brother-in-law William III reigned for twelve important years from 1702 until her death in 1714 whereas Victoria succeeded her uncle William IV when she was seventeen, reigned for almost sixty-four years and restored some moral fibre and respectability to the royal house which had been viewed through the reigns of Georges I to IV as having been run by mercenaries. One other snippet for the record books when Elizabeth II became Queen: it was the first time in history that Britain had three living queens but no king.

Elizabeth was 3,000 miles from home and relaxing in a sitting room at the Sagana Lodge, on the banks of the Sagana River in the Aberdare Forest in Kenya, when she learned of the King's death. The lodge was a wedding present to Elizabeth and Philip from the people of that country and they had spent a few restful days there after a busy round of public engagements. The previous night had been a memorable one; one of those nights of eternal memory, bearing in mind the events which followed. They spent it at Treetops, the famous observation post perched on a platform in a giant fig tree overlooking the water-hole and salt-lick in the game reserve, watching elephants, baboons, waterbuck, rhinos and other assorted animals, emerging from the forest for a drink. It was probably while filming these scenes at the water-hole with her cine-camera that Elizabeth became Queen.

That night they did not go to bed, resting in chairs at Treetops between their excursions to view the sights on the ground, which included a herd of forty-six elephants appearing out of the bush a few feet from where the princess was standing. Eric Sherbrooke Walker, owner of Treetops, commented to her, 'If you have the same courage, ma'am, in facing whatever the future sends you as you have in facing an elephant at ten yards, you are going to be very fortunate.'[1] Grimy and tired, they made their way back to Sagana during the morning after a breakfast of scrambled eggs at Treetops. They freshened up and then went fishing, Philip apparently anxious to see how the trout were biting, and then they returned to Sagana for an early lunch. Soon after 1.30 p.m. local time, three hours ahead of Greenwich Mean Time, Elizabeth's maid Bobo Macdonald and Philip's valet John Dean sat on the steps of the lodge cleaning the shoes. The princess's private secretary, Major the Hon. Martin Charteris, was on his way to the Outspan Hotel on the opposite side of the valley for lunch when he was informed by a reporter from the *East African Standard* that there had been a Reuter's message that the King was dead, though there was no official confirmation. Martin Charteris telephoned Sagana Lodge. Elizabeth and Philip were still in the long sitting room that ran the length of the lodge and the telephone was answered by Lieutenant Commander Michael Parker, Prince Philip's private secretary. Charteris reported what he had been told and said he would try to get the news confirmed. They agreed to say nothing to either until confirmation could be obtained. Charteris could not raise anyone at the Governor's house in Nairobi; the Governor and his staff were at that time aboard a train travelling to Mombasa for the departure ceremony the following day when the royal couple were due to begin the voyage to Australia aboard the liner *Gothic*, already moored and waiting at Mombasa. A pile of cipher telegrams at his virtually deserted official residence had not been dealt with.

Almost an hour passed. Parker meantime had got hold of a radio and though he had gleaned no real confirmation, he presumed from the tone of broadcasts that the news was correct. He went to the lodge and through the great bay window of the sitting room, which framed the breathtaking view of Mount Kenya, he beckoned Prince Philip. Parker told him the news. 'Philip looked as if half the world had just dropped on him,' the aide recalled. It is an oft-quoted remark but one which cannot be improved on. Philip knew he was not just conveying the news of the death of a loved one, the one most dear to her; he was the instrument of deliverance that brought Elizabeth finally to her moment of destiny and there is no way of putting that realisation into mere words. Philip went back inside where his wife who was now queen still sat relaxing and unaware of the drama. They walked outside and he relayed the news beside the tranquillity of the Sagana where royal tears could be shed in private.

The holiday atmosphere had, until then, pervaded Sagana Lodge. The staff, the servants, the police and the Askari guards went about their business. It was demolished in an instant and an uneasy silence enveloped all those within that circle. People talked in whispers and the trumpeting of the elephants seemed so much louder. It was the Queen who by her own activity brought them to attention, put them at ease and made the whole situation more endurable. This, in the heart of the African bush miles from civilisation, was the start of a reign in a style to which her governments and people would quickly become accustomed: firm but a touch nervous, formal but compassionate, caring for others first and herself last, and inwardly steeling herself, fists sometimes visibly clenched and jaw set. She was in total control. This description, stripped of sycophancy and based on true and honest observation of the moment, was to become the hallmark of Elizabeth II.

The formalities demanded by protocol and the constitution were quickly brought into play and the Queen took an instant lead, like an army officer thrust prematurely into command, while Prince Philip began to sort out the logistics of returning to England. What seems like trivia forty years later was vitally important detail at the time, not least of which was how she wanted to be called, the name she would use, since it was by no means a certainty that she would take her first given Christian name. Her father and great-grandfather, for example, were both Alberts, but became George and Edward upon accession. The Queen had been christened Elizabeth Alexandra Mary and could have chosen any of those names, or any other if she had wished, or if her government had prevailed.

Charteris ventured the question.

'Oh, my own name, what else?' replied the Queen, seated in one of the two red and grey chintz armchairs positioned at each side of the stone fireplace. She moved over to a desk, near the bay window and there began her first tasks which were to be recorded over the signature 'Elizabeth R'. The next matter of constitutional discussion was whether she should sign herself in that style before the Accession Council had been called to its meeting in London to authorise the proclamation; it was an important point in view of the Queen's immediate task of sending a clutch of telegrams to the governments in the Dominions who were to have hosted her forthcoming visit, informing them she could not now attend. She also sent messages to her mother, the Queen Consort, her grandmother and her sister. An informal discussion between Charteris and Prince Philip took place at which the Queen did not speak. Then, when a cipher telegram arrived from London requesting permission to call the Accession Council, she proceeded in signing all her correspondence as 'Elizabeth R', a snap decision which was eventually found to be constitutionally correct, and it is one of those asides to the scenario in the bush which demonstrates the way in which propriety, at each step, had to be followed. In London, her Prime Minister Winston Churchill had called a Cabinet meeting for 11.30 a.m. to discuss the 'grievous news' and called another one in the afternoon when he heard from the Queen.[2]

Prince Philip had, meantime, discovered that the Argonaut Atlanta in which they had flown from London to Nairobi had just returned to Africa carrying members of the household who were to join the onward journey to Australia; even in those days the transport facilities available to the royal household, that is, the planes, boats and trains, were fully utilised without much regard to cost. Fortunately, the aircraft was still on the tarmac at Mombasa and it was arranged that it should be sent on to Entebbe in Uganda, where the royal couple could link up by taking a small Dakota of the East African Airways from the nearest airport at Nanyuki. The Queen called her maid Bobo Macdonald to check that mourning clothes had been packed. They had, as a matter of course, but they were among the clothes aboard the liner *Gothic*. A messenger was promptly sent to retrieve the black dresses, stockings, coat and hat and have them stowed aboard the Argonaut. As Philip supervised the arrangements for the return, the Queen sat at her desk and signed numerous photographs of herself, another necessity for the packers of royal luggage, which she handed out to members of the staff at Sagana. It was a tearful ceremony; her African chauffeur flung himself to the ground and kissed her feet. And then the small royal party began its forty mile journey along the dusty roads occasionally speckled with the fallen jacaranda blossom, towards the tiny airfield from which they would begin the 500 mile journey to Entebbe. At the little airport, lined with local officials, sightseers and a small posse of newspaper photographers were asked not to take any photographs of the Queen. Because her mourning clothes had been sent to the Argonaut, she was still wearing the summery beige-flowered dress and white hat; only Prince Philip had been able to show a mark of respect by wearing a borrowed black tie. There are no photographs in existence of the Queen on her day of accession in Africa, save for the holiday snaps and cine-film shot beside the water-hole at Treetops.

They were warned by the pilot that the journey to Entebbe might be a bumpy one; thunderstorms were reported and one struck with all its tropical ferocity as they neared Uganda. The storm was fierce enough to delay the take-off of the Argonaut for three hours and it was almost midnight before the Queen and Prince Philip were guided across the rainswept tarmac by Sir Andrew Cohen, Governor of Uganda, to board their flight to London. The aircraft was fairly spacious, with only the necessary staff travelling, and the Queen retired almost immediately to her sleeping compartment at the rear of the plane. She carried with her a message from her Prime Minister Winston Churchill, radioed earlier to the Dakota, which read, 'The Cabinet in all things awaits Your Majesty's command.'[3]

The Alps were in sight when Queen appeared for breakfast as the plane continued north crossing the Mediterranean. She was now in full mourning clothes. Time was slow in passing and light was already fading into a late afternoon gloom when the Argonaut finally touched down at London Airport where a small party of politicians was waiting for her in the bitter cold of that February day. As the plane came to a halt and the steps were manoeuvred into position, the group moved forward to position themselves at the bottom of the steps. Before the formal part of the arrival, family matters were dealt with. The Queen's uncle the Duke of Gloucester came aboard the aircraft with Lord and Lady Mountbatten. They paid formal homage to the new Queen and then embraced in their exchange of mutual sympathy.

'Shall I go down alone?' the Queen asked.

'I think you should,' Mountbatten replied.

And so it was decided that Prince Philip should hold back, until the Queen had reached the tarmac for the formal welcome and acknowledgement by her senior Privy Counsellors before he joined her, in what would be, according to protocol, the position he must adopt on every public occasion, behind and in her wake, unless required to support her arm.

At the bottom of the steps, Winston Churchill, Clement Attlee and Anthony Eden stood forlorn in raven black, top hats in hand and bareheaded. Beyond them was Lord Woolton, leader of the House of Lords, who remembered it as a period of 'deep emotion for everyone'. Beside him was Harry Crookshank, leader of the House of Commons. Was it the whistling wind making their eyes run? Or were these tears in the eyes of men? In Churchill's case, they were certainly tears. His daughter Mary Soames remembered that when King George VI died 'none among his subjects felt sadder than Winston, who not only cherished the memory of the close relationship which had developed . . . during the war years, but was genuinely personally devoted to the King. Now the accession of the young Queen Elizabeth aroused in him every instinct of chivalry.'[4] Attlee too shed a tear when the King died.[5] He, likewise, would become a favourite of the new Queen in spite of earlier differences.

Then there was the Foreign Secretary and Churchill's own heir apparent, Anthony Eden, pale and drawn and already a sick man; and who could have predicted then the traumas in which he would involve the monarchy before many years had passed in the new reign. He greeted her sadly and warmly, and for the moment perhaps remembered when he first met her as a young princess with her grandfather George V in January 1933 when the young princess and her mother the Duchess of York showed Eden around the stables. She was a slip of a girl but then, as now, older than her years, and now here she was coming towards him, head high, without veil and courageous . . . and he wrote of the moment, 'the sight of that young figure in black coming through the door of the aircraft, standing there poised for a second before descending the gangway to the duties which lay before her is a poignant memory.'[6]

For Uncle Dickie, Lord Louis Mountbatten, back inside the aircraft and waiting to follow his nephew's wife, the Queen, there were the emotions that stem from being in the family and the realisation, in self-aggrandisement so typical of him, that perhaps he himself was now the most influential male member of the family to whom his niece by marriage might turn for advice. Such thoughts were not far away from the minds of other influential people in the corridors of

Westminster, where it was already being suggested that Mountbatten should be given an overseas posting lest his power over the new royal court might be too great to bear.* Regardless of his personal aspirations at the court of Elizabeth II, one thing did please Mountbatten beyond words on that day of days. It was that the woman who stepped from the aircraft on to British soil as queen was a Battenberg wife. Harder to credit, he seemed to truly believe that his most earnest wish might now be granted, that the ruling house of Britain would become Mountbatten, the surname adopted by his nephew. This was a secret ambition which, according to Lord Beaverbrook, he had nursed for years 'in a devotion to his heritage which is little short of fanatical'.[8] The new Queen's grandmother, Queen Mary, had already been warned of such aspirations and, as we shall see, acted promptly to halt them.

The old Queen, grief-stricken by her son's death, was no less punctilious about all the ramifications of paying homage to a new monarch. She gave instructions that she was to be informed the instant they left London Airport and so at 4.27 she was driven out of Marlborough House so that she could be waiting at Clarence House when the Queen and Prince Philip arrived soon after 5.00 p.m. to begin their new life

*It was purely coincidental, however, that he left the British shores for Malta two months later to become Commander-in-Chief of the Mediterranean Fleet. The appointment was made before the King died. However, London was very soon awash with rumours that Mountbatten was sent abroad to prevent him from being able to 'influence Lilibet and Philip', a fact which he acknowledged in a letter to his wife.[7] There were plenty around who considered him a dangerous man to have so close to the monarchy, especially Lord Beaverbrook. Not least of the reasons discussed, or possibly broadcast, by the dirty tricks department of Westminster was the fact that Mountbatten's lifelong friend and 'secretary' Peter Murphy, a homosexual socialite whom he met at Cambridge, was once a card-carrying member of the Communist Party. Murphy was very close to the Mountbatten hub, often residing at the family home. The word put around was that Murphy was a Russian spy, and with barely six months having elapsed since Burgess and Maclean took flight, Murphy was investigated by MI5, a move which Mountbatten said was at his own instigation. The report came back clearing Murphy and he continued to be close until his death in 1966.

and the new Elizabethan Age, Elizabeth to take her position supreme in the court which would now bow before her. 'Her old Granny and subject must be the first to kiss her hand,' said Queen Mary to her companion.[9]

Similarly, the Duke of Norfolk was also there to offer his advice and support. The slightly pompous, blue-cheeked and very officious holder of the hereditary title of Earl Marshal, in charge of weddings, funeral and coronations, was waiting to ask the Queen whether she would prefer a naval or military funeral, or what? In less than half an hour, he had whisked her through his proposals for the arrangements and she agreed to leave it all to him, though it is unlikely that she gave him permission to issue the formal instruction that 'all persons put themselves in mourning' which brought criticism from several quarters. Meanwhile, she was informed by telephone from Sandringham that the King's body was still lying on the bed in which he had died, should she wish to drive there to see him before he was placed in the coffin. She declined; she wished her memories of her father to be happier ones.

The following morning, the constitutional formalities had to be enacted. The Privy Council gathered at St James's Palace, Prince Philip taking his place among the fullest of attendances of men each of whom, apart from Philip, was at least twice her age. They bowed before her in unison and she made her Declaration of Sovereignty in a clear voice, pausing occasionally and hardly faltering in the speech where, twice, she had to mention the name of her father. Everyone present was very kind, later applauding her stamina at facing what must have been a considerable ordeal. When it was over, Philip stepped forward and led her back across the courtyard from St James's Palace to Clarence House where he ordered a couple of stiff drinks and she cried on his shoulder; then she made history by becoming the first monarch to watch her own Proclamation on television as the heralds shouted it from the ramparts of St James's Palace and other points in London.

After lunch, she and Philip left for Sandringham for a private and emotional reunion with her mother and her sister, for whom the death of the King has brought to an untimely end the very world of that cosy foursome which had become synonymous with British life. The two children, Charles and

Anne, who were staying with their grandparents while their own parents were away, barely understood what was happening. As the Queen and Prince Philip made their journey that afternoon, Britain's national newspapers were preparing for another day of emotional eulogies to King George VI and of quite unprecedented welcome to the new Queen. There was no abdication to heighten the drama, as on the last occasion, yet the whole press coverage was fuelled into a total overkill that became commonplace by the nineties but which was thoroughly new in the fifties.

The King was loved principally for his morale-boosting efforts during the war; few monarchs had begun their reign under such difficult circumstances or in the face of such considerable public indifference. He won the hearts of his people through his ordinariness and his qualities of simple resolution and dedication to service and the nation was shocked by his death. Women wept quite openly. People stopped their cars and chatted to each other about the King. Internationally, tributes, formal and genuine, came like a torrent and Harry Truman entered in his private diary a poignant little note, 'He was grand man. Worth a pair of his brother Ed'. Even the American papers gave massive coverage, as Sarah Churchill, Winston's actress daughter who was in the United States at the time, recalled in a letter to her parents. 'It is amazing to see the detailed and affectionate recordings by the press . . . the papers suddenly seemed all English and there was no other news, and American friends seemed to grieve as if he were their friend and King; it really was remarkable. How glad I am that Queen Elizabeth has Papa at her side for comfort and guidance and the glory of the two are so right to start another Renaissance.'[10] Winston Churchill in his speech to the House of Commons once again best summed up the feelings of the nation, especially in regard to George VI's wartime activities: 'The late king lived through every minute of this struggle with a heart that never quavered and a spirit undaunted . . . I who saw him so often knew how keenly he felt personally all the ups and downs of this terrific struggle.' And then he spoke of the 'fair and youthful figure . . . she comes to the throne at a time when tormented mankind stands uncertainly poised between world catastrophe and a golden age.'[11]

The King Is Dead. Long Live the Queen. The impact of having an attractive young woman as monarch, a mother of two, gave sustenance to a new phenomenon – hysteria in public reaction mirrored in the newspapers. Nothing quite like it had been seen before and old-time courtiers were shocked and worried about the extent of it. Preparation for the funeral also received blanket coverage. One snippet that did not get into the newspapers was Lord Mountbatten's attempt to grab pole position in the funeral cortège walking immediately behind the gun carriage that carried the coffin, which he claimed was his by right, the precedent having been set when his father was granted that place for the funeral of Edward VII. The Duke of Norfolk angrily rebuked this attempt at putting himself in front of everyone, including the new monarch, not to mention senior dukes and assorted European royalty. He wrote to Mountbatten suggesting he might care to reconsider his request. 'I am sure that on reflection you will not press for what you have asked . . . and in fact be the only individual to be between the Queen and her father.'[12] Mountbatten reluctantly accepted, but did write a formal memorandum stating that at least the precedent had been recognised and could thus be drawn upon in future.[13]

One who would have been exceedingly upset by the granting of such precedence was the Duke of Windsor. He still regarded himself as an important member of the British royal family, whereas the rest of them regarded him merely as 'family', a wandering black sheep with a wife to match. It was his brother, the late King, supported wholeheartedly by Queen Mary and Elizabeth, the Queen Consort, who had ruled that the Duchess of Windsor should receive no royal recognition as afforded to all others of her title, that of the prefix Her Royal Highness. Windsor earnestly hoped that this might change under the new management of Buckingham Palace; it seemed wishful thinking especially when he was told by telephone from Buckingham Palace, even before the new Queen had arrived back from Africa, that Wallis would not be welcome at the funeral. This prompted a discussion between himself and Wallis as to their prospects as they sat in their eighth-floor apartment in the Waldorf Towers, New York. They gloomily concluded that while Queen Mary and 'Cookie', their nickname for the Queen Mother, were alive nothing would alter and the estrangement which had existed since December 1936 would continue unabated. Wallis urged him to try to see the new Queen and discuss the whole thing. 'After all, there are two sides to every story,' she said.[14] Nor did the idea that he might be offered a job by the British government seem any less remote, a realisation which had dawned only a few months before the King's death. His perpetual overtures for some kind of a role that befitted an ex-king had been rejected, one after the other. He and Wallis were shaken but not especially grief-stricken by George VI's death; they had been apart and out of touch for too long. Even so, it seemed in bad taste, as perhaps was now to be expected, that Windsor should choose to hold a press conference on the sundeck of the Cunard liner *Queen Mary* on which he had secured a hasty reservation to take him to London for the funeral. Surrounded by the streamers and decorations and the partytime atmosphere that accompanied any sailing, he read aloud to a collection of rather brash newshounds from notes he had scribbled on a piece of paper. His words were no less pointed than the surroundings in which he chose to make them: 'This voyage on which I am embarking . . . is indeed sad and it is all the sadder for me because I am undertaking it alone. The duchess is remaining here to await my return.'[15] When he arrived at Southampton on 13 February, he was less bitter and played a softer tune. 'My brother drew strength in his heavy responsibilities from what I once described as a matchless blessing, a happy home with his wife and children. So as we mourn a much loved monarch our hearts go out to the widowed Queen Mother, and her two daughters in their grief.'[16]

The duke was driven to London and went straight to see his mother at Marlborough House, where he was to stay for the duration. She had arranged for him to take tea with the Queen and the Queen Mother that afternoon. It was a strained meeting; though they had not seen each other face to face since 1936 they had surprisingly little to say. Windsor later made a brief memo that the level of the conversation was hardly raised above polite exchanges to which 'Cookie listened without comment and closed on the note that it was nice to be able to talk about Bertie with someone who had known him so well'.[17] Windsor was not provided with any cause for hope by the Queen, who he surmised would be unlikely to change instantly the obvious antagonism that remained towards his wife by his mother and the Queen Mother. Queen Mary, a woman of firm principle, was unmoved; she was not going to give way merely for the chance of reconciliation with her son. Confirmation was not long in coming; he was not invited to a private dinner party that evening at Buckingham Palace, at which some of Philip's relations, notably the King of the Hellenes and Prince Ernst Augustus of Hanover, were guests of honour. He went instead with his mother and his sister Mary, the Princess Royal, to Westminster Hall where his brother's body lay in state. He stayed for just under fifteen minutes and fell to one knee as he left in silent tribute. The coffin had been brought from Sandringham on Monday 11 February to begin the lying-in-state at Westminster. There a short service was attended by the Queen, the Queen Mother and Queen Mary. Selwyn Lloyd* remembered the moment vividly:

> The three Queens stopped just opposite where I was. They were clad in deep black with black veils. Queen Mary talked all the way up Westminster Hall . . . I felt sorry for the Duke of Edinburgh who had Queen Mary, the Queen Mother and Queen Elizabeth to look after . . . he looked as if he felt anything might happen to any one of them at any time . . . in fact they all played their parts with great dignity and composure.[18]

It is an interesting use of the phrase 'played their parts' that Selwyn Lloyd chose in this reference to the ceremony; it is an old-fashioned phrase that was meant to describe how well a person had performed a particular task. In a way, it also had a more literal meaning, because they were playing a part, acting out the ceremonial which they now do on a much grander scale and with a much greater cast. In fact, the scenes during this 9-day period from death to burial were extraordinary and took on proportions that were more akin

*Conservative MP for Wirral 1945–76; Minister of Defence 1955; Foreign Secretary 1955; Chancellor of the Exchequer 1960; Leader of the House 1963; Speaker 1971; life peerage 1976.

to some Hollywood epic, when thousand upon thousand queued to file past the coffin during the lying-in-state, 305,806 in total, and thousand upon thousand lined the streets of London on the morning of the funeral which ended, finally with the Queen, a lonely figure, sprinkling symbolic earth upon his coffin as it was lowered into the royal vaults under St George's Chapel within the castle at Windsor.

It was shortly afterwards that Queen Mary received some disturbing news on the palace grapevine; Lord Mountbatten was heard boasting to Prince Ernst Augustus at Broadlands on 17 February, that since 7 February the House of Mountbatten occupied the throne of Great Britain, Northern Ireland and the Dominions by virtue of the Queen being married to his nephew.

Mountbatten's claim was only slightly at variance with the view of the editor of *Debrett*, Cyril Hankinson, who suggested that Elizabeth was the last of her House of Windsor and that unless steps were taken to change the name of the dynasty, Prince Charles would be the first to rule as a member of the House of Mountbatten.[19] Either way, Queen Mary was outraged at the very idea and was not going to stand for it. No Battenberg marriage, she retorted angrily, was going to depose the House of Windsor, founded by her husband *in aeternum*. She summoned a messenger to take a note to Churchill's private secretary John Colville who carried back to his boss the old lady's fears. Churchill, fired by some colourful rhetoric from Beaverbrook against his old enemy, declared that Mountbatten was trying to take over the British monarchy and called a Cabinet meeting immediately to stop him.[20] During the next few weeks, the issue became bitter and difficult. The Lord Chancellor drew up a lengthy legal document outlining the position and examining point by point all aspects of what was described in Churchill's secret Cabinet papers as 'this delicate issue'. He concluded that under the Letters of Patent drawn up in 1917, when King George V changed his name, the Queen never had a surname. But 'it cannot be questioned that it was the intention of George V that his descendants should be named Windsor'.[21] Aware of the Cabinet attempts to retain the House of Windsor, Mountbatten urged his nephew to prepare a strongly worded memorandum and send it directly to Winston Churchill. This

Prince Philip did on 5 March, seven pages protesting against the proposed move to disallow the Queen from taking his surname, pointing out that on her marriage to Prince Albert the British royal house had assumed Albert's name of Saxe-Coburg-Gotha. Philip's letter annoyed Churchill intensely and he flung it down upon his desk and began penning a fiery response, effectively telling Philip that under no circumstances would he permit the change of name, and he believed his Cabinet would be unanimous in supporting him. This was indeed the case, when eventually the Lord Chancellor's own memorandum was discussed; the Cabinet decided, upon Churchill's personal application, to authorise the Queen to retain her family name as the House of Windsor, and all her heirs to be so titled. Churchill himself was left to 'advise' the Queen of the Cabinet's decision and it was made official by Order in Council on 21 April 1952.

Mountbatten, not to be outdone, recorded in his personal book of heritage, entitled 'The Mountbatten Lineage', that he had been preparing since the year of his nephew's marriage to the Queen, this typically self-congratulatory sentence: 'The House of Mountbatten reigned for two months but historically it takes its place among the reigning houses of the United Kingdom.'[22] Nor would he rest until achieving at least part recognition.

The widowed Queen Consort also chose the days immediately following her husband's funeral to clarify her own position, issuing a long and quite intimate message of intent to the nation, representing an unprecedented manoeuvre from one with no true official rank, for according to the constitution she ceased to exist at the moment of her husband's death. Technically, she should have taken the title of Queen Dowager, or she could have reverted to Duchess of York. She personally chose the title of Queen Elizabeth the Queen Mother and wrote a 'little note' to her people to explain why; as the *News Chronicle* leader-writer described it, 'a statement without parallel in the history of kingship'.[23] It showed a remarkable determination, at the most difficult moment in her life since her husband was forced to take on the mantle of king, which had now killed him. As Penelope Mortimer put it, she had spent 'thirty years creating a king out of unpromising material, a king she had intended to last

. . . to grow old with dignity. But her artefact had fallen to pieces . . . and she had very little to show for it.'[24]

And so the Queen Mother set her stall out, swearing allegiance to her daughter Lilibet, the Sovereign, and commending to the nation 'our dear daughter: to give her your loyalty and devotion; in a great and lonely station to which she has been called she will need your protection and love'. She went on: 'Now I am left alone, to do what I can to honour that pledge without him. Throughout our married life we have tried, the King and I, to fulfil with all our hearts and all our strength the great task of service that was laid upon us. My only wish now is that I may be allowed to continue the work we sought to do together.'[25]

Continuing the 'great task of service' sounded then more like a threat than a promise, especially in royal circles where there was still a memory of the dear, deaf and widowed Alexandra who pestered her son George V beyond measure with her letters and memos. Or would she adopt the formidable stance of her mother-in-law Queen Mary, the most regal of recent queens and icily fierce, too, when she wanted to be? She was still close at hand for advice, should the Queen ever require it. Temporarily, the Queen Mother had remained in Buckingham Palace and she and the Queen and Prince Philip had a discussion some days before the funeral as to the couple's future living arrangements. Clarence House, which had been their home for three years, had been refurbished to their own requirements, with installations such as the white maple panelling which lined Philip's study designed like a ship's cabin, a wedding present from the Canadian Pacific railway, or Philip's combined bedroom and dressing room which came as a gift from the City of Glasgow, complete with fourteen items of fitted furniture and gadgets that opened secret panels. The Queen's own suite, overlooking St James's Park, was definitely the best in the house, warmly furnished in rosewood with drapes of red rose and cream, on thick satin and rose pink walls. Her own personal favourite was the Lancaster Room, one of the main reception rooms, which came as a gift from the people of Lancashire.[26] They were both very fond of Clarence House, especially since they had put up with the considerable uproar about the cost of the place. Philip suggested they should try to stay put. The Queen Mother could retain a residential suite at Buckingham Palace, while the Queen and Philip and other members of the royal entourage could commute from Clarence House for day-to-day business which would continue to be conducted within the palace. As the formal link between the Queen and her government, as opposed to the informality of her private talks with Churchill, the Queen's private secretary inherited from her father, Sir Alan 'Tommy' Lascelles, first broached the subject to Churchill on the Queen's behalf. Churchill would not hear of it; in fact he was quite emphatically against the whole idea. The Queen even thought she could 'win him round'[27] by her own persuasiveness but Churchill remained adamant. Buckingham Palace was the symbol of the British monarchy and nothing less than the permanent residency of the reigning monarch would do and so by the middle of April, after several weeks of trying, the Queen gave up and agreed to move.

There was no respite for any of them. Foreign dignitaries had poured in for the funeral from around the world and it was the Queen's duty to meet many of them and receive the condolences of her governments abroad. Not least of these was the meeting she had with Dr Adenauer, the German Chancellor, and her own Foreign Secretary Anthony Eden on discussions for the future sovereignty of Germany.[28] In fact, she virtually flung herself into getting to know all aspects of government life and meeting the ministers of her government, personally. Lord Alexander, Governor-General of Canada, for example, brought the request that she might spend more time in that country and maintain a permanent palace from which she could be seen to be Queen of Canada,[29] which proved to be wishful thinking on someone's part. The logistical problems were bad enough, considering her other world commitments but, in the event and as Canada became more nationalistic in its outlook, such a move would not be welcomed. Thereafter, in the following month, she held meetings with virtually every one of the government's most senior ministers and instructed her business managers to fit in as many public engagements as they possibly could. It was as if she had made a decision to throw herself in at the deep end, and sink or swim. She swam. In the five months to 31 May, she carried out 140 engagements, and added another 308 to the total in the remaining seven months of the year. They marked the end of court mourning with the release of a special photograph portrait of the Queen and Philip at the end of May, and this was snapped up by the newspapers.

It had of course been a year of 'firsts' and especially the first State Opening of Parliament by the Queen, in November, and what a stir that caused in the royal household. In her day, Queen Elizabeth the Queen Consort sat on a throne of equal size alongside her husband King George VI on a dais four steps up from floor level. Philip, however, was not officially a consort and since 6 February he had been offering to take over some of his wife's workload as the previous Queen Consort had done, only to find doors slammed in his face by establishment courtiers at the palace, to whom he was an outsider and a nobody. Now, the public humiliation came when he discovered he would not be allowed to sit alongside the Queen's throne in the House of Lords, but below, four steps down in the chair that Prince Charles might one day occupy as Prince of Wales. Fury, as the tabloids would say, evacuated itself from his lips and Cecil Beaton's verbal portrait of the scene is perhaps the best. The royal photographer was in the public gallery, viewing what he saw 'entirely as a theatrical production'. He thought the Queen was a real personality with her erect stance and rigid little head. But Beaton's description of Philip, who was then thirty-one showed how much of a bad day it was for him: 'The Duke of Edinburgh . . . seemed nothing more than an adequate consort. He looked extremely ill, eyes hollow, his complexion green and his hair already beginning to thin. I doubt if he will live long.'[30]

There was concern from another quarter also, this time over the Queen. Doctors writing anonymously in the *Lancet* said:

> Of late the medical profession has become more and more aware of the physical price paid by those subjected to too frequent or continuous strain nowadays imposed on Royalty. As doctors, therefore, we should have special reason to welcome an assurance that, by deliberate decisions taken in advance, Her Majesty's health and

> vitality will be protected from Her Majesty's hereditary sense of duty.[31]

And since this 'concern' might also apply to long-suffering members of the royal household whose hours were long, whose pay was not spectacular and whose marriages were put under especially severe strain by the amount of time they spent away from their families, there was a little postscript to the end of the year which would have considerable implications. In December, Group Captain Peter Townsend, former equerry and much relied-upon aide to King George VI, divorced his wife who had some time ago decamped with John de Laszlo, son of the artist who painted one of the most acclaimed portraits of the Queen. And with Townsend 'free', thoughts of true romance stirred elsewhere in the palace, to emerge later in what promised to be a somewhat spectacular, if problematical, year. And in cynical 1952, some whose recent memories of the past were none too happy and who had doubted postwar promises for a new and better world, may not have shared the sentiment expressed in the Queen's first Christmas message to the Commonwealth when she said, 'Many grave problems and difficulties confront us all, but with a new faith in the old and splendid beliefs given us by our forefathers, and the strength to venture beyond the safeties of the past, I know we shall be worthy.'[32]

Chapter Two
Coronation
(1953)

There was so much in the newspapers about 'the fairytale Queen' in the first twelve months of her reign that criticism, or at least expressions of concern, about the public's apparent lusting for 'royal' stories was a foregone conclusion. This was only the start of it; publicity on such a massive scale was not only unprecedented, it was unnatural. Prince Charles said as much, thirty-eight years later, in an interview in December 1990 when he pleaded for less intrusion and trivialisation by newspapers; this had been happening in an upward curve ever since his mother took over. This kind of complaint had been around long enough. In 1910, when Winston Churchill was Home Secretary, the *Daily Mirror* was accused of intruding on private grief when it published a photograph across its centre pages on 21 May of King Edward VII lying dead in bed, which it acquired for a fee from a court photographer. To this the *Mirror* responded that it was merely reflecting the interest of its readers whose appetite 'for details of the Royal family is insatiable and sells newspapers like no other topic can.'[1]

In the first year of the New Elizabethan Age, few who had listened to the tabarded heralds shouting her Proclamation would even consider trying to rationalise her accession. For the mass of the public at large, they wanted Elizabeth to go on living the fairytale that they had been watching unfold like a story by Hans Christian Andersen since she was a child. They wanted her as their glamorous figurehead, because she was too young to take on the role of national matriarch which actually lay in reserve for the Queen Mother after the death of Queen Mary. Disagreement on this perception came largely from political quarters and radical writers and it is worth recounting, for a moment, some of the warnings. Lord Ardwick (formerly John Beavan), a Fleet Street colleague of the author, wrote an especially telling piece for the *Manchester Guardian* just prior to the Coronation:

> The Queen lives in a blaze publicity. Cameras and microphones record every public act . . . Since accession, hardly a woman's magazine has dared to go to press without an article on the Royal Family while in the popular newspapers she has taken the place of the film star . . . and students of the constitution have asked whether there is not some danger of letting the daylight into the magic and of dissipating the mystery which Bagehot* thought was the very life of the monarchy.[2]

Miss Jennie Lee, MP, the wife of Nye Bevan, also took up the cudgels in various articles she wrote on the monarchy and not unexpectedly, considering her position on the left of the Labour Party, she turned it into a political discussion, too. Her barbed comments about the press could well have been written to support Prince Charles's complaint in 1990: 'there should be limits set by good taste and ordinary courtesy. They [the royals] ought not to be dragged in to fill the headlines every time there is a shortage of hot news. They ought to be spared the pert innuendo and the ghastly sycophancy that they are forced to put up with from some quarters.'[3] But it was not entirely the fault of the newspapers. Elizabeth's significance was, as one American writer colourfully described it, no more and no less than the fresh young blossom on roots that had weathered many a season of wintry drought.[4] The British, as weary and discouraged as the rest of the world in the early fifties, saw in their new young Queen two things: first, the reminder of a great past and secondly, and perhaps

*Walter Bagehot, eminent Victorian writer and constitutional expert whose book *The English Constitution* became the definitive work on the role and perception of the monarchy.

more importantly, the focal point for hope – a fresh start and the emergence from wartime sadnesses and postwar austerity. This year, 1953, was coronation year and that would be the beginning of a new era. It was all a bit of a mirage. At the beginning of the year, on 19 January, Chancellor R. A. Butler produced for Churchill's Cabinet a confidential and gloomy assessment of the nation's ills. The country was impoverished by war, but still carrying the old burdens of a major power and the new ones of becoming a welfare state, and Butler said, 'Only the most powerful and convincing action can prevent a major calamity for sterling'.[5] He called for resolute action to 'stop the rot' and a fortnight later introduced his austerity programme including cuts in consumer goods, increased NHS charges and reductions in overseas travel allowances. Meanwhile coronation fever was being whipped up and if Jennie Lee was correct, the Conservative Party saw this as an ideal moment to use the Queen as the figurehead. Jennie Lee believed that Churchill and his men had talked the Queen's advisers into joining the conspiracy, in recommending the Queen at the outset of her reign to prepare to behave like Queen Victoria, with lots of pomp and splendour in the foreground, so that the people forgot about poverty and squalor and food rationing in the background. Under cover of the brightness that shone on the Queen, the government continued to dose the nation with its unpleasant medicine, including (in April) a cut in Argentinian beef imports and (in May) cuts in overseas spending and defence budgets. Looking back, it is now possible to see that Jennie Lee was probably correct, though her colourful and fiery language tended to obscure her point at the time. The Queen was surrounded by toadying but often devious advisers who were certainly very closely in touch with the Churchill camp, and who incidentally made a point of keeping Prince Philip out of reckoning by slamming doors upon him lest he should prove to be too much of a disruptive influence; it was no secret that he had already been given a rocket by Churchill though the reason remained a secret – as did a number of 'royal incidents' that year.

Philip was already talking about 'modernisation' with such suggestions as getting rid of the debutantes' 'coming out' circus which began each year with presentations at the Palace.

He had also just persuaded the Queen to accept an invitation to dine with Douglas Fairbanks Junior (actor and friend of Mountbatten). Mixing with show people, whatever next! What Lee warned of happened, certainly in the first couple of years. There was lots of pomp, lots of circumstance and a few eccentricities from within the royal family added for good measure which ensured that they were seldom off the front pages. But what the public saw was all a pretence, a charade; the royal family was surrounded by people in rented morning suits, moth-eaten robes and incredible snobbery while trying to make the public believe that they were just an ordinary family; wealthy, but ordinary. It wasn't working and it wasn't the Queen's fault. She was inexperienced and relied heavily on the advice of her father's old hands, 'crusted old operators tending the constitutional juggernaut' Philip called them,[6] accepting their order and judgement at face value, which she would eventually learn, after being warned constantly by her husband, was not the thing to do.

Louis Wulff, the doyen of court correspondents of the day, tried somewhat vainly to defend them when he wrote: 'The secret is that the Queen and her family represents to us all . . . the idealisation of ourselves. She, with her husband and children, epitomises all decencies of domestic life, the sanctities of the family circle. Our Queen and her family belong not to one narrow restricted class of society but to all of us.'[7] The *Mirror* would soon take up the similar call for the Queen to show herself as being more approachable and in touch with the 'common man'. And thus, sooner or later she would, with Philip's help, have to find a proper balance between simplicity and sumptuousness, between debutantes and Lancashire dole queues, and between majesty and democratic example. Whether she could ever achieve that, or even have the power to, and establish a true second Elizabethan Age is really what her reign would be about; it is also the thread that runs through the next forty years of this story.

If the first eleven months had been trying enough, the year of 1953 would prove to be something of a vintage royal year in terms of newspaper coverage. It was as if some hidden hand had decided to paint them a picture of what it was going to be like for the ensuing forty years, and in the next twelve months provided a whole collection of epoch-making events, ranging through death, divorce, scandal, coronation, crisis and political shenanigans of the highest order, and Wulff's entreaties about the 'sanctities of the family circle' would, at the end of it, ring a trifle hollow.

The Queen sailed on into her uncharted waters with her second-in-command who was more used to choppy seas, but on this occasion Philip couldn't see the storm brewing either. They were simply overwhelmed by events and work. There was so much to be done, so many meetings and engagements to attend, so many formalities to withstand, so many of the idiosyncrasies of British constitutional life to contend with and, not least, so many changes to their personal life.

Dealing with the latter first, Elizabeth tried deliberately and conscientiously to maintain some semblance of family life to run alongside her monarchical duties. Whatever else had passed in her years of 'presumptive' training and regardless of the obvious limitations of the intellectual side of her upbringing, she had arrived at her destiny as an exceedingly well-balanced young woman who was publicly visible as being capable of happiness and sadness, of marriage and motherhood and of performing with grace and dignity all the daunting ceremonial duties expected of her. She was, according to those in her close-knit little circle of friends, unspoiled and remarkably nice, though capable of putting her foot down with ice-cool determination and displaying flashes of Hanoverian arrogance which forty years later had still not been dulled. It was noted that at functions when she was ready to leave and Philip was still off somewhere engrossed in conversation, she would send an aide to his side to whisper 'The Queen is leaving now!' In her official and constitutional duties, she was the boss, otherwise and in private they were much like any other couple, engaged in the struggle for domination of their personal affairs. Philip's humble background, his naval discipline and his obvious comfort at being in hearty masculine company rather than the aesthetic and intellectual, made him more naturally outgoing.

Occasionally, he would need to interject with one of his ice-breaking witticisms if her patience was tested and her face set in that familiar Hanoverian glaze which Princess Anne also inherited. Together, they worked out a programme that would ensure they spent as much time as possible with the children, in the homeliest of atmospheres, although often her engagements would make heavy inroads into this 'home' time. A normal day which did not involve external engagements would begin at around 7.45 a.m. with a fairly leisurely breakfast with Philip, each reading their personal letters and their favourite newspapers while also listening to the radio news programme. Philip would frequently interject into this peaceful piece of palace domesticity his own running commentary and interpretation of some significant event. Outside the privacy of their own quarters he could not be seen, or have the effrontery, to offer advice to the Queen but it would be unnatural, especially for him, if he did not make his personal views known over breakfast.

Soon after 9.00 a.m. the two children, Charles and Anne, were brought to them by Nanny Helen Lightbody, with the corgis trailing behind. If the weather was fine enough, they would all go out into the garden; the day's events would mean that their schedule even for this family get-together would be strictly timed so that forty-five minutes later the Queen and Philip would go to their separate offices to begin work with their secretaries, planning engagements and dealing with day-to-day palace business. At 10.00, on a normal day, she would meet with her then private secretary Sir Alan 'Tommy' Lascelles, going through the important business. Lascelles was an early influence of the new Elizabethan reign. As a former servant of her father, and soon to retire, he had a long experience of life at the palace and was rigidly bound by protocol established years earlier by his distinguished predecessors, Wigram, Hardinge, Stamfordham, Knollys and Ponsonby. They were powerful men, whose voice was officially not heard yet whose words more often than not came from the mouths of the monarchs they served. 'He taught me how to be king,' George V once said of Stamfordham. Lascelles had been around for a long time. He became assistant private secretary to the then Prince of Wales (later Edward VIII) in 1920. He thought Edward was 'the most attractive man I have ever met'[8] but resigned from the post eight years later, angry and disillusioned with his playboy master. He returned to Edward's service when he became King and they fell out again over Wallis Simpson, whom Lascelles hated; the feeling was entirely mutual. Later, after the abdication, he joined King George VI's staff as deputy private secretary, eventually succeeding to the prime position and able to wield the most formidable power in the tradition of the old-style courtiership to which he belonged.

A dour but honourable man, Lascelles was none the less blinkered by these traditions and was awesomely protective of the absolute formalities of palace life. And thus, while the Queen, and especially Prince Philip, were trying to break down a few barriers and sweep away the dusty cobwebs of the past, relationships with palace staff remained unpleasantly tense because of his overpowering presence. The Queen forced her own requirements over the way it was mapped out for her by her aides.

At 11.30 a.m. she would hold the first audiences of the day, a foreign ambassador presenting his credentials, perhaps, or a visiting governor-general from one of the Commonwealth nations whom she made a point of treating with warmth and respect.[9] Some visitors would stay longer than others, usually reflecting the state of that nation's friendship with Britain. For a Russian in those days, for example, the interview would be brief and strictly formal and Andrei Gromyko could escape quickly enough from the presence of the royals whose relatives his party had massacred thirty-five years earlier. She was more relaxed with the friendly nations and occasionally invited their representative to lunch, though it would be short and sweet, seldom longer than an hour and a quarter, and the fare would be plain and straightforward. She lunched as often as possible with Philip in the most informal surroundings and occasionally the children were brought down. This would be followed in the afternoon by attention to state papers, which the Queen would do privately in her study, or possibly by an outside engagement. At least one afternoon a week in these early days was given over to discussions over her clothes, hairdressing requirements and other matters of appearance and attire that would not normally have troubled a male monarch; once a king has acquired his wardrobe it merely needs occasional updating.

She discovered that her wardrobe had to be extended

considerably and despite the difficult times she could not afford to skimp on clothes. She needed to be fashion-conscious and that meant that many more dresses and coats and gowns were added. She took the advice of Norman Hartnell who had gained the tag of 'the Queen's dressmaker' and it was he whom she consulted for the design of her coronation gown. Hartnell reckoned the Queen knew exactly what she wanted. There were already decisions to be made about the extensive wardrobe the Queen would need for her long and diverse tour of the Commonwealth after the Coronation, and for almost a year before the departure date Hartnell was making frequent trips to see her, accompanied by his models who would discover, on occasions, the Queen, the Queen Mother and Princess Margaret sitting together on a sofa eagerly awaiting their private mannequin show, with mother and sister helping the Queen to select clothes for a New Zealand summer or a night under the stars watching festivities in Fiji.

The children might come down for tea if the Queen and Philip were in the palace, and invariably they were all together for an hour before the children's bedtime. This was sacrosanct, and even the Prime Minister's weekly Tuesday audience, which had been at 5.30 p.m. with the King, was put back an hour to allow her more time with the children. The point of relaying all of the above in more detail than might otherwise be necessary is to illustrate that here in Britain, approximately twenty years before women were 'liberated' and feminism became fashionable, was this slight young woman with a 25 inch waist and golden eyebrows, mother of two, with a handsome swashbuckling husband, who was, granted, one of the world's richest women, choosing her dresses and hats, caring for her children and yet surrounded by men of stature, men of power, men of letters, men of years.

As head of state she was equal in status, but not power, to leaders of other countries whose representatives and ambassadors had to bow before her and walk backwards from her presence. In station she ranked alongside famous, if not infamous, names like Stalin (until 5 March 1953 when he died), Franco, Mao and Tito, men who had no respect for their own monarchies. Indeed, other precarious monarchies were still falling; those recently ejected included Egypt's portly and odious Farouk, and Prince Philip's cousin Constantine, King of the Hellenes, was forced to flee Greece in the wake of the Junta; another of Philip's cousins, King Michael of Romania, was forced to abdicate at gunpoint. There was US President Eisenhower whom she would soon meet; and there was Konrad Adenauer, the German Chancellor desperately fighting to get the phoenix risen, to which cause Prince Philip was perhaps naturally sympathetic; and there was Winston Churchill who had thrown a protective arm around the new Queen as if she was his own daughter, but who needed a protector himself to ward off the back-stabbers in his party. Already on the horizon was the Queen's first major political constitutional crisis.

Just as the new year dawned, Harry Crookshank, one of Churchill's ministers, was among those talking openly about his future as Anthony Eden recorded: 'dined with Harry Crookshank . . . he was convinced than W was an increasing liability to us; that if he had not been leading at the general election we should have had another sixty seats . . . Harry said no one could tell when a general election might have to be called . . . therefore W should go at the Coronation. There was an historical precedent for it.'[10] And knowing, as we now do, what a débâcle the Tories made of choosing a new leader, there was trouble brewing on the constitutional front for the new monarch.

The Coronation was being seen as one of those focal points in history which might be used for a variety of things. Queen Mary, frail and in her eighty-sixth year, decided with some premonitory, some say calculated, wisdom that she might not be around for it and made a new will leaving everything to her granddaughter, with the exception of a few items for her staff and great-grandchildren. She added the codicil directing that if she should leave for the next life before the Coronation, on no account was there to be any extended mourning to upset the arrangements. She went so far as calling the Duke of Norfolk to Marlborough House and extracting a promise from him that the Coronation would go ahead regardless, which was just as well, because on 18 March she wrote to a friend that she felt 'weary and unwell';[11] then in the style that she had personally followed throughout her life, in everything be swift and to the point, she passed to the other side six nights later. This unexpected event in the middle of preparations for the Coronation, led by the Duke of Norfolk and Prince Philip, brought a sadness to the Queen that was barely seen publicly, except during the funeral.

Apart from her father, Queen Mary had been the Queen's foremost tutor in the complexities of court life, its foibles and its eccentricities and, above all, the need to uphold its formalities of which the old queen had been one of the great participants through the six reigns she had experienced in her life. She was appreciated for that; often stern and upright, Queen Mary had been the toughest female in the royal household since Victoria, and occasionally the coldest according to her eldest son the Duke of Windsor. Certainly, she never wasted words. Her sole broadcast, launching the liner that bore her name, was done in twenty-eight words. One of her brief publicly recorded talks was to a group of children who were emigrating to Australia: 'Remember that life is made up of loyalty. Loyalty to your friends, loyalty to things beautiful and good, loyalty to the country in which you live, loyalty to your king and, above all, for this holds all other loyalties together, loyalty to God.' That code perhaps best personified her instruction to her granddaughter. Now, on a darkly wintry day, very dark considering the time of year, thousands of her loyal subjects lined the route of the procession, silent and bareheaded as the roll of funeral drums and the stamping of military boots to the Death March accompanied her coffin to Westminster, and then on to Windsor. There were very few in the nation that day who could recall a time when Queen Mary had not been a figure of British life, the quintessential royal. 'Queen Mary did not cling to insubstantial shadows of what might have been,' said Winston Churchill in a broadcast tribute. 'She moved easily through the changing scenes.'[12]

One who might have disagreed with those words was the Duke of Windsor. He was in no better humour because it was as plain as the nose on his wife's face that the Duchess of Windsor was to be no more welcome at Buckingham Palace now than when his mother was alive. News of his mother's closeness to death came when they were once again in New

York enjoying their socialite whirl and before he set sail for England he had been apprised of the fact that neither the Queen nor the Queen Mother would think it appropriate that the duchess should accompany him. So she stayed in New York and on the very night of the funeral she was to be found camping out with her exceedingly rich homosexual playmate, some say lover, Jimmy Donahue, the Woolworths' heir whose outrageous behaviour had long since become an established part of gossip column life. Nor was the point lost on the columnists that while the duke mourned at his mother's funeral, his wife was out on the town, and undoubtedly this news was relayed back to London.

Two days after the funeral, the Queen was guest of honour at a luncheon of the Commonwealth Parliamentary Association. Churchill was the speaker and he seized upon the current mood of the nation as his theme: 'All around we see proof of the unifying sentiment which makes the Crown the central link in our modern changing life.'[13] Certainly, the Coronation had become the central focus of the year. The Queen was deluged by palace work, coronation preparations and planning the long tour due to start in November. She gave Philip some tasks including the presidency of the committee advising the Royal Mint on the design of new seals, coins and medals which she was especially keen to get right; they would after all be around for rather a long time in unalterable metal form. But the most controversial of Philip's appointments by the Queen was his chairmanship of the Coronation Commission as well as acting as the Queen's spokesman, using her name occasionally to push through a decision or two against the advice of a few of the old courtiers he was facing. There were numerous disagreements as they discussed the complicated tasks involving precedent and protocol and who was going to perform what job and who was going to sit where. But there was one aspect of the planning that Philip could not handle himself and on his advice the Queen stood firm against such voices as Churchill and Dr Fisher, the Archbishop of Canterbury, and especially Tommy Lascelles. It was on the question of allowing the actual Coronation to be televised live. The commission and the Queen's own advisers had been arguing for months with the BBC over the extent of the 'vulgar intrusion' of their planned coronation coverage. Eventually, the commission ruled against allowing this new medium to film any part of the ceremony because they felt it would detract from the religious solemnity, in spite of firm public opinion in favour and some colourful comments in the newspapers, such as John Gordon's in the *Sunday Express*, hitting out at 'the tight-knit group of palace officials whose determination to keep people as far as possible away from the throne never diminishes. What a bunch of codheads to run the Queen's business.'[14]

This piece of precision bombing was placed at the behest of Mountbatten who was, for the time being, on better terms with his old enemy Lord Beaverbrook. However, Churchill remained certain that it would all place too much strain on the Queen and anyway 'Why should the BBC have a better view of my monarch than me?'[15] Tommy Lascelles thought the implications went much deeper than religion or pressure and with hindsight it is now possible to see that his reasoning was, of all the objectors, the most sensible. Lascelles pleaded with the Queen, respectfully and quietly, to bar the cameras because he felt that the monarchy owed much to myth and mystique. Lascelles argued that there was a danger that under the enormous glare of those early heavy duty lights, the mystique might begin to fade. He was probably right, but he lost his case. The nation protested, and newspapers like the *Daily Express* trumpeted, 'The sooner Mr Churchill can announce the ending of the (television) ban, the sweeping aside of the ruling of the palace officials, moved only by protocol, the sooner the nation will be able to express its gratitude.' The *Express* quoted and requoted seven vital words from the Church of England Coronation Service, that the sovereign should make her oath 'in the sight of all the people'.[16] And as we now know, the Coronation became the first major televised royal spectacular of the Elizabethan Age, to be improved and enlarged with each royal event whose culmination would be the balcony scene at Buckingham Palace, when they would all gather to wave to the adoring crowds thronging forth down the Mall. That's where it began – a few weeks before the Coronation and the British

Royal family was about to be thrust into the realm of truly global celluloid celebrities.

In the meantime there were extensive preparations. A couple of months before she died, Queen Mary advised the Queen and Philip to 'talk Coronation'. She told them to think about the symbolisms; talk about the ceremony; try to get it all into perspective so that it did not loom large as a nerve-shattering event. Without doing that, she warned, it might easily become too daunting to accept. And so they talked, and they rehearsed, and the Queen chose her people to do various jobs and Philip argued her case with the commission. In the privacy of their apartments, and often watched by the children, she would practise walking with a 5 pound weight on her head, as if it were the Crown of St Edward which she would wear on Coronation Day. Later, they set up posts and tapes in the Buckingham Palace ballroom and there, with the accompaniment of gramophone records of her father's Coronation and with a large white bed-sheet pinned to her shoulders like the train of her gown, the Queen rehearsed her manoeuvres until they were certain there could be no accidents.

As the day neared, she joined the weeks of rehearsals and the dress rehearsals, a task shared by several thousand participants. Often there were frayed tempers and Philip would be called upon to shield his wife's tears. Or perhaps it might be her turn to be firm and his to get it wrong, and she would say, 'Don't be silly, Philip, come back and do it again.' The Queen was a natural worrier in these early days of her reign, especially over the smaller details of large events. She worried over everything from her portrait for the new postage stamp to the high cost of carpets and curtains for their new suite in Buckingham Palace. She worried about protocol, and she worried about Philip's latest passion of flying and where had he got to if he was late home. She worried about not spending enough time with the children and she worried about the suggestion that Philip should not be allowed to travel in the Gold State Coach for the Coronation, which was a serious proposition, supported by those in the palace who wanted to keep him firmly in his place. There was no precedent. Victoria was unmarried at the time of her coronation, so of course was Elizabeth I, and Queen Anne was carried to her coronation by chair. In the end, the Queen decided that Philip should travel with herself in the gold coach; it was just another notch in the tension that was now reaching its peak.

Secretly, she was also seriously worried about another family bombshell delivered to her door by her own sister, Princess Margaret. So much has been written about the romance of Princess Margaret and Group Captain Peter Townsend that there can be barely a detail left which remains unfamiliar to the reader. However, it is necessary to recall the sequence of events and to include some items of previously undisclosed matter, culled from private sources and from Public Records Office documents released thirty years later, in order to discover the impact of this news upon life at Buckingham Palace at this crucial and historic time. Townsend and Margaret had been thrown together, or perhaps reunited might be more applicable, in 1952. They had long been friends, of course, and their closeness blossomed especially when the handsome Townsend, then an equerry whom the King trusted like a son, accompanied the King and Queen and the two princesses on their tour of South Africa in 1947. Townsend often found himself in the role of Margaret's minder.

In 1952, when he became comptroller of the Queen Mother's household, he and Margaret were naturally brought closer again since Margaret was also her mother's constant companion. 'We found increasing solace in each other's company,' Townsend recalled,[17] 'with the change in her own family situation, living alone with her mother (whom she adored) and the breakup of mine.' After his divorce in which he was the innocent party, Townsend and Margaret spent more and more time in each other's company. It reached the point where one afternoon at Windsor Castle, when the rest of the family was away, Townsend gazed into the eyes of his princess and said the fateful words, 'I love you.' To which she replied, 'And I love you.' Their feelings for one another took no heed of wealth, rank, or other conventional and establishment barriers and this mutual disclosure, while joyous in one respect, was at the same time highly problematical. The question was would they be allowed to marry, he being a divorcee and she still third in line of succession to the throne? They decided that they must tell the Queen as soon as possible and try to obtain her consent to marry.

The moment they chose came a few days later when they were both invited to spend an evening in the company of Elizabeth and Philip at Buckingham Palace. The Queen took the news sympathetically and calmly. Philip, as was his way according to Townsend, tried rather sheepishly to look on the funny side of this rather dramatic situation. At least, he did at that moment. Later, he became seriously opposed to the whole business. The Queen Mother was also informed. She knew the couple faced dire problems but was too charitable and kindly to say as much. And so, the family had been told and the initial shock-waves had not been great; in fact they had all displayed tact and charity.

The serious nature of the affair did not begin to dawn, perhaps, until Tommy Lascelles, figure of authority and pillar of the establishment, was told by Townsend who had decided that he must immediately resign from the Queen Mother's household. In the large office of the Queen's senior adviser, Townsend stood before the darkly inquisitive eyes of the man he actually regarded as a friend and began to relate the whole story; Margaret had warned him not to expect any sympathy. Townsend knew from his long association with Lascelles that he would get none though he hoped for understanding, at least. He received neither. Out came the now oft-quoted remark: 'You must be either mad or bad,'[18] said Lascelles as the vision came to him of what ructions the last divorcee to become entangled with one so close to the throne had caused. It was Lascelles's view that Townsend should not merely resign but should accept some overseas posting immediately and make no further contact with the vulnerable, lovesick princess. He was scared and haunted by thoughts of the abdication crisis of Edward VIII with which he had been so closely involved and immediately saw this developing situation as a rerun of the events of 1936, right at the very point of the Coronation. Lascelles decided in his own mind that it was his bounden duty to protect the Queen and the monarchy from another damaging scandal which, by its very nature, would grab the attention of the world's press.

If it leaked out, the whole solemnity of the Coronation

would be overwhelmed by trivialisation and he could imagine the packs of baying reporters at the palace front door and the great barrage of reaction that would follow. Lascelles, who could quote the Royal Marriages Act of 1772 by heart, went straight to the Queen and reminded her that under this Act Princess Margaret would have to obtain Her Majesty's consent to any marriage made before her twenty-fifth birthday. Thereafter she would be exempt from this requirement but would, as a member of the royal family, still need the consent of Parliament and the Parliaments of the Dominions, too. More crucial, said Lascelles, was the Townsend divorce and in the eyes of the Church it mattered not a jot that he was the innocent party. The Queen, as titular head of the Church of England whose canon number 107 of 1603 forbids divorce, could not constitutionally give her consent unless her Prime Minister and thus the Cabinet agreed. Lascelles had no doubt in his mind that the marriage should not be permitted and yet curiously he did not tell the Queen as much. He merely replied in the affirmative to her question as to whether the marriage was possible yet almost immediately began taking steps to ensure that the whole sorry business was halted before it went any further.

Lascelles told the Queen that he thought the Prime Minister should be informed if the couple planned to pursue their ambition to marry. He then personally, and privately, made sure that Churchill was alerted immediately. He sent for Sir John Colville, a former courtier who was now the Prime Minister's private secretary. Lascelles left Colville in no doubt that the love match must be stopped and over lunch at Chequers the following weekend, Colville revealed all to Churchill, though the Prime Minister did not apparently grasp the implications immediately and commented, 'What a delightful match'. He thought Townsend was a hero and a gentleman. When Colville pointed out that Townsend was a divorcee and that Tommy Lascelles was worried lest a new scandal of 1936 proportions hit the royal family, Clemmie Churchill interrupted and said, 'Winston, if you are going to begin the abdication all over again, I'm going to leave. I shall take a flat in Brighton.'[19]

The upshot was that Lascelles got his way. Churchill advised the Queen that Margaret should be told that she could not marry a divorced member of the household. She must wait until she was twenty-five and if she was still of the same mind, she should apply again. There was no doubt that a strong argument could be put forward that if, by some awful happening, the Queen and her two children died, Margaret would become queen. She would be married to a man whose marital status was not recognised by the Church and thus any children of the marriage would be immediately precluded from the line of succession. It was, in that respect, a complete mirror of the situation facing Baldwin at the time of Edward VIII's wish to marry Mrs Simpson.

The Queen accepted the advice in part only, insisting that Townsend should remain at the side of the Queen Mother who she knew relied heavily on his abilities; also she could not bring herself to exile a man who had been such a loyal and devoted servant to her father. Thirty years later, Princess Margaret told a confidante that the trouble was that no one actually said, 'No, you cannot marry'.[20] If they had, it is most likely that she and Townsend would have agreed to part there and then, thus avoiding the great furore that followed. But Lascelles never said, 'You can't'. He was more concerned with the Queen's happiness than Princess Margaret's and did not want to place on Her Majesty's shoulders at that particular time the burden of such a decision and so he tactfully and deviously engineered a postponement. And so the Queen never said, 'You can't'. And Churchill, though saying 'No', added, 'Apply again later.' Everyone allowed them to continue believing that at some point in the future the dream might be realised, and they could marry. Only Prince Philip showed a touch a realism and said, 'Forget it'. But no one listened to him. So there it rested and by now the Coronation was almost upon them. The Margaret problem was put to the back of their minds and everyone except she hoped that it might go away; of course, it would not, and as a matter of fact it would be on Coronation Day itself that the affair would burst into the open publicly for the first time.

By then, lots of serious words were being written about the Coronation itself; yards of column inches in every newspaper and magazine in the land analysed every minute detail of the life and times of the Queen and her immediate family and took the enthusiastic nation inch by inch along the procession route and word by word through the Coronation ritual. The artists, the poets and the musicians were all busy composing special pieces for the ceremony. All over the United Kingdom, and in the Commonwealth too, extraordinary things were going on. The dream sequences were coming to fruition; the fairytale was going to be assured of a happy ending and the nation beavered away, in spite of the rationing, to make sure that Cinderella went to the ball. And nobody listened to the likes of Manny Shinwell, leftist Labour MP, who said it was all such a waste of time and money and that the aristocracy of Great Britain was 'doomed and almost damned'. Churchill's Cabinet chipped in by increasing food supplies for the celebrations and street parties. Everyone was allowed the bonus of an extra pound of sugar and 4 ounces of margarine or cooking fat. Street parties were allowed special concessions and makers of such scarce delights as crisps and toffee apples were provided with additional supplies.[21]

The symbolic importance was best summed up by the renowned BBC commentator Richard Dimbleby whose exactness for detail and devotion to the royal family were often mistaken for sycophancy. 'The truth is,' he wrote, 'the monarchy has long since become our way of life. For us, it means justice, respect for the rights of the individual and freedom . . . the system . . . which flourishes best, it seems, where there is a monarchy, where there is at the head of affairs one person willing to sacrifice herself entirely to the good of her people.'[22]

One who was once king but never crowned, the Duke of Windsor sat miserably viewing the preparations from afar. He had already discovered that any hope of an invitation for himself and his wife would not be forthcoming and he was not prepared to go alone; he therefore became one of Europe's most senior royal figures who would *not* be attending his own niece's biggest day. He held a press conference to issue a statement, which he first had cleared by Churchill, in which he claimed unconvincingly that it would be 'contrary to precedent for any sovereign or former sovereign to attend'. Instead, he watched the ceremony on the television of an American friend in Paris, apparently enlightening the assembled company with the most informed commentary of the day, aided by the acid, and often insulting, wit of the duchess who was less able to hide this fresh and greatest humiliation by her husband's relatives across the Channel.

The crowds gathered, the rain fell, and *The Times* welcomed even the television coverage, stating:

> Posterity may judge it one of the wisest acts and the most far reaching in its consequences . . . yesterday for the first time in perhaps a thousand years, the sovereign was crowned within the sight of many thousands of the humblest of her subjects. Yesterday, by penetrating at last, even vicariously, into the solemn mysteriousness of the Abbey scene, multitudes who had hoped merely to see for themselves the splendour and the pomp found themselves comprehending for the first time the true nature of the occasion.[23]

The Times added that 'no mere report' could have impressed so strongly those who looked upon this deed of dedication in which they too, silently and reverently, participated.

Viewers of television and the films which were rapidly flown to major cities throughout the world for an audience of hundreds of millions, witnessed one of the greatest historic spectacles of lavishness, pageantry and sheer splendour that was, and still remains, capable of being staged anywhere on earth. And with the incantations of 'Vivat Regina Elizabeth! Vivat! Vivat! Vivat!' still ringing in her ears, the Queen returned to Buckingham Palace in the gold coach drawn by eight Windsor greys, to the rapturous cheers of the thousands who lined the route, passing each throng as its crescendo reached the peak, thus being met by one continuous sound of cheering. The British had got their pomp and their circumstance and their glamorously, passionately historic occasion to give them new heart. They were still there at midnight, hundreds deep outside the palace and down into the Mall shouting her name and succeeding finally in forcing her to make one final appearance as the last hour of the day was rung out by Big Ben.

One thing the television cameras did not pick up during the day was the touching little scene in the annex of Westminster Abbey, when Princess Margaret casually flicked some fluff from the lapel of Peter Townsend's uniform. An American reporter saw it, and the look in her eyes, and the following day the American press, reacting to a story which appeared first in the *Journal-American*, was agog with the news that there was another royal romance in the air. There had already been some speculation in the continental newspapers and now it came out with the full force of American headlines. The British newspapers remained, for the moment, unusually silent and on this occasion there was no conspiracy, as there had been with the press lords to keep the name of Wallis Simpson out of the papers and certainly unrelated to the then King in the months before the Abdication. Curiously, the Queen's advisers chose not to inform her of this developing situation. Neither she nor the Queen Mother were told of the stories circulating in the foreign press, though the palace press secretary Commander Richard Colville must certainly have been aware of them, and equally must have felt it his duty to warn Tommy Lascelles.

The two men were in much the same mould; Colville was a thinnish man with a narrow face which set naturally into a kind of bland expressionless form made more formal by his straight-cut black hair and thin black-rimmed spectacles. He came straight to this post of press liaison from his gallant wartime naval service, and had not managed to improve relations with the nation's media one bit. He was constantly criticised for his formal, dismissive air and to some degree this remained the tone of press contact long after he had gone. Anyway, Colville knew but didn't say that a certain storm cloud was looming. It took fourteen days for a British newspaper, the *Sunday People*, to pluck up the courage to mention what was being openly discussed abroad and even then it chose that time-honoured route of discounting the rumour as 'utterly untrue. It is quite unthinkable that a royal princess, third in line of succession, should even contemplate marriage with a man who has been through the divorce courts.'[24] The *People* would have been in touch with Colville for a comment; none was forthcoming. Peter Townsend said later that had Colville warned Princess Margaret or himself earlier of what he must have known might occur when the story first appeared in America on the day after the

Coronation, 'there would have been time for me to fade out before the storm burst'.[25] But Colville did not warn him or anyone else, except perhaps Lascelles and this, said Townsend, was the first of a series of incomprehensible blunders.

Cries of scandal were overtaken by the popular press who, encouraged by overwhelming public support by way of opinion polls, were urging the couple to ignore protocol and the stuffed shirts of constitutional life and announce their engagement. Of course, it would never happen. The headlines raged for days with one 'sensation' after another, quieted only when Margaret took off with her mother for a tour of Rhodesia and while she was away, Tommy Lascelles finally got his way and Townsend was exiled to Brussels. Even in that scenario, the palace manipulators tricked the couple by telling them that there would be a chance of a meeting upon the princess's return, scheduled for 17 July before Townsend left the country. And so their goodbyes to each other in Clarence House on the day the princess left were performed in the expectancy that they would see each other again very soon. No sooner had she taken off than Townsend was told by Tommy Lascelles that he should pack his bags and be out of the country by 15 July, the day before Margaret returned. The power of Lascelles showed itself once again; he was intent on assuring that his beloved monarchy would not be tainted further by this unwanted and unsavoury incident, and it was his earnest hope that he would now end it for good. The Queen, however, did not appear so heartless or unforgiving. The next day, Townsend accompanied her and Philip on a visit to Ulster. On their return and as she left the plane at London Airport, she made a point of stopping for a chat with Townsend, lined up as he was with other staff and the pilots. In full view of reporters and photographers, she shook his hand and smiled warmly. And though Margaret was away and Townsend was being sent aboard, they both retained a hope that in two years' time, when Margaret was twenty-five, a way would be found for them to be together. The 'Margaret problem' had temporarily subsided, but was simmering away on the back-burner waiting to explode.

Shell-shocked by this barrage of headlines which had rained down upon them unceasingly for fourteen days, following as it had the months of relentless press and newsreel coverage since the death of her father, the Queen might well have been lulled for a moment into the thought that nothing more could happen of an untoward nature. She was looking forward to a holiday at Balmoral, scheduled between August and early October, before beginning one of the most extended of royal tours she had yet undertaken. Suddenly, and surprisingly, she was thrust into the eye of a constitutional hurricane, the true seriousness of which was to be withheld from the public at large. Winston Churchill suffered a stroke on 23 June. Serious though it was, under normal circumstances Churchill's illness would not have been a particular problem since he had an able Foreign Secretary in Anthony Eden who had been seen by many as Churchill's heir apparent. However, Eden himself was recuperating from an illness and was almost as unavailable for important decisions as Churchill himself. In April, Eden had what should have been a relatively simple and straightforward operation. However, the surgeon's knife apparently slipped and a biliary gland was accidentally cut, causing blood poisoning and fever. Eden was critically ill for some days and, once again, the real seriousness of his condition was kept from the public. Even so, while he was away recuperating, Churchill was often apt to telephone him on the slightest excuse 'and waste a great deal of time. The outside world had no idea just how difficult the Prime Minister had become.'[26]

There was certainly no question of Eden returning to duty when Churchill had his stroke and with them both out of action, the national, not to mention international, view of the British government's ability to govern could have been seriously questioned especially at that crucial time of troop movements around Suez and Soviet ambitions in eastern Europe. A vague medical bulletin about Churchill's condition, that he 'needed a rest', was therefore put out by his doctor, Lord Moran. In private, Moran was telling Churchill's closest confidantes and relatives that his active professional life was over. His private secretary John Colville took further defensive action by summoning friendly press lords, including Beaverbrook and Camrose, to Chartwell. It was all 'quite a conspiracy', his daughter Mary Soames later admitted.[27] As Colville described it, the press lords 'achieved the all but incredible and, in peacetime, unique success of gagging Fleet Street – something they would have done for no one but Churchill'.[28]

The constitutional channels were also alerted by Colville who telephoned Tommy Lascelles. The seriousness seems even to have been kept from the Queen, if her letter to him on 26 June was anything to go by: 'I am sorry to hear from Tommy Lascelles that you have not been well . . . I do hope it is not serious.'[29] Well aware of the monarch's prerogative of being there to be consulted, to encourage and warn her Prime Minister and fascinated by her own father's closeness to Churchill, the Queen was apparently unaware that a 'secret' plan had been worked out by Tory leaders. If it appeared, as was then likely, that Churchill might have to resign, Lord Salisbury would advise the Queen that he would form a caretaker government until Eden was fit enough to take over. Naturally the opposition party would have launched a searing attack on the government, demanding that no such responsibility should be placed upon the shoulders of the young Queen and that there should be a general election immediately. That is why the Tory Party managers decreed it imperative that Churchill's stroke should be kept secret for as long as possible. And so, on top of all else, the Queen was unknowingly thrust into what threatened to become a major crisis, the likes of which had not confronted a reigning British monarch since the early thirties. The extent to which Churchill was incapacitated was described by his daughter Sarah who had been warned on her arrival at Chartwell to 'prepare yourself for a shock'.[30] She said her father had suffered a stroke down his left side which had left him almost totally paralysed. 'The shock of seeing a great oak tree felled,' she recalled, 'is as close as I can get to describing what I felt. My father was in a chair. I went over to him . . . his eyes flashed brilliantly but of course he could not answer and his face was naturally distorted on the left.' The Queen asked that she be allowed to visit, but Clemmie Churchill thanked her warmly and suggested that if she did so, people might think he was dying. The first Eden heard about it, incidentally, was five days later when his wife Clarissa received a confidential letter from Colville.[31]

Early in July, Colville wrote again, stating that there was

a surprising improvement in Churchill's condition, and slowly he improved, until stage by stage his voice returned, and then movement in his paralysed limbs, and finally the facial distortion became less pronounced. By the time the *Daily Mirror* stumbled across the truth, he had recovered sufficiently for the serious nature of the stroke to be denied. Thereafter, Churchill began to set himself goals; that he would be fit to go to the Tory Party Conference in October, and then that he should remain in office while the Queen was away on her tour. Slowly, the crisis subsided and few people outside of the Queen and the Churchill family circle were aware that, for almost three months, Britain had had neither Prime Minister nor Foreign Secretary.

The Commonwealth Coronation Tour loomed large before her now: on 23 November she was to set out on a journey that would take her from the shores of England for six months. By then, Winston Churchill was back in the House of Commons having given true credence to that old phrase 'a miraculous recovery'. From there, frail but for the moment the immovable leader of Her Majesty's Government, he said of her, 'It may well be that the journey the Queen is about to undertake will be no less auspicious and the treasure she brings back no less bright than when Drake first sailed an English ship around the world.' Always one for going slightly over the top in his remarks about the royal family, Churchill nevertheless summed up the importance of this tour, important not merely to the Queen as head of the Commonwealth, but to Britain's immediate status in the world, too.

There was one postscript to the year which was directly linked with the Queen's travels, which increased the possibility of accidents, or worse, befalling her. It also represented a further demeaning of Princess Margaret. Under the Regency Act of 1937 brought in to clarify the position regarding the Duke of Windsor should anything untoward happen to George VI, it was ordained that the person next in line of succession and over twenty-one years old would become regent until the heir to the throne reached the age of eighteen. As that stood, Princess Margaret would become regent if anything should happen to the Queen. Prompted by Lascelles, this was brought to Churchill's attention and discussed in Cabinet. Churchill proposed a new Regency Act of 1953, under which the Queen acknowledged that 'in the event of a Regent becoming necessary in my lifetime, my husband should become Regent and charged with the guardianship of the person of the Sovereign'.[32] The documents relating to this decision were lodged in files under the 30 year rule at the Public Records Office at Kew. In that year also, nine other files out of eighteen concerning the Queen and the royal family including Philip's memo to Churchill on the name change – were ordered by the Prime Minister to remain on the secret list; two were to remain closed for fifty years, the remaining seven for a hundred years.

Chapter Three
The Travelling Begins (1954–5)

'I want to show that the Crown is not merely an abstract symbol of our unity but a personal and living bond between you and me,' said the Queen in her Christmas broadcast to the nation and the Commonwealth as she began what was to be a particularly hectic year. Regardless of her personal thoughts, what lay ahead typified in every way the sentence written by Walter Bagehot in 1867 during the reign of Queen Victoria, that 'the use of the Queen, in a dignified way, is incalculable'.[1] The most important royal tour since George VI took his family to South Africa in 1947 and, for different reasons, Edward VIII cruised the Dalmatian coast with Mrs (but not Mr) Simpson in 1936, was about to commence in the continuing, unabated glare of worldwide public interest. The Queen had spent months in preparation, in between her commitments for the Coronation. Often, on a quiet Sunday afternoon the whole family could be found sitting on the floor, with maps spread out before them, going through the route and studying the mounds of reading matter provided by the tour organisers; years later, it all became rather routine. Every possible aspect of life in the fifteen countries to be visited was typed out in advance. This included everything from political and economic notes, to strange customs and anticipated climates. The preparation was important not merely for the quite personal knowledge she would require, so that she could converse without fear of upsetting the natives, but also in terms of planning her wardrobe for the next six months. There were dozens of other incidentals, such as the need to carry gifts, medals and honours to be distributed to various people she would meet on her travels, not to mention the gross of personally autographed photographs that would be handed out on her behalf; all of this had taken months to prepare.

Before the Queen and Prince Philip left, the Queen Mother threw a small farewell party for them at Clarence House on the evening of 20 November; 'just a few friends' and, as became something of a regular feature of palace life, a few notable celebrities were invited from the world of show business to entertain. Noël Coward was among them. He sang 'Mad Dogs and Englishmen' and other songs from his famous repertoire and Peter Ustinov did some impressions. There were only about thirty people present, but the party went on into the early hours. The Queen and Philip did not leave until shortly before 3.00 a.m. The following Monday, Noël Coward watched their departure from London Airport on television. It was, he noted in his diary in his typically patriotic prose, 'immensely moving . . . the Queen looked so young and vulnerable and valiant and Prince Philip so handsome and cheerful . . . true glamour without any of the Windsors' vulgarity'.[2]

The Queen set a great deal, personally, on the first Commonwealth tour arranged to show herself to her people abroad, and the vastness of the journey which was to take her from the country for 173 days, at that time unique in its conception and in its compass, would include a number of 'firsts'. She was, for example, the first reigning British monarch to fly the Atlantic when she set off for Bermuda on the first leg of her journey, the first to circumnavigate the earth, the first to visit New Zealand, the first to open the Australian Federal Parliament, to mention the most significant. The whole project was carefully planned and commissioned to succeed on behalf of the British government in three main aims: to express through the Queen a belated personal thank-you to the people of the colonial empire and the Commonwealth for their help during the war, something which George VI had wanted to do, though he had managed to visit only South Africa before illness struck; secondly to consolidate the bond between the mother nation and its farthest-flung territories through the best public relations effort currently available anywhere in the world; and thirdly to bolster the cause of British commercial interests. These were the political reasons, but for the Queen there was a personal target: to throw herself totally behind the ideals on which the Commonwealth is based.

This would remain her aim throughout her reign in spite of the nations and countries who, for one reason or another, would prefer to cut the ties with Britain. It would, eventually, prove to be one of the areas that she consistently fought to uphold, very often showing more concern and enthusiasm for the Commonwealth than a lot of her ministers in successive governments. She clung to her dream of Britain and its Commonwealth nations remaining as 'one big happy family' (her words) rather like an updated version of the empire and reminiscent of the days when Victoria was queen to more than half the world's population, though Elizabeth's own determination to promote the Commonwealth ideal dated back to the more recent past, when India gained independence and King George VI, bereft of the jewel in his imperial crown, could no longer be described King Emperor. The disappearance from the King's stationery of the initial I, for *Imperator*, bestowed upon his great-grandmother by Disraeli seventy years earlier, marked the passing of the Indian Empire that had such close ties with the Crown. He was depressed that the old British Empire had virtually gone but he was more worried that some nations in the new Commonwealth which replaced the Empire were making uncomfortable rumblings about discontinuing their allegiance to the British Crown. The King impressed upon his daughter the need to keep the Commonwealth afloat and she pursued that goal quite dramatically for years to come.

It was a new world she was visiting, as she set off on her tour that cold November day in 1953, and no doubt it was with some mixed feelings that nations like India who once had bowed to Victoria as Empress would merely give Elizabeth acknowledgement as its first citizen, or that many of her black subjects on the continent of Africa were rising to the Mau Mau chant of 'Death to all white men', or that her white subjects on the same continent were talking openly of a South African republic. She was also unaware of an unseemly discussion over the cost of the trip which had been going on at 'secret' level between her own government and the richer Commonwealth countries she was due to visit. Originally, Australia and New Zealand had agreed to pay a substantial portion of the costs – until it was discovered just how much it would be. The new royal yacht *Britannia* was not completed in time and the government had to charter the liner *Gothic* for the journey at a cost of £280,000, plus another £1 million for on-board costs.[3] A protracted correspondence took place and the Cabinet concluded that the 'matter of reimbursement should not be pressed if it were to cause embarrassment'. Australia did eventually make a contribution and, indeed, publicly the welcomes could not have been warmer.

The only comparable royal tours in modern times were those of Edward, Prince of Wales in the early 1920s when he was given the task of travelling throughout the empire to express the nation's gratitude for assistance rendered in the First World War. Just as the Queen set out to do in 1954, Edward was advised to try to make the subjects overseas feel that he was their very own prince, and he reported back his success in Canada to his father, King George V: 'I'm rubbing it in that although not actually Canadian born I'm a Canadian in mind & spirit & come here as such & not as a stranger or a visitor & that goes well! These Dominions do appreciate being put on the same level as the U.K.'[4] His mother Queen Mary responded with a warning, 'I feel angry at the amount of handshaking and autograph writing you seem compelled to face . . . this does not sound dignified.' To which her loving son replied apologetically, 'I quite understand what you say about shaking hands and allowing myself to be mobbed & I can assure you that it isn't my fault as you may imagine; you just can't think how enthusiastic the crowds have been . . . one is powerless.'[5] His right hand became so bruised and swollen that eventually he had to shake with his left.

History was about to repeat itself, as it so often does in royal progress, and no doubt the new royals would take the past into account. The Queen and Philip separately often made studies of what their predecessors had done and how they had tackled various tasks and in that winter of 1953 through to the spring of 1954, they went on their travels in a style that was to set its own pattern for the future. The Queen was mobbed in each port of call, and one was 'powerless' no doubt to curb her people's enthusiasm – not that the Queen, in her day and age, would even contemplate such a move.

Moving on from Bermuda, her first visit on the Coronation tour, the Queen learned of an embarrassing oversight that she would have to put right in the next port of call, which would be Jamaica. As they left Hamilton, a local coloured lawyer, Mr E. T. Richards, pointed out that the British were obviously not ready to discard the colonialist attitudes of the past, since to the welcoming dinner for the Queen not a single black person was invited. News of that nature travels quickly and the Queen had to make amends by ensuring her next stop, in Jamaica, was not marred in any way by lack of attention to the native population. That would have been difficult anyway; since this was the first visit paid to the island by any British monarch, most of the population turned out to take a look at the new Queen who would reign over them, and perhaps a few might have pondered whether her accession would make any difference to their lives. By and large, it would not and early indifference to the presence of the white Queen was displayed by the Jamaican Chief of Maroons (Negroes) who twice failed to turn up for an audience with her. He owed his allegiance to the God-King Haile Selassie.

The liner *Gothic* was moored at Jamaica harbour ready to carry them on the next part of their voyage of discovery. The new royal court was on board. Tommy Lascelles had retired before the tour began and his place was taken by Sir Michael Adeane, a young modernist, with Martin Charteris as his assistant. Things were looking up. The new men were neither crusted nor old (as Prince Philip once described the Queen's courtiers), being forty-two and thirty-nine respectively. Fleet Street saw their arrival as a breath of fresh air flowing into musty palace life, though they still had the po-faced Commander Richard Colville to contend with as press secretary. Lady Pamela Mountbatten joined the tour as one of the Queen's two ladies in waiting; and Viscount 'Johnnie' Spencer was appointed acting Master of the Household while on board ship. It was, according to the well-informed Helen

Cathcart, no accident that the two were selected. The Queen it seems was trying a spot of matchmaking to bring together two good friends and if she had succeeded might well have changed the course of her own family history, since Althorp's younger daughter Diana eventually married her own son and heir. The matchmaking was in vain. Pammy and Johnnie made a humorous twosome but never became a pair. Mountbatten's youngest, then twenty-five, stayed single for another six years before marrying interior designer David Hicks, while Johnnie, then aged thirty, had already lost his heart to a slip of a girl, Frances Roche, the seventeen-year-old daughter of the Queen Mother's old friend Lady Fermoy and by the time he was due to sail, they were already thinking of marriage. For Frances, it was more of a schoolgirl crush than a romance and Johnnie, never one to hold a young gel's affections for long, felt himself rather fortunate that he had been able to attract such a charming, and engaging young prospective partner. On the day he sailed on the *Gothic* for the royal tour, she turned up at the dockside with her mother to wish him *bon voyage* and present him with a specially painted portrait of herself in non-perishable red oxide, to hang in the cabin that would be his quarters for the next six months. Johnnie, a well-known royal socialite and occasional escort of Princess Margaret, was intent on marriage as soon as possible upon his return – and to begin a family that would include a daughter named Diana.

In Fiji, as etiquette demanded, the Queen courageously swallowed a drink of the soapy-tasting Yaqona, followed by at least a taste of a spread of the most exotic foods. She would remember for ever the nose flutes that welcomed her to Tonga and the two-mile-long cavalcade of small boats that accompanied her into Sydney Harbour as she filmed and photographed the sights for her children, occasionally remarking how much her sister Margaret would have enjoyed it. The schedule was so energetic that the Queen lost weight, down to well below 8 stones, and her maid had to alter a number of her dresses which had suddenly become too loose. The extent of the journey and the workload she and Philip undertook which, forty years later, remains unsurpassed on any succeeding tour, is best explained in one simple set of statistics recorded from the moment she left London until her return: they made 51 separate journeys by aircraft totalling 18,106 miles; 75 by ship, boat, or ferry totalling 19,644 miles; 702 trips by car or jeep totalling 4,006 miles; 44 by rail totalling 1,857; the complete round the world tour extended to 43,618 miles. For collectors of royal trivia, here are a few other facts: she opened seven Commonwealth parliaments, held eleven investitures, attended 223 receptions, made 157 speeches (and sat through 328 delivered by other people) and when they went ashore at New Zealand, it required two trucks to carry their luggage. In Australia alone, she shook hands 4,800 times, listened to the National Anthem on 162 occasions, acknowledged the curtsies of 2,536 women and received 190 gifts. It was a pattern that would be repeated over and over again.

'In the wider sphere of world affairs,' said the Queen as she carried her message to nations bound by historical ties, 'the British Commonwealth and Empire have shown to the world that the strongest bonds of all are those which are recorded, not in documents, but in the hearts of the people who share the same beliefs . . . bonds of human friendship and unity which come from sharing the same heritage and aspirations and the same loyalty.'

It would perhaps be too cynical to highlight the naivety of her words especially when the return journey covered a route which today would be unthinkable, with stopovers at Ceylon, Aden, Entebbe Uganda, Tobruk Libya, Malta and Gibraltar. Then, however, the welcomes were grandiose and generally warm-hearted. Indeed, Tobruk was chosen as the point at which the Queen should take delivery of her new royal yacht *Britannia* with Prince Charles and Princess Anne, then five and three respectively, on board.

The children had been staying with the Mountbattens in Malta for the previous ten days and Charles has since recalled that his first impression of his great-uncle was of the tall figure standing on the quay at Valletta to meet them. Mountbatten was excellent with the children whom he seemed to regard more as 'honorary grandchildren' than great-nephew and great-niece; he would play boisterous games with both and keep them amused for hours with his stories, usually about his own exploits rather than, as Philip Ziegler put it, 'fairy stories' though Lord Beaverbrook would maintain there was no difference. The relationship between Mountbatten and the future king which was to become so important to the latter began there in Malta, while waiting for his parents to arrive home.

Mountbatten arranged for the children to meet the Queen and Philip at Tobruk and they were so taken with the family reunion that it was more than an hour before they were ready for a conducted tour of their new ship which would become their floating palace for dozens of future tours. The *Britannia* replaced the old *Victoria and Albert*, which was scrapped in 1939 after George VI was warned that it was not seaworthy. Plans for a replacement were postponed because of the war and a new yacht was finally commissioned in 1950.*

When they sailed on to Malta for the state visit to the George Cross island, Mountbatten was waiting with his Mediterranean fleet to give the Queen a spectacular welcome and let Philip show what the *Britannia* could do alongside a naval flotilla. For days, Mountbatten had been practising with typical egotism a manoeuvre with his fleet to greet the Queen which involved sailing his ships towards the *Britannia*

*The word yacht in this context is one of the royal anomalies that no one bothers to explain to the taxpayer. It is a ship, an ocean-going liner, in every sense of the word: 126.65 metres long, it cost £2.1 million and provided state apartments plus accommodation for fifty guests, with a crew of 21 officers and 265 ratings, manned entirely by Royal Naval personnel on a rota system, distinguished by white instead of the customary red badges and caps bearing the title *Royal Yacht*. Though commissioned in 1950, in the early days it was dubbed Philip's Folly, when he was being bombarded with criticism over the cost of various high-tech 'toys' with which he equipped himself, such as a helicopter, new racing yachts, a car telephone and a newfangled filing system at the palace. Philip was responsible for some of the extra costs, however, after the *Britannia*'s launch; he ordered certain modifications, which included making the dining room larger, to seat 56 people instead of 32. Since it was completed, the *Britannia* has had numerous refits costing between £2 million and £10 million a time, the last one being in 1991. One of those was for its use during the Falklands War and it was said at the time of its commission that it could double as a military hospital if required. In fact, it turned out to be totally unsuitable for that purpose.

at 25 knots as she approached and then turning inwards so close that the royal observers watching from the deck of *Britannia* were actually splashed. It had not apparently occurred to him that one steering error aboard just one of his ships could have caused a 'disastrous accident'.[6]

By the time they headed home for London, the media and nation were showing signs of withdrawal symptoms. The extravagant newspaper, newsreel and television coverage of the Queen's world tour was hardly a replacement for the real thing and consequently much was made of the welcome home. On 15 May, they sailed jubilantly down the Thames in their new yacht to Westminster Pier with 200 jet aeroplanes roaring overhead. And amid another display of London royal pageantry, they transferred by car to Buckingham Palace, through a route lined with cheering crowds. Winston Churchill insisted upon going out to the mouth at the Thames to join the royal ship and failed to recognise his Queen, waiting to greet him as he came aboard. She had not yet changed into her 'welcome home' clothes and was still relaxing in casual slacks and blouse. 'And who is that young woman?' asked Churchill as his suntanned Queen walked towards him.

They relaxed in their new quarters in Buckingham Palace, freshly decorated and with all their personal furniture and wedding presents moved over from Clarence House. They spent a week getting to know the children again, and going through the photographs and the films with the Queen Mother and Princess Margaret. They had barely had time to settle back home when Johnnie Spencer's wedding was upon them. Spencer had flown back from Malta ahead of the royal party to join in the arrangements for his marriage to Frances Roche. Naturally, with so many royals in attendance, it was a very public wedding at Westminster Abbey and the Scots Greys, with whom the bridegroom served in Europe in the Second World War, formed a spectacular guard of honour with arched swords. Spencer, whose own godparents included Queen Mary and Edward, Prince of Wales, was heir to the great estates of the seventh Earl Spencer, largely in Northamptonshire where their country seat of Althorp was located. There was some question whether the eccentric earl would attend his son's wedding. He was a forbidding man who was given to answering the front door himself, often carrying a shotgun over his arm. In younger days, Winston Churchill who went to Althorp to research the biography of their common ancestor, the Duke of Marlborough, reported that the earl snatched the cigar from Churchill's mouth and stamped on it. He was also nicknamed the curator earl because he could recite the history of virtually every piece of furniture and work of art in his house. In spite of his father, Johnnie Althorp, a warm and jovial man, was the catch of the social circle to whom the Spencer–Fermoy wedding became the event of the year. The groom was kept waiting for ten minutes because the Queen was delayed by palace business and the bride dare not enter the church before she had arrived. And so they were there to witness the betrothal of the two who would, unbeknown to anyone on that day, produce a future bride to the Queen's own heir.

During the previous week, the Queen had held her own party, a cocktail party for her ministers and the Shadow Cabinet of the Opposition, and then she went off to a welcome-home luncheon thrown by the City of London at which, traditionally, royal travellers give accounts of their journeys. 'I set out to learn more of the peoples and countries over which I have been called to reign,' she said, 'and to try to bring them the personal reality of the monarchy. The structure and framework of the monarchy could easily stand out as an archaic and meaningless survival. We have received visible and audible proof that it is living in the hearts of the people.' This, at least, reassured the residents of Buckingham Palace that they were not a dying breed; others in the ranks of public comment were not so sure.

The red boxes began arriving again just as soon as the flag went up. It was a purely symbolic duty and one which monarchs used as background on the occasions they chose to offer counsel to their ministers; but it was none the less very informative, providing the Queen with all the information she needed to know about the current workings of her government and intelligence from aboard via Foreign Office telegrams. It was viewed as a chore by her Uncle David, Edward VIII, who used to leave the boxes lying around, or showed the papers to Mrs Simpson and thus became the first monarch in British history to have all confidential documents screened for security reasons before they were delivered to him. His brother, King George VI, was conversely an absolute stickler for what he considered to be a prime area of his responsibility, making a thorough study of the contents of the boxes which included minutes of Cabinet discussion and other secrets from the various government ministries, to acquaint himself fully with his government's business. In this, Elizabeth followed her father exactly, even down to the little game he used to play, apparently handed down, that they should try to catch their ministers out on some detail or report. Churchill bemoaned the fact to his secretary John Colville one day when he returned from his weekly audience. 'She caught me out,' Churchill would say, noting that the Queen had questioned him in the closest detail on a report which he had not read. Later other of her prime ministers, especially Harold Wilson, used to get flustered about the same experience.

The red boxes, in those less security-conscious days, were brought to the palace daily in a spritely little horse-drawn carriage whose maroon doors displayed the royal arms. It would clip-clop into the cobbled royal mews where the Queen's messenger would be waiting to carry the boxes through the half mile of corridors within Buckingham Palace to the Queen's second-floor office, pleasantly and warmly decorated now in feminine colours and with her mahogany desk right-angled in the huge bay window overlooking the palace gardens. There, she went through the daily routine of reading the memoranda and secret reports flown in from all over the world. No other person apart from herself is permitted to view the contents of the boxes, whereas in Victoria's day permission was given for Prince Albert to read them with her. If, for example, a Foreign Office box of top priority is brought, only she and the Foreign Secretary will possess the gold keys that open it.*

There was much for the Queen to catch up on in the field

*In May 1936, the British secret service put 'dummy' reports into a Foreign Office box because they suspected a leakage and that the leak was coming from within Buckingham Palace, i.e. through Mrs of foreign affairs occurring during her absence, as her Foreign Secretary Anthony Eden pointed out. He was back in harness after further surgery, this time by a specialist in America, though according to Hugh Dalton 'Eden's stock is falling fast . . . if Winston went it would be Butler as PM and Macmillan at the Foreign Office. They say he (Eden) is nervy and always losing his temper in cabinet, foreign office and elsewhere.'[8] Darker rumours suggested Eden was in some way addicted to, or affected by, the long months of painkiller drugs he had been taking after his illness and surgical accident. In spite of Hugh Dalton's speculation about Mr R. A. Butler, then Chancellor of the Exchequer, taking over from Churchill, elsewhere it seemed a foregone conclusion that Eden was the heir apparent. And as the pressure began mounting that summer against Churchill, pressure from within his own ranks, the Queen would soon find herself thrust into what was one of the most dramatic, yet secret, pieces of political theatre in modern British history, with herself waiting in the wings to exercise her royal prerogative in the selection of a new Prime Minister.

Churchill was firmly in favour of the Queen's prerogative, under which the new Prime Minister is invited to form a government by Her Majesty. The occasions when the Queen is called upon to do what, in the fifties and sixties, amounted to the appointment of the Prime Minister, stemmed not so much from her own constitutional role or involvement in politics – in fact she was expressly unable to involve herself in any dealings directly with the House of Commons – but from difficulties that arose more out of the rather lax method the Conservative Party followed for the selection of a leader. There was then no formal election procedure for the Conservatives to choose their new leader, who would merely 'emerge'. Churchill, according to Colville's own recollections,[9] was of the view that he should not 'advise' the Queen as to his successor unless he was specifically asked to do so.

Simpson's gossiping with her friends, who included Joachim von Ribbentrop the German ambassador. The leak was substantiated according to reports in the FBI general file on the Duke of Windsor.[7]

The situation she would soon face had all the makings of a messy transfer of power, one which was fraught with serious constitutional problems and remains to this day one of the most hotly debated questions whenever the topic of the Queen's prerogative is discussed. In that year, there were those in the ranks of government who challenged not merely Churchill's ability to lead the party but also the suitability of his heir apparent, Eden, but it seemed unlikely that they would be given the chance to express their views by any democratic process. This lack of procedural mechanism also undoubtedly contributed to the months of internal strife within the Conservative Party, many of whose MPs were torn between their love of Churchill and their desire to see him replaced. Churchill meanwhile seemed determined, for his own reasons, to hang on. The Queen was discreetly made aware that at some time in the not too distant future, she might have to call upon a new Prime Minister. As his Cabinet went off for the holidays, and the knives were temporarily sheathed, Churchill retired to Chartwell where he became engrossed by the situation in which he found himself and spoke repeatedly to Colville of the treachery that surrounded him. Colville noted, 'As the days went by he became less reconciled to giving up office and adumbrated all sorts of reasons why he should not. Never had a P.M. been treated like this, that he was to be hounded from his place merely because his second-in-command wanted the job . . . it looks a terrible and painful struggle.'[10]

Eden meanwhile was recording his version of events. He wrote in his diary for 27 August that he had consulted Butler and Macmillan who were convinced that Churchill had decided to stay on, in spite of the nearness of the next general election, when Churchill would be eighty. They were all gloomy. After the meeting, Eden went to see Churchill; 'Interview opened stiffly . . . he launched out into a long rigmarole as to how he felt better (he didn't look it & his argument was often confused). He also argued it was a bad time for him to go; not possible for the new administration to make its mark in the last year.'[11]

The long and painful struggle over the leadership predicted by Colville became a reality.

Though speculation as to Churchill's departure was

surprisingly low-key, the Queen was informed of the subcurrent of activity through various channels. It carried on through February and Colville noted with a somewhat despairing tone, 'He was ageing month by month and was reluctant to read any papers . . . facts would be demanded from government departments and not arouse any interest when they arrived; it was becoming an effort even to sign letters and a positive condescension to read Foreign Office telegrams. And yet on some days, the old sparkle would be there.'[12] In February, Eden became firmer in his resolve and finally extracted a promise from Churchill that he would retire in April.

In March, Churchill made what many believe to be one of his greatest speeches in the House of Commons in the big debate on defence. Thereafter, his words became much quoted: that Britain's possession of the H-Bomb may compel peace so that 'safety will become the sturdy child of terror'. On 29 March, he had his usual Tuesday audience with the Queen; the meetings often now extended beyond the normal half an hour. Sometimes, he would stay for an hour and half and when his staff inquired occasionally what he and the Queen managed to talk about for such a length of time, he would reply, 'Racing . . .'

On Monday, 4 April the Churchills had arranged a dinner party for the Queen and Prince Philip and a few other friends; the date had been chosen some weeks beforehand but since it was now realised it would fall on the eve of his resignation, invitations were hurriedly extended to about fifty people, including most of his family and high-ranking staff, leaders of his party and of the Opposition, among them his old adversary Clement Attlee, together with a selection of other notable figures from his past, such as Montgomery.

Churchill, proposing a toast to the Queen, reminded his assembled company that it was a toast he used to enjoy drinking when 'I was a cavalry subaltern in the reign of Your Majesty's great-great-grandmother, Queen Victoria' and he was proud to have reached 'the wise and kindly way of life of which Your Majesty is the young and gleaming champion'.

His devotion was evident to the last, and the Queen in proposing his own health, made a short speech of praise for 'my Prime Minister'. The next day, 5 April, Churchill presided over his last Cabinet meeting and in the afternoon went to Buckingham Palace, wearing his frock coat and top hat, to formally tender his resignation. Eden was summoned to Buckingham Palace and accepted the Queen's invitation to become Prime Minister. What has remained an intriguing mystery ever since is how she arrived at the decision to call him and not R. A. Butler who mistakenly gained the impression that she might, or even the ambitious Harold Macmillan. There are few quoted insights into what exactly transpired between them. According to Colville, the Queen did not mention Eden's name during Churchill's last audience as Prime Minister[13] nor did the outgoing Prime Minister, a stout defender of the 'Queen's prerogative', presume to advise her before he left. He considered it an important constitutional point that he should not do so. If that assessment is correct, Eden was appointed as Prime Minister by the Queen alone and without advice, and there appears to be no available documentation to contradict this view.

What we do now know, largely from previously classified documents or unpublished papers released in 1989 and 1990, is that the much-quoted statement by Churchill that 'no two men will ever change guard more smoothly' was true only in its execution by the Queen. The smoothness masked eighteen months of internal strife and bitterness amongst senior colleagues in government as they anguished over how they could get rid of him. That the handover appeared smooth was also aided by the fact that it happened in the middle of the longest newspaper strike in history!

Anthony Eden called an immediate general election, set for 26 May. Against Clement Attlee, whose National Health spectacles and drawn cheeks presented a picture that was too much of a reminder of the postwar austerity programme he introduced, even the pallid Anthony Eden actually cut a promising figure, in spite of what Clementine Churchill had described as his 'odd colour', referring to the yellowish look of his cheeks. He was aided by last-minute own goals by Labour such as the dock strike, now in its seventh day, and a newspaper report, planted by the Tories, that if Labour won then their left-wingers would depose Attlee immediately and make Aneurin Bevan the Prime Minister. On the day,

Eden won a comfortable overall majority of fifty-eight.

Two days later, having accepted the Queen's invitation to form a government for the second time in two months, Eden brought her into the first of the several crises that would punctuate his short tenure at No. 10 Downing Street and tarnish the sovereign herself. One of the first actions of his Cabinet was to declare a State of Emergency to deal with the effects of two major strikes, in the docks and on the railways, the latter having been called from midnight on 28 May. Eden had to ensure by legislation that supplies of food were maintained and public order upheld. On 31 May the Queen's signature for such a Proclamation was received at a special meeting of the Privy Council at Balmoral.

If omens were to be heeded, this was a bad one by any measure; the social upheaval that confronted the new government weighed on the Queen's mind, while Eden privately blamed the ineptitude of the last days of the Churchill administration for the trouble in which he now found himself. As yet inexperienced in matters that involved the well-being and social order of her subjects at grass-roots level, the Queen listened intently to the implications of the Proclamation she was required to sign. The emergency powers were needed, it was explained, to be used against anyone 'who threatened to deprive the community of the essentials of life'. She asked questions from a woman's standpoint, inquiring of the threat to food supplies and to children and she listened as Eden broadcast his warning to the nation, 'I am not going to leave you in any doubt as to the deadly seriousness of what is happening in our country . . .'

The strikes caused discomfort to her nation and damaged its trade but were over within weeks. Other pressing problems concerning the economic ills of the country also taxed Eden's thoughts and there is a telling phrase that became all too familiar in future years, in a memo he wrote to his Chancellor of the Exchequer that summer: 'We must put the battle against inflation before anything else.'[14] But looming up fast on the rails, almost unnoticed, was a personal matter concerning the royal family that would explode into a barrage of headlines that no mere political crisis would wipe from the front pages.

It had nothing to do with politics, or at least it ought not to have done. Princess Margaret was approaching her twenty-fifth birthday; the date, 21 August 1955, was circled in the diaries of every news editor in Fleet Street where reporters were poised for action, and the possible return from exile of Peter Townsend. In the two years that had elapsed since the last débâcle of the princess's romance with a divorced person, nothing had changed in their feelings for one another and neither had anyone told Margaret that marriage was definitely out of the question. During this time, she had become a familiar figure in the social pages, being portrayed variously, and generally sympathetically, as 'the little princess who has hardly smiled' and the elegant woman about town, adorned with sophistication, jewels and long cigarette-holders, for whose hand in marriage a number of notable eligible bachelors aspired. And though often photographed with male escorts like Billy Wallace, Colin Tennant, or Mark Bonham Carter, Princess Margaret was still consumed by her love for Townsend; separation had, in truth, been painful. She had patiently waited to reach that magical age of twenty-five, blithely assuming she would be free to marry. This belief was only enhanced by the arrival as Prime Minister of Eden whom she expected could be counted upon for support. Though a formal man, he had been around since the days of her grandfather, and a regular visitor to the palace ever since. They had met on many occasions; he had been house-guest of her father and of her sister. More importantly, he had also gone through a divorce in 1950; he had parted from a wife, Beatrice, who hated politics, and was remarried to Churchill's niece Clarissa. His Cabinet, she knew, also contained two other divorced persons, in Peter Thorneycroft and Walter Monckton. And so, what could possibly stop her now in her hopes and dreams to marry the man she loved? What obstacles could now exist?

There were to be plenty. Two days before her birthday, the *Daily Mirror* pounded out their now famous headline: 'Come On, Margaret! Please Make Up Your Mind'. The ball was rolling and for the next two and a half months, it bounced from one set of headlines to another, ranging across the full gamut of emotions, from the support of the mass public to the vitriol of the extremist churchmen, the most prolific of whom were still using as their case for the prosecution the fact that if perchance some misfortune collectively befell the Queen and her children, Princess Margaret's children by Townsend would eventually come to the throne – but in the eyes of the Church they would be illegitimate and so the royal family would become extinct. And so it went on, and on and on.

October arrived and the word went around that Peter Townsend was coming home. The Queen had a plan. Townsend and Margaret should be allowed to meet and if they so wished, she would make every effort to smooth a path for her sister to be married by seeking the approval of Eden's Cabinet. Philip was against it and so was the Queen Mother who had already been approached by her old friend Lord Salisbury, Lord President of the Council, who suggested that her late husband would not have permitted the marriage under any circumstances. The Queen, however, dearly wanted to safeguard her sister's happiness if it was at all possible.

Townsend returned to London on Wednesday, 12 October; it was arranged that he should stay with friends in the royal circle, the Abergavennys in Lowndes Square. The next day, Princess Margaret and the Queen Mother returned to Clarence House from Balmoral. Though now assuredly against the marriage, the Queen Mother continued to regard him with nothing but sympathy and kindness. The large posse of reporters and photographers who tracked his every move even down to buying a new pair of breeches from his tailor's in Conduit Street and a box of fancies from a baker's shop in Chelsea, reported back to the office, 'He's been inside for two hours'. Speculation became volcanic and the inundated commander of the Queen's press corps, Richard Colville, merely fanned the flames with a badly worded statement indicating there was no announcement regarding Princess Margaret's future contemplated 'at present'. What did that mean – 'at present'? Townsend retreated to less public accommodation in the country, to the home of the Hon. Mrs John Lycett, a cousin of the Queen, at Allanbay Park, Berkshire; Princess Margaret was invited to join them for the weekend. Also present were several dozen uninvited persons, hanging from trees with cameras clicking every time a bird took flight, and filing stories for Monday's paper which gave the waiting nation a moment-by-moment account of Margaret's idyllic weekend. Well, that just about sealed their fate. On 18 October Anthony Eden took a plane to Balmoral where the Queen had hoped to remain and deal with her family situation unhurried and calmly. Of course, he said, he had every sympathy for Princess Margaret but, realistically, the marriage could not be approved by his Cabinet and he had refused to put it to the vote. Lord Salisbury was already threatening to resign from the government if the marriage were allowed and others might follow. The Cabinet could not, therefore, give its consent[15] and if Margaret were to proceed, she should understand that she would be required to renounce her right to the throne and it would be necessary for her to leave the country for the time being, and, of course, her income from the Civil List would be discontinued immediately. Still, the Queen refused to be rushed and on 24 October *The Times* published a thundering leader, written by its editor Sir William Haley, solemn and sermonising: that Margaret had but two choices, either to renounce her happiness for the love of the Commonwealth, or to renounce her royal status and marry, which would damage the Queen's own position as a symbol of goodness, especially in family life. Margaret went to see the Archbishop of Canterbury, Dr Geoffrey Fisher, who apparently thought she had come for guidance. 'Put the books away,' she told him. 'I've come to give you some information, not to ask for it.' She and Townsend had already decided it was over; they could not go on. The archbishop beamed, 'What a wonderful person the Holy Spirit is.'[16] Some newspapers tried to rouse them into a last-minute pledge of marriage but Townsend was already packing his bags and Margaret was showing the statement they had written between them to the Queen: 'I have been aware that, subject to my renouncing my rights of succession, it might have been possible for me to contract a civil marriage. But, mindful of the Church's teaching that Christian marriage is indissoluble, and conscious of my duty to the Commonwealth, I have resolved to put these considerations before any others.'

It was over. *The Times* expressed grateful thanks on behalf of the nation. In truth the nation would have preferred them to have married and only the *Manchester Guardian* was prophetic in its assessment: 'her decision . . . will be regarded by the masses of the people as unnecessary and perhaps a great waste. In the long run, it will not redound to the credit or influence of those who have been most persistent in denying the princess the same liberty as is enjoyed by the rest of her fellow citizens.'

The diarists among them scribbled their impressions. Harold Nicolson wrote of the 'great personal sacrifice'[17] that Princess Margaret had made, and said it would be awkward for him because he was meeting the Duke of Windsor for dinner that very evening the news broke. The duke might well have been reflecting that he ought to have made the same sacrifice twenty years earlier. He was, Nicolson reflected, putting on a front of being busy and happy but the truth was that he remained unoccupied and miserable.[18]

Noël Coward also sided with the establishment, though for different reasons, when he observed:

> Poor Princess Margaret has made a sorrowful, touching statement that she will not marry Peter Townsend. This is a fine slap in the chops for the bloody press which has been persecuting her for so long. I am really glad that she has at last made the decision but I do wish there hadn't been such a hideous hullabaloo about it . . . it would have been an unsuitable marriage anyway. She cannot know, poor girl, being young and in love, that love dies soon and that a future with two strapping stepsons and a man eighteen years older than herself would not really be rosy . . . private sorrow is bad enough, but public sorrow is almost unbearable.[19]

Royal duties could not be interrupted by family matters and there were already plans in the pipeline to send the Queen back on her travels; they seemed determined to make her the most travelled monarch in history – and of course they would eventually succeed. One matter had occurred to the Treasury, however, regarding the costs of overseas trips. Since air travel was still fairly new for the royals, the procedure set up when the Queen first flew across any long stretch of water was still in place; it called for her route by air to be worked out with the Royal Navy and the Royal Air Force so that British ships could be posted where possible at regular intervals along the route and sail in the same direction as her plane, while the RAF would first send a reconnaissance aircraft to monitor air miles, timings and landing facilities and then provide escort aircraft. The whole procedure, complicated and costly, was put in motion whenever a member of the royal family travelled on long flights abroad. Cabinet discussions on the topic provided the solution, that in future the ships would only be posted for the Queen.[20]

Chapter Four
Rich in Crisis (1956)

The new year was almost upon them and as the royal family relaxed at their traditional Christmas gathering at Sandringham they must have been looking forward to less turbulent times. Surely there would be some respite from the headlines? They might well have asked themselves that question but they would have needed more than a crystal ball to foretell that the Queen was on the threshold of what would be described retrospectively as a period rich in crisis, and what had gone before so far in her short reign would pale in its significance. Her task, it seemed, could be likened to pushing a boulder up a never-ending hill.

She was, that Christmas, already well advanced with plans for another overseas tour, again with the double aim of letting her be seen by her people and of bolstering her government's trade and overseas ambitions. A 3 week tour of Nigeria was being described as 'one of the most important journeys in the Queen's life' as the politicians attempted to retain some influence in remaining 'possessions', and there was a touch of unfortunate irony in the fact that the very week of the visit saw the fifty-fifth anniversary of the defeat by British troops of the last rebel emirs of Nigeria in January 1901 on what was the last day of Queen Victoria's reign, a fact which the Colonial Office who had planned the tour of Nigeria had apparently overlooked.

The Queen and Prince Philip left England for their visit on 27 January 1956. She was the figurehead of the fading colonial rule in Africa, the Queen of all Nigerians – though at best, all she could eventually hope to achieve was to provide the nation with the monarchy's umbrella of unity if they wished to use it. Nigeria was important; it was the largest of Britain's colonies, the largest African territory and Britain's largest trading post in Africa. The country was also in the throes of campaigning for independence within the Commonwealth, yet was split by the tribal and regional loyalties that eventually formed the basis for civil war. There was actually little hint outwardly in the country of the extent of troubles that were soon to come, though Colonial Office and Foreign Office intelligence was already predicting unrest, hence the Queen's visit as, hopefully, a calming and unifying spirit.[1]

Wildly excited crowds lined the 13 mile route from Lagos Airport into the city and the whole pattern of welcoming ceremonies as she progressed through the country developed into the most spectacular and colourful scenes the Queen had ever witnessed and which could only be reminiscent of the Delhi durbar staged for King George V in India in 1911. The Queen and Prince Philip dined in state with twenty-two Nigerian ministers and noblemen, bringing together tribal chiefs who had never been in each other's company, sitting under a vast cream punka, the only one remaining in the country. This, it was said, was a symbolic meeting with the punka representing the universal cover of the Queen's sovereignty. As she travelled out into the regions, she was entertained by the chiefs and emirs who, like the Indian princes when they tried to outdo each other in their gifts of jewellery to King George V and Queen Mary, arranged massive displays of tribal ceremony to greet her. At Kaduna, for example, 8,000 warriors with painted faces and in traditional dress surged forward to present themselves and fierce and frightening horsemen of the Jahi tribe galloped forward at breakneck speed across an arena, pulling up inches short of the Queen's covered dais. Then the warriors swept down out of the Sahara in centuries-old custom, to the sound of silver trumpets and brass cymbals which were made before the reign of Elizabeth I.

At Kano, once the biggest slave-trading city of all Africa, Muslim horsemen, turbaned and wearing armour which was made at the time of the Crusades, formed a guard of honour as they met the emirs of Kano, Gumel, Hadeija and Kazure whose ancestors were among the last to accede to British rule at the turn of the century. And so it went on, throughout the country, with the men of noble ancestry brought forward by the white colonial officers to pay homage to the white Queen on a scale never seen before, nor to be seen again.

At each stopping point she quietly (but perhaps warily) lectured them. 'Tolerance is necessary not only in religious matters but also towards those whose views and traditions differ. It is by this spirit of understanding that the people of various races and tribes will be brought together.'[2] The tour was billed as a great personal triumph for the Queen; it was indeed a huge success in all kinds of ways, and especially as an example to the rest of Africa which was being overtaken by the mood of independence from imperial rule. The politicians, and the Queen herself, set great store by arousing public feeling and demonstrations of devotion to the monarchy. The people were more taken by the personality and the glamour of the Queen, and by the pomp of their own native pageantry, for the visit did not halt the desire to end colonial rule. Four years later, Nigeria was granted independence and ran into the bloodiest period of its history.

The Queen came back to a Britain in the grip of freeze and squeeze. The coldest day since 1895 had just been recorded and on the very day of her arrival home, 17 February, the new Chancellor of the Exchequer, Mr Harold Macmillan, hoisted the bank rate to 5½ per cent, the highest since the financial crisis of 1931, introduced tighter curbs on hire purchase and credit, and cut government subsidies for milk and bread. 'The nation must pause in the pursuit of higher living standards,' said Macmillan, and added that ominous sentence which continues, still, to reverberate through the corridors of Westminster, 'Inflation is obstinate and serious.'[3] The brakes were put on the great fifties consumer boom which the following month showed itself in an incredible balance of payments deficit of £103 million; the government's economic planning was not ready for the materialistic age which sought the electronic goods like televisions and hi-fis, washing machines and cars that were in abundance across the Atlantic in those days of breaking out from postwar privations. World trade was expanding rapidly yet this vigorous upturn in Britain's economy was accompanied by what Prime Minister Anthony Eden described as the 'plagues of prosperity'.

It was an age that also sought icons and heroes and heroines, like James Dean, Marilyn Monroe and Marlon Brando, and rejected religion. The Queen and Prince Philip were slotted into that kind of mould and the Queen herself realised it. 'I do not want to be dressed like a film star', she snapped one day when Norman Hartnell brought some clothes that she thought were too extrovert. The phrase was not a one-off and obviously it was a matter of concern to her that she was being seen in that light. Her footman Ralphe White recalled one day being asked to go upstairs to get the Queen a coat because she was going out for a walk in the grounds. 'I came back with one of her fur coats. She looked at me horrified. "No not that," said the Queen. "I look too much like a film star in mink." I had to go back upstairs and bring down one of her tweed overcoats.'[4]

Out of the limelight, the Queen insisted upon a simple elegance in her appearance, of which Malcolm Muggeridge was to write: 'duchesses, but not shop assistants . . . find the Queen dowdy, frumpish and banal'.[5] The trouble was, of course, that there were no other people to compare with, other than film stars, who were so often in the public eye and who were so physically attractive; who else was mobbed every time they stepped off a plane or out of a car? Who else could draw a crowd by their very presence? Only the likes of Elizabeth Taylor (4,000 Londoners stood vigil outside Caxton Hall, London to catch a glimpse of her when she married Michael Wilding). Too awful a comparison? Perhaps so but then, suddenly, the two examples of public interest merged in real life on 19 April, when the fairytale syndrome was trotted out again for the marriage of movie star Grace Kelly to Prince Rainier of Monaco which was considered of sufficient importance for twenty-five nations to send representing dignitaries, standing shoulder to shoulder with Hollywood's finest. The ceremony was televised worldwide and now Hollywood had its very own 'queen'. The public loved it, just as they did the Queen's own fairytale. And there was an underlying and serious similarity between film stars and royalty which Malcolm Muggeridge identified in his article that year for the *New Statesman*, entitled 'The Royal Soap Opera'. The piece has been the focus of attention on many occasions as the starting point of a series of critical attacks on the Queen herself, though, as Muggeridge complained, his words were not properly read. 'No one reads these days,' he moaned after the umpteenth newspaper had paraphrased and misquoted his thesis. What he was really trying to point out, as was made clear when the article was reprinted in *The Listener* in 1981, was that the masses, the Queen's people of the materialistic fifties, had no real religion and that they had discovered an ersatz religion, a substitute for deity, in the monarchy.

There was a volume of written adulatory material after the Coronation to support Muggeridge's view, with some writers going to the extremes of describing the New Elizabeth Age as being inspired by the 'spiritual exultation' which had 'so recently sanctified a godly and united nation around the Crown'.[6] Though rites of initiation in the ceremony were much the same as they were when Edward the Confessor and William the Conqueror were crowned in the same building in the eleventh century, some observers felt that there was a new kind of adulation emerging for the monarchy, a kind never experienced before. *Reynolds News*, a popular Sunday paper among what was then termed as the working classes, ran a survey of its readers' views towards the monarchy and concluded, 'For thousands of Britons reverence for royalty has become a national religion, everything about the monarchy being tinged with a mystical piety.' It quoted from interviews taken across the country a publican who 'hardly dare draw a pint when royalty appears on the bar room television . . . the atmosphere is like that in a church'. And there was the husband who rowed with his wife because she insisted he stood up in their own home when the National Anthem was played on the radio.[7]

Much the same kind of idolatry, incidentally, was being accorded at the same time to James Dean and Elvis Presley. As one *Reynolds News* reader pointed out, 'What's the difference in teenagers who scream at Elvis and thousands who stand in the rain just to wave a little flag when the

Queen's car rushes past. Half of them don't even see her.' Gwin Steinbeck, wife of the author of *East of Eden*, said after Dean's death in a car crash in 1955, 'Many people have no emotional roots and are without a basic faith. Dean became a substitute Christ and as such they are even trying to resurrect him.' Nor was it unknown for past monarchs to see themselves as deities. 'For myself,' said Queen Elizabeth I, 'I was never so much enticed with the glorious name of King or Royal authority of a Queen as delighted that God made me his instrument to maintain His truth and glory and to defend this kingdom from peril, dishonour, tyranny and oppression.'

Star worship was certainly nothing new but it was new to royal figures, with the possible exception of the Prince of Wales in the twenties. In this consumer age, in which acquisitiveness was seen as a prime virtue, heroes and heroines were required to be looked at, to be read about, to be modelled upon and to be swooned over. That is not to say that by making this comparison, the Queen was being placed in the same iconophilic category as Elizabeth Taylor and Grace Kelly; it was undoubtedly true, however, that for glamorous reasons the sheer impact of her presence in public life was drawing unprecedented attention wherever she went in the world, be it from Fijian natives, or hordes of Nigerian horsemen, or simply adoring crowds in the cities of the civilised world and the danger was, as we can now view from a distance of thirty or more years, that the unity the Queen was supposed to represent and the very serious nature of her constitutional role in life were in danger of becoming swamped by hysterical adulation.

Muggeridge had spotted this turn of events and argued caution because the popular monarchy was a very recent invention. He was right. The transition to a popular monarchy from an aristocratic monarchy, so hated by the politicians of the eighteenth and nineteenth centuries who had to deal with the first four Georges, had been in progress for a mere fifty years. Queen Victoria's reign quelled any kind of public clamouring for royalty because she ruled, in the end, by remote control and having created the legend of 'The Widow of Windsor', all that remained was for her to live up to it, which she did. She was seen by the public so infrequently that indifference to the 'parsimonious German frau' set in and even republican groups began to spring up. Edward VII only just saved his reputation in the latter days of his life, though he never lived down the image of a bloated, lobster-jowled royal playboy whose life had been one long round of self-indulgence and his critics did not hesitate to say so. Nor did his aristocratic court stop covering up for his incredible womanising which his humiliated wife Queen Alexandra accepted and even condoned, in the end, by bringing one of his mistresses to his death-bed. George V and George VI were thankfully more simple men, reserved and totally committed to their life of service; nothing would deter them from it. They too, however, continued to be served and surrounded and protected by class-conscious aristocratic courtiers whose style, and even whose very existence, was going out of favour in Britain in the fifties.

Queen Elizabeth II found herself torn between pleas to stay on the royal pedestal and pleas to come down and meet the common man, as the *Daily Mirror* – then heading for the historic peak in its circulation of over 5 million copies a day – insisted upon calling working-class people. There was precedence for that too, in a way, as recounted by the Duke of Windsor when he was Prince of Wales and put himself about rather too much for the likes of some of his staid Georgian courtiers.

'If I may say so, sir,' the Keeper of the Privy Purse Sir Frederick Ponsonby protested, 'I think there is a risk in your making yourself too accessible.'

'What do you mean?' asked the young prince.

'The monarchy should always retain an element of mystery . . . not show itself too much. The monarchy must remain on a pedestal.'

'I do not agree. Times are changing,' Edward replied.

'I am older than you, sir, and I have been with your father, your grandfather and your great-grandmother . . . they all understood.'[8]

That little exchange took place in the twenties, and could easily have been held again when Edward became king in 1936. The question was, could it now be applied to the fifties and beyond? Would the monarchy fade if the mystique was chipped away? With the benefit of seeing the result of

Edward's reign and his brother's attempt to repair the damage of it, it was certainly true that if the Queen listened to the critics and turned herself into a social monarchy which mirrored the ordinary family life which she was supposed to symbolise, there were great risks of vulgarisation and debasement which she could, perhaps, not have foretold then, and so whatever changes were required would need quite delicate handling. That apart, she was also being used by the self-interest of politicians, courtiers, the media and at least one member within the family circle (Mountbatten).

Regardless of all the pomp and circumstance that had been a deliberate feature of the opening of her reign, and the protocol and formality that surrounded her, the image was still to be 'glamour' and if the word had not been so hopelessly debased, even in 1956, hers could be said to be the most glamorous life in the world. She was surrounded, still, by the sycophants and flatterers who are always attendant upon monarchy and the dangers have always been visible. In those days, there was usually a row when someone spoke out of turn, yet surprisingly not a lot was said of Muggeridge's article when it was first published, though, as we shall see, it would inspire a huge controversy in the autumn of 1957 when it was reprinted in America. When the attacks came, as they surely would, it was upon the royal family that the cudgels rained and the Queen, just trying to do her best, who would soon take the brunt of the criticism; all of it lay just ahead, along with some other tarnish not of her making . . .

The summer months of 1956 were awash with visiting VIPs from overseas, including Harry S. Truman and his wife who lunched at the palace in June, Sir Robert Menzies, the Australian Prime Minister who was given an audience as were the prime ministers of India, New Zealand and South Africa. On 16 July, King Faisal II of Iraq, a mere twenty-one years old, arrived for a state visit with his influential uncle, the Crown Prince Abdulillah, and was received by the Queen in suitable magnificence; they talked about things that reigning monarchs talk about, especially world affairs and more especially the situation in the Middle East. Faisal, a modest young ruler who had the deepest sense of caring for his people,[9] impressed everyone with his sincerity and charm.

He struck an immediate rapport with Prince Philip and later they went sailing together. His grandfather, who founded the dynasty with British backing, had ridden with Lawrence of Arabia. Doubtless a topic for discussion amongst them was the tide of Arab nationalism being aroused by Colonel Nasser in Egypt from whose country British troops had recently departed for Cyprus to help combat EOKA's terrorists. The old world order of British imperialism had certainly left its problems. Faisal and his uncle warned that Nasser could become a problem to the western world and his words may still have been ringing in the British politicians' ears when the intelligence community began to sound more alarm bells.

On the evening of 26 July, what the King had warned of came to fruition. He was dining at No. 10 Downing Street with Sir Anthony Eden when one of the Prime Minister's private secretaries rushed in bearing a written message on a folded piece of paper. Nasser had seized the Suez Canal by force and had nationalised the Anglo-French company which operated the shipping lane; this, said Nasser, was in retaliation for the Americans' refusal to finance the building of the Aswan Dam.

Eden's Cabinet went into crisis session the following day after receiving news of Nasser's takeover of the canal. The newspapers were screaming 'Foul!' and comparing Nasser to Hitler. *The Times* leader on 1 August was fairly typical and in view of 1990 developments in the Gulf it is interesting to be reminded of what was being said in 1956: 'If Nasser is allowed to get away with his coup all the British and Western interests in the Middle East will crumble.'[10]

On the afternoon of 2 August, Eden brought the Queen into an affair that would leave its sorry mark on British history and a stain on the Crown. She was staying with the Duke of Norfolk for Goodwood races and was already in the Duke of Richmond's private box, waiting for the 2 o'clock race, when a messenger arrived bearing a sealed envelope from the Prime Minister. Eden was due to make a statement to the Commons that afternoon and one of the elements of that speech was the government's intention to call up 20,000 British Army reservists for which he required a Proclamation signed by the Queen. She read the document, but did not sign it. She was unable to make any observations or ask any questions; she said, however, she would approve it if her Prime Minister so wished. Eden was informed by telephone and in his speech to the Commons, he read out the Proclamation, as yet unsigned by the Queen, said that as a precautionary measure a number of army, navy and air force units were being sent to the eastern Mediterranean and made the following promise: 'the freedom and security of transit through the canal can only be effectively secured by international authority. It is upon this that we must insist.'

In further statements that would sound all too familiar when Saddam Hussein grabbed Kuwait in 1990, Eden said that half the west's oil passed through the Suez Canal and he could not allow a man like Nasser to 'have his thumb on our windpipe'.

The following day, on 3 August, a special Privy Council meeting was held at Arundel Castle, the Duke of Norfolk's home. It was called specifically for the Queen to sign the Proclamation to call out the reservists, which she could have done just as easily the previous day. Constitutionally she could not refuse to sign, though she did have the prerogative to ask for information. The question that she would undoubtedly have asked was, 'Is Britain going to war again?' The call-up of reservists surely meant that the eventuality was likely. The discussions of that meeting remain on the secret list, as do the subsequent discussions which Eden had with the Queen. Eden did admit, however, that the question of the reservists was 'one of our difficulties'[11] in the preliminary discussions not merely because of the war prospect but also because they would be taken from important work in civil life.

In the dramatic scenes of international diplomacy, and conspiracy, which now began to unfold, the Queen as head of state effectively stood at the helm, waiting to advise, encourage, or warn, just as her father had done with Winston Churchill in the last war. How much would she be told? How closely would Eden keep her informed? Eden, who resigned as British Foreign Secretary in 1938 over Chamberlain's appeasement of Hitler over the invasion of Czechoslovakia, had no intention of appeasing Nasser whom he saw as a man in a similar mould to the German dictator. But Hitler was also too fresh in the minds of the British and the nation quickly split. These divisions became bitter as the days and weeks rolled by and more and more troops of an Anglo-French consortium headed eastwards to Suez while Nasser held firm and steadfastly rejected various resolutions from the United Nations and an eighteen-nation plan for the operation of the canal. Israeli Foreign Minister Golda Meir flew to Paris to conclude negotiations on the question of an Israeli strike, backed up by the British and the French; when the details were finalised, Eden was personally apprised of the plan by the French and outlined it to a shell-shocked Cabinet on 3 September. It was the first of four Cabinet meetings at which no minutes were taken on Eden's personal orders, and thus the records remain to this day remarkably silent on what transpired.[12] Eden carefully omitted these facts in his memoirs. He had even instructed that the head of MI6, Dick White, should not be told about covert collusion at the time.

This shroud of secrecy imposed upon the whole operation by Eden was so effective that President Eisenhower and the US Secret Service were unable to discover what was happening. Although Eden continued to brief the Queen, American Secretary of State John Foster Dulles telephoned his brother Allen, then head of the Central Intelligence Agency, on 18 October and complained that 'we do not have a clear picture of what they are up to . . . they are deliberately keeping us in the dark'.[13] The Russians seemed to be rather better informed. Just as the whole Suez crisis was about to erupt, tanks rolled into Budapest on the night of 26 October and Soviet troops killed 3,000 people on the first night of their action against the Hungarian 'revolutionaries'.

On 29 October, heavily armoured Israeli forces swept across the 120 mile border with Egypt as a 'reprisal for Egyptian attacks on Israel's land and sea communications'. Within forty-eight hours, RAF Vickers Valiant bombers were taking off from Cyprus to begin bombing raids on military airfields near Cairo and in the Canal Zone as a preliminary to the allied British and French forces being put ashore from troopships. The troops began fierce hand-to-hand fighting to regain control of the Canal Zone. The Americans were furious and the whole adventure was halted within twenty-four hours by a demand for a ceasefire from the United Nations which for the first time in history Russia joined with America to support. The following day, the day on which Russia completed its own brutal dispersion of the Hungarian uprising by sending in 4,000 tanks, Marshal Bulganin sent Eden a personal telegram threatening immediate force 'to restore the situation in the Middle East' and made veiled threats of even a nuclear attack on Britain, which was a sabre-rattling cover for the Soviets' own despicable deeds in Hungary.

On 6 November, Eisenhower was returned as President with a bigger majority, which he took as support for his stand over Egypt. Eden, Selwyn Lloyd and their close supporters still wanted to continue their military action in the Middle East but Chancellor Harold Macmillan brought news that day which finally and completely ended the Suez adventure for Eden – and his political career. Macmillan reported that there had been a wave of panic-selling of the pound, which seemed to have been orchestrated by America. Britain's gold reserves had fallen by £100 million in a week; it was Macmillan's understanding that unless Britain gave an undertaking by midnight to end its occupation, the US Treasury would not support efforts to shore up the nose-diving pound. Macmillan, who until then had maintained a hawkish stance, became what one of his colleagues described as 'the first of the bolters'.[14]

It took years for the truth of the Anglo-French intervention to emerge – that Eden had made a secret deal in advance with the Israelis under which Israeli forces were covertly encouraged to make incursions into Egypt so that the British and French could go in behind them on the pretext of securing the canal, which they were entitled to do under the 1904 treaty. Yet in the week after the invasion, rumours of collusion were strongly and repeatedly denied by Eden himself.

Tempers ran high; nerves were frayed after many late-night sittings at the House of Commons. In the aftermath that continued with much vitriol for weeks, the Commons was suspended on several occasions through grave disorder and uproar among MPs in which even some Tories sided with Labour in their insistence that the government's handling of the Suez crisis was a national disgrace; even some of Eden's own ministers resigned in protest. Later, there were questions raised as to the Queen's knowledge of and part in the affair: had she been told of the attack in advance? Had she known of the secret deal with Israel? Had she approved? Eden maintained until his death that the Queen had been kept 'fully informed' of the crisis as it developed and was aware of her Prime Minister's plans, as relayed to her during his weekly audiences in the run-up to the invasion. She acted in the correct and proper constitutional way of accepting his reports and intentions with impartiality. However, Eden continued to be economical with the facts when his memoirs were published in 1960, and even Harold Macmillan sustained their vow of silence until after Eden's death. At the time, however, it was taken by some on the left of politics that the Queen must have given a positive gesture of approval, and there was great anger in many quarters that Eden had involved the Queen in his duplicity.

Lord Mountbatten, who was at the centre of the storm by virtue of his role as acting chairman of the Chiefs of Staff Committee, and was utterly and vehemently opposed to the attack on Egypt, also defended the Queen when the topic came in for renewed discussion in the late 1970s. Mountbatten said the Queen did not give her nod of approval, or indeed any kind of approval. She was, like himself, opposed to the Suez operation though constitutionally there was nothing she could do to prevent Eden taking the action he had by then already embarked upon.[15] The Queen, perhaps with the benefit of informal chats with Lord Mountbatten, while her husband was away on tour, was distressed that she should be drawn into it in such a way. Churchill, Montgomery and Eisenhower were as one in condemning the Suez action as ill-conceived and ill-executed.

Eden's critics were to be additionally outraged when the Queen suddenly found herself at the centre of yet another Conservative Party leadership crisis, which only she could resolve by calling for a new Prime Minister. This she would very soon be forced to do, amid shouts from the left, summarised by Sydney Jacobson (later Lord Jacobson) who said the Queen had been forced into doing the Conservative Party's dirty work. In a dramatic midnight communiqué from No. 10 Downing Street on 19 November, it was announced that Sir Anthony Eden was suffering from severe overstrain which made it impossible for him to carry on in office for the time being.

He fled the country four days later for Jamaica where he had been given use of 'Goldeneye', the island home of the James Bond creator Ian Fleming, brother-in-law of the Queen's deputy private secretary Martin Charteris. This offered the dual purpose of recuperative climate and getting him out of the firing line of political and press criticism. The crisis was such that Winston Churchill intervened on 23 November with a 'secret' and poignant letter to Eisenhower, imploring him to consider the special relationship between Britain and America. 'There is not much left for me to do in this world,' he wrote, '. . . but I do believe with unfaltering conviction that the theme of the Anglo-American alliance is more important now than at any time since the war.' Thereafter, Eisenhower dealt closely with Butler and Macmillan, to the extent that some have accused him of meddling in British politics to save the Conservative government, and the immediate crisis passed.

When Eden returned, looking bronzed and much fitter on 14 December, it was merely a matter of time before he announced his resignation, by now being sought from a crescendo of voices on the left, baying at the scent of the possible downfall of the government, yet unaware of Churchill's plea to Eisenhower to keep them afloat. On 8 January 1957, the Queen was still at Sandringham with her family when she received a request from Eden to receive him. She invited him and Clarissa to dine that evening and stay the night. He explained that he had sought three separate medical opinions, and they were all of the same view that his health was such that he could not continue. She expressed her profound regret that he had decided to retire and asked him if he would like an earldom; he said that would be an honour he would like to accept, at the appropriate time. 'Poor Anthony has resigned, given up,' Noël Coward recorded and added the view shared by many, '. . . tragic figure who had been cast in a star part well above his capacities'.[16]

The departing Prime Minister did not advise the Queen on his successor though, like Churchill, he was a firm supporter of the system of employing the Queen's prerogative in the selection process. He spoke not to the Queen but to her private secretary Sir Michael Adeane and suggested that a senior Cabinet minister should be asked to take unofficial soundings of the Cabinet, and at the same time he gave a nod towards the man he thought should succeed, R. A. Butler. The Edens returned to London the following day, and the Queen prepared to leave Sandringham for Buckingham Palace; the press office gave out a cover story that she was returning to see her dressmaker. Eden summoned Macmillan and Butler to Downing Street, along with Lord Salisbury, the Lord President of the Council, and told them in confidence that he was resigning. They all appeared shocked at the news, though none could seriously say it had not been expected. Salisbury gained the impression that he would have a significant part to play in the succession, and went to see Lord Kilmuir, the Lord Chancellor, who was unequivocal in his judgement that the Queen was fully entitled to seek and receive advice from anyone she wished in order to discover who commanded the support of the majority in the House of Commons. Kilmuir ruled instantly against a vote being sought from a party meeting or election, in spite of the prospect of a clear division amongst Conservatives as to who they might choose. He said the decision lay with the Queen, who should not wait, in fact ought not to wait, for any such procedure and so Adeane was advised that the 'soundings' would be taken by Salisbury and Kilmuir. He based this on precedent which had been followed religiously, with the single exception of the selection in 1922 of Bonar Law who insisted upon his party's endorsement before kissing the King's hand in acceptance of office. Cabinet ministers were summoned individually to Salisbury's room in the Privy Council office; Kilmuir was apparently amused to discover that almost each one, upon arrival, began the conversation by saying, 'This is like being called to the headmaster's study'. To which Salisbury responded tersely in his short-tongued vernacular, 'Well, which is it? Wab or Hawold?'

The majority apparently chose Hawold, yet outside in the cut and thrust of political life, the national press were taking their own 'soundings', as always, and by a rapid poll of both grassroots opinion in the constituencies and Conservative MPs, decided that the popular choice, by a large majority, was Butler. It was a natural assumption, therefore, that Butler would be summoned to the palace. The man himself was confident enough to discuss that night with his sister what he should say in his first television broadcast to the nation as Prime Minister. Macmillan, with more of an eye for political showmanship than his quieter opponent, gave the press a photographic opportunity by strolling around Downing Street with his wife and daughter. However, the morning after the Cabinet soundings had been taken – and regardless of popular opinion – Salisbury was summoned to the palace and reported to the Queen that the majority in cabinet voted for Macmillan; he made no other recommendation. Even then, the Queen did not rely solely on this advice. In accordance with her rights under which, as Kilmuir ruled, she could seek advice from whomever she wished, the Queen spoke to Winston Churchill who arrived at Buckingham Palace at her own request soon after Salisbury had left. He recommended Macmillan, in spite of strong reservations which had once inspired him to warn Eden about his misgivings over him – 'he was the only politician Churchill ever warned me about'.[17] He felt Butler was indecisive. Churchill's son Randolph was a lone voice that day in predicting Macmillan in his article for the London *Evening Standard*, tipped off not by his father but by Lord Beaverbrook. And then finally, the shock – Macmillan was summoned to an audience with the Queen at 2.00 p.m. and invited to become Prime Minister.

A political storm followed instantly with some Tories talking openly of their disappointment, if not astonishment, at Macmillan's success and Labour, now led by Hugh Gaitskell, launched into a spectacular attack, highly critical of the constitutional implications of the selection process which had effectively given the Queen responsibility for choosing the successor. Sydney Jacobson also thundered:

> At the age of thirty, after less than five years on the Throne, the Queen had to decide who was going to be the next prime minister. And she had to do this against a background of crisis, in a tense and perplexing political situation, at a time when she was deprived of the support of her husband. No wonder many Conservative MPs argue that it is wrong that the young Queen had to make the decision on such limited advice.

Yet the royal family seems to have been proud of its involvement – if the comments of Helen Cathcart, the royal biographer whose work all but carries a palace stamp of approval, are to be taken as a guide: 'Her (the Queen's) wisdom has been enriched by experience, including the crises when she probably shaped the course of world affairs by choosing astute Harold Macmillan as Britain's prime minister instead of unyielding 'Rabbie' Butler.'[18] In the aftermath, the political pundits reckoned that Butler's criticism of the Suez intervention cost him dear and thus he became 'the best Prime Minister Britain never had' and the Queen's choice of Macmillan seemed to some a sign of her further condonement of the fiasco, which we now know it was not. However, her farewell note to Eden revealed her sympathy for the man and the close bond of friendship that had existed between them, never quite to be repeated:

> My dear Anthony . . . I want to thank you not only for the loyal and distinguished service you have given me . . . I am anxious that you should realise that that record which has indeed been written in tempestuous times is highly valued and will never be forgotten by your Sovereign.[19]

Clarissa Eden, meanwhile, commiserated with Butler in a note 'to say what a beastly profession I think politics are and how greatly I admire your dignity and good humour'. The 'good humour' was not an entirely appropriate description on the night of the selection. Butler was overflowing with bitterness and for some time afterwards referred to the Queen sarcastically as 'our beloved monarch'.[20] Sydney Jacobson and others on both sides of the political commentating spectrum also questioned the right of the Tory aristocracy to hand over the selection of the nation's leader to the Queen who, in turn, had chosen to rely exclusively (he did not know about Churchill's advice at the time) on the advice of the Queen Mother's friend Lord Salisbury, 'straight from the glaciers of Tory nobility'.[21] And, incidentally, Macmillan was connected to those circles too, unlike Butler. And that brought him one great advantage, said one of his Cabinet members Reginald Maudling later, inasmuch as he was assured of the overwhelming support of the one key area of the Tory Party that mattered – the 'blue blood and thunder group'. Lady Dorothy Macmillan was the sister of the tenth Duke of Devonshire whose family had been at the peak of the aristocracy and the centre of the court circle for many decades. The Dowager Duchess of Devonshire was the Queen's Mistress of the Robes and close to her ear; as such she was a highly influential woman who was not averse to using that power when necessary. It is hardly likely that the Mistress of the Robes had much to do with the selection of the new Prime Minister but her power and influence could be counted upon to help keep the family scandals under lock and key.

And here is the biggest mystery; that Macmillan's personal traumas and eccentric private life, of which certain close friends and associates might have been aware, were never taken into account in his selection. If they had become known in today's climate of newspaper stridency, Macmillan would never have become Prime Minister; of that there is no doubt. With his wife's long-standing affair with Lord Boothby 'still rumbling on',[22] the fact that Boothby, and not Harold Macmillan, was the true father of Sarah Macmillan, and that Sarah, the illegitimate daughter, herself had an illegal abortion because had she borne her own illegitimate child it would have 'ruined her father's career' – all these facts would have ruined Macmillan's chances. The man must have lived permanently on a razor's edge, indeed they all must have feared exposure of these facts at any time.

It is now possible to observe, from a distance in time, the ruthless hypocrisy in that group of men who had selected a new Prime Minister with so many skeletons in the family chest, but who also had the temerity to castigate Princess Margaret for falling in love with a man who had two failings – that he was middle class and had divorced the wife who had deserted him.

So there it was. The Queen had exercised her prerogative once more and Harold Macmillan arrived to kiss her hand, and the feeling expressed in some quarters that the monarchy had suddenly turned back towards eighteenth-century traditions more akin to the Georges was not helped by the fact that Macmillan soon afterwards began appointing several of his relatives to key positions. Through all of this period, there are a number of unsolved mysteries as to the depth of the Queen's knowledge and involvement. Intriguingly a batch of files concerning Cabinet or Prime Ministerial discussions with or about the royal family during Eden's tenure between 1955 and 1956 remain classified at the Public Records Office at Kew; five folders all carry the mark 'Closed for 100 years'.[23] There is simply no way of knowing whether they relate to government business or something more personal . . .

Chapter Five

On with the Motley (1957)

'Thank goodness Philip isn't here,' the Queen remarked to one of her aides one day during those early winter months of 1957 with a brief moment of respite as the eye of the hurricane passed by. He would, she said, have been 'impossible to live with' through all the drama. Philip wasn't there because he was making what he described as his personal contribution to the Commonwealth ideal. This, whichever way you looked at it, could only be considered a rather arrogant statement, especially as in so far as the constitution of the nation was concerned, and that also covered the Commonwealth, Philip did not exist. The journey that was to take him out of the country for almost five months, and around the world again, was first suggested in the spring of 1956, when Buckingham Palace agreed that he should open the Olympic Games in Melbourne in November 1956.

As he discussed the trip with some of his friends, like the yachtsman Uffa Fox and the naturalist Peter Scott, the idea was conceived for a much broader trip, not merely a flight to Melbourne and back. Why not take the royal yacht *Britannia* and visit some of the island outposts and communities normally considered too small for a royal visit? The Queen approved the idea, and so did the government. What a good idea, they said, seemingly paying no regard to the £1.8 million cost of such a trip which seemed to expand in its conception with every discussion. How he managed to obtain government approval for it still remains a mystery, and there appears to be no recorded discussion of the topic in cabinet, where it was surely raised, unless it was among the closed files on royal family matters which cannot be inspected for 100 years.

How were they to know that the nation would be on the very edge of bankruptcy through the Suez crisis when Philip was on his travels? And so a small party of friends was put together, including the artist Edward Seago and Raymond Priestley, the Antarctic explorer and president of the British Association, and Philip's brand-new Lagonda was loaded aboard the *Britannia* for use on shore leave, and with a small contingent of personal staff the yacht set sail with a rear-admiral on the bridge and 275 other officers and crew under his command.

The yacht was to rendezvous with Philip in Mombasa and just after lunchtime on 15 October, the Queen headed a small party of royalty at Heathrow Airport to wish him *bon voyage* as he boarded a VC-10 of the Royal Air Force, adapted to his requirements to carry him on the first leg of the journey to Africa to join the *Britannia*. The onward route aboard *Britannia*, with himself often on the bridge reacquainting himself with the joys of his truncated naval career, went via the Seychelles, Ceylon where he was once stationed as a naval junior officer, Malaya, Papua and New Guinea, Australia, New Zealand, the Falklands and Antarctica and finally back to Africa and Gibraltar. There was lots of sport at sea and on land; crocodiles were shot in Darwin where Philip claimed one big enough to make handbags for the Queen, Margaret and the Queen Mother; there was polo, sailing – Philip's own yacht the *Bluebottle* won a bronze in the Melbourne Olympics – football on ice and whale-hunting, all of this occurring long before His Royal Highness became so concerned about endangered species of wildlife. The critics of such an extensive and costly adventure were ferocious in their attacks, punctuated as they were by the rumours of lively parties and a seemingly carefree existence in Australia, while Britain herself suffered the traumas of the Suez crisis.

Sir Raymond Priestley made a valiant attempt at defending the trip. 'The tour did a lot of good. True, it was a chance for the prince to enjoy himself in informal company, doing things he wanted to do. It was all his own idea and he was as enthusiastic as a schoolboy . . . overall he made the tour a pleasure cruise for all his companions.'[1] All the same, Philip's talk of the 'sacrifices' he made by being away from his family for so long in the cause of the Commonwealth ideal, did not appease those who felt the whole trip was just an excuse for a damned good adventure with amiable company which happened along its route to call in on several remote communities, many of whose inhabitants had no idea who he was.

As the weeks and months wore on the press corps back home was getting a touch restless, especially in view of some of the speculation in continental and American newspapers and magazines* implying that the Queen's marriage was in trouble, and the *Daily Express* gave great prominence to a series of articles entitled 'The Woman of the World with an Absent Husband'. This talk had been circulating among the gossips even before he left London and was the result of the prince's own now well-documented social life in which he continued to enjoy the friendship of highly colourful sporting and artistic companions. These were the rumours which those close to the hub reported that the Queen refused even to consider and the whole scenario was echoed thirty-five years later when the Prince and Princess of Wales were subjected to similar widespread allegations about the state of their marriage. Even so, Philip might just have slipped home without too much fuss had it not been for one hugely unexpected incident, already brewing as he commenced the homeward leg of his tour. Eileen Parker, the wife of Prince Philip's private secretary Mike Parker, made an appointment to see the Queen's press secretary Commander Richard Colville. The news came as a bombshell: Mrs Parker was giving the press office of the palace due warning that she

*The continental press was to become a continuing blight on the Queen's life. In 1972, *France-Dimanche* analysed its press cuttings on the Queen and Philip over the past fourteen years and discovered that in the European media alone, the Queen was preparing to abdicate on 63 occasions, was divorcing Prince Philip in 73 stories, had fallen out with Lord Snowdon in 115 stories, had fallen out with Princess Grace of Monaco 17 times and was pregnant 92 times!

intended to sue her husband for a legal separation as a prelude to a divorce action. Naturally such an announcement would be accompanied by something of a furore in the newspapers. Another woman was involved and was the straw that broke the camel's back after years of her putting up with an absentee husband whose attendance upon his employer had been well beyond the call of duty. 'Quite frankly', said Mrs Parker, to an aghast Commander Colville, 'I've had enough of it. The children hardly ever see him.' Colville was sympathetic, though naturally his first thoughts were of his own employers and his mind quickly conjured up visions of an abundance of lurid headlines. Once more, he decided not to inform the Queen of these impending probabilities. The news came in the midst of the Queen's own constitutional crisis, over Eden and Macmillan; Colville pleaded with Eileen Parker to think again. Was the situation beyond reconciliation? It was.

There was no alternative, said the wife, but she did agree to hold off at least until her husband returned home. Colville's hopes that the Parker divorce would remain under wraps until they were all back in England, so that at least he might be able to contain the damage, were shattered when Rex North, the *Sunday Pictorial* gossip columnist, picked up the story: Philip's best friend and secretary was being sued for divorce. D-I-V-O-R-C-E. There it was again. The Queen and Prince Philip suddenly found themselves splashed across the pages of newspapers and magazines the world over for something they seemingly had no part in. The Parkers' marital problems instantly became a 'royal scandal' and were taken by some continental publications as confirmation that all was not well in the royal household, either. If Michael Parker was being sued for divorce then, by some strange logic, it followed that Philip might suffer the same fate. Parker resigned immediately, to save the royals further embarrassment and this act, far from quelling the storm, actually fuelled it.

Even Eileen Parker added to this confusion when she later wrote, 'My first instinct was to blame sheer panic for Mike's abrupt decision [to resign] but then upon reflection I started to wonder if his resignation was a smokescreen for something, or somebody, else.'[2] Abroad, big hints were dropped about the 'bachelor' lifestyles of the two men and the *Baltimore Sun*, the Duchess of Windsor's home town newspaper which kept the locals abreast of their famous daughter's famous relations, stretched it to the very limit, suggesting that Parker's divorce was linked inextricably to rumours that Philip 'had more than a passing interest in an unnamed woman and was meeting her regularly at the apartment of royal photographer, Baron'.[3] By now, Philip had reached Gibraltar and the telephone lines between him and Buckingham Palace were red-hot. Sir Michael Adeane, the Queen's private secretary, took the unusual step of personally issuing a press statement denying that there was anything wrong in the royal household. 'Why are they saying these cruel things about us?' the Queen asked sadly. And it was a good job she was not in America, otherwise she would have been devastated by the coverage there; whole front pages and hundreds of thousands of words were devoted to the 'royal scandal', *World Press News* reported. In Britain, the customary newspaper poll came out in favour of Parker, concluding that he should have stayed in his job. The Queen, meanwhile, continued with her plans to go to Portugal for a state visit, arriving on 17 February. She was there to meet the plane carrying Prince Philip to join her and went aboard to see her husband for the first time in four months and two days, and just to lighten the proceedings she pulled a false beard out of her pocket and put it on her chin – to match the beard Philip had grown while he was away.[4] The plane was surrounded by hundreds of the world's press clamouring for pictures and story. Portugal's President Craveiro Lopez put the presidential car flanked by police outriders at their disposal and it sped away from their pursuers to a lonely bay in the Sebutal Peninsula where the royal yacht was waiting. In spite of the furore that surrounded them, according to Philip's cousin Queen Alexandra of Yugoslavia, 'Philip and Elizabeth had planned their reunion with ardent anticipation . . . a couple need to contrive an occasional romantic new meeting with one another'.[5] In her description of this romantic liaison, Alexandra seemed to have overlooked the several hundred small craft of every shape and size hooting their sirens, several thousand cheering people on the shore, along with cameramen and reporters in chartered craft anxious to satisfy their editors' demands for the low-down on the royal marriage.

As is always the case with such stories, later to be experienced almost to the letter by the Queen's son and daughter as their own marital problems were scrutinised to a tedious degree decades later, half truths which had some basis were lumped with rumours which did not and the whole was turned into a case for the prosecution. The media claimed that the Queen's marriage was all but over. It was not, nor could it ever be, except by death of one of the partners. True, the marriage had been under pressure. It was well known, and very obvious, that Philip suffered from extreme frustration at being regarded, still, as something of an outsider and would have been largely ignored if he had not made his own presence felt. Those close at hand knew that he had to get out and mix with the boisterous male company of his navy days to save his sanity. This does not excuse some of his exploits, but at least explains them. The Queen seemed to accept this, according to both her friends and servants, who are often better placed than most to give an honest assessment from close quarters, and the Queen's footman of the period, Ralphe White, maintained that the reports of a split were simply 'far wide of the mark'.[6]

The fact that there had been no additions to the family since 1950 was also used in evidence. But the Queen seemed to have decided, first, that there could be no more children until the Coronation was behind them and then, in succeeding years, it became virtually impossible as she surveyed the continuous round of engagements and tours that her government demanded of her. It began to become something of an obsession with royal watchers, as she reached the end of the decade . . .

They returned to England under the glare of what Stanley Baldwin once described as the 'cruelty of modern publicity'. The Parker divorce was the touch-paper which, when lit, exploded like delayed action fireworks all summer long and on into the autumn. It was, and remains still, one of the worst years the Queen had ever experienced in terms of criticism, about herself, about the monarchy and about her family. First of all, the *Daily Mirror* had attacked the royal court with a major article under the headline 'Is the New Elizabethan Age Going To Be a Flop?': 'The circle around the throne is as aristocratic, as insular and – there is no more suitable word for it – as toffee-nosed as it has ever been.' The *Daily Express* then accused the royal family of being philistine: 'none of them patronise the arts or opera', Lord Beaverbrook moaned. The *Women's Sunday Mirror*, counting the cost of Prince Philip's round-the-world cruise, said the Crown was spending too much money and pleaded with Buckingham Palace to trim its costs, or the royals to pay more for themselves. Writer B. A. Young also complained in Lord Altrincham's *National and English Review* that, though the Queen had a very active diary and attended many engagements, she was not being overworked and had ample time for relaxation at one of her several homes. Young calculated that 'thirty public appearances in ninety days is hardly a backbreaking programme for a company whose principal raison d'être is the making of public appearances'.[7] This was a somewhat harsh assessment; as Brigadier Stanley Clark recounted in his *Palace Diary*, the Queen had completed over 200 engagements by the end of May, though many were of course within the confines of the palace. The Lord's Day Observance Society launched into a bitter tirade about the Queen seeing politicians on a Sunday and continued its attack over the Queen's visits to polo matches on the Sabbath to watch her husband riding fast and furious, with herself giving encouraging shouts from the sidelines of 'Go on . . . go on!' This, said the society's honorary secretary, was 'in our opinion unfortunately typical of the national disregard for the sanctity of God's Holy Day'.

Though a polite response from one of the Queen's aides was received, clearly the reprimand had no effect on the head of the Church of England who continued to be seen in excited animation watching her husband swirling his polo stick around Cowdray Park or Windsor Lawns.

A small bandwagon was rolling, and the League Against Cruel Sports jumped aboard when reports from the annual shoots at the Queen's Sandringham estate indicated a plentiful bag. In March they voiced a protest about the huntin' and shootin' activities of the royals at large – 'we know who our worst enemies are, and the Queen is certainly the worst'. She was, one of its members pointed out, one of the best shots in the family; it was something of a monarchical tradition.

George V, Edward VIII and George VI were all excellent marksmen: George VI kept meticulous records of his shooting activities in his game book, noting, for example, the number of woodcock he shot from 1911 to the last at Sandringham shortly before he died. They numbered 1,055. Wildfowling was another popular royal sport. George V never managed to shoot any in flight; George VI sent them up from the haunt at Sandringham and took 526 duck in flight. Though Sandringham was the scene of much of their game-shooting where daily averages of 300 to 400 birds a day are not uncommon at the start of the season, Balmoral provided what they considered sport *par excellence*, that of deer-stalking. The Queen's own game book records that her best shoot was twelve stags from three stalks and she shot one of the five best deer taken by women in Scotland; the stag's head, with its huge twelve-point antlers, was mounted and hung on the walls of Balmoral. Despite their concern for conservation and the eclipse of endangered species, the Queen and Prince Philip saw no paradox in their sporting activities, either then in the fifties or today in the nineties, explaining as Philip often does that 'interest in wild animals and plants combined with a love of the countryside sports has never ceased to cause problems for rational thinkers who convince themselves that the two characteristics are incompatible';[8] however, though they easily swept such criticism aside, some of it would stick, as the Queen was to discover, later in that year of 1957.

On 8 April, the Queen was off on her travels again, to make a state visit to France to revive the former *Entente Cordiale* which had become somewhat fractured in the light of recent events . . . 'Our emotions will be shared by all my people,' she said in response to the warm welcome. Two of her people who were not present, however, were her Uncle David and Aunt Wallis who had slipped quietly out of Paris some days before, heading across the Atlantic once more, and extended their stay in New York to ensure they were not around when the Queen and Philip arrived. If they had been, the observance of protocol would have required a meeting, at least with Windsor himself who demonstrated his feelings later when Prince Philip came to Paris but failed to call on him: 'Maybe neither he nor I would find the encounter rewarding,' the duke complained in a letter to Mountbatten. 'Still, as former king as well as an uncle by marriage, I consider this behaviour to me in a foreign land extremely bad manners.' He added that in training his nephew for the role of prince consort to Elizabeth II, Mountbatten had 'left off the curriculum the simple practice of courtesy'.[9]

Protocol could not be satisfied when the Queen arrived and anyway, it was a bad time for a meeting. The Windsors' twentieth wedding anniversary was but a month or so away and since that date was, firstly, a reminder to the Queen of her father's Coronation and to Windsor that his brother had decided to withhold the prefix of Her Royal Highness from his wife, the duke had no desire to settle the family feud without recognition for Wallis. The feeling was clearly mutual. When the Queen Mother came to France in June with the Duke of Gloucester to unveil a war memorial, the Windsors had returned from America; no meeting was arranged and Wallis was wondering whether she would have to wait another twenty years before she finally came face to face with her sister-in-law. She scoured the papers the following day and scowled at the photographs. 'Cookie's getting fat,' she remarked to her husband. 'Or should I say, fat-ter.'[10] There was another reason, apart from the Wallis factor, which fuelled the continued coolness that year and which also contributed to the pressure being placed on the Queen herself.

What they all knew, and worried about, was that in a few weeks' time certain documents captured by the Allies during the war were to be made public; the date in July had long been pencilled in the royal calendar. The Queen had been warned by Churchill when he tried to suppress their publication in 1953 that they contained damaging references to the Duke of Windsor who was also warned in advance of their publication. In spite of it, he had continued to maintain an unashamed contact with former sympathisers of fascist and Nazi rule in Europe and in America and, of course, the Windsors' closest friends in Paris were Sir Oswald and Lady Diana Mosley. The foursome was considered a continual embarrassment at the British embassy in Paris, where the ambassador Sir Gladwyn Jebb had given specific instructions that no member of his staff should remain in the room if Sir

Oswald and Lady Diana walked in, a rule which he applied wherever possible through his tenure from 1952 to 1960; such an instruction presumably had the prior approval of London. It was made especially difficult, however, when the Mosleys walked in with the Windsors. Diana Mosley's sister Nancy Mitford believed that the friendship of the former King and the former leader of the British fascist movement, who was interned in Britain during the war, stemmed largely from their shared nostalgia for the era of the Third Reich in Germany. Nancy said, 'They want us all to be governed by the kind clever rich Germans and be happy ever after. I wish I knew why they all lived in France and not outre-Rhine.'[11] That nostalgia was to burst forth and haunt them as the Nazi documents came due for public release. Some years had passed since the Americans, in answer to pressure from historians, had begun preparing to release the documents. Churchill, then back at No. 10, was horrified to discover this news, coming as it did just before the Coronation of Elizabeth II. The implications were obvious and the great British party of national celebration would have been badly spoiled by the awful revelations. Churchill fired off a letter to his old friend Eisenhower, the new President of the United States. In a letter marked 'secret and personal', he pleaded with his 'Dear friend . . . to exert your power to prevent publication'.[12] Between them, Eisenhower and Churchill merely managed to delay the fateful day of revelation. That day was now upon them in 1957.

Earlier that year, Sir John Wheeler-Bennett visited the Queen at Balmoral and he later recounted that she took him on a long walk of about eight miles, and he was neither shod nor dressed for such a jaunt. They returned to Balmoral for lunch after which the Queen Mother took him for another walk, almost as long as the one he went on with the Queen. At the end of it, Wheeler-Bennett was noticeably flagging and the Queen Mother remarked, 'Did my daughter, by any chance, take you for one of her walks this morning?'

'Yes, ma'am, she did.'

'Then,' said the Queen Mother, 'champagne is the only remedy.'[13]

Wheeler-Bennett was instrumental in securing the eventual publication of what became known as the 'Lisbon Incident', recounting through telegrams and documents damaging evidence of Windsor's admiration of the Third Reich, of his consorting with enemy agents and of statements which were bordering on treason. The Macmillan government carefully stage-managed the release of the Windsor papers in Britain, disowning them as coming from a 'tainted source'. The Duke of Windsor instructed his solicitors to state that attempts by pro-Nazi sympathisers were made to persuade him not to take up his appointment in the Bahamas but 'at no time did I entertain any thought of complying with such a suggestion which I treated with the contempt that it deserved'.[14] It took the wit of Noël Coward to add a dry perspective. 'Secret papers have disclosed his pro-Nazi perfidy which, of course, I was aware of at the time . . . Poor dear, what a monumental ass he has always been.'[15]

The mass of publicity that the documents inspired was an unwelcome addition to a difficult year, and brought back painful memories, especially for the Queen Mother who remembered the strain that these events of 1940 had placed upon her husband. By and large, the German documents and the duke's reaction to them were reported without much hostile comment and the royals could breathe a sigh of relief. They knew very well that it could have been much worse. In fact, having resigned himself to the worst, Windsor was not especially distressed. He was more concerned with what Wheeler-Bennett had written about him in the King George biography and asked to see a copy of the manuscript before publication 'since you are writing part of the history of a living former Sovereign'.[16] He was also convinced that the cooperation Wheeler-Bennett had received from 'that evil snake' Tommy Lascelles would ensure that 'I am shown in as bad a light as possible'.[17] Windsor finally wrote to the Queen; she declared that he would not be allowed to see it until the book was in proof form.

It so happened that on the very day of the release of the Windsor documents, the Queen was the host at a garden party in the grounds of Buckingham Palace, to welcome 4,000 members of the influential American Bar Association to London. Macmillan was rebuilding the bridge of Anglo-American relationships and the Queen would naturally become an ally to this cause; in fact both she and Winston

Churchill had been actively involved in mending the fences after Suez. Churchill sent Eisenhower a copy of a letter the Queen had written him stating 'I hope it means that the present feeling that this country and America are not seeing eye to eye will soon be speedily replaced by even stronger ties between us.'[18] It had already been agreed that she would visit the United States for the first time as Queen later in the year. And so, to offset those nasty stories about her uncle and Hitler, there she was being photographed in the palace gardens where hot-dogs were being served to her American guests, shortly before retiring to Balmoral for the summer.

It was but a brief respite. The August issue of a small magazine entitled *National and English Review* would, under normal circumstances, have passed anonymously into yesterday's news as had the previous issues. This one, however, was devoted to a discussion entitled 'The Monarchy Today' and the editorial was written by the magazine's owner and publisher, Lord Altrincham. It contained one sentence which flashed around the world, made Altrincham famous and sent the Queen's champions immediately to arms: 'The personality conveyed by the utterances which are put into her mouth is that of a priggish schoolgirl.' He described her voice as a 'pain in the neck'.[19]

Before proceeding with the story of Altrincham's criticism, it is worth reverting for a moment to 1938, when a private in the British Army overheard a stranger make what he later described as a 'grossly offensive remark about two members of the royal family'. Outraged by these comments, the soldier turned upon the speaker, knocked him down and killed him. He was charged not with murder, but manslaughter, and the fact that he was attempting to uphold the good name of the royals was taken as a good enough reason for provocation, regardless of whether the dead man had been speaking the truth or not – and in all probability, he was. The soldier was all but praised for his actions. He was bound over to keep the peace for two years, and was set free immediately. Most seemed to believe that justice had been done and the newspapers felt the story merited little or no coverage.

In 1957, soon after Altrincham had made his statements about the Queen, a member of the League of Empire

Loyalists gave the young peer a wallop in the face. He was arrested, found guilty of a breach of the peace and fined £1. Thus, it could be seen where the sympathies of the establishment judiciary lie although, going by past precedent, had the loyalist shot the peer, the defendant might even have escaped the fine. The judge also commented that the face-slapper had the knowledge that '95 per cent of the nation are disgusted and offended at what was written by Lord Altrincham'. He was actually wrong; a poll in the *Daily Mail* showed that one in three agreed with the writer and so what began as an attempt at constructive comments on the Queen's performance so far, suddenly turned into a barrage of criticism. Altrincham's description of the Queen as sounding like a priggish schoolgirl, remained the focus but it is interesting now to bring out another paragraph from his editorial which did not receive much publicity at the time. It was by way of a warning: 'When she has lost the bloom of youth, her reputation will depend far more than it does now upon her personality. It will not be enough for her to go through the motions; she will have to say things which people will remember and do things on her own initiative which will make people sit up and take notice.' He later added to this assessment these words: 'The Queen is still young and the hopes of her subjects are still infinitely stronger than their regrets. She has a unique opportunity. The future is hers if she will only grasp it.'

The reaction to Altrincham's study of monarchy in 1957, which remains to this day a perceptive and wholly worthwhile series of essays, was still being heard as the Queen neared her next major tour, arranged partly to help rebuild Anglo-American bridges which had come tumbling down during the Suez crisis and partly as an exercise in boosting British trade and tourism. And as she was heading west to begin the tour of Canada and the United States in October, the *Saturday Evening Post* in New York revived Malcolm Muggeridge's article of the previous year on the Royal Soap Opera, and ran it under the headline of 'Does England Really Need a Queen?' It was quickly fed back across the Atlantic and attacked by the British press who chose to run major castigatory articles on Muggeridge as a route to reprinting and paraphrasing almost everything he had said. This time, they focused on the soap opera syndrome, which Muggeridge reinforced during interviews when he said, 'It has become a kind of show, hasn't it? It just goes on and on, in the same way as The Archers. A little boy [Prince Charles] gets mumps and goes to school. Princess Margaret has the Townsend affair. All her escorts come and go. There are these awful reports about the Queen and Prince Philip. Such is popular monarchy.'*

And so the whole palaver was in full swing when John Osborne, the newly styled angry young man whose new play, *The Entertainer*, had just opened in the West End, wrote in the CIA-financed magazine *Encounter*, that what was happening to royalty in Britain was symptomatic of a sick society – 'the gold filling in a mouth full of decay'. It was evidence of bankruptcy within the nation's culture. 'It bores me, it depresses me that there should be so many empty minds, so many empty lives in Britain to sustain this fatuous industry; and no one should have the wit to laugh it into extinction.'[20]

Muggeridge was sacked by the BBC, the Press Council refused to condemn newspapers for distorting his remarks, he was unwanted and unloved, for the time being, and Altrincham was attacked at all levels. The Queen, puzzled by his comments, thought Altrincham 'must be mad'; some of her supporters turned upon him hysterically, one nobleman suggesting he should be hung, drawn and quartered; he also received letters smeared with excrement. The attack was also brought up at Cabinet level but merely noted.[21] Clearly, Britain was not ready for such a relentless attack on their Queen as had been witnessed during the previous three months, coming as it did on the heels of the sustained barrage of unsavoury press headlines over Mike Parker's divorce. Prince Philip, however, was not one to disregard constructive

*As with most other things, nothing is new in the history of monarchy. Napoleon once likened royalty to the then equivalent of soap operas, remarking that 'to be royal is like playing a part at the theatre, with the exception that monarchs are always on the stage'. Charles I, in similar vein, spoke of the fickleness of his public: 'The English nation are a sober people,' he observed, 'but there are occasions when they lose their heads and it is at such moments that monarchs have to be most careful.'

criticism out of hand. 'We ought to take account of this,' he remarked to his wife, midway through the battering; he at least could be counted on for a positive reaction as opposed to the dismissive comments of the palace hierarchy.

The Queen actually overwhelmed this bad press very quickly. The newspapers were filled once again with the glamour of the monarch and with the pomp and the adulation as she proceeded on her way through another 'triumphant' tour of her former colonies, broadcasting to the Canadian people and being described by the enthusiastic Americans as a 'living doll' as reporters and television cameras mobbed her – in Washington no less than 2,000 newsmen fought to get close to her.

Chapter Six
Prisoners of the Past (1958–9)

The public face of the monarchy which had been shown so vividly in all its contrasting aspects during the first few years was, and is, the mere icing on a very substantial cake. Behind this facade existed a huge machine which even Prince Philip criticised and wanted to change; the Queen and the Queen Mother were less certain that it should be tampered with. The palace system is governed by customs and practices dating back to the Middle Ages and the Queen was, in the mid-fifties, still surrounded by the musty old traditions which existed because they had always existed; many remain in place in the last decade of this century, still. Other palace residents, in the past, had tried and failed to update them but after the months of relentless criticism the Queen had faced, with much of it directed towards the courtiers who surrounded her and controlled her life, it became obvious now that a 'fundamental if not critical'[1] readjustment was necessary. The attacks had been unprecedented; nothing like it had happened since 1936. The false concept of 'fairyland' which began in 1952 had come home to roost, along with a few other troubles as the nation itself stumbled from one condition to another and a certain hysteria developed in the appraisal and suspicion of the one constant force in the British caste system, though it must be said that this stemmed more from writers and newspapers than directly from the public. In many respects, the monarchy had become a prisoner of its own past.

They discussed it amongst themselves, the Queen, the

Queen Mother and Philip, and a number of changes were already in the pipeline, but it was obvious to all that it was going to be a difficult task to drag the monarchy into the second half of the twentieth century. Philip said they had to start within the confines of Buckingham Palace itself; he'd made a study of it, just as the Duke of Windsor did when he was king – and the duke recalled in his memoirs, 'I was soon to find that any tampering with tradition is fraught with trouble.'[2] There was heavy resistance to the most trifling change. Philip would be accused of being domineering, bombastic and unreasonable, which was probably true.

Spurred on by his uncle, Philip was the Queen's strongest advocate of change, telling her constantly that they had to adapt and stay flexible to modern demands and he warned, 'Most monarchies of Europe were really destroyed by their greatest and most ardent supporters'. Much of the 'old guard', as it was known, still ruled the roost within the palace and Philip was soon complaining to the Queen that the door was often being slammed shut in his face when he tried to study their procedures and suggest new methods. True, the Queen had acquired a small number of younger advisers but she had inherited a band of snobbish old courtiers who jealously guarded their positions as well as the duties of the 230 staff at the palace and the 120 at Windsor Castle, not to mention the additional unpaid courtiers who were so many and varied that they could never be accurately counted. It is only when the huge staff and job descriptions are analysed that it is possible to see why it was so difficult to introduce change.

In an influential and powerful monarchy such as Britain's, the Sovereign and her court are at the epicentre of national and international life, not merely as it affects politics and worldwide diplomacy, but spreading through pretty well every aspect of public life, right down to small voluntary organisations. And so the administration of the royal household is considered by those who run it to be of the utmost importance if the British monarchy is to remain. That self-assessment was one which only a thorough investigation of the traditions and the ceremonial could confirm, and apart from Philip's own tinkering with the system, it remains today largely unaltered.

The officers of Her Majesty's Household, many of whose posts are hereditary, fall into three main categories. The senior figures are the Great Officers of State whose titles have been handed down through ancestry. The second rank are officers of the Queen's Household who are appointed by the Prime Minister of the day and the third rank, who are the most important to the Queen personally, are officers and staff of her Domestic Court who handle all the day-to-day administration of palace life.

The higher echelons of these strange and pompous heraldic creatures who emerge from their castles and stately homes colourfully caparisoned and hugely decorative for great state occasions, seemed to inspire in foreign observers raptures of admiration for British traditions or, conversely, questions as to the nation's sanity for continuing with them. They are harmless if not important links with 1,100 years of history in which royal continuity has been broken, briefly, only once. The Duke of Norfolk, the most prominent of the Great Officers of State, claimed his right to the title of Earl Marshal; the title can be traced back to the days of the Norman kings and has been in the Duke of Norfolk's family since 1672. Then there is the Lord Great Chamberlain, a title which has alternated between the Marquess of Cholmondeley and the Ancaster and Carrington families, who has charge of the Queen's Palace at Westminster and has authority over the buildings of both Houses of Parliament when the Houses are not sitting. There is also a Lord High Steward, a Lord High Constable and a Lord High Admiral, titles which are traditionally held by high families.

The political officials whose duties are largely ceremonial are appointed by the government and tend to be drawn from the ranks of junior ministers. They include a Household Comptroller, a Treasurer, a Vice-Chamberlain of the Household, the Captains of the Gentlemen at Arms and the Lords in Waiting.

The Queen herself relies almost exclusively on her own household which is quite independent of the government. The Lord Chamberlain, not to be confused with the Lord Great Chamberlain, traditionally heads the list. He is concerned with the internal organisation of, and invitations to, all state occasions, banquets, dinners, and the garden parties at which the Queen entertains about 25,000 a year. He also has control over all officers, servants, tradesmen, medical staff, musicians and even comedians (and any other artistes who may be employed for palace functions). The Lord Steward runs the domestic economy of the palace while the Master of the Horse is concerned, as the name implies, with the provision of horses, carriages, cars and royal processions. There are also many more titles of considerable antiquity below this management structure with ancient names such as Goldstick, Silverstick,* the Ladies of the Bedchamber, the Mistress of the Robes, the Groom of the Robes, the Ladies in Waiting, the Permanent Lords in Waiting, the Gentlemen Ushers, the Extra Gentlemen Ushers, the Bargemaster, the Clerk of the Closet, the Keeper of the Swans and the Queen's Permanent Representative at Ascot race course.

Then comes the administrative layer of the palace executive which includes her closest aides, such as her private secretary, and his deputy and two assistants; her press secretary and staff; her chief clerk and the rest of the civilian personnel on whom the Queen relies for the running of her now quite vast organisation of which the above gives but a mere flavour. It was amongst these various layers of court protocol and precedence that the targets of recent attacks, the 'insular', 'toffee-nosed' aristocrats were to be found. They were the people whom Lord Altrincham has described as the 'tweedy' country gentry who still formed 'a tight little enclave of English ladies and gentlemen around her'. But, really, could that ever change?

Prince Albert tried to get to the bottom of the system when he began what he called his palace 'investigations' soon after his marriage to Queen Victoria. Like Prince Philip, Albert came from a relatively poor court, constantly ridden with financial problems – just as Philip's immediate family had been since his father's enforced exile from Greece. Albert

*As the Queen is Colonel-in-Chief of all the Guards Regiments, there is close daily contact between her and her Guards through the offices of Goldstick and Silverstick whose duties are performed by colonels in the Life Guards and the Royal Horse Guards; among the duties of the Goldstick is to receive daily from the Queen in person the parole and countersign.

soon became acutely aware of the inefficiency and overspending at Victoria's court and aided by what the local palace staff called his own 'imported German spies' he began a total review of palace life. He found it absurd, for example, that, as he put it, 'The Lord Steward finds the fuel and lays the fire; the Lord Chamberlain lights it and provides the lamps but the Lord Steward must trim and light them. The inside cleaning of windows belongs to the Lord Steward's department; the outside must be attended by the Office of Woods and Forests . . .'

He uncovered one scandal after another, such as the cottage industry that was traditionally operated among palace staff in 'palace ends', in which footmen went dashing up to the West End to sell bags of leftovers from state occasions and general day-to-day life. The candle scandal was a prime example. Each day, every single candle in the palace was replaced, even those in the servants' quarters, whether they were burnt low or not; many had never even been lit. This amounted to several hundred candles a week, available for sale to eager tradesmen. Albert also discovered that a single order for a particular colour of candle which Victoria had requested for a state ball resulted in the same order being delivered to the palace every week for years.

When Philip began his 'investigations', he first studied Prince Albert's old records and found similar anomalies and similar resentment to these inquiries. He was puzzled by a fresh bottle of whisky that appeared in the Queen's bedroom each night, even though she did not drink. The staff could not enlighten him as to why this was done until, after a further search of the archives, it was discovered that Queen Victoria, plagued with a cold one day, asked for a bottle of whisky to be sent to her room. The next day, it was replaced by a fresh one and the custom continued through four reigns. Philip began a study of work procedures and would stop members of staff wandering through the maze of corridors and ask them what they did for a living. He found it ridiculous that uniformed flunkeys were walking around carrying messages on silver trays, passed between other senior members of staff or between members of the family. He discovered that if he and the Queen were working in their office and required a drink or a sandwich, it took four separate members of staff to convey the message and deliver the food after the first had been summoned by bell. So the Queen agreed to his suggestion that they should introduce an internal telephone system. This is one small example of the changes he began introducing into palace life; because of the vastness of the operation, it was an ongoing revolution. 'The Queen and Philip were always discussing ways of improving things – it was a constant topic,' said Ralphe White.

The elite of the court were horrified as Philip continued to press the Queen into sweeping away some of the old traditions that were choking the system, even though she was not always in agreement. 'He either had to beat them or bow to them, and Philip was not in the business of bowing to anyone,' said one of his aides. Philip approved Basil Boothroyd's description of his battle against the old guard 'who closed ranks . . . hoping to rumble on without a lot of tinkering from a newcomer for whom there was literally no place'[3] and who, above all, was a Battenberg. He had to draw on all his powers of persuasion to get the Queen to authorise some of his suggestions and to discontinue some of the antiquated state balls, levées and unnecessary audiences which took up so much of their time.

He engineered some fairly controversial discontinuations; the most lively debate surrounded the ending of an absurd annual practice, the presentation of the current crop of debutantes to the reigning monarch. The highlight of their coming-out, it was another of those traditions, whereby each year four or five hundred of the gels would parade before the monarch, with the allotment of five seconds each to curtsy and receive the response of a bow, thus securing the confirmation of their daughter's social position for the proud parents looking on. It was, truly, one of the worst examples of snobbery; shock and horror hit the court and even the Queen Mother protested, 'But the girls do so look forward to it.' To which Philip responded, 'And so did all the hangers-on who are getting a rake-off'. Apparently the Queen Mother was surprised to learn that some of the less wealthy sponsors of the debs were actually taking a small consideration to ensure that certain daughters of the upper classes received an invitation from the Lord Chamberlain.

Another innovation already in place was the beginning of

informal lunches at the palace at which the Queen wanted to bring in people from all walks of life to Her Majesty's table for light, informative conversation. The first few tended to favour the establishment, with people like the editor of *The Times*, Sir William Haley, heading the guest list, but they got better. Actors, artists, architects, businessmen, churchmen eventually found themselves receiving a note from the Lord Chamberlain, in which they were informed that Her Majesty requested the pleasure of their company for lunch; it turned out to be a 90 minute 'experience' at the Queen's luncheon table which most praised, though some derided it as being filled with meaningless small talk and platitudes. Philip, meanwhile, began his own 'think tanks', inviting industrialists, businessmen and church leaders to dine to pick their brains on current issues and to take the temperature of views on a wide variety of issues – including the monarchy.

The content of the Queen's speeches at banquets and opening ceremonies had also been scrutinised after Lord Altrincham's attack, and one of her speech-writers, her then deputy private secretary Sir Martin Charteris,* welcomed the opportunity of giving her more meaningful lines to read. In fact, during a debate at Eton a year after he retired from palace service, Charteris actually complimented Altrincham for 'doing the monarchy a great service' by his constructive criticism. One of the problems that all her speech-writers faced was the difficulty which the Queen – and most royals – had in making her speeches sound spontaneous. One of her later ministers in Harold Wilson's government, the ex-lord Tony Benn, says she 'can't say good morning without a script'[4] and this difficulty has not improved with age. In public she finds it almost impossible to deviate from the written word and even more difficult to force humour through the Hanoverian jaw. 'I am simply not a performer,' she once retorted quite angrily when suggestions were being made as to how she should tackle a certain speech. But until this point in time, the dour and unimaginative speech-writers of the fifties had failed completely to comprehend the Queen's difficulties in making any speech sound as if it truly came

*Later Principal Private Secretary, 1972–7.

from the heart and not, as Altrincham suggested, as if it was being read by a schoolgirl; because that is exactly what most of them did sound like, and just as naive. Furthermore, they had totally failed to account for the fact that the electronic age of television and transistor radios meant that her speeches were being heard more often, for longer, and by many more people. As some of the top comedians in the country discovered, all of their best material quickly became stale, although catch-phrases or familiar opening lines became well known. The Queen was no different in that respect, and since she began most speeches with the phrase 'My husband and I . . .' she had suddenly become the butt of the mimicry of countless comedians.

New script-writers were brought in; speeches were tightened up and an element of controversy was added whenever possible, just as Philip had done in his own speeches. He had been able to be rather more outspoken, since he represented no one and spoke on behalf of no recognised constitutional authority. He was well aware he could fuel a debate in the newspapers which would not only be critical of himself, but also bring public attention to the royal family in a more serious way; thus the headlines – when they appeared – would not merely contain references to their private lives. He fought hard to try to force the balance of coverage across the whole spectrum of the monarchy, so that the trivia was counterbalanced by publicity of their more serious work. The only way he could do it was by being controversial, if not downright rude.

They tried this with the Queen's speeches, although because of the restriction on content, they did not usually include any headline-hitting material. The key, as far as she was concerned, was to improve her presentation, to make it a delivery instead of a recitation. This was why, when the idea was suggested that she might make her annual speech to the nation on television rather than on radio, it took several months of internal, and quite secret, debate about how the Queen could be shown in her best light.

The BBC had made the approach, tipped off by Mountbatten that she might consider going on television. They produced for the Queen's private viewing a special film, starring their most famous presenter Miss Sylvia Peters, who went through the various ways in which the Queen might broadcast the speech. They filmed five different ideas in which the cameras might capture the Queen, ranging from an 'eavesdropping' approach, looking in on her as she made her radio broadcast, to looking directly into camera and reading the speech from a script prompter. The BBC had some equipment delivered to Balmoral during the Queen's holiday so that she could rehearse; it came in useful because a month later she made her first live Canadian television broadcast as she read her speech at the opening of Parliament. Throughout the Canadian and American tour, the changes in her style and approach were obvious to seasoned followers of the royal troupe. On their return from America, there were more rehearsals at Buckingham Palace, and again at Sandringham from where the actual broadcast was made, before the Queen felt confident that she had honed her technique as far as she could; Philip often stood on the sidelines giving her advice and Prince Charles and Princess Anne wandered casually in and out. When the broadcast was finally made, it was received by millions on screen and heard all over the Commonwealth. Diarist Harold Nicolson, who listened, noted, 'She came across . . . with a vigour unknown in pre-Altrincham days.'[5]

Her secretary, Sir Michael Adeane, also went to great lengths to improve the Queen's image in other areas. He made a study of the royal tours, both at home and abroad, and discovered that many of the Queen's hosts still believed that they had to lay on the earth in terms of hospitality for their royal visitors, another throwback to a past age where huge and glittering, colonial-style receptions and 4 hour banquets were set out and enjoyed by some of her predecessors. The Queen, naturally enough, found them time-consuming, largely unproductive and often exceedingly boring. So in 1958, Adeane compiled a confidential guide amounting to 6,000 words on twenty pages of Buckingham Palace foolscap intended 'to help those who were drawing up plans for a royal visit' and more specifically to enable her to be seen by as many members of the public as possible at wherever she stopped.

They were hints which would show the Queen's personal preferences as well as giving an indication where hosts could cut through the tedium of long speeches and avoid surrounding her with local dignitaries thought to have a prior claim on her attention. It listed a wide range of dos and don'ts even down to the minutiae: the Queen likes to receive flowers, but not wired bouquets; she likes to receive gifts and often tries to wear items made for her, but the colour magenta should be avoided because the Queen doesn't like it. Lunchtime meals should be planned to last no more than a hour where possible. The Queen does not normally drink alcoholic drinks at lunchtime, merely bottled water, Prince Philip might take a lager or champagne before meals. Formal evening dinners should not be endless affairs, and the Adeane hints suggested that an hour and a half would normally be sufficient and that included the time allotted for speeches. The Queen and Prince Philip were prepared to taste local dishes in moderation, though they generally tended to avoid exotic fish dishes. Oysters were definitely 'off' the menu and her favourite, lobster, would be allowed only by prior approval. On her tours, the Queen insisted that children be given preference at all points, whether in terms of crowd position or presentation of bouquets. It 'is the children who must take an important place in every tour or visit', said Adeane's memo and to ensure that every child present was able to get a good view of the Queen, an open-topped vehicle such as a Land Rover was preferable so that she could drive slowly through lines of assembled youngsters.

The Queen preferred all her visits to be kept as simple as possible. She did not normally undertake the laying of foundation stones, but liked to plant commemorative trees instead. She hated huge motorcades, with masses of motorcycle outriders, because they reminded her of the newsreels she saw of Hitler during the war. In church services, the offertory plate or bag should be handed to the Queen or Prince Philip in the usual way; they each normally carried £1 for such occasions. Sunday was considered a day off, with the exception of private church services, although during overseas tours they were prepared to participate on Saturdays and take Monday as a day off so that weekend crowds were not deprived of the opportunity of seeing her. And finally, lists of all people to be presented must be submitted to the palace for vetting by the tour organisers. On the home front, all royal visits were carefully monitored so that every city in the land received a 'fair share' of attendances either by the Queen or another member of her family.[6] When the Lord Mayor of Manchester, for example, complained to the Prime Minister's office that 'no one ever visits Manchester' the President of the Board of Trade replied that during the previous ten years Manchester had done rather well – twelve royal visits. Satisfying all demands placed 'a tremendous burden on the royal family . . . an endless stream of engagements', said the memo.[7]

And so, the pattern was being established here, for what would become her working routine for many years to come. It was a new style of royal roadshow that had to take account of modern times and requirements. All of the above were changes which could be very quickly introduced, some of which came in direct response to criticism, and over the following five or six years the Queen slowly introduced other streamlining of her palace operations, including the replacement of some of the 'old fogies'.

If adjustment was necessary in her image and presentation and style, a rather more drastic change would also be required in a way that affected her personally and in her position as head of the Church of England, which capacity, the nation was constantly being reminded, meant that divorced people were still to be excluded 'from the inner royal circle'.[8] Unlike some recent ancestors who seemed prepared to uphold the rule in so far as it did not affect their own pleasures, the Queen knew that according to tradition – and the exceedingly stern strictures of her grandmother Queen Mary – divorced people were to be excluded from the inner circle. Under Queen Mary's interpretation, no divorcee was allowed in her presence, nor in the royal enclosure at Ascot, unless of course you happened to be a prime minister or prime minister's son, like Randolph Churchill. That is why when Mrs Wallis Simpson was divorced, it had to be achieved with her husband Ernest's cooperation so that, ridiculously, he became the guilty party with a fake co-respondent, leaving Wallis's reputation seemingly unsullied and innocent, which it wasn't. Queen Mary saw through the scheme, of course, and never once allowed her daughter-in-law to come within her presence for the rest of her life.

And so entered the second agent of change, whose arrival on the royal scene would have, eventually, untold implications to the divorce rule, not to mention the deflation of some of the unhealthier aspects of royalty.

The young Mr Antony Armstrong-Jones came permanently on to the royal scene at the beginning of 1958 and heralded the introduction of a new factor that would have to be taken into account by the Queen. In fact, the 'Tony' problem became the catalyst to a good many things in the royal household, though the most significant would be the first divorce at the heart of the royal family for five centuries. He first became noticed by the royals when he was employed as an assistant to the occasional court photographer Baron, discovered by Mountbatten, who became one of Prince Philip's closest friends and, incidentally, whose reputation brought the Queen and Philip much anguish through the rumour factory. Baron's parties were notorious, especially for their sexual content, and Philip was linked by association but not by hard evidence. Baron had photographed numerous members of the royal family which was a novel experience for Antony Armstrong-Jones, his young assistant who turned to photography from Cambridge after failing his architectural exams.

Later, Armstrong-Jones received a surprise invitation to photograph the Duke of Kent on his twenty-first birthday and in the autumn of 1957, the Queen asked him to take some photographs of Prince Charles and Princess Anne in the grounds of Buckingham Palace. He was young and modern and achieved a relaxed, comfortable relationship with the children. Though Cecil Beaton hated the tag of 'royal' photographer, he was jealous of the position and regarded Antony Armstrong-Jones as a threat to it. Beaton wrote cattishly that he 'didn't think A. A. Jones's pictures are at all interesting but his publicity value is terrific. It pays to be new in the field.'[9] At the time, however, Princess Margaret obviously continued to prefer Beaton as a photographer because she summoned him to the palace in February 1958 to discuss his taking some new photographs of herself. All of the royals admired Beaton's work and he was in constant demand taking formal and informal photographs of the family, some of which were released for public view and to the newspapers, while others were kept for their private albums.

Margaret's preference for Beaton was short-lived. Two nights after her meeting with him, she was attending a dinner party at the home of Lady Elizabeth Cavendish in Cheyne Walk. Her ladyship, a willowy 31 year-old who was one of Margaret's oldest and closest friends, was also her lady in waiting. The connections went deeper; she was also the sister of the Duke of Devonshire, and their mother, the Dowager Duchess, as we know, was the Queen's Mistress of the Robes. Lady Elizabeth meanwhile indulged in certain intrigues at court and elsewhere, and was especially friendly with the poet John Betjeman, later to become poet laureate. At her dinner party on the evening of 20 February, the unattached 'PM', as Margaret was always known, became overtly taken by the conversation of the unattached 28 year-old society photographer, AAJ. He was, she observed some time after this first meeting, totally unfazed by the fact that she was the sister of the Queen, which she found unusual in first-time encounters, and she enjoyed his relaxed, unpompous chat. He was, it appears, unimpressed by her social status and she found him more exciting, even dangerous, company than what remained of the old 'Princess Margaret set'.

She was also in her twenty-eighth year, which was quite long enough to remain single, as many of her friends observed, fearful that she would end up a middle-aged spinster. It might even have been an embarrassment to her that she was still living with her mother, because princesses don't have apartments on their own. All she had to invite her friends home to was a sitting room in Clarence House. She was the most attractive young princess in the world, alluring, available and vulnerable. She spent the first half of her twenties waiting for a romance that could never be, and was left high and dry. She desired good company, she needed a relationship badly. She did not work especially hard and the Queen worried constantly about her sister's social excesses. It was not hard to see that Margaret had in a way become the foil; the press could have a go at her, call her names, like spoilt, or unpredictable, or fun-loving. Margaret rather lived up to the reputation, and the sophistication of earlier years slipped a little as the cigarette-holder-and-glassin-hand photograph became far too commonplace. That's what the Queen worried about.

Antony Armstrong-Jones came along just at the right time. More than that, it was another opportunity for the princess to reject, consciously or not, the royal life and the boring titled suitors who were lining up. He was a mere photographer, a nobody, and very soon after Lady Elizabeth Cavendish's dinner party, they were seeing rather a lot of each other, secretly of course. She would go to his tiny little house by the Thames and friends would arrange weekend dinner parties. Months went by before the Queen learned of her sister's new friend; by then they were rather committed to each other . . .

We shall return to the ferment of Margaret's new friendship shortly, but in the meantime in 1958, the press, who were totally unaware of the new man in the princess's life, focused their camera lenses on a new subject – the Queen's son and heir, then coming up to his tenth birthday. Some time previously, the Queen's press secretary Commander Richard Colville had sent the first of several letters to Fleet Street newspaper editors on his employers' behalf:

> I am commanded by the Queen to say that Her Majesty and the Duke of Edinburgh have decided that their son has reached the stage when he should take more part in more grown-up educational pursuits with other children.* In consequence, a certain amount of (Prince Charles's) instruction will take place outside his home . . . the Queen trusts therefore that His Royal Highness will be able to enjoy this in the same way as other children without the embarrassment of constant publicity.[10]

Charles's prep school tuition in Knightsbridge passed with relative calm, after the first day's barrage of photographs

*Until this point in time, Prince Charles's education had been almost exclusively in the hands of his governess Miss Catherine Peebles, Mipsy to the children. She ran the palace schoolroom until Charles was eight and he began to receive additional tuition; at that point three other girls of known families were bussed in to join Princess Anne when she became the sole royal pupil.

when he was spotted as the only child arriving in a grey overcoat with a black velvet collar. But the next stage of his education came when he moved on to Cheam in 1958, a choice which the Queen finally accepted against the advice of her mother and her father's relatives who all felt that the conventional route of Ludgrove and Eton would be preferable. Philip, supported by Lord Mountbatten, favoured Cheam and Gordonstoun which had been the education provided for himself by the Mountbatten family. By now, past undertakings from national newspaper editors were long forgotten and as the prince moved to Cheam, reporters and photographers from home and overseas laid siege to the area. For weeks, barely a day went by without a story or photograph of Charles appearing, especially in the continental magazines who seemed fascinated by him. The press had found another star, and here in that year of his first term at Cheam he achieved his initiation into the spotlight that would focus ever more fiercely upon him, through times good, bad and indifferent. Three weeks after he arrived, the Queen paid a private visit to see how her son was settling in. His detective, on constant duty, reported that he wasn't being given a chance by the press and on her return to the palace, the Queen summoned Colville to her study. 'Isn't there anything we can do?' she asked. 'What if I talk to the newspapers personally?'

Colville suggested a conference of editors; she agreed and they were informed that the Queen was so concerned about the effect of the publicity on her son's education that unless it was curtailed she would seriously have to consider taking him away from Cheam and returning to the system of private education at the palace, which would have been a pity. As Colville had already pointed out, Charles was the first heir to the throne in history who had joined the external educational system to join 'ordinary' boys at an 'ordinary' school. If this decision had to be reversed, said Colville, the press would be to blame. They calmed down for a time, though they could hardly be blamed for a strong revival in interest which accompanied the Queen's announcement at the end of July that henceforth her son was to be known as the Prince of Wales. Charles was back in the headlines where, give or take the odd day or two, he would remain *ad infinitum*. However, the Queen continued to try to protect him and

Commander Colville wrote to the Press Council to state that 'the private lives of the royal family are being increasingly disrupted by certain sections of the press' and he sought guidance as to how it could be curbed. As the *Guardian*, reporting this approach, pointed out: 'The covering of news in a snob way for the entertainment of the establishment is almost a thing of the past. Pressure for more and more intimate details of the royal family and more and more candid camera shots of them has been building up for years.'

The Press Council could do little, other than repeat the request Colville had already made twice on behalf of the Queen to editors – to leave Charles alone. Cheam was his term-time home for almost four years during which time there were said to be fifty-four separate incidents logged by school staff of intrusion into school grounds or premises by adventurous newshounds seeking the lowdown on Charles, the scholar and school sports competitor. Enough is enough, said Colville to the Press Council. And the Queen became even angrier soon afterwards and decided upon more drastic action. The Press Council was as toothless then as it was upon its demise in 1990. In January, the following year, the Queen resorted to law when one of her former employees, Charles Ellis, a former superintendent at Windsor Castle, sold an article to the *Sunday Pictorial*, entitled 'The Queen in her Castle'. He was brought before the Queen's Bench Division where his lawyers eventually gave an undertaking that he would write no other articles appertaining to his employment by the Queen.

There was hidden benefit to Princess Margaret in the diversion created by Charles. No one outside of a small group of close friends had rumbled her new romance. And come the start of 1959, the family scattered all round the globe on a series of tours, mainly within the Commonwealth, as a further distraction. Prince Philip took off on a working tour, travelling to India, Pakistan and the Far East. He was away for three months and then missed his wife's thirty-third birthday by carrying straight on to another long-standing engagement to celebrate the 350th anniversary of a British settlement's being established on the island of Bermuda. On his return, he joined the Queen at Windsor

Castle for what his cousin Queen Alexandra of Yugoslavia mischievously described as 'an unusually long weekend'. The Queen Mother went off to Kenya and Uganda, Princess Margaret was booked for a tour of the Caribbean, the Duchess of Kent and her daughter Princess Alexandra went to Latin America while the Duke and Duchess of Gloucester were planning their visit to Nigeria in the face of the pressing demands for independence.

The Queen, in the meantime, was preparing for two more major tours, one to Canada in the summer and the second to Ghana in the autumn to reaffirm British ties to the former colonial territory that was once known as the Gold Coast.* The Canadian trip was another vast undertaking planned to last almost six weeks to enable the Queen to travel coast to coast and spend time in as many of the nation's major cities as possible. She also planned to meet up with the American President Dwight D. Eisenhower and his wife Mamie for the official opening of the St Lawrence Seaway.

Her business and tour managers could not have imagined in their wildest moments the unexpected news, confirmed almost on the eve of departure, that she was expecting her third child, due to be born early in the new year. She ruled out the cancellation of the Canadian trip, but one of her private secretaries was sent to Ghana to inform Dr Nkrumah personally and explain that she would not, after all, be able to make her planned visit, and would he kindly keep her news a secret for the time being. Even before she knew of her condition, Canadian officials were already questioning the intensity of the Queen's Canadian schedule. Esmond Butler, her Canadian press secretary, came to England to discuss the final arrangements and, without knowing that the Queen was pregnant, suggested that some of the visits might be curtailed. He pointed out that on a single day when she was to visit Port Arthur, Fort William and Calgary, for example, there were thirty-two entries on her schedule between 9.00 a.m.

*Under its Prime Minister, Dr Kwame Nkrumah, Ghana became the first of Britain's African colonies to be granted independence within the Commonwealth in March 1956. Dr Nkrumah told a cheering crowd who watched the lowering of the Union Jack to delight in 'the casting off of imperial chains'.

and late in the evening. The day included taking the royal barge into Port Arthur for meetings in that town with local dignitaries, a hospital visit, a drive through the streets to meet the children, a drive to Fort William, an official luncheon, more receptions, another hospital visit, more children, a baseball game, an exhibition of square-dancing, a flight to Calgary, more tours through the streets, more children singing and dancing, more presentations, a visit to an Indian village, chuck-wagon races and a barbecue all timed to split-second precision. That pattern was to be repeated over and over again and Esmond Butler relayed the concern of some of the newspaper editors he had spoken to that it was simply too much. 'Let the mayors and dowagers repine and royalty will have an easier time,' wrote the editor of *Maclean*'s magazine. To which the Queen responded, 'I am going there to work, not for a holiday'.

The reality of the tour was even worse than it appeared on paper. They had failed to take into account the extremes of weather, 90 degrees in Toronto and a squalling thunderstorm in Port Arthur while the royals were travelling in an open-topped car; nor had they planned fully for the delays to the schedule that occurred through the sheer volume of the crowds. There was also a day trip to the United States, to Chicago, where the Americans had laid on a massive reception – twenty-four US warships formed a guard of honour for the royal yacht *Britannia* and five squadrons of jet fighters flew overhead. A 200 foot barge filled with flowers was moored at the landing stage; guns, ships' sirens and bells rang out in a loud greeting and trumpeters blared out the British National Anthem and 'Rule Britannia'. One and a half million people lined the streets below banners which read 'Welcome to the Windy City, Liz and Phil'. Then she visited the International Trade Fair and walked along 2,500 feet of red carpet specially laid for her arrival, watched a display of fire floats, walked around the Chicago Art Institute and Museum of Science, went to lunch with seven US state governors, 45 mayors and 300 other dignitaries, and after an afternoon of tours, went to dinner with a similar number of people in all, thirteen hours of engagements.

By now, the Queen was being affected by morning sickness and the attendance of her physician, Surgeon Captain D. D.

Steele-Perkins, gave rise to some rumours. 'Was she pregnant?' someone whispered, and so she had to let the Canadian Prime Minister John F. Diefenbaker in on her secret. The tour went on, with a train ride to Ontario, a cruise of Lake Superior and another train journey through the Rocky Mountains. Vancouver provided another daunting schedule and by the time the royal party reached Nanaimo where she was to be installed as an honorary Indian princess, she looked exhausted. Onwards, still, for a trek through the Yukon and the North-West Territories, and she rejected Diefenbaker's suggestion that the tour should be cut back. The latter proved too much, and she was ordered to bed for a day's rest before a flight to Edmonton and a 4 day whistle-stop tour of the Prairie Provinces. By the end of it, Steele-Perkins was getting worried and at his suggestion the plan to sail home in *Britannia*, calling at the Shetlands and the Orkneys on the way, was abandoned and the Queen flew straight home to London.

Balmoral that summer saw a gathering of the family. Lady Pamela Mountbatten brought David Hicks, an artist and designer, and soon they were formally requesting the Queen's permission to become engaged. Princess Margaret managed to get an invitation for Antony Armstrong-Jones who stayed at Birkhall, the Queen Mother's home. The two newcomers to the royal circle represented fresh blood, especially with both coming from their artistic background. It was during that month of August that the Queen's pregnancy was officially announced. The engagement of Princess Margaret to her Tony was, however, to be kept under wraps. The Queen was, naturally, delighted that her sister had found happiness at last. But there was an obvious pitfall, two in fact, and though the Queen and Philip did not wish to throw a wet blanket over the princess's plans yet again, they had to face reality. The first problem was an obvious one: the Queen's sister, third in line to the throne, was planning to marry a commoner. Well, wasn't Philip a plain 'mister' when he became engaged to the Queen, having renounced his Greek princehood for British nationality? And wasn't that problem overcome by the King providing him with a bagful of titles? Ah yes, but Philip was a prince, of true royal birth with a pedigree that stretched back somewhere into the dark ages. Well, Tony might accept a title. That would solve it, wouldn't it? But there was another nagging problem: his parents were divorced, and both had remarried. Tony's mother was now the Countess of Rosse, titled at least. His father's second wife was the actress Carol Coombe, from whom he was also divorced, and he was about to take a third wife, Jennifer Unite, an air hostess who was barely a year older than her stepson. What would Mr Macmillan's Cabinet think of that?

Obviously, the princess's engagement would have to be relayed to the Prime Minister, and Margaret and Tony agreed to keep their decision to marry – and even their association – an absolute secret. Macmillan, meantime, had more important matters on his mind. He was running high in public opinion, having assured the British public recently that they had never had it so good and reaffirmed Britain's position as a world power during a highly successful televised fireside chat with President Eisenhower from No. 10 Downing Street on 31 August. Dubbed the Ike and Mac Show, the apparently impromptu conversation which made such a big impression was followed by a small motor tour along streets lined with cheering crowds. Cynical observers noted that they drove through some of the Conservatives' marginal constituencies and talk of a general election proved to be fully justified. A week later, Macmillan set the date for 8 October and on the ninth of that month he was invited to form a government, having been returned with a thumping majority.

Three matters concerning the royal family came before the Macmillan Cabinet in the latter part of 1959; they remain on the 'secret' list at the Public Records Office in Kew and will not be revealed until well into the next century. Two of the secrets can now be identified. One was almost certainly cabinet discussion of the proposed engagement of Princess Margaret to Antony Armstrong-Jones, since there is no record or mention of that subject and it is known that it came before the Cabinet. Because she was past the age of twenty-five Princess Margaret no longer needed the permission of the Sovereign under the Royal Marriages Act of 1772; she was, however, bound by her royal status and Civil List allowance to give notice to the Privy Council of her intention to marry and to inform Her Majesty's Cabinet. No one could stop her marrying the man of her choice, though there were certainly a few raised eyebrows and it was within the scope of the Cabinet, if not Parliament, to question the decision if it so wished. Macmillan himself was in agreement and he eventually informed the Queen that the Cabinet wished to pass to the princess their good wishes and congratulations. The timing of the announcement, however, dragged on for what to the princess seemed an interminable time; they had to continue to keep their secret for several weeks yet.

The second matter on which cabinet discussion remains classified concerned the Queen's name change. Having been advised by Churchill in 1952 that the name of the royal house and family should remain Windsor, and not Mountbatten as would have been the case if she taken her husband's adopted surname, the Queen had personally put forward another proposal, that it should be changed to Mountbatten-Windsor; she had made the approach to Macmillan in December.

According to Lord Beaverbrook this plea came as a result of continued pressure from Lord Mountbatten who

> suggested that even if the name Windsor be retained, the name Mountbatten might be included. Prince Philip was less concerned than his uncle . . . though he took pains to see that the Prince of Wales should know his heritage. He sent German genealogists to secure a complete family tree for Prince Charles to see. Through all this the Queen has remained steadfast in one respect. She could never see the name Windsor, chosen by her grandfather, abandoned by the royal house. On the other hand she sympathises with her husband's feelings and more particularly with the overtures of his uncle. So the compromise . . .[11]

Again, this adjustment of the family name had to be discussed in cabinet. Harold Macmillan referred to it obliquely in his memoirs as 'The Queen's Affair'. There was apparently considerable discussion on the name change and it was clear that the Macmillan Cabinet would not approve a straightforward addition of Mountbatten hyphenated to the family name of Windsor. In fact, when the full discussion came up in cabinet, Macmillan was away on his African tour, and the acting Prime Minister R. A. Butler was forced to take over the 'delicate negotiations'. Butler discovered only at the last minute the background to the Queen's name, and the memorandum prepared by Prince Philip in 1952 – 'of all this Winston had told me, as a senior member of cabinet at the time, absolutely nothing'.[12] The Lord Chancellor re-submitted lengthy and complicated proposals, so complicated that legal experts argued over their meaning. There was considerable discussion in cabinet, chaired by Butler who noted that 'several of our colleagues expressed serious regret that this step had to be taken but while recognising the dangers of criticism and unpopularity, particularly attached to the husband, none felt the Queen's request should be refused'.[13] As Macmillan described it, it meant in a nutshell 'the name of the House, Family and Dynasty to remain Windsor; the name of any 'de-royalised' grandson etc of the Queen and Prince Philip to be Mountbatten-Windsor'.[14]

More precisely, the ruling decreed that all the Queen's children and her descendants who had the title of HRH Prince or Princess would remain Windsors; all others would become Mountbatten-Windsor, thus ensuring the retention of the existing name of the royal house for the line of succession. Female descendants who married, for example, could adopt the Mountbatten-Windsor style. This was something of a loop-hole, and certain Cabinet members were somewhat disturbed to discover that it was not just distant descendants who would use the new hyphenated name; Princess Anne became the first to do so when she married Captain Mark Phillips, although her birth certificate, registered by Philip himself, ambiguously fails to give any surname whatsoever. In this, Macmillan, Butler and the rest of the Cabinet had 'reckoned without the fast footwork of Mountbatten'.[15]

Chapter Seven

A New Family (1960–62)

A crop of spectacular births, marriages and deaths opened the new decade and not least among the discussion these events provoked was the question of why the Queen had waited so long before adding to her family, with a gap of almost ten years since Princess Anne was born. In effect she started a second family with Prince Andrew's birth in February 1960, to be followed four years later by Prince Edward's, and with other additions to the family coming by way of marriages and births to new royal couplings, it was therefore perhaps no accident that the overriding royal theme of the sixties was to be one of family life, with the virtues of the family group being projected and emphasised regularly throughout the decade. As to why the Queen had waited so long, the question almost answered itself: she had simply been too busy since the Coronation to allow her personal wishes to interfere with the succession of critical events in her reign. There were those who would have preferred to have been able to pinpoint other reasons, such as difficulties in her marriage – as speculated upon by the gossip writers from overseas – but those close to the family have steadfastly denied that this was ever the case. The plain fact was that the Queen had been worked off her feet – over 4,800 engagements in the first ten years of marriage – and one year soon rolled on to the next in circumstances of national crises and family drama, so that she may hardly have dared to become pregnant. In that time, she had also made seven major overseas tours, visiting twenty-eight countries. In fact, she and her husband were so often away from home and their two existing children that any psychiatrist might have recommended no further family until they had a more settled life in prospect, but that in turn would have been an interminable wait. These demands on her time had often prompted the question: what kind of mother can she be, with so much of her time taken elsewhere? She strove to bring up the children as 'normally' as her situation would permit and stipulated that they should have plenty of contact with the outside world, enjoy a wide circle of friends and normal interests. It was a simple enough statement of intent, but exceedingly difficult to achieve. 'Considering everything,' said a member of the household, 'she is really an ordinary mother . . . she joined in their games, took an interest in everything they did, supervised their education – not wanting to send Charles away to school, but philosophical that eventually he would have to go; ensuring that neither Charles nor Anne was shown special privileges. These were the basics she concentrated upon.' They played family games, like charades and Scrabble, went riding and swimming together. The Queen loved to play duets on the piano with Princess Margaret, and to sing choruses of old songs. All the things that families do when they are together were on the menu, though performed as a group with far less frequency than she would have liked. She also desperately wanted to enlarge her family; the Queen Mother said that six or eight months off for maternity leave was a blessing in disguise and the Queen returned to some of the female tasks that she had neglected, like going shopping, sneaking privately into the theatre with Philip after the lights had gone down or visiting old friends.

The break enabled her to initiate a long-held ambition to remodel the guest suites in the King Edward III Tower at Windsor Castle, summoning the architect Sir Hugh Casson to supervise while she went shopping for new wallpaper and curtains. Although she had allowed the press to photograph her new home when, as Princess Elizabeth, she moved into Clarence House upon her marriage, the renovations at Windsor were kept under wraps as the Queen became more determined to try to curb the intrusion of publicity into her private life. She also looked in on the work being carried out at Queen Mary's former home, Marlborough House in the Mall, which she had presented as a new Commonwealth Centre.

Come January, however, she was confined to quarters to await the arrival of her child and was unable to attend the first of the year's weddings, that of her former lady in waiting, Lady Pamela Mountbatten, to David Hicks on 13 January. That did not stop Lord Mountbatten staging a wedding for his younger daughter that had all the trappings and pomp of a major royal occasion; the whole German clan, along with the factions from pretty well every other remaining royal house in Europe, arrived for the ceremony in a swirling blizzard to make up a glittering guest list of 1,300. Princess Anne was a bridesmaid, along with two of her cousins, Clarissa of Hesse and Frederica of Hanover. Prince Philip proposed the toast to the bride and groom and his uncle welcomed the first untitled male to the family. An interior decorator, however distinguished, was not 'what he would have chosen as a recruit for his family'.[1] Once his daughter had made up her mind, however, he supported her wholeheartedly. Much the same feelings must have been in the minds of the Queen and the Queen Mother as Princess Margaret began planning her own marriage.

The family joy of Pamela's marriage was soon to be overshadowed. The day after the wedding her mother, Lady Edwina Mountbatten, went off on her travels, as restless as ever and driven by a mixture of duty and ambition. Long gone were the days of her scandals and notorious affairs; her life in the twenties and thirties was consumed by wanderlust and a search for far more excitement than her husband could provide as a serving naval officer. Even her biographer Richard Hough, who wrote her story with Mountbatten's cooperation, described her lifestyle as 'decadent, self-indulgent, meaningless', a life in which the rules of the game were 'generously flexible'.[2] From the war years onwards, when the last of her great love affairs which had threatened to destroy her marriage to Mountbatten was over, she flung herself into charity and good works. From then on, there was no other goal than to work hard for the deprived and starving wherever in the world she might find them. When she returned from India after Mountbatten had guided the country towards independence, she became an international figurehead of, among other things, the Save the Children Fund which her great-niece Princess Anne later took over. She set a pattern of service which other young royals, especially those up and coming in the nineties, would find an unbeatable example. In January 1960, she embarked on a gruelling tour of the Far East for the St John Ambulance Brigade of which she was also head. On 20 February, she suffered a heart attack after a long day of engagements in Jesselton, Borneo and died in her sleep. She had lived long enough to learn that her nephew had just become a father again . . . the Queen gave birth to Prince Andrew on 19 February – the first child born to a reigning British monarch since Victoria had Princess Beatrice in 1857. And so for the space of two days, the newspapers were full of the arrival of the Queen's new son, followed immediately by the glowing obituaries of the Countess Mountbatten of Burma whose notorious early years were obliterated by her recent role which the newspapers recorded had verged upon that of national heroine. Her body was flown home to England for a burial at sea, which she had requested. It was a spectacular event in itself, and a fitting end to a life led to the full, with an escort of ships including a frigate sent especially from India, and Mountbatten was overwhelmed by the acclaim, expressed in hundreds of telegrams he received from kings, queens, presidents and prime ministers the world over.

Two days after Edwina's death came another blow for the Queen and the Mountbattens. Queen Victoria's last surviving grandson, Alexander, Marquis of Carisbrooke, died in his grace-and-favour apartment at Kensington Palace, aged seventy-four. He was, coincidentally, the eldest son of Princess Beatrice and Prince Henry of Battenberg. The Queen ordered a week of official court mourning for both and it was an odd moment, therefore, to unleash the next item of very personal news in the royal calendar: on 26 February seven days after her son's birth, five days after Edwina's death and three days after Cousin Alex's death, the Queen gave the go-ahead for the announcement of the engagement of her sister Princess Margaret to Mr Antony Armstrong-Jones.

The collective impact of these events was substantial, as

were the headlines and pictures of the latest bombshell. That was the word. Though the rumours had been around in the inner circle of Margaret's friends, the engagement came as stunning news to the nation and to the press whom Harold Nicolson observed had been well and truly 'scooped'. Not a hint had slipped out previously and it was greeted with total astonishment. In fact, Buckingham Palace had carefully planned the announcement to follow the birth of the Queen's third child, though they had not taken the two deaths into account. The Queen consulted with the family and decided that the announcement should be made regardless of the mourning; the plans had been set and should be adhered to – they all knew at Buckingham Palace that there was an element of risk in how Margaret's engagement would be received, and in terms of damage limitation there was nothing to gain in holding it back. Anyway, time was marching on; the couple had been unofficially engaged since the previous October and the wedding had already been booked for May. And so in spite of the deaths, the news of their betrothal was released with military precision by the Queen Mother's own press secretary Major Griffin who chose to reveal it in a short statement at 6.00 p.m. that Friday evening, thus commandeering the evening news programmes on television, mass coverage in the Saturday morning papers and huge follow-ups in the Sundays. If there was to be any press-baron objection or rent-a-quote disapproval from the 'tweedy' set who could not bear the thought of their Princess marrying an arty-crafty commoner with divorced parents, it would be overpowered by the sheer weight of the publicity, and reaction from the public. And it was.

In the afterglow of genuine public happiness for the Queen countered by the sadness over Countess Mountbatten, Margaret's engagement was received with wholehearted approval. Even *The Times* was positive, informing its readers, who might have been concerned over the princess marrying a mere photographer, that the news would be 'enthusiastically welcomed throughout the Commonwealth on the simple assurance that Her Royal Highness is following her own heart and the Queen is delighted with her choice'.[3] Later the analysts began analysing and an anonymous writer in the *New Statesman* predicted that Margaret had half closed the door on her magical and mystical world and eventually her public engagements and public persona would diminish accordingly. Tony Armstrong-Jones was to be portrayed as 'a most unlikely candidate';[4] his Bohemian friends were examined, his reputation for unorthodox girlfriends revealed and his father's small but beautiful collection of wives was noted. But seriously, Tony Armstrong-Jones would bring new blood into the royal family and it was badly needed. So three cheers for Tony.

Meanwhile, the sacks of parcels of newly knitted baby clothes and every kind of toy being delivered to Buckingham Palace from well-wishers around the world were now joined by van loads of cards offering congratulations to Margaret and Tony. The public mood had changed quite dramatically. There was romance in the air, another wedding and another party, so why be cynical? Britain was on the crest of Macmillan's wave, in spite of a recent 1 per cent hike in the bank rate, and at times like this there was nothing better than a bit of sentimental patriotism and, as something of a rehearsal for the great state occasion to come, thousands turned out to line the streets of London to welcome General de Gaulle. His arrival in London in April marked the re-emergence of the Queen to public duties. De Gaulle stayed at the palace for the duration and the royals and politicians and old wartime comrades came out in force to give him the red carpet treatment.

The day after de Gaulle left, the Queen returned to family matters – helping to prepare for the wedding and posing for photographs of the new family. Cecil Beaton, who now considered himself to be Armstrong-Jones's rival for palace work, did not share the nation's glee at the forthcoming nuptials. 'He's not even a good photographer,' was his bitter cry when he heard the news and concluded that he could personally better this 'Cinderella in reverse' story only by rushing off and marrying Greta Garbo.[5] Only Noël Coward was noticeably prophetic in his assessment of the engagement: 'Whether or not the marriage is entirely suitable remains to be seen', although Coward did discover that not everyone in the royal household was as ecstatic about the news as we had been led to believe. He lunched with Marina, Duchess of Kent and Princess Alexandra and found a distinct *froideur* when he mentioned the subject.[6]

Meanwhile, Tony Jones, as the *Mirror* insisted upon calling him, was removed to a safe haven; he was provided with a guest room at Buckingham Palace to shield him from the white heat of public interest that had suddenly swung into his direction. Did he pinch himself, that first night in the palace? Who wouldn't? Cecil Beaton was still grumpy, though it pleased him that in spite of Armstrong-Jones's new prominence, he was summoned to the palace to photograph the Queen, her new baby, Charles and Anne in advance of the christening in April. He didn't like babies at the best of times, and he especially didn't like babies with bossy fathers like Prince Philip. The infant was carried into the room some minutes before the Queen by a nurse who was followed by Charles and Anne. On seeing them, Beaton said, 'Oh well, I suppose we had better start photographing right away if that would be all right.'

'Well, I don't think it will be,' said Princess Anne and Beaton loathed her on sight.

Soon, the Queen and Prince Philip arrived and Beaton struggled to make this conventional group look interesting. 'I felt as if I was being chased in a nightmare,' he wrote afterwards. 'The family stood to attention. I said something to make them smile . . . and I clicked like mad at anything that seemed passable.'

Philip did not like Beaton at all. He kept suggesting ways of taking the photographs and making other irritating comments, ending by stating that he wanted to take some pictures himself. Finally, Philip called the session to a halt by saying to the Queen, 'Surely we've had enough. If he's not got what he wants by now he's an even worse photographer than I think he is (ha . . . ha . . . ha . . . ha).'

The Queen and Philip left the room and Beaton began taking some photographs of the children who had been left in the care of the staff. He placed Princess Anne by the window: 'The wretched girl shrugged her shoulders and pulled a face. Yes, I said like a demon, You hate it . . . but hate it by the window there, hate it looking this way, hate it looking that way. Now detest it looking straight at the camera.' Suddenly, Prince Philip came back unexpectedly and said in amazement as if Beaton was not there, 'Now he's started again. He's taking Anne now!'[7]

In spite of these technical problems, Beaton was the official photographer at the palace for the royal wedding in May. He was still critical of the royal dresses and rather uncomplimentary about the bridegroom who he thought looked 'extremely nondescript, biscuit complexioned, ratty and untidy. The fact that this man is of little standing, that he is in no way romantic (even as Townsend was) makes no matter for he is the man the princess has fallen in love with and so all must be made perfect in the eyes of the world. The fact remains, the young man is not worthy of this strange fluke of fortune, or misfortune, and because he is likeable and may become unhappy makes one even sorrier.' So now Beaton had joined Noël Coward in the foreboding.

The biggest royal spectacular since the Coronation was stage-managed to perfection by the Duke of Norfolk, the Queen's Earl Marshal, called to the fore again to relish his hour or three of pageantry and glory. Richard Dimbleby, speaking soft and low and respectful, had secured an exclusive eyrie inside Westminster Abbey and 300 million television viewers saw the 'most beautiful princess anywhere on this earth' given away by Prince Philip to her common man. There were, in this mêlée of celebration, two or three points that could not go unnoticed. Buckingham Palace admitted that an unprecedented number of wedding invitations were declined; a closer scan of the guest list showed that a surprising number of continental royalty had shunned the wedding which was later explained by one of them as being 'tit for tat', because of the ten royal weddings in Europe since the war, the Queen had attended only one.* The Duke and Duchess of Windsor did not even have the opportunity of declining; they were not among the 3,000 who received one of the gold-embossed invitations from the office of the Lord Chamberlain which bore the words 'The Queen Mother is Commanded by Her Majesty to Invite . . .' Happy families! The bride's uncle and aunt had no contact at this time with the royals in London and, like millions of others, had to be content to watch the ceremony on television. 'I do not know

*Actually the Queen could not be blamed; she was not permitted to visit any country as a private individual; protocol required a formal invitation and a state welcome before she could return privately.

the gentleman,' said the duke icily when questioned by reporters about his view of the groom. 'But I wish my niece and her husband every happiness.'

In spite of all the sentimental outpourings, the family did not escape without a complaint about the expense of it all. In fact there was a good deal of ill-feeling over costs, which was then and has remained one of the blind spots of royalty. It became known that the government had authorised the spending of £56,000 to refurbish a fairly modest apartment at No. 10 Kensington Palace for the newlyweds and that the nation would bear the cost of the honeymoon, estimated at £10,000 a day, Caribbean cruising in the royal yacht *Britannia*. That passed, but on reflection the Queen could not have hoped for a better overall reaction to her sister's wedding; perhaps more importantly, the monarchy itself was helped by virtue of the young and romantic imagery that had been trawled up in its wake.

The development of the Queen's own family continued to dominate the home front for some time to come. But it was her other 'family', that of her Commonwealth, that provided the greatest headaches in the new decade, and by choice she remained in the front line of what was going to be a bumpy ride. Quietly and away from the public glare of family hyper-activity, matters of state, with much overseas involvement, continued. The official boxes never ceased to arrive, even during her confinement, and in the latter stages her Prime Minister Harold Macmillan made sure she would not become bored by sending her lengthy reports on his African tour at the beginning of the year. What he did not reveal to her that winter, or anyone else for that matter, was a dark plot in South Africa whose aim was to de-recognise the Queen as the head of the Commonwealth. Support for this move would undoubtedly have been more widespread, had it not been that it was South Africa proposing it. The news would have caused some sensational headlines for the Queen of a different kind had it been known and it came, not without coincidence, the day after Macmillan had made his famous 'wind of change' speech . . .

Of all her first ministers, before and after, Macmillan was the most prolific in his contact with the sovereign. His memoirs are scattered with the reference 'I wrote to the Queen to inform her . . .' and she apparently looked forward to receiving his highly documented and very literate observations on the various matters of government business that currently occupied him. It was a deliberate policy on Macmillan's part, which he began soon after taking over at No. 10, regardless of the fact that she had no power to alter anything. 'It is true the monarch must in the end yield to the formal advice given by ministers,' he wrote, 'but the Queen has an absolute right to know . . . to criticise . . . to advise – duties which are so important and may well in a critical situation become vital.'[8] Macmillan's reports to the Queen began when he found that the arrangements for the weekly audience in the late afternoon each Tuesday were timed to fit in with her seeing the children and were not always convenient in terms of giving him the time he required.

He also did not wish to appear to be standing in front of her reciting a monologue without discussion, or, as Queen Victoria once described Mr Gladstone's visit, addressing her as if she were a public meeting. So Macmillan devised the scheme whereby he would send her notes concerning the main points of the matters he might raise during audience. This, eventually, developed into a rather more detailed affair which, the Prime Minister recounted later, was due to the 'assiduity with which she read and absorbed the vast mass of documents circulated'. It also helped Macmillan himself because in writing the report to the Queen, he was often able to crystallise his thoughts on a particularly trying topic. She would sometimes reply, especially when he was abroad, occasionally in her own hand if it was to be a short note but often she sent a longish and detailed one through her secretary Sir Michael Adeane, setting out her observations. It was this relationship with Macmillan that really put the Queen on course for her dealings with future prime ministers.

Macmillan's African tour in January and February of 1960 was punctuated by some emotive speeches on both sides. 'The wind of change is blowing through this continent,' he told the South African Parliament in Cape Town, 'and whether we like it or not this growth in national consciousness is a political fact.' In reply, Dr Henrick Verwoerd, the South

African Premier, was loudly cheered when he retorted, 'There has to be justice not only for the black man in Africa but also for the white man'. The following day, at a private meeting, Verwoerd told Macmillan that there was a great feeling against retaining the Queen as head of the Commonwealth. Macmillan said he was surprised by this statement, especially as nearly half the white population of South Africa was of British descent. However, Verwoerd said he was considering raising the issue at the next meeting of the Commonwealth prime ministers, in May. It ran out of control long before then. Macmillan wrote to the Queen about his fears for Africa and on his return told her that there were many difficulties to be faced.[9] Britain was torn between seemingly condoning South Africa's apartheid policies even when it did not, and splitting the Commonwealth. The immediate dilemma for Macmillan resolved itself, in a way, barely a month later at Sharpeville when police massacred fifty-six demonstrators. The issue went straight into the United Nations where various resolutions demanded an end to apartheid. Older, and white, members of the Commonwealth such as Australia wanted Britain to give what was tantamount to support to Verwoerd by using its power of veto against any UN moves against South Africa.

The Australian Premier Sir Robert Menzies, secretly supported by the British government, felt that there should be no external intervention in 'what is, though tragic and terrible, a domestic problem for the Union of South Africa'.[10] The newer Afro-Asian members of the Commonwealth would be furious with Britain if it did nothing and Macmillan warned the Queen that the Commonwealth was in imminent danger of disintegration through racial quarrels. 'My supreme task is to try to steer us through this crisis,' he wrote on 3 April 1960.[11] The May Commonwealth conference developed into a behind-the-scenes slanging match which was only briefly set aside for Princess Margaret's wedding to which many of the protagonists had been invited. The Queen, realising the temperature would be somewhat heated, invited all of her Commonwealth prime ministers back to Windsor for dinner, instead of the customary meal at Buckingham Palace. She did not leave until after midnight, by which time some of her ministers were visibly flagging, especially the South African Foreign Minister Eric Louw – representing Dr Verwoerd who was nursing a bullet hole in his head after an assassination attempt in Johannesburg the previous week. Louw was now canvassing opinion about South Africa remaining in the Commonwealth if it moved to become a republic, thus rejecting the Queen as head of state. The answer to this, as Menzies later revealed, was a very definite No, even though Ghana's Dr Nkrumah had just done exactly the same thing and remained in the Commonwealth. Macmillan while refusing at present to intervene in the affairs of South Africa 'steered his course' to placate the black and Asian nations and the Queen nodded her approval. Nigeria, Sierra Leone and Uganda were all coming up for independence; Ghana was facing desperately troubled times following its own declaration of independence and there were fears it would descend into the likes of the bloody civil war raging in the Congo. Any overt support for South Africa at that time would have meant the disbandment of the Commonwealth and to ensure that the member countries knew just exactly where her sympathies lay, her Prime Minister reported at audience on 3 May that the Queen had been formally invited to visit the republics of India, Pakistan and Malaya. The Queen said she was very pleased; though she stuck rigidly to the ideal, the Commonwealth would yet prove one of her greatest tests of endurance. Nor would they be able to prevent South Africa leaving the Commonwealth. Its people voted by referendum to de-recognise the monarchy and become a republic; but at least it saved the Queen from the continued embarrassment of being Queen of South Africa. Following the United Nations' Security Council condemnation of apartheid, echoed by the black leaders of the Commonwealth countries, Dr Verwoerd decided they were no longer welcome in the club, and would leave in May. On the same day, there were some early indications of another rising problem when Sir Roy Welensky, Prime Minister of the Central African Federation, flatly rejected Britain's plans for increased black representation in Northern Rhodesia and called up 3,000 territorials to help put down the expected insurrection.

The rest of the year was largely taken up by domestic events.

Margaret and Tony came home and faced months of scrutiny and camera lenses stuck up their noses. The Queen's engagements were kept to the home front and included such historic events as the launching of the Royal Navy's first nuclear submarine, *Dreadnought*, which followed the launching of the first guided missile destroyer *Devonshire*. The nuclear age and deterrent concept so heavily promoted by Harold Macmillan had become a burgeoning industry in his bid to build up a strong and competent atomic arsenal of missiles and H-Bombs and it was perhaps significant that Macmillan chose to place the royal stamp on these two most important additions. He knew it was a political hot potato and that the Labour Party's autumn conference would contain emotive calls from the powerful left for unilateral disarmament as the Labour leader Hugh Gaitskell, perspiring with anguish, pleaded, 'There are some of us who will fight and fight again to save the party we love.'[12]

The costly atomic toys were all part of the New Elizabethan Age about which there had been so much hope; now hope had faded to the acceptance of another kind of Britain. The expense of these aspirations to remain a world power lay heavily on an economy struggling with the demands of its welfare state and requests from its former colonies for loans to help them into independence. The resources of the nation were being spread too thin, especially when industry rested too much on past laurels, thinking the world owed it a living, and did not hustle too greatly in the world markets. The unions did not help, with more strikes one infamous two weeks the previous spring than in Germany for the previous seven years. It became known as the 'British disease' and the continued inflationary plague on the British economy led Prince Philip to demand of the nation's bosses and workers alike, 'Get your fingers out . . .' Philip was able to say such things and get away with it, or at least get no more than a roasting from a hostile press.

The Queen's speeches remained undemanding and uncontroversial; in these days of the plunging temperatures of the Cold War, her government saw her most important contribution as her appearances abroad, helping to keep the nations of the Commonwealth within the family and ensure that their leaders did not misuse their new-found independence and align with the Soviet Union. This was undoubtedly among Macmillan's greatest fears, that Asia and huge chunks of Africa would go Communist; already Nkrumah in Ghana seemed on the verge of defecting and there were fears that it would spread like a bushfire through the African continent and the Asian nations, as these governments sought aid and goods from whomever could supply them. All this was happening at the very time that Khrushchev was sabre-rattling, boasting of a treaty with East Germany and banging his shoe on the woodwork at the United Nations, deriding American lackeys and stooges, while the Americans themselves were in the middle of a critical election, which saw the arrival of John F. Kennedy at the White House.

The tense international politics prevailed as another demanding tour was being planned for the Queen, and lest one believed the messages of the government information services that this was being arranged purely for the benefit of her peoples who had yet to see her in person, a closer scrutiny would reveal that she was to travel through strategically important countries who might easily be wooed by the Russians. The tour was to last six weeks and included in the royal party was Lord Home, Macmillan's new Foreign Secretary. It began in Cyprus, the newest independent Commonwealth state which lies 40 miles from the nearest point in Asia Minor and 60 miles from Syria. In most recent history, it was, of course, the scene of so much bloodshed in the fifties which was now to be washed aside as Archbishop Makarios, once exiled and imprisoned, welcomed the Queen as head of the Commonwealth, though not as their monarch. The island that had been a British colony since 1925 was granted republican status in 1960, save for an area of 99 square miles for British bases. Onwards to Delhi, arriving just half a century after her grandfather's great Delhi Durbar at which he was installed as Emperor of all India. This time the British monarch was witnessing the country's Republic Day Parade and she tried to make a virtue of it, using as her theme for her speeches as she travelled across the country that it was all 'a triumphant vindication of the vision of the statesmen who changed the old Empire into a free association of equals', and the millions of dark-skinned, poverty-blighted people who lined streets in every city cheered in a kind of spectacular mass hysteria that had no root cause other than some strange and mystical throw-back to the past in which she was the embodiment of the Raj, encapsulated by a great parade of 325 elephants or by her sailing down the Ganges on a decorated barge. She may have been brought slightly down to earth on learning that Nikita Krushchev had not long before slept in the same bed as Her Majesty at her vice-regal lodge. That was a touch of irony that perhaps helped bring this true extravaganza into reality and undermine the lie that this tour was for the people, and not a giant public relations exercise for the promotion of backdoor political influence. There was a time and place for it all, once, and what the Queen and the onlooking world were witnessing in these few days, though they did not know it, was the last such great demonstration of Indian expression towards a reigning British monarch. And the likes of it are unlikely to be seen again.

There was one other throw-back: the tiger shoot in India which the Queen and Prince Philip joined and never lived down. Philip shot one of these huge majestic creatures straight between the eyes and a photograph of himself and the Queen, and their hunting party, surrounding the unfortunate dead beast was flashed around the world and used in bold reproduction in many newspapers. Still, it wasn't as bad as when George V and his party went tiger-shooting after his Delhi Durbar. They shot thirty-seven tigers in one day. It was the beginning of another of those inexplicable royal paradoxes in that two months after the tiger incident for which he was heavily criticised Philip joined his friend Peter Scott in the formation of the World Wildlife Fund.*

After India, they travelled on to Pakistan, Nepal, Turkey and Iran for more welcomes, and more brickbats. In Nepal, the Queen and Prince Philip's hunting party went on another tiger shoot and this time shot and killed another of the world's

*It was perhaps ironic that ten years later the tiger population of India had dropped to such alarming levels that the World Wildlife Fund had to invest $100,000 to attempt to restore the balance and save it from extinction; the programme was largely successful by the time Prince Philip became international president of the WWF in 1981.

rarest animals, the white rhinoceros. Philip did not claim this one; he had an infected trigger finger. The animal took two bullets, one from the Queen's private secretary Sir Michael Adeane and the other from her Foreign Secretary Lord Home who commented with all due aristocratic insensitivity, 'I am certain it was my shot that killed it . . . but we're sharing it . . . I'm having the horn and front feet and Sir Michael is having the back end. I'm not sure what we shall do with it – probably make waste paper baskets out of it.' Exceedingly loud public and media indignation followed, into which the Queen by association was dragged and perhaps not undeservedly. As one of the leader-writers quite rightly asked, 'When will they ever learn? The British love animals almost as much as they do the monarchy.'

The Queen returned to England exhausted and slightly bruised. Though not as long as some previous tours, the journey had been difficult and occasionally quite tense. The Queen had been back barely two months when they were off again, this time on a state visit to Italy which included an audience with Pope John XXIII at the Vatican, the latter stirring up the usual flurry of religious fervour that always accompanies the British royal family's recognition of the existence of the Roman Church.

For the rest of the year until late autumn when yet another overseas tour was planned, the royal calendar was taken up with another clutch of additions, through marriage and procreativity. Prince Eddie, the Duke of Kent, finally persuaded Miss Katharine Worsley, a northern lass, to risk the daunting prospect of life in the royal goldfish bowl and marry him. The wedding in June was at York Minster and again became a major television production, this time using nine commentators. The Queen was already aware that Eddie's sister Princess Alexandra would be next, and indeed she became formally engaged a year later to Angus Ogilvy and they were married in similarly public fashion early in 1963.

Almost unnoticed that summer was the arrival of a child to Viscount 'Johnny' Althorp and his wife Frances; they were apparently disappointed it was another daughter, their third; she was christened Diana at the local church at Sandringham where the Althorps were the more modest neighbours to the royal estates. Unlike the two previous Althorp daughters – and the son, Charles, their fourth child – Diana was the only one who did not have a royal godparent, the Queen Mother and the Duke of Kent being among the earlier sponsors, and in this royal countryside the new Althorp child took her first breath towards her unknown destiny, as a future queen alongside Charles, who was then twelve and a half.

One other birth before the year was out delighted the British nation as much as it did the family: Princess Margaret was safely delivered of a son, David Albert Charles, the Lord Linley, whose title was assured only one month before his birth when his father finally buckled to pressure from the palace and his wife and accepted an earldom to become Lord Snowdon, otherwise Lord Linley – the Queen's first nephew – would have been plain 'Mister Jones', and twenty years later was wishing he was. Lord Snowdon soon grew into his title, much too much according to many of his friends, and the *Guardian* spoke rather wistfully of the disappointment that he should have had the title thrust upon him. Perhaps it was inevitable that he should become totally involved in the family in terms of titular recognition. With the Queen and Philip away so much of the time, Snowdon and Princess Margaret had assumed an increasing number of engagements, though those present would record that he often looked uncomfortable and politely bored; symptoms of a gastric ulcer soon developed. That wasn't the only pain he suffered. The 'Margaret and Tony' love story had already soured in the press and while the Queen was off doing her good works and being glorified by all and sundry, Princess Margaret and her husband became the patsies, though in many respects this was due to their own insensitivity to public feeling. They became rather obvious sitting targets.

In their cramped surroundings at Kensington Palace, the Snowdons were unable to keep their occasionally emotional marital convulsions private, until the day came when their rather badly paid staff, a butler named Cronin and a maid named Ruby, resigned before Christmas. Reporters with chequebooks in hand came running and the two defecting persons from below stairs spilled the beans about tantrums and other troubles. They never seemed to be out of the spotlight. Ten weeks after Lord Linley was born there was some especially damaging publicity about Margaret and Tony getting an entire first-class cabin in a BOAC jet to themselves as they went off to the Caribbean for a holiday, leaving their newborn with the nanny, thus depriving the airline of some £5,000 in payable fares. Attacks came from every quarter, decrying her cost to the taxpayer and even her clothes. An American magazine put her in the list of the world's worst-dressed women and then Cecil King, chairman of the Mirror Group, personally approved a 'Page One Comment' in the *Daily Mirror* – which in 1961 signalled the onset of high drama in the newspaper world – suggesting that it was perhaps time that Princess Margaret considered retiring from public life completely; this was no idle suggestion nor was it one to be taken lightly. . .

Another tour was coming up, and the Queen's courage would temporarily rescue the family from the less desirable headlines. She was down to visit Ghana starting on 9 November to make the visit that had been postponed two years earlier when she discovered she was pregnant. In the meantime, Nkrumah's Ghana had been granted republican independence within the Commonwealth and the country had become a one-party dictatorship with murders, strikes and urban unrest. On 3 October fifty of Nkrumah's political opponents were arrested and imprisoned. Macmillan sought an audience with the Queen and suggested that though she should continue with her tour of the rest of West Africa, perhaps Ghana should be deleted from the itinerary. The Queen replied that she wished to go ahead with Ghana, regardless, unless she was specifically instructed by the government that she should not do so. Macmillan admired her 'outstanding courage'.[13] On 18 October Macmillan secretly contacted President Kennedy.*

* Kennedy had visited Britain earlier in the year with his wife Jackie and they dined at Buckingham Palace. The Queen had a special connection with the Kennedy family; during the war years as a young princess at Windsor she introduced one of her Guards officers, the Marquis of Hartington, to John Kennedy's sister Kathleen. The two had married but were ill-fated; the marquis was killed in Normandy: Kathleen later died in a plane cash.

In a note marked private and confidential, Macmillan sought Kennedy's help in trying to calm the situation in Ghana ahead of the Queen's visit, pointing out that time was short.[14] The Americans were on the verge of giving Nkrumah financial aid towards the Volta Dam project. 'If you were to decide to go ahead,' Macmillan wrote to Kennedy, 'it would be a great help if this could be announced before the Queen's visit . . . it would have a calming effect throughout Ghana and would go a long way to reducing the general temperature.' The Prime Minister added an alternative. If, on the other hand, the American mission recommended that no contribution should be made, 'then I earnestly ask you not to let this be known until after the Queen has left Ghana'. If such an announcement was made during the Queen's tour, it would 'seriously increase the risk to her safety and well-being'.[15] In reply, Kennedy could only promise that no negative response would be made during the time the Queen was in Ghana.

As each day passed, the situation became more dangerous. During a Commons debate on 19 October, a number of MPs demanded that the Queen's visit should be called off, not merely for the Queen's safety but as a display of Britain's displeasure at recent events in the country. Macmillan told his Cabinet that the Queen still wanted to proceed, and he warned of the alternatives if she did not: that Ghana might proceed with its rumoured intention of leaving the Commonwealth and that the Russians, who were on the verge of sending a military mission to Ghana, would move in permanently. Having said that, he was also sure that the decision rested not on political considerations but solely on the question of the Queen's safety. Churchill weighed in with a long letter, imploring Macmillan to dissuade the Queen from going. 'I have no doubt Nkrumah would use the visit to bolster up his own position . . . no doubt Nkrumah would be much affronted if the visit were now cancelled and Ghana might leave the Commonwealth. I am not sure that this would be a great loss. Is it too late for the Queen's plans to be changed?'[16] Sir Anthony Eden, recently created Lord Avon, agreed.

Macmillan sent the Queen a long memo on 3 November, stating that the Colonial Secretary Duncan Sandys had visited

Ghana and was of the opinion, supported by local officials, that it was unlikely that there would be any attempt on Her Majesty's life, nor demonstrations of hostility against her. However, there was very strong risk of an attempt on the life of President Nkrumah while in her company.[17] That prospect became only more apparent the following day when bombs exploded in the centre of Accra. Hasty telephone calls between No. 10 Downing Street and Buckingham Palace continued for the next twenty-four hours, until Macmillan decided to ask Duncan Sandys to return immediately to Ghana and get a first-hand account of the situation. Macmillan also suggested he should warn Nkrumah that if he was considering pulling out of the Commonwealth, he should say so frankly. If it were to happen soon after the Queen's visit, assuming that went ahead, there would be serious repercussions and the United States might wish to reconsider its attitude to Ghana and 'in particular the Volta Dam project'.

Sandys worked out his own plan for testing the water or, as he put it, 'trying it on the dog'. On arrival in Accra, he persuaded Nkrumah to drive with him in a stately procession along the royal route proposed for the Queen's tour. Nkrumah agreed, with Sandys sitting beside him in the same car that would be used for the royal visit. He was able to report to Macmillan that he had 'emerged to tell the tale'.[18]

The drama heightened; Tory MPs were joined by Labour members in calling for the tour to be halted. Macmillan summoned his security advisers who reported that the risks were no greater than they had been in India, Pakistan, or even a visit to Belfast. The Queen told her Prime Minister that she still remained firm, that she was determined to go. 'If I do not,' she reportedly told Macmillan, 'we will look foolish if Nikita Krushchev goes instead. And you wouldn't like that, would you?' The Cabinet also supported her wishes. But now Macmillan faced a critical constitutional situation which he could not, and did not, relay to the Queen because of its delicate political nature. If he made a statement to the House on the night before the Queen was due to leave, there might well be a call for an adjournment debate. Labour could grasp the opportunity and vote against, not on the grounds of opposing the visit but for reasons of the Queen's security, along with a possible eighty to one hundred Conservatives who the Whips estimated were strongly opposed; the government would be defeated. Macmillan would have refused to alter his advice, and admitted he would have been forced to resign that evening, probably at about 11.00 p.m. after the vote. He also considered the position if the Queen, as she might, refused to accept his resignation. She would fly off on her visit, he would probably be impeached and the Queen would face an unprecedented constitutional crisis for apparently disobeying the wishes of her Parliament. 'All of this,' wrote Macmillan later,'we discussed during these anxious days . . . it all seemed too absurd to be true.'

In a swift tactical move, he contacted the Labour leader Hugh Gaitskell and informed him it was the Queen's personal wish that the trip should go ahead; perhaps to Macmillan's surprise, he found Gaitskell cooperative and unwilling to go against the Queen. Macmillan, in his eventual speech to the House gave this assurance:

> on the information and advice available to them, the Government have formed the view that the explosions (in Accra) do not indicate any intention . . . to perpetrate acts of violence during the Queen's visit. We have therefore no reason to fear that this journey will involve any special and additional risk to Her Majesty's safety. On the other hand, there can be no doubt that the cancellation of this visit, so long promised and so eagerly awaited by the people of Ghana would seriously impair the invaluable contribution made by Her Majesty's journeys towards the strengthening of the ties that bind the peoples of the Commonwealth.[19]

Gaitskell did not deter. He spoke of the House's loyalty and affection for Her Majesty and added 'All the life of royalty and the tours of Her Majesty involve considerable risks. She accepts them proudly . . .'

Was it worth it? Was the risk of the Queen's life and what Macmillan described as the 'most trying week of my life' (he wrote that before he'd heard of Christine Keeler) all made in the cause of her personal dedication to duty and the Commonwealth concept? Or was it more deeply and politically rooted in those old colonialist dreams, coupled with keeping the Russians out of Africa? Whatever it was, the Queen's tour was described as another great triumph, though some of the more realistic commentators were nearer the truth when they assessed that the loud public reaction to the Queen in Accra had no deep or lasting significance. Perhaps it did not but it was not for the want of trying on her part. A week after the Queen's return home Nkrumah got his money from President Kennedy to build the Volta Dam and a couple of months later, the Russians awarded him the Lenin Peace Prize.

The Queen's knowledge on such topics as Ghana became legendary. Typical was the description given to the author by Sir Geoffrey de Freitas who was made High Commissioner to Ghana in 1961 (later to become Labour MP for Kettering). He recalled that when he went to Buckingham Palace for his audience with the Queen – as is the practice for all her newly appointed or returning diplomats – he had been told beforehand that it was unlikely she would keep him more than five or ten minutes. 'It was quite extraordinary. She gave me an impromptu talk which lasted about forty minutes in which she told me all I would need to know about the place, its customs and its politics. She warned me about certain aspects and people. It was knowledge I could not possibly have acquired in the six or seven weeks previously, when I'd been searching through the archives in Whitehall trying to find out about the place.'

Chapter Eight

Goodbye, Harold – Hello, Mr Wilson (1963–4)

There was a joke below stairs at Buckingham Palace. Someone asks, 'What does the Queen do with her old clothes?' Chorused reply: 'She wears them.' It was true that she certainly kept them and now that Princess Anne was growing up she could have some of her clothes cut down for her. It was noticed. Poor Anne. The fashion pundits spotted it and made a point of mentioning in 1963 that not only was Anne, the attractive young princess, having to wear her mother's cutdown cast-offs, her own clothes were obviously being lengthened by letting down the hem. Other beneficiaries of the Queen's vast selection of hand-me-downs were some of Prince Philip's many continental relatives who found a never-ending supply of Norman Hartnell's finest creations to suit an endless supply of young princesses to whom the Queen was Aunt Lilibet. That was an obvious good avenue to channel the Queen's old clothes, rather like the Oxfam concept; she was determined to get the fullest use out of them. It was one of many penny-saving ideas that came into the Queen's mind. The children's clothes had new pockets and cuffs sewn on so that they would last longer. The children were all taught to care for their possessions; once Charles lost a dog lead and the Queen asked if he had searched for it. He had looked everywhere, one of the staff explained. 'Well, he must go back tomorrow and look again,' said the Queen, 'and this time he must find it.' She was frugal and abstemious in all she did, and moaned at belowstairs for the palace's ungenerous pay scales which kept the servants barely above the poverty level, although the live-in people did have a fairly good standard of upkeep in terms of food. The poor pay was probably one of the reasons why so many of them sold the stories of life in palace employ: John Dean, Philip's first valet, Marion Crawford, the Queen's former governess, and Michael Parker's wife Eileen all wrote books which provided a through-the-keyhole look at life in the royal households and did quite nicely out of them. Though the royal family disliked their secrets getting into the newspapers, there was one advantage from the readers' point of view. From these articles and personal anecdotes from members of staff, who were generally truthful people, it was possible, for those interested in royal trivia, to glean otherwise carefully hidden moments in royal life that prove they are all actually human, and find it necessary to use the bathroom, like the rest of us. Footman Ralphe White's recollections illustrate the point perfectly. Just before she was to due to speak at a magnificent banquet in Australia, the Queen was overcome by hiccups and her speech had to be delayed until she was able to get rid of them by holding her breath and drinking gulps of water. Family life, and the ability to prove that at home they are 'just like normal people', can often only be confirmed by these moments, witnessed by servants or close members of the family. There was the day, for example, when the Queen Mother came into the house at Sandringham and found the door open. 'Whoever left the door open? This place is like an icebox,' she shouted. 'That was me, Mother,' came the reply from the Queen. 'I thought the house was bit stuffy.'[1] There were other moments to treasure; the Queen sitting on the floor at Balmoral searching one of the corgis for fleas, or playing football with the children among the antiques of Windsor Castle, or when she lapsed into one of her mimicking accents when it started to rain and she remarked in Eliza Dolittle language, 'Coo-er, it's raining and I ain't got me brolly.'

Several ex-servants did rather well selling tales of life at the palaces to the newspapers or secretly supplying gossip columnists with regular tit-bits, which was why so many stories of a personal and intimate nature surfaced in the press. It all turned sour when the continental journals, in particular, used the servants' stories as a basis for invention and the most outrageous fiction began appearing, especially in German magazines. That is when the Queen and Philip moved to put a stop to story-telling by getting royal servants to sign a legal agreement, which the royal family has been willing to enforce at the slightest hint of infringement, to safeguard the privacy of palace life. However, this bar on book-writing did not extend to certain friends and relatives. Ex-Queen Alexandra of Yugoslavia supplemented her declining fortunes with a *Family Portrait of Prince Philip*. 'She meant well,' wrote Helen Cathcart, one also close to the family and who has written biographical portraits of most of them.

Helene Cordet, otherwise known as the Night Club Queen of London, also had her autobiography published which became of particular interest to those seeking a link between her and her childhood friend from Paris, Prince Philip. She seemed to admit to being the 'mystery blonde' – or one of them – with whom he was said to have been seen and it did nothing to quell the rumours that they had had an affair. 'There had been a lot of talk about it,' said Larry Adler, one of Philip's former friends and co-founder of the stag luncheons known as the Thursday Club, that used to be held at Wheeler's Restaurant in Soho. 'There was supposed to have been a child by her. It was before he got married though.'[2] Helene, in fact, had two children around the time of her renewed friendship with Philip during the war years in London, but has denied that either was his. These rumours were to flare up again later in the year, and regularly thereafter, though as successive reporters have discovered, evidence of any infidelity was hard to come by; everyone had a tale to tell about Prince Philip's exploits and in the upper echelons of British society, where he was not liked because he was not one of them, there was considerable sympathy shown for the 'poor Queen' whenever the matter was discussed. Almost thirty years later, the same situation existed: lots of stories, lots of rumours and a plentiful supply of alleged names – but no evidence.

The Queen very seldom went out, in the social sense, except to the homes of a very small and select group of people, less than half a dozen couples, with whom she could relax in comfortable clothes, no jewellery and no make-up. She seldom indulged herself in anything other than racing, and clothes actually became something of a chore to the Queen because they were invariably associated with her working life. As Lord Mountbatten said, 'Why should she go around looking like Marlene Dietrich? She shares her mother's cautious rejection of needless extravagance. The royal style is usually one of largesse. But the Queen inherited from the Queen Mother a respect for thrift. She likes dressing very, very simply. Boots and breeches or tweeds and light cotton dresses. When people say that she is dressed in dowdy clothes and old style, that is good.'[3] She preferred to slip on a headscarf and thick, comfortable clothes and flat brogue shoes, but she did indulge herself by buying Philip things. He had nothing, of course, when they became engaged, nothing except the suit he stood up in and just a few pounds in the bank. The young husband of the world's richest woman needs to look the part and gradually his list of acquisitions began to mount up in the early sixties, to a degree that they were noticeable by their very existence and the high profile of the user. The Queen bought him a new racing yacht, *Bloodhound*, in 1962 for £10,000; he also had three smaller sailing boats, one of which was given to them as a wedding present, and which went out on loan to Dartmouth College when he wasn't using them. The royal yacht *Britannia*, moored for the duration of Cowes Week, was always a good target for the critics of the royal good life. The Lagonda bought in 1956 was replaced by an Alvis Convertible costing £3,110 in 1961 and in 1963 he added to his car collections with the new Reliant Triplex which he ordered at the motor show. His selection of guns and firepower for a variety of game-shooting was also of the highest quality and included a pair of James Purdy hammerless ejector double-triggered game guns.

His greatest pride and joy was his string of polo ponies which also provided him with his form of escapism from the frustrations of his royal life, usually on Sunday afternoon – much to the consternation of the Lord's Day Observance Society who never let up in their expressions of aggravation at seeing the Queen following her husband's fortunes on the polo field. Philip had not done at all badly for a man who had nothing, not even a name. Leonard Mosley, the writer, once compared him to the husband of a mythical tycoon's daughter, richer and more influential than the man she married. And he would probably spend the rest of his life (a) trying to persuade her that he really did take her for love and not money, (b) trying not to resent the power of her bank balance, (c) quelling the suspicions of his enemies that he would never have got anywhere in life if it had not been for her influence.[4] This, of course, was an especially vitriolic expression of Prince Philip's predicament, written for the arch-enemy of the Mountbattens, Lord Beaverbrook. Unfortunately, it was also quite true except that Philip was too thick-skinned even to bother about it.

The Queen indulged herself in 1963 in her only area of considerable personal expense for sheer pleasure; she decided to update her horse-racing activities which had declined in terms of success over the previous three or four years. It was and is her one great obsession. She inherited the royal racing stable from her father who was nowhere near as interested in the sport as the Queen Mother and her daughter. Queen Elizabeth II became the first monarch since Queen Anne to register her royal colours, purple body with gold braid and scarlet sleeves, and quickly became one of the principal money-winners on the British turf. More than that, she had a personal connection with several courses and especially Ascot, founded by Queen Anne, which remains her personal race-course and which she also administers through permanent staff. The success of the fifties, however, had faded. Her racing manager, the once sharp and dandy Irishman Captain Charles Moore, was eighty-one in 1963. A former racing manager for her father, the Queen owed him a lot and he had chosen classic-winning horses for her stable. His advice had also taught her how to make a good deal in buying racehorses when she was still in her teens and now he boasted that she was as good a judge of horseflesh as himself. Sir Gordon Richards, whom she knighted in Coronation year, would recall that he could remember her in her teens when she was brought down to look over the Beckhampton stables of the great trainer Fred Darling. The horses would be led around and Darling would name them as they went past. Within a few minutes, the young princess would 'have them off pat'. Later, when he was riding for her, the Queen's eye for the conformation of a horse was brought home to him when she said of one of his mounts, 'Gordon, that one looks like a camel'. Richards replied, 'Yes, ma'am and it gallops like one, too'. Another royal jockey, Harry Carr who rode in the royal colours for seventeen years before he retired, said, 'She's a real authority on breeding and the whole business of racing. You can tell it as soon as you talk to her.'[5]

Her interest just grew and Moore had steered her racing team to the peak of success in the late fifties when she had thirty-eight horses at stables, including seventeen new yearlings, nine of them home-bred, several brood mares and twenty horses in training. She was able to present to Captain Cecil Boyd-Rochfort a silver cigarette box engraved 'To Cecil Boyd-Rochfort, leading trainer, from Elizabeth R., leading winning owner'. She was the leading winning owner in 1954 when Aureole won her almost £25,000 in one season, and again in 1957. Boyd-Rochfort was still her trainer and Lord Porchester, her lifelong friend and racing expert, was advising her as she began building her new team to replace Captain Moore, whom she persuaded to retire, much against his will, to a grace-and-favour apartment at Hampton Court early in 1963.

While at Sandringham that winter for Christmas, she would often drive herself over to Newmarket at the crack of a cold and crispy dawn to watch the first string of horses going out on the heath for the early morning work-out, then stay on for much of the day, before driving herself home in the evening. As with everything in the Queen's personal life, however, she had to rely on delegation and the supervisory powers of others, whether it was her horses, her estates, her homes, or her children. The continuity of her own active participation was constantly broken by the demands of the job.*

*It is interesting here just to tot up a few more figures as she reached the tenth anniversary of her reign: she had travelled 250,000 miles, visiting 21 countries, made state visits to 13 others, had spent in total 402 days overseas, and countless other full days in travel at home. She received 13 return state visits, had held 95 investitures,

* * *

She was going to have to delegate for another of the children's birthdays – Prince Andrew's third. Her government had arranged another extensive overseas journey and at the beginning of February 1963 the Queen and Prince Philip flew off on a 6 week tour that would take them via Canada to Fiji, New Zealand and Australia. It was being openly speculated, though denied in official circles, that the tour had been hurriedly arranged to placate the most ardent of her Commonwealth members, upset by Britain's overtures to join the Common Market and talk of cutting some of its trading ties with Commonwealth nations. At the time the tour was being planned, it was expected that by the time the Queen arrived in Australia, Britain would have been accepted as a member of the EEC to which it formally applied for membership in August 1961. However, two weeks before the Queen set off for her tour, General de Gaulle, who had been so pleasant when he stayed with her some months earlier, turned nasty and called a press conference on 14 January to declare that Britain must sever its links with the Commonwealth as a price for EEC membership. The *Non* was firm but Macmillan's chief negotiator, Edward Heath, maintained that, though the French terms were unacceptable, he would fight on.

The governments of Australia and New Zealand were still rather worried that the mother country might yet desert them, and that could have a drastic effect on their exports of butter

---

75 inspections and reviews of the armed services, 8 sessions of Parliament, 142 meetings of the Privy Council, attended 56 social church services, met 165 ambassadors to receive their credentials, given 177 luncheons or dinners at Buckingham Palace, 18 garden parties, attended 68 galas, operas, charity film premières and theatre performances, 21 exhibitions, 136 special engagements; she had visited 210 separate towns or cities in the United Kingdom, most for a day; she had received in audience Churchill 27 times, Eden 41 times and Macmillan 142 times, Commonwealth prime ministers 91 times, Cabinet ministers 271 times and 'other individuals' 1,864 times. Average number of persons presented to the Queen officially or present at her garden parties amounted to around 28,000 in a single year and on an average working day she might sign her name 50 times.

and lamb. The Queen took with her a calming speech approved by her Prime Minister, which she delivered to the opening of the New Zealand Parliament. 'The movement among countries of Western Europe towards closer economic and political association has important implications for New Zealand and other Commonwealth countries. The broader developments of today require a close and searching appraisal of additional measures to provide New Zealand and other developing countries with the wider opportunities they need for international trade.'[6] In other words, Britain wanted to join the Common Market as soon as possible and really the Commonwealth nations who were until now very good trading partners would do well to look for other markets. There was a definite edge to it all and this was apparent in two instances, when there was a telephone threat of an acid attack on the Queen and, more light-heartedly, when a group of students in New South Wales shouted 'Taxi!' as her car passed by. There was talk of this 'being the beginning of the end' for the Commonwealth ties and republican thoughts were certainly being stirred in Australia, though it was the last thing the Queen personally wished.

If these thoughts troubled the Queen, as they surely did, she showed no outward sign of it. When occasionally she let the smile drop and allowed the familiar pursing of her lips and set jaw take hold, giving the impression that she was depressed and slightly gloomy, it was for personal reasons. The Mayoress of Blenheim, New Zealand, asked outright, 'Is there anything wrong, Your Majesty?' The Queen replied that she was missing her family, and particularly her youngest, Andrew. She explained that she had bought him a tractor from a toy shop in Regent Street before they left, and it was to be presented to him on his birthday with a note from her, which his nanny was to read out. The Queen telephoned her children regularly from the royal yacht *Britannia*, which had gone ahead to New Zealand to be there when she arrived. 'It is always a worry,' she told the mayoress, 'that the children will forget us whilst we are away on these long trips.'

The row with de Gaulle which temporarily eased the strain there might have been in Australia for the Queen, had other repercussions of which the Queen was kept informed.

Princess Margaret had been due to make a state visit to France that month; Macmillan cancelled the visit as a deliberate act of revenge against the French leader's intransigence over the Common Market. The French people were not unduly worried, though it might have occurred to the Queen more than once in those few weeks that she and her family were increasingly being used as pawns in Macmillan's international political dealings. It was a rather inept act on his part, and he was widely criticised for it. But his 'usage' of the royals had become so obvious: attaching them to the launching of politically controversial matters like nuclear submarines, visits to America to patch up Anglo-American relations, several Canadian jaunts to bolster trade and quell republican feelings, Africa, India, Pakistan and Ceylon to shore up the Commonwealth and to keep the Russian influence at bay, now Australia and New Zealand to smooth over strained feelings over the Common Market.

They returned home to a political scene bubbling with gossip and rumour. Before the year was out, it would involve her in more high political drama.

An article in *Queen* magazine, ironically by William Douglas-Home, included what became the quote of the year: '. . . called in MI5 because every time a chauffeur driven Zis drew up at the front door out of the back door into a chauffeur driven Humber slipped . . .' It was one of the first reports that had ever appeared in print on what became known as the Profumo Affair. The Queen was back in England when, on the afternoon of 22 March, while Mr John Profumo, her Secretary of State for War, and Mrs Profumo had joined the Queen Mother at the races, MPs in the House of Commons were demanding to know if there was any truth in the allegations connecting a government minister, unnamed, with Miss Christine Keeler who was in turn linked to a Soviet diplomat. They implied that people in high places were concealing vital information. Mr Profumo was contacted at the races and was told of what was being said. He returned to London and informed MPs, in a personal statement, that there was 'no impropriety whatsoever'[7] in his acquaintanceship with the 21 year-old Miss Keeler. He lied, of course, and there began the summer-long scandal which lurched from one set of revelations to another and daily provided Fleet Street with more sex and scandal than it would normally have been able to print in a month of Sundays, Sunday being *News of the World* day; the world waited expectantly for another insight into the lives of Christine Keeler and Mandy Rice Davies whom Noël Coward described as 'those miserable little tarts'.[8]

It was unfortunate that as the scandal gathered steam, Miss Rice Davies was arrested by Scotland Yard on 24 April 1963 as she was about to leave the country on the very afternoon of Princess Alexandra's wedding to the Honourable Angus Ogilvy, second son of the Earl of Airlie; and this major event in the royal calendar had to share the following day's news with the 'sensational' arrest of a girl no one had ever heard of until three weeks earlier.

However, the royal wedding did not suffer and was made into a great European occasion, because of the connections of the bride. Her father was the late Prince George, Duke of Kent – the Queen's uncle who was killed in an air crash in 1942. Her mother was Princess Marina, Duchess of Kent who was Prince Philip's cousin, sister of Princess Olga of Yugoslavia, cousin of ex-Queen Helen of Romania. There were more guests than for Princess Margaret's wedding, including the King of Norway, the Queens of Denmark, Sweden and Greece, ex-Queen Victoria Eugenie of Spain and ex-Queen Helen of Romania. The Queen gave a dinner party for 100 of her favoured guests at Windsor before the wedding, and it was followed by the largest ball to be held at Windsor for more than a century, with 1,600 guests, some of whom were doubtless craning their necks to see who was there and who wasn't, and if two half-expected, yet unlikely, guests had turned up. The bride's late father was the Duke of Windsor's favourite brother and, like him, was known for his kicking over of the traces. The groom was also the nephew of the duke's former equerry Bruce Ogilvy and with this knowledge, it might have been possible that Uncle David and Aunt Wallis would at last receive an invitation to join their relatives for such a massive gathering of the clan. He would have liked to have been invited; but he was not. Apart from the continuing ice-coolness between Windsor and his sister-in-law, the Queen Mother, the bride's mother Princess

Marina had her own unpleasant memories which she could never forget. When her husband was killed in his air crash, she did not receive one word of condolence from either the Duke or Duchess of Windsor from their wartime exile in the Bahamas. The Windsors were not only ignored for the wedding, the Duchess was ignored completely in a special souvenir programme produced for the royal day. In the bride's family tree, all her relatives were listed with their spouses – all except one; the Duke of Windsor was merely credited with being a former king and no mention was made that there existed a Duchess of Windsor or even that he was married. Amongst such a gathering of royalty, they were not especially missed.

An interesting little poser arose as to how to keep such a galaxy of kings, queens, princes and princesses amused on the day that remained before the ceremony. The Queen solved it by hiring two buses for a sightseeing tour of Windsor and its surrounds, with Philip as their guide. They all ended up having a 'pub lunch' at Maidenhead – if the pre-warned landlord's serving of lobster and champagne could be described as such.

The wedding provided a mere breather in the gathering storm. As Macmillan gloomily recorded in his diary, the newspapers had produced 'one mass of life of spies and prostitutes; day by day the attacks developed'. On 5 June Profumo resigned from the government, admitting with 'deep remorse' that he had lied to the Commons over his association with Christine Keeler.[9] An appointment was made for him to be received by the Queen, whom he knew well, so that he could hand in his seals of office, as is usual when a minister resigns or retires. However, Conservative MP for Bournemouth John Cordle, outraged at Profumo's behaviour, protested that for this man to set foot inside Buckingham Palace would be an affront to the Queen. It was therefore arranged that Profumo should return his seals quietly by courier to save any further trouble. Later, the Queen sent him a personal message expressing her regret that his career had ended in the way that it had.

On it went: Macmillan looked a broken man but hoped he had been saved by Profumo's belated honesty; he said as much – 'The matter is now closed'. Harold Wilson had other ideas and continued the attack, viciously and correctly accusing Macmillan of indolently gambling with the nation's security for political reasons.[10] On 10 June, Dr Stephen Ward, the society osteopath, appeared in court, charged with living off immoral earnings; he was seen as the central figure, the link between high society and low life and the man who procured girls for famous names. It was at Ward's rented cottage on Lord Astor's estate that Keeler had frolicked naked around the swimming pool.

The Queen's family provided a brief and welcome interlude to these revelations with one of those royal stories that is guaranteed to make every front page. It was the most famous one of Prince Charles's early years; on 17 June, he and three friends from Gordonstoun, where he was in his second year, had been given permission to go out to the cinema while on a canoeing expedition at Stornoway, accompanied as ever by the royal detective Donald Green who was on permanent assignment to Charles and had quarters in Gordonstoun. A small crowd gathered, recognising Charles and so Green took the group into the Crown Hotel, while he went off to book the cinema seats. The crowd continued to peer in and Charles, who hated it, took refuge in the next room, which turned out to be the hotel bar. According to the official version of events,[11] he was acutely embarrassed by this discovery and rather than leave, he ordered himself a cherry brandy – at the very moment a woman journalist walked in. The rest is history: 'Underage Heir to Throne Orders Drink at the Bar' was too good to miss and though initially denied by the palace, it was eventually admitted. There followed what the popular newspapers gleefully term as 'uproar' and the story went right around the world, with the temperance movement joining in to berate the royal family. The local police issued a summons against the hotel for serving a minor, though it was later withdrawn on the assurance by Gordonstoun's headmaster, quoted in *The Times*, no less, that they had their own system of awarding punishment, if necessary; a cane was kept for that purpose. On 24 June, the school reported that the 'incident is now closed' but refused to state if Charles had been caned. The Queen was angry on that day, though not especially over Charles's escapade; Prince Philip had become the latest target.

Some photographs had turned up in the Profumo case; they were allegedly from Ward's private collection and some of them had got into the safe at Odhams Press, part of the Mirror group. Labour's mischievous Richard Crossman was in a London restaurant when he saw Hugh Cudlipp, editorial director of the Mirror Group. 'How are the pictures the Secret Service took?' he asked Cudlipp.*

Cudlipp said nothing, but smiled in his enigmatic way. Crossman observed later, 'He knew I was on to something'. And so did a number of Cudlipp's executives who were present in the room. The photographs, it was being alleged, included one showing Prince Philip and his photographer friend Baron taken some years earlier. Ward was an acquaintance of them both and later a good friend of Baron's who had taken him several times to the luncheon club at Wheeler's Restaurant which Philip attended on occasions in the late forties and fifties. On 23 June, Cecil King, chairman of IPC which owned the *Mirror*, personally approved the devotion of the entire front page of the following day's *Daily Mirror* which ran: 'The foulest rumour being circulated about the Profumo Scandal has involved a member of the royal family. The name mentioned is Prince Philip.' It was a very flimsy piece of journalism that might have been read for what it did not say, rather than what it did; no explanation was given as to the rumour but the report added that it was 'utterly untrue', an old newspaper technique for bringing a matter to public attention. The *Mirror* was reported to the Press Council which agreed that the story was in bad taste but took no further action. So now the Queen's own family had been dragged into it.

Another mystery developed; at the time Ward was due to appear in court, a sale of his art was being held by exhibition at a gallery in Holborn to raise money for his defence. He was an accomplished artist and his sketches included those of several members of the royal family who sat for him between March and July 1961. They included portraits of Prince Philip, Princess Marina, Lord Snowdon and the Duke and Duchess of Gloucester which were commissioned for the

*Ward somewhat misguidedly believed he was working for MI5, who later disclaimed all knowledge of this possibility.

London Illustrated News whose editor Sir Bruce Ingram was a friend of the Queen's late grandfather. Ward had also drawn Macmillan, Churchill and Selwyn Lloyd. Ward found the royal sitters most cooperative, especially Philip. 'Good lord,' said Philip when he met him at Buckingham Palace, 'I did not connect you with this appointment.' Ward recalled that Philip had been to one of his parties at his flat in Cavendish Square before he married Princess Elizabeth and he remembered him. During the sitting they 'talked about the old days, polo and the fact that he had a rare condition called rider's bone in the thigh. He was a wonderful sitter.'[12] The royal portraits were embarrassingly on display at the very time Ward came to trial, until one morning a tall bowler-hatted man from the *Illustrated News* walked in. He produced a bank draft from his case and bought up every one of the royal likenesses and left. The trial opened at the Old Bailey and the touts were selling tickets; there were numerous well-known faces in the public gallery on the first day, including Lady Plunket, the wife of the Queen's friend and equerry David Plunket, and the television personality Katie Boyle.

On 31 July, on the eighth and final day of his trial for living off immoral earnings, Stephen Ward was found unconscious from a drugs overdose at a friend's flat in Chelsea and remained in a coma while the jury returned a verdict of guilty on two charges. He died three days later and thus took with him to his grave several unanswered questions that might have eventually come out in what was the greatest scandal to hit any government this century.

For Macmillan it was just one hammer blow after another or, as Lord Hailsham described it, a government in 'a slow decline from its peak of the 1959 election' and 'punctuated by a series of what have since become known as banana skins'.[13] The case of the Admiralty spy, William Vassall, jailed a year earlier for his six years of damaging spying for the Russians was still fresh in media minds, as was Kim Philby who vanished while in the Middle East in January, 1963. On 1 July, the government – and Harold Macmillan personally – was finally forced to admit that Philby had defected to Moscow and that he was the 'third man' who tipped off his Foreign Office colleagues, the traitors Guy Burgess and Donald Maclean, so that they could defect in

June 1951. This admission was doubly hurtful as far as Macmillan was concerned because it was he, as Foreign Secretary, who had given Philby official clearance from suspicion after he had been named in the House of Commons by Mr Marcus Lipton in 1955. As yet, in that summer of 1963, the 'fourth man' in the affair was still to be revealed; he was not far away – working for the Queen at Buckingham Palace.

The Queen and her family repaired to Balmoral, as usual, for the summer and they must have felt glad to get away from the hub of activity but soon she was to be at the centre of it again, for two reasons. No one paid much attention to the arrival at Balmoral Castle of a local Scottish doctor, George Middleton, but on 15 September, final confirmation was obtained and Commander Colville broke the news to the press: 'The Queen is cancelling all future engagements for the time being.' She was expecting her fourth child. This news was quickly followed by the discovery that Princess Margaret was expecting her second, and this meant that there were now four expectant mothers in the royal family; Princess Alexandra and the Duchess of Kent were also both pregnant.

Ten days later, on 26 September, the countdown to political crisis started and the Queen began to prepare to return from Balmoral to London as it became clear that her royal prerogative might be called upon once again. The first development was the publication of the Denning Report into the Profumo Affair which, though considered by many to be a fairly comprehensive whitewash of the whole business, was none the less critical of Macmillan and his government. The baying hounds of the Labour Party who had been demanding Macmillan's resignation since June, were now joined by many MPs from within his party who felt he had personally avoided the truth of the Profumo business until it had become such a devastating scandal. Even so, the Prime Minister had, according to his own recollections of the events, decided to 'stay and fight', having stayed up all night without a wink of sleep anguishing over what he should do. The next morning, 7 October, having decided to inform his Cabinet of his decision to stay, he collapsed with 'excruciating pain . . . I was seized by terrible spasms'.[14] He was admitted to hospital immediately with inflammation of the prostate gland which it was feared could be malignant, though in the event it was not, and he was operated on without delay. There now began ten days of political wrangling which Macmillan, though occasionally fuzzy through drugs and operations, fought to control at every step. The Conservative Party's management had moved *en masse* to Blackpool for its annual conference which became the scene of the most dramatic leadership struggle the party had ever known, with candidates becoming personalised in the style of an American convention. There was, still, no formal election procedure and the frenzy of the conference had not entirely accounted for the fact that it was the Queen who would summon the new man, and the Queen had already stated to Macmillan that she would be guided by his advice.

What transpired in the ultimately very bitter contest was a *coup de main* carefully plotted by Macmillan; the Queen was, perhaps unwittingly, to play an integral part in the final step. He drew each of the candidates to his bedside. Lord Hailsham thought he was the 'chosen one' because, on the eve of the operation, Macmillan had sent his son Maurice and son-in-law Julian Amery to warn him to be ready. Afterwards, Hailsham had the 'distinct impression that he had done another of his famous somersaults. So he had . . . it was another retreat . . . another Suez.'[15]

As in 1957, 'soundings' were being taken within the party and as before, when Butler lost out to Macmillan, the whole process was to become tainted by bitterness as the struggle developed. Especially vociferous were those who simply could not accept that the decision should rest, as it did, with an 'emergence' worked out between Macmillan and the Queen. Home's majority, if it ever truly existed, was clear only in the Cabinet and in the House of Lords. A poll in the *Daily Express* was more decisive: Butler was ahead with 40 points, Hailsham second with 22, Maudling was on 11 and Macmillan's candidate, Home, was last, polling only 9. It was, by any token, a highly unsatisfactory state of affairs, yet on the strength of his 'soundings', Macmillan prepared a long memorandum for the Queen which he placed in a gigantic envelope. Thursday 17 October was the night of the famous midnight meetings, at which ministers and supporters

Then, as now, royal couples willingly posed to show off the latest addition to the Royal Family. This photograph of the then Duke and Duchess of York (later King George VI and Queen Elizabeth) was the first, taken two weeks after their daughter Elizabeth was born in April 1926.

A bonny baby snap, one year later.

The first major formal event for the young Princess Elizabeth was in 1934 when she was bridesmaid for her uncle George, Duke of Kent at his marriage to Princess Marina of Greece. It was also one of the last family occasions at which the three brothers would be pictured together: Edward, Prince of Wales abdicated two years later, the Duke of Kent was killed in a plane crash in 1942 and Elizabeth's father died in 1952.

Grandmother, mentor and guide to a future destiny, Queen Mary poses proudly with Princess Elizabeth in the autumn of 1927.

The corgis became an ever-present ingredient of royal photographs, especially so for the Queen who was and is devoted to her dogs. This study is one of the first, taken in 1936.

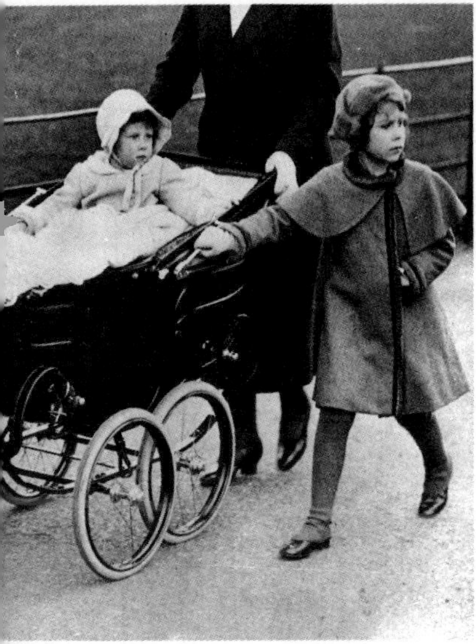

The 'two little princesses' were inseparable during childhood, and seldom was there a photograph of one without the other. Above, a nanny takes them for a stroll in Hyde Park in the spring of 1933 and (right) they are pictured for a fancy dress party given by Lady Astor in 1934.

At the start of the war, the royal family were seen to be 'doing their bit', and the young princesses were no exception. Indeed, their photographs, such as this one in which they are seen knitting socks for the forces, verged on propaganda to inspire the nation's youngsters into similar good deeds.

A significant moment in history for the young Princess Elizabeth when she officially became heir presumptive on the Coronation of her father as King George VI in May 1937, and by the solemn expression upon her face in this study by Dorothy Wilding, she seemed to recognise the importance of the moment.

The war years were especially confined for the two young princesses and Queen Elizabeth did her best to get them involved in normal activities and provide them, and Elizabeth in particular, with confidence-building experiences which would help them in their future lives of public appearances. Regular participation in the Windsor annual pantomimes and entertaining the family with a piano recital were ways of at least providing some training for what lay ahead. All three pictures were taken towards the end of the war, the last (below right) was in February 1945 when they sang a duet of 'Swinging on a Star'.

The war's end also marked the blossoming of the Princess Elizabeth from teenager to young adult and the progression is evident as she was allowed out of the restrictive confines of Windsor Castle. She found enjoyment mixing with other girls her own age, such as those in the ATS where she trained as a Second Subaltern in 1945, or in the Sea Rangers which she and Margaret joined and are pictured (top left) on an exercise aboard the motor torpedo boat the *Duke of York* in July 1946. But perhaps the most striking picture of her emergence was the portrait, right, again by Dorothy Wilding, taken for release at Christmas 1946 when there were abounding rumours of her forthcoming engagement.

The year of 1947 was a momentous one. Mounting speculation of an engagement was brushed aside by Buckingham Palace while Princess Elizabeth herself began in earnest her public duty. She travelled abroad for the first time, on a major tour of South Africa with her parents and broadcast to the Commonwealth dedicating her life to the service of her people. This photograph was issued for the occasion, showing her at work at her desk in Buckingham Palace. On 10 July 1947 Buckingham Palace finally announced her engagement to Lieutenant Philip Mountbatten, a former Greek prince who had renounced his title and just paid £10 to become a naturalised British citizen.

Philip's good friend and occasional court photographer Baron was commissioned to take wedding photographs and this relaxed study of the bride was captured after the ceremony. Outside Buckingham Palace and down the Mall as far as the eye could see thousands glad of the break in the austere gloom of postwar Britain, cheered and chanted until the newlyweds appeared on the balcony of the palace in what was the largest spontaneous display of public affection towards the royals in recent memory.

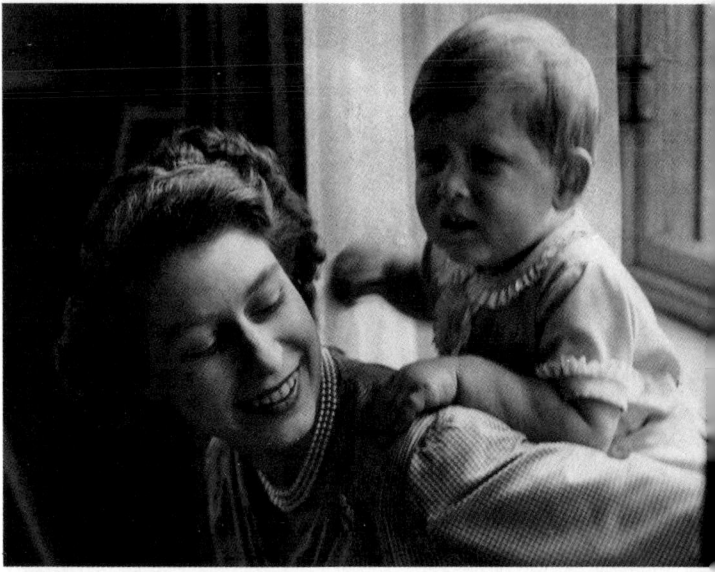

'Our family, us four, the "royal family", must remain together with additions at suitable moments,' King George VI wrote to his daughter Elizabeth the night before she was married. The additions had arrived in the three years since then and 'us four' had become 'us seven' much to public glee, whose perception of them as a warm family group was greatly enhanced by the skills of Cecil Beaton when he introduced a new informality to royal photographs like the one (top) of Elizabeth and Prince Charles, though a shattering development was already looming when they gathered for a group portrait in 1951 (below). The King had by then but a few months to live.

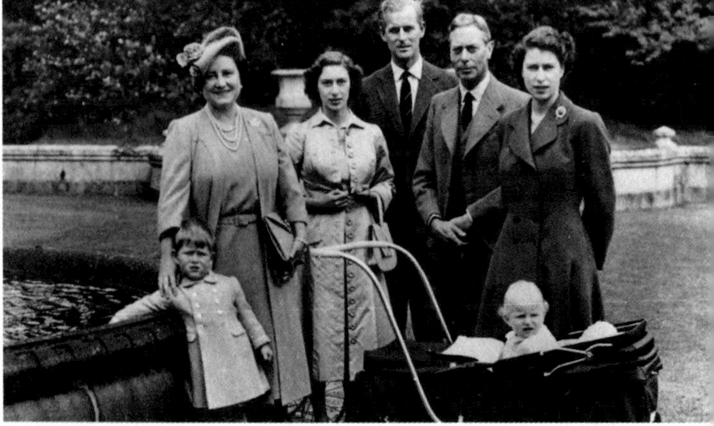

And now she was Queen . . . this remarkable study by Dorothy Wilding was the first official portrait of the Queen after her accession in 1952, taken while still in mourning for the dead King. She wore a black taffeta gown designed by Norman Hartnell, with frilled neckline, nipped waist and billowing skirt, to which she added the simple elegance of her English rose and foliate diamond necklace, an earlier gift from an Indian prince, the Nizam of Hyderabad.

The moment of destiny: months of planning, marred in the final stages by the death of the Queen's beloved grandmother, Queen Mary, finally arrived. The expression upon the young Queen's face told the story as the greatest example of historical pomp and circumstance anywhere on this earth was watched for the first time on television by an audience of 500 million around the world. The Queen's St Edward's Crown tipped the scales at 2.25 kilograms, and she wore it around Buckingham Palace beforehand to get used to the weight.

In the years immediately following her coronation, the Queen embarked upon a series of world tours that could only be compared with the travels of Edward, Prince of Wales in the twenties – except the Queen's would continue for the next four decades and more. There was another difference; the empire was all but done for, although the Queen was treated as if she was still Empress of India when she arrived there in 1961. A million people turned out to hear her at this rally (above) and they were treated to her own radiant enthusiasm (right). It was an important moment in history, if only for being the first and last time such a spectacle would be witnessed.

The Queen's visit to India had the dying ingredients of the last days of the British Raj about it, including the traditional tiger shoot. The last monarch to go on such a jaunt was George V in 1911 and his party shot 37 in one day. This time, Prince Philip shot one between the eyes and all crowded proudly round the corpse, though the Queen looked decidedly indifferent – perhaps contemplating the furore that burst forth the following day when the picture was published on every front page. Philip never shot another one and in fact eventually returned with charitable funds to help save the Indian tiger from extinction.

of Butler anguished over how they could get the Macmillan plan halted.

Macmillan merely dismissed these overnight developments as 'distasteful' but made a hand-written addendum to the memo he had prepared, and proceeded with his plan to resign, sending a letter to the Queen which was handed in at Buckingham Palace at 9.30 on the Friday morning. At 11.10 a.m. the Queen arrived at the Edward VII Hospital to see him. For the occasion, he had taken off his pyjama jacket and put on a white silk shirt; he was also wheeled, complete with all the tubes and attachments, to the hospital boardroom for the meeting with the Queen. Macmillan recalled that she was 'very upset' about his decision to resign and she paid tribute to the almost seven years of his time in office.

The Queen then asked, 'Have you any advice for me?'

'Ma'am, do you wish me to give you any advice?' Macmillan inquired.

'Yes, I do . . .' the Queen replied.

'Since you ask, ma'am . . .' said Macmillan, 'here it is.'[16] He read out the memorandum to the Queen and replaced the manuscript in the envelope. Macmillan's parliamentary private secretary Knox Cunningham handed over the large envelope to Sir Michael Adeane, the Queen's private secretary, a short and portly man who reminded Knox Cunningham of Tenniel's drawing of the Frog Footman in a scene from *Alice in Wonderland*.[17] The envelope, Macmillan suggested, might be placed in the royal archives as evidence of his advice. He also suggested that the Queen 'should move quickly' to appoint his successor. Even as this scenario was taking place, Butler, Hailsham and Maudling were meeting privately with Iain Macleod, in his position as party chairman; Hailsham and Maudling agreed to serve under Butler and that he should make this position known to Macmillan.[18] By then, it was all too late.

The Queen returned to Buckingham Palace and, according to Macmillan in his memoirs, without taking further significant advice, summoned the fourteenth Earl of Home, as he still was, to attend her. She asked him if he would 'see if he could form an administration', though according to Selwyn Lloyd he did not formally kiss her hand in total acceptance of appointment as Prime Minister, because he would need to 'consult with his colleagues',[19] which was a polite way of saying that Home was not at all sure that he could actually form a government.

Even so, Home knew he was a compromise candidate and thought seriously at one stage of pulling out altogether. He was also establishment, culled from the hierarchy of the aristocracy, and from the Queen's point of view he was a man she knew well in a private capacity, and trusted.

It took a long weekend of 'sheer horse-trading' before Home's position was secure and he presented his ministers to the Queen at a Privy Council meeting on 21 October. Selwyn Lloyd, a former Minister of Defence and Chancellor of the Exchequer, was standing in a corridor waiting to go in as the new Leader of the House in Home's government when Prince Philip came along to go into the meeting. 'They haven't brought you back again, have they?' said the Prince[20] on seeing Lloyd, a remark which perhaps summed up the ending of another great leadership crisis in modern British politics. The internal strife caused by successive Conservative Party leaders involving the Queen in the process of choosing a leader, left a deep and lasting gash. Iain Macleod, in an article for the *Spectator*, accused the Tories' 'magic circle' of aristocrats of acting against the party's democratic wishes, and dragging the Queen into controversy. Enoch Powell, meantime, compiled immediately an account of the events of the past ten days which he then deposited at his bank; he, more pointedly, accused Macmillan of giving the Queen inaccurate information, 'thus having deprived the Queen of the exercise of her principal prerogative'.[21] At the end of the day, the Queen would have been excused if she had quoted the words of one of her ancestors, George IV, who commented to the Duke of Wellington during a similar crisis in 1827, 'Might not they organise a vote to elect their own leader?' Wellington replied, 'No, sir. It is the royal prerogative to choose and the only personal act the King of England has to perform.'

In the Queen's defence, the new Prime Minister who had renounced his earldom to become plain Sir Alec Douglas-Home, later maintained that she had not done the choosing. The Labour Party's ridiculing of the system clearly stung, however, and it invoked a national debate among politicians and historians as to the validity of the Queen's prerogative. Typical of those who saw her powers remaining intact was historian Robert Blake, who said, 'It is the one power on which she does not have to accept advice because when a prime minister has resigned there is no one to give her binding constitutional advice so there must always be an element of royal prerogative in the choice.'[22] Yet, witnessing first-hand the divisions it had caused and the damaging criticism of the monarchy's role that followed, Sir Alec himself ensured that never again would the royal prerogative be called upon in this fashion. He personally initiated a new system, published in 1965, which would rely on a properly constituted ballot and which, in the end, saw in the next three leaders of the Conservative Party, Mr Edward Heath, Mrs Margaret Thatcher and Mr John Major. Even so, as was seen with the election of the latter, that system would require some honing. As far as his own dealings with the Queen were concerned during his short tenure at No. 10, Douglas-Home, like his predecessors and his successors, spoke highly of his weekly meetings with the Queen.

> I can only say I found it of great value. The Queen has very wide experience and happily ever-lengthening experience, because she knows every Commonwealth Prime Minister and I should think every Commonwealth statesman personally. At the [Tuesday] meetings the political business of the week plays an important part and there are always international events going on. But there are many other areas of conversation going on – for instance, the Church. You might have an unchurchy Prime Minister and an unworldly archbishop. In that case, the Queen would be a very valuable bridge between church and state. So there are many areas in which the Queen and the Prime Minister talk about many things.[23]

The Queen's 'family' theme for the sixties was renewed again in the new year with the succession of royal babies. The births came fast and furious and royal correspondents were soon describing it as a vintage year: Princess Alexandra had a Leap

Year's Day baby, James Ogilvy born on 29 February; the Queen gave birth to Prince Edward on 10 March; the Duchess of Kent had Lady Helen Windsor on 28 April; and Princess Margaret had a May Day baby, Lady Sarah Armstrong-Jones.

The additions to the family brought an obvious new glow of warmth which for once accurately reflected the Queen's own peace of mind. She had never been happier and looked forward to a relaxing summer, surrounded by her closest relatives, though the relaxation part of the proceedings would be short-lived; more drama lay in store for the remainder of the year.

In the summer of 1964, MI5 learned, with the cooperation of the FBI, the identity of the fourth man in the Burgess, Philby and Maclean spy network. He was Sir Anthony Blunt, the homosexual Surveyor of the Queen's Pictures, a courtier for some thirty years and a third cousin of the Queen Mother. Even before he was confronted by this allegation, it was established in advance that Blunt was to be offered immunity from prosecution if he confessed. Sir Roger Hollis, head of MI5, had taken the step of consulting the Home Secretary and, in turn, the Queen's private secretary Sir Michael Adeane before any approach was made. Adeane insisted that 'the monarch should not be dragged into the affair and this would be best served by a secret deal. Adeane knew, even if Hollis did not, that if Blunt ever came to trial there was the risk of another, even more explosive royal scandal.'[24] Legend had it that immediately after the war, King George VI sent Blunt – then an MI5 officer – to Germany to retrieve from the attic rooms of the Hesse family's Wolfsgarten Castle certain documents which compromised the pro-Hitler activities of the Duke of Windsor and the Duke of Kent[25] about which Blunt informed the Russians. Controversy surrounds the existence of such documents; Philip Ziegler, in his authorised biography of the Duke of Windsor, doubts their existence. However, US Attorney John Loftus, formerly with the US Department of Justice, an expert on Nazi intelligence who requires government clearance on all his writings, told the author he had seen top secret documents relating to Windsor and had interviewed two US officers who had found the files in Wolfsgarten Castle. One of them confirmed the documents related to communications between Hitler and the Duke of Windsor.[26] John Costello, author of the acclaimed *Mask of Treason*, is not alone in suggesting that the secret deal to give Blunt immunity from prosecution and allow him to continue working for the Queen, arose directly because of this information which he possessed. Peter Wright said in *Spycatcher* that attempts by MI5 officers three years later to interview Blunt further were halted 'by the highest authorities'. And so the Queen, that summer, unwittingly and reluctantly became a key figure in one of the great spy scandals of this century. The question of exactly how much she was told of the affair is not, and perhaps never will be, answered. Only assumptions can be made, that because of the top secret nature of the affair and because of its seriousness, Adeane would have told her all the salient facts of the case to this blatant cover-up. More would yet come out on the affair when Mrs Margaret Thatcher would be forced to reveal that it did indeed occur . . .

That autumn, the Queen was travelling again, booked to go to Canada at the beginning of October for an 8 day visit to mark the centenary of the first meeting of the Fathers of the Confederation which led to the British North American Act and the birth of Canada as a nation. The Queen was due to cover the path of the founding fathers from Prince Edward Island to the city of Quebec which, as the time of her visit neared, was seething with French nationalism which, in itself, was stirring up Canadian republican feelings. There had been several shooting incidents and a couple of gun battles with the police. 'The Queen is not necessarily in danger,' said the leader of one of the nationalist groups, though he added ominously, 'but you can never be sure. It only takes one bullet . . .' The graffiti in French spelled out the dangers: 'Chez-nous'. The question was raised, of course, whether or not the Queen should go, especially as the Canadian authorities had already sent troops into Quebec to search for bombs or extremist gunmen. 'No one is going to harm me,' she insisted and since the government allowed her to proceed with the journey, observers of her recent travels might well have gained the impression that, whenever there was trouble in the Commonwealth, the only solution her ministers seemed to have was to send in the Queen. She did it again, this time calming Quebec and also stating that the time had come to look at the possibility of updating the Canadian constitution. So another success was chalked up.

Philip continued on to the Bahamas and Mexico but the Queen had to return home. Constitutionally, she had to be in the country for a general election – called by Sir Alec Douglas-Home, for 15 October. Not unexpectedly for a man devoid of personality or charisma and who was saddled with the task of trying to hold together a badly damaged party, he lost.

For the first time in her reign, the Queen faced a Labour government, nor was Philip immediately on hand to offer a few choice observations; that may have been a blessing. The prospect of receiving a Cabinet full of men who were rather more passionate about the political cause than those they were replacing must have been somewhat daunting. They were a diverse band, whose views ranged across a broad spectrum of socialism, from moderate to strong left-wing, with the likes of the mercurial George Brown declaring, 'Brothers, we are on our way' and the man she was about to invite to form a government, Harold Wilson, walking across the threshold at No. 10 and quipping, 'Nice place we've got here'.

And there was another sign of the times when Wilson arrived at Buckingham Palace to receive the Queen's official invitation to form a government. He was not wearing the customary morning dress – and he had his wife, sister and father with him in the ministerial car. Some of the Queen's courtiers, more used to the loving devotion of Churchill, the friendship of Eden, the total formality of patrician Macmillan and the gentleness of the Scottish laird Douglas-Home, simply gasped with horror!

The whole gamut of policies pursued and put in place by Macmillan was up for dismantling. Wilson talked of 'criminal Tory neglect' and his colleagues looked forward to increasing state intervention in a variety of industries. The Tories were gone; Douglas-Home was out of office but the Queen had to carry on. And as one who had kept totally up to date with her government's business these past dozen years, it was she more than the politicians who would face a period of severe readjustment because even though she might not have agreed with everything the Tories did, they had become so familiar to her that their policies had become, in a way, hers.

Not least up for change was the attitude of the men and women who were to become her ministers. She could no longer be assured of their undying love, devotion and respect. In fact some would readily have done away with the monarchy for good, there and then. And perhaps there is no better description of the scenario that faced the Queen than that of Richard Crossman, one of Wilson's ministers, as he and his colleagues prepared for their first audience:

> Undoubtedly the most fantastic episode was the kissing of hands and the rehearsal . . . when we new ministers were summoned to the Privy Council offices to rehearse the ceremony of becoming a Privy Councillor. I don't suppose anything more dull, pretentious or plain silly has ever been invented. There we were, sixteen grown men. For over an hour we were taught how to stand up, how to kneel on one knee on a cushion, how to raise the right hand with a bible in it, how to advance three paces towards the Queen, how to take the hand and kiss it . . . how to move back ten paces without falling over the stools which had been so carefully arranged so that you did fall over them. Oh dear. At 12.15 all of us went out, each to his own car and drove to the palace and there stood about until we entered the great drawing room. At the other end was this little woman with a beautiful waist and she had to stand with her hand on the table for forty minutes while we went through this rigmarole. Then at the end informality broke out and she said 'You all moved back very nicely' . . . and then she pressed a bell and we all left. It was two-dimensional . . . it's the thinness of it all that astonishes me.[27]

A month later, Crossman was back at the palace, this time with his wife for a reception of Cabinet ministers. He recorded that they were shown into a magnificent room where they were served quite ordinary gin and tonics. In due course, the Queen entered, and spoke to each minister and wife for ten minutes

> In our ten minutes she talked, as I am told she always does, about her corgis (two fat corgis, roughly the same size, lay at her feet) . . . I asked her what good they were and she said they were Welsh dogs, used for rounding up cattle by biting their legs. Then the Queen got on to talking about cows . . . and said how terribly pleased she was when she entered for the dairy shows for the first time and won the championship for Jersey cows . . . it was a fairly forced performance.[28]

Crossman's view of the Queen as a person mellowed considerably in the years to come, though his liking for the institution that she represented certainly did not. But at the very least, the Queen could expect colourful variation to the political life on whose periphery she circled.

Chapter Nine
Family Matters (1965–6)

Nothing less than a funeral of great state occasion was due to Winston Churchill who died on 24 January 1965. He had been like a surrogate uncle to the Queen, though never crossing the invisible line that divides politician from monarch, and she was determined that he would be buried with all the pomp and ceremony that he adored. Her horses and carriages and household staff were placed at the disposal of Sir Winston's relatives, even down to the little hot water bottles that the royals keep in the carriages to warm their hands on cold days, and Saturday 30 January was a bitterly cold day. For the first time in her reign, she broke all custom in attending the funeral and laid aside her usual precedence which would have meant she would be the last to enter St Paul's Cathedral and the first to leave. Instead, she and her family were already in their seats when the dramatic funeral cortège arrived and the bearers' party walked slowly down the pale blue carpet towards the glistening cupola to the sound of a soft and dignified choir singing the words 'I am the Resurrection and the Life'. Later, in the springtime, the Queen invited Lady Churchill and her son Randolph to Windsor Castle for lunch, followed by a moving private ceremony for the handing back of Churchill's insignia of the Order of the Garter. In the afternoon, almost all her family were present for another poignant service which signifies the memorial to a knight in St George's Chapel, Windsor. The Queen's personal tribute to her greatest commoner[1] was completed in May when she bestowed a life peerage on Clementine Churchill, who took her seat on the cross-benches as Baroness Spencer Churchill of Chartwell.

One day after the funeral, the Queen and Philip flew straight off to 'another overseas tour', a 3,700 mile non-stop flight to Ethiopia (and later, Sudan), then still under the control of a royal ruler whose opulence would look obscene, set against the tragic developments of starvation, poverty and death that engulfed the people of the nation within a few years. These were indeed the final death throes of British attempts to retain influence in the area, as indicated by the precision with which the Foreign Office attended upon the visit. The Queen dubiously regarded the Emperor Haile Selassie whose titles included King of Kings, Elect of God and Lion of Judah, to which Her Majesty bestowed one more, bringing with her a baton to appoint him Honorary Field Marshal of the British Army. A further gift of a stallion sired by the Derby winner Nimbus had been shipped out ahead as a token of the British monarchy's alleged esteem for the precarious ruler who had survived recent attempts to oust him as Macmillan's so-called 'wind of change' blew dangerously in his direction. In return, the Emperor presented the Queen with a pearl necklace and a gold tray. For Philip there was a gold sword and a gold and silver fruit bowl; a gold watch for Charles, a gold bracelet for Anne and two golden medallions for the two young princes; to look at Ethiopia two decades further into history, the Queen, like the rest of her subjects, must have wondered what in heaven's name it was all about. Whatever the Foreign Office had in mind failed to be sustained and this was to be the last such exchange of niceties between the British sovereign and one of Africa's last surviving dynasties; he was soon to be overthrown and the nation foundered in the hostilities of opposing factions, famine and disease. In the end, Princess Anne would return to try to help bring relief.

From Ethiopia, the Queen moved on to what her advisers had cautiously warned might be a doubtfully volatile reception in neighbouring Sudan where she had expected to be greeted by the military ruler, General Ibraham Abboud. Unfortunately, the general had been overthrown since the invitation was extended and there were doubts as to whether the Queen would even be welcomed by the new rulers amongst the historically sensitive surrounds of Khartoum. In fact, she received a rousing welcome with hundreds of thousands of people lining the streets, and members of the Presidential Council who now ran the country drawing lots to decide who should be the first to greet her. There was only one minor demonstration, when a rotten tomato was thrown at the Queen's car when she visited Omdurman, scene of General Kitchener's victory in 1898 over the Khalifa – at which, incidentally, a young Winston Churchill took part in the cavalry charge by the 21st Lancers.

Soon after her return to England, a private message was delivered to Buckingham Palace by the Dowager Viscountess Monckton, widow of the first Viscount Monckton of Brenchley, who had died a fortnight before Sir Winston Churchill, on 9 January. As Walter Monckton, KC, the viscount had been one of the Duke of Windsor's oldest friends and closest advisers for more than half a century. He was one of his staunchest allies during the abdication crisis, and thus another link with that historical moment had passed on. Lady Monckton made her contact with the Queen after visiting the Duke of Windsor on his arrival at the London Clinic on 23 February for an operation for a detached retina. The duchess came with him and spent most of the time with her husband in his suite of rooms. Their arrival had been given prominence in the newspapers, who carried front page photographs of the duke in black-lensed spectacles and looking weak and frail and much older than his seventy years after a recent abdominal operation in Houston, Texas.

On that day, the Queen was alone at Buckingham Palace, suffering from a chill, the result of coming from the hot climes of Africa into the cold and damp February of London. Philip had gone off alone on another engagement and the Queen Mother was making an official visit to Jamaica, where she also visited Noël Coward at his villa, Firefly, atop a long and twisting mountain road and they sat looking across the bays, drinking a Coward cocktail speciality, called bullshot, and eating curry in coconuts, followed by rum cream pie which he had prepared himself.[2] When the author visited the villa some years later, a photograph of the Queen Mother, taken on that day, was still displayed in pride of place in a silver frame on top of one of the two back-to-back pianos in Coward's cramped little den; photographs of other members of the royal family were scattered around the room.

The message from Lady Monckton thus reached the Queen while she was alone. It said simply that her uncle would be 'cheered and invigorated' by a visit from members of his family.[3] Her private secretary Sir Michael Adeane who knew of the message was in favour; he was already 'concerned' about the recent criticism in the newspapers of the continued exclusion of the duke and duchess from the British royal circle, albeit a two-sided quarrel which had been equally enforced by the duke because of the continued lack of royal recognition of his wife. It would later become apparent that the duke also wanted to try to bridge their differences as he saw his life edging closer to its end.

Outstanding matters such as the place of his eventual burial as well as the final resting place of his wife needed to be considered. Although he had earlier, more in anger, bought a joint burial plot in America, he now especially wanted them both to be buried in the royal cemetery at Frogmore and to be assured they would both receive suitable religious recognition with funeral services at St George's, Windsor. Time was of the essence; it needed to be settled, as did his concern that the £10,000 a year he received from the Queen annually in compensation for his life's interest in the Sandringham and Balmoral estates, which he passed to his brother King George VI upon abdication, would continue to be paid to his wife after his death. Discussion of these delicate family matters had never seemed possible in the climate of distant coolness which had existed between both sides for the past twenty-nine years.

The key to the warming of family relationships lay with the Queen Mother; according to those in her circle, the bitterness had subsided with the passing years and on her return from Jamaica, when the Queen told her of the contact by Lady Monckton, she did not object to a visit though, even now, she did not feel able to go herself. In the meantime, the duke had undergone three separate operations on his eyes by the time the Queen arrived in her Rolls Royce outside the London Clinic shortly after 6.00 p.m. on the evening of 15 March. No other member of the family went with her; she was accompanied merely by Sir Michael Adeane and her private detective Inspector Albert Perkins. The duke's doctors and surgeons, the clinic's matron and its chairman were on hand to receive the Queen before she was shown to the Windsor suite, where nervously the duchess was waiting to greet her; it was to be their first ever formal meeting and only the second time the Queen had met her – the last time was almost exactly twenty-nine years earlier when the Princess Elizabeth was ten years old and had a brief, chance encounter with the then Mrs Wallis Simpson. 'Aunt Wallis', a description which had probably never crossed the lips of any member of the family except perhaps in sarcasm, went down almost on one knee in a deep curtsy. The duke, dressed in silk pyjamas and dressing gown and with his left eye heavily bandaged, rose from his armchair and bowed, and they kissed, almost formally rather than in the style of a long-sought reunion of uncle and niece. Indeed the official atmosphere pervaded, with the presence in the background of Adeane who was ready should the Queen require any advice on matters the duke might raise. They chatted for a while, before the duke raised the question of his concern over his eventual burial site and said he would write a formal note to his niece.

The Queen's visit lasted little more than twenty minutes, but it was the signal, finally, for the years of accumulated bile and torment to be partially eased for the Duke and Duchess of Windsor; in the days that followed, they were to receive more royal visitors.

The first was the duke's beloved sister, Mary the Princess Royal, Countess of Harewood, who came on 17 March, carrying a bouquet of flowers, and stayed for almost an hour. She kissed her sister-in-law Wallis on the cheeks; it was their first embrace and only the second time they had met since the Abdication. It was also, though no one could have guessed then, the last time the princess would see either; she collapsed and died barely two weeks later.

The Princess Royal was followed by Princess Marina, who quelled her own distaste for the Windsors for their lack of contact after her husband the Duke of Kent was killed. Her daughter, Princess Alexandra who had never met Wallis, also came. Then Mountbatten arrived and what memories came gushing into the room as he stormed in like a military invasion, grasping the slender, bony hand of his cousin. For years, Mountbatten had been the constant companion and aide to the Prince of Wales and his affectionate and supportive companion on two of the great empire tours. Then, they were the two most handsome young bachelors in English society, the model of dress and style for millions of men and the heart's desire of a larger number of women. Mountbatten was still handsome and strong and alongside him the duke, lined, thin and bandaged, looked a tired and pathetic figure. The mere comparison of their lives which had been side by side in their progression to family aspirations in the twenties, was itself a telling synopsis of Windsor's abject failure. Mountbatten's had been full of vigour and zest and action; often criticised and often derided, he had none the less accumulated enough honours, awards and naval CV to fill a yard of closely printed small type. Windsor, who once showed such great promise as the young Prince of Wales, had thrown his life away on wanton pleasure in the twenties and early thirties, turned his back on the duty and service he was bred for, and after eleven months as uncrowned monarch, departed the shores of England to make no further significant contribution to the world, except to keep the gossip columnists in business and provide a constant thorn in the side of his relations. That the Queen Mother had continued to withhold any kind of recognition for this couple was perhaps understandable. She knew the secrets. Those who have sought to offer explanations and apologies for the Duke of Windsor's wasted years, never managed to produce a convincing case. And though Mountbatten had his faults, and many of them, his presence that day alongside the wrinkled shell of the ex-king must have inspired thoughts of what life might have been for Windsor had he not decided to give up everything for the dubious prospect of life with Wallis Simpson; but then as Tommy Lascelles, the Queen's former private secretary, once said, 'Thank God he went'. Mountbatten remained for forty-five minutes, apparently unaware that his once 'oldest friend' had long ago been converted by Wallis's ardent dislike of him; she regarded him as an 'ambitious, untrustworthy, self-seeking snob'.[4] When he left, she turned and said in a voice full of acrimony, 'I thought he'd never go. Too boring. He talked of absolutely nothing but himself the whole time.'[5]

The Queen made a second visit to her uncle a few days later, when he had moved to a recuperative suite at Claridges. She came this time with her assistant secretary, Sir Edward Ford, and stayed for tea. Five days later, the duke took a telephone call at Claridges from Buckingham Palace. It was to inform him that his sister, the Princess Royal, had died suddenly that afternoon after collapsing while walking in the grounds of her Yorkshire home with her son, the Earl of Harewood. She was sixty-seven.

The Duke of Windsor was pronounced medically unfit to travel to Leeds for the family funeral and thus the prospect of his and Wallis's meeting the Queen Mother did not arise; instead, they went to a memorial service which was being held at the same time in Westminster Abbey, quietly slipping into their seats by a side door almost unnoticed except by those immediately around him in the 2,500-strong congregation. And if in that time of illness and family grief, observers and close friends believed, for a moment, that past differences ought to be set aside and allowed to fade into the past with age, they were shortly to be given a jolt back to reality. Early in May, the film version of the Duke of Windsor's autobiography, *A King's Story*, opened in London bringing with it a resurgence of all that the Queen Mother hated about the story, with interviews and talks with all the protagonists drawn mainly from the duke's side of things. The royals hated the original book, as did many who were close enough at hand to know the truth, and believed that Windsor had been somewhat economical and one-sided in his recall of the facts.

The film was historical in that it showed a senior member of the royal family, talking to camera for the first time about matters directly concerning the monarchy. It did not help the cause of family harmony one bit and though it had been rumoured that the Queen would soon formally recognise her aunt by receiving her at Buckingham Palace, no such meeting now appeared imminent; but at least there had been some contact which, as Lady Monckton told the duke, was a move in the right direction.

Other broken bridges, leading to the other side of the Queen's family, were about to be mended, thus renewing the monarchy's official contact with German relations which had lapsed since 1939. It was to be a historic moment, not merely for the constitutional and political value of a state visit to Germany by the Queen, but allowing her to visit the homes of her husband's relatives for the very first time in her life. From the political standpoint, it was important as the Cold War became deeper. Whereas Germany was once viewed suspiciously as a defeated enemy, it was now seen as an important ally in the front line of the eastern front against Communism, in a jittery international scenario made worse by the entry of American troops into the Vietnam War.

The journey that would mean so much to Philip had its beginnings in 1964, during the brief tenure at No. 10 of Sir Alec Douglas-Home. The Queen mentioned during an audience one day that she was unable to visit half of her family; it was impossible to make a private visit to any country to which she, as reigning monarch, had not made a state visit. When, in the past, the possibility of a visit had been mentioned the Queen – apparently at Philip's suggestion – quoted the precedent established by Queen Victoria, who had more relatives there than in England. The same was true of Prince Philip and no one was quite sure of the relationship of two of Prince Edward's German godparents the previous year, Princess Sophie of Hanover and Prince Louis of Hesse. The inclusion of these names who were rather mysterious as far as the British public was concerned, amongst the godparents of the Queen's fourth child actually served to demonstrate how much the Queen wanted to recognise the existence of her husband's relatives and it masked one of her most earnest wishes, to be able to visit them in their own homes and castles.

Philip had always made the journey alone, or had taken Charles and Anne. Successive ministers had always maintained, though often they would not admit as much, that such a visit, even a private one, might arouse too much public feeling, especially in view of the cool public reception given to West Germany's President Heuss on his state visit to Britain in 1958; years later no return visit had been arranged. Ministers were also anxious, even in the sixties, that there might be a public backlash if the full extent of Prince Philip's

German connections became known. His four sisters, all Greek princesses who like him had spent years in exile in Paris, had married into elite German families in 1930–31 and three of the husbands became high-ranking Nazi officers during the war. Princess Sophie, the youngest, was first married to Prince Christopher of Hesse who was an ardent Nazi attached to Goering's personal staff and who eventually became head of the notorious Luftwaffe 'research' office which was the most efficient internal security organisation within the Third Reich. It was perhaps fortuitous that he was killed in a plane crash in 1942, otherwise he would certainly have stood trial before a War Crimes tribunal. Sophie's brother-in-law, Prince Philip of Hesse, was indeed arrested by the Americans at the end of the war; although he had been tossed into a concentration camp after falling out with Hitler, he was put back into internment as a 'Nazi activist', listed as target number 53 on the Allies' list of wanted war criminals.[6] He was held for two years, brought to trial soon after Princess Elizabeth married Prince Philip, and quietly freed, having been sentenced to serve two years and partially stripped of his property and estates.[7]

Princess Sophie married again in 1946 to Prince George of Hanover who was, of course, directly linked in ancestry to the Queen herself. Prince Edward's German godfather, Prince Louis of Hesse-Darmstadt, was a cousin of Lord Mountbatten and a second cousin of Prince Philip. His brother George Donatus, Grand Duke of Hesse, married Prince Philip's fourth sister Cecile. Tragically, however, Cecile and George and their two sons were killed in an air crash in 1937 while on their way to Croydon, London to attend the wedding of Prince Louis to the Hon. Margaret Geddes. Just how deeply the family was split by the war is perhaps best demonstrated by the fact that Prince Louis, having married an English bride, was then seconded to the German embassy in London, under Joachim von Ribbentrop, on Hitler's personal instructions for the specific and perhaps innocently performed task of keeping contact with the British royals. The Mountbatten clan, which included Philip's mother Princess Alice who was Lord Mountbatten's sister, originated from a morganatic branch of the Hessian dynasty and had a straight line of descent through the German royal house. Lord Mountbatten must, therefore, have had difficulty in keeping a straight face when he wrote to his cousin in 1939, 'I'd hate to be German.'[8]

Philip's sisters Princess Sophie of Hanover, Princess Margarita of Hohenlohe-Langenburg and Princess Theodora of Baden were all still alive. By the mid-sixties, however, the Queen's ministers clearly decided it was now possible to risk what Helen Cathcart described as 'these inconvenient German connections'[9] being brought into the public arena by official attachment to the christening of Prince Edward, third in line to the throne. In fact, it passed virtually unnoticed. The background of these relations was not made a public issue and thus the Queen, egged on by Philip, felt able to broach the subject to Sir Alec Douglas-Home. He was somewhat amazed that the visit to Germany had been withheld for so long.

In May 1965, it was all to be put right; a state visit to Germany had been arranged. It would be the first such visit by a British sovereign (excluding the ex-king Edward VIII who went as Duke of Windsor to see Hitler in 1937) since King George V and Queen Mary visited Kaiser Wilhelm for a family occasion four months before the outbreak of the First World War. Before the visit took place there was a totally unprecedented amount of newspaper and magazine coverage. Week after week, huge sections of magazines were turned over to the British royal family and Prince Charles was unfortunate enough to experience his first major brush with the press. One of his exercise books had been stolen from Gordonstoun; there was a good and ready market for such things in the continental media. It was eventually tracked down by Scotland Yard detectives who took possession of it and returned it to the palace.

By then, however, excellent photocopies had already been made and sold to the German magazine *Der Stern* for £1,000. The magazine discovered the book contained two essays of particular interest, one arguing the case for democracy in which the prince deplored the tendency to vote for a party rather than the merits of a particular candidate and the other on the freedom of the press which he was firmly in favour of. However, neither he nor his mother was in favour of giving the press freedom to publish stolen property. The

Queen called her advisers and they decided there was little they could do. She did become exceedingly angry soon afterwards when *Time* magazine in America alleged that the prince might have sold the exercise book himself to get money and that he was not averse to taking cash for his autograph. To that, Commander Colville was ordered to respond rapidly in these words, personally approved by the Queen:

> There is no truth whatever in the story that Prince Charles sold his autograph at any time. There is no truth whatever that he sold his composition book to a classmate. In the first place, he is intelligent enough and old enough to realize how embarrassing this would turn out to be and second he is only too conscious of the interest of the press in anything to do with himself and his family. The suggestion that his parents keep him so short of money that he has to find other means to raise it is also a complete invention.

And it was just one of the many preambles to the Queen's visit to Germany, including a complete A to Z of British monarchy to which one magazine devoted an entire issue. But sometimes, all publicity turns out to be good publicity and on this occasion the Queen could not have been better received if she had landed in Cheltenham. Prince Louis of Hesse was on the tarmac when she arrived on German soil and accompanied them for much of the tour to which, belatedly, had been added the Berlin wall. For some reason, Berlin had not been originally included but was put in by Prime Minister Harold Wilson, reviewing the schedule.

'Your country and mine,' the Queen said, 'stood on opposite sides. This tragic period in our relations is happily over . . .'

It may have been over, but was certainly not forgotten by certain sections of the battery of British media who followed the Queen. The *Sunday Times*, then owned by Lord Thomson, ran a leader welcoming the visit as 'a sign that this country has at last realigned its views about the Germans and accepts them genuinely as human beings'. To underscore this new mood of reconciliation, Lord Thomson invited the new German ambassador to London, Herr Herbert Blankenhorn, to lunch; all went well until copies of that week's *Sunday Times* magazine arrived, with a front cover devoted to a Nazi wartime hit-list of British VIPs and details of the invasion that never came. Herr Blankenhorn, whose own wartime background had been the subject of a Commons discussion, retired coldly. Elsewhere in Fleet Street, the press reported the ecstatic welcome the Queen had received – she 'stunned the German nation'. Though joining the rest with massive coverage of the Queen's 'triumph', the *Daily Express* could not let the moment pass without due deference to Lord Beaverbrook's memory. 'It is with great sadness,' leader-writer and associate editor Derek Marks wrote, 'that we watch the Queen . . . they are precisely the same people who held the dagger to our throats.' And he went on to recall Auschwitz and Belsen.

Still, the Queen's visit received greater attention from the British media than any of her tours since the year of the Coronation. In the first three days alone, the BBC and ITV screened seven hours of coverage between them, and the BBC devoted two hours and twenty minutes to the Berlin visit alone.

When the formalities were over, the Queen could make her own pilgrimage, sailing up the Rhine to Wolfsgarten, the country home of the Hesse family which was crowded with relatives, including fourteen nieces and nephews. Schloss Wolfsgarten was steeped in history that the Queen was anxious to get the feel of; she was shown the room that had been Queen Victoria's favourite during her many visits there and the measuring board, still there, on which the heights of Lord Mountbatten and Tsar Nicholas II were marked when they were boys, to which later was added Prince Philip's first when he was ten and then at fifteen.[10]

The dynastic home of the Hesse-Cassel family, Schloss Friedrichshof in Kronberg, had darker memories. It was here that Anthony Blunt, when working for MI5, came immediately after the war bearing a royal warrant signed by King George VI to collect documents and letters found in the attic room of the castle by invading Allied soldiers, many which were said to date from Victorian times and were personal family records. It was in the grounds of this castle that Allied troops found buried cans of microfilm which formed part of the collection of captured German documents brought to England for study after the war. It was in this castle which was commandeered as a GI rest centre at the end of the war that three members of the American forces – alerted by the arrival of Anthony Blunt seeking documents from the attic – carried out a systematic search of the building and discovered a walled-up compartment in the cellars. Behind it, they discovered an underground vault in which the Hesse family had buried its valuables in a lead-lined box soon after the start of the war. The three stole the contents and the theft was discovered only in 1946, on the eve of Princess Sophie's wedding to Prince George of Hanover which was attended by Prince Philip. The Hesse women, who sought permission to go back into the castle to retrieve their jewels, found that virtually everything had been plundered. The American military was informed, and after an investigation lasting some weeks, the three officers, one of them a woman, were arrested and subsequently jailed. Most of the jewels, then worth £1.5 million, were recovered from various hiding places in America, including left-luggage lockers in Chicago railway station. The haul was collected and sorted at the Pentagon, and it included dozens of historical pieces, including tiaras, brooches, rings, necklaces and bangles set with the finest stones. Many of the stones, prised from original settings, were loose in brown paper bags. The strong box also contained nine volumes of letters from Queen Victoria to her family, bound in black leather etched with gold.[11] Later, the Queen was able to visit the castle at Salem where Prince Philip's brother-in-law, Theodora's husband Berthold, the Margrave of Baden, had been headmaster of Philip's first school after Cheam. It had been founded with the help of Kurt Hahn, who was deported after falling foul of Hitler and repaired to England to build a similar school at Gordonstoun. Philip stayed at Salem for only a year but could not attune to the heel-clicking regime and Heil Hitler salutes of German youth and was despatched back to the care of his Mountbatten uncles in England by his German relatives 'for his sake as well as ours'. He left his mark, however, in the form of initials carved on his desk, which was still in the castle for the Queen to see. These were the memories and matters of recent history that so affected all of those who, by her visit, were now finally reunited as a family; few people in England fully appreciated at the time the importance of this visit to the Queen and her family.

Politically too, she left an unusually pointed and futuristic notation with one of her final speeches. 'The rising generations in Europe and indeed the whole Western world are now united by common interest . . . it is our task to defend this civilisation in freedom and in peace. That is why we stand together in NATO; why so many of our armed forces are serving in Germany. It is why we wholeheartedly support your natural wish for peaceful reunification.' It was a speech which Harold Wilson had written, and for which he was strongly attacked.

Back home, she walked straight into another public row, caused by the first of the Queen's Birthday Honours lists produced under Harold Wilson's premiership. He had decided to popularise the awards by adding what he described as the 'common touch', that is, bringing in more people who were immediately recognisable to the masses instead of restricting them largely to faceless civil servants, diplomats and community workers; as in the New Year's Honours list when Stanley Matthews became the first ever footballer to be knighted. The actor Jack Warner of the popular TV series Dixon of Dock Green was awarded an OBE, which was fair enough, and no one seemed to mind when Mary Quant was awarded an OBE for her services to the British fashion industry and even actress Vanessa Redgrave came forth for a CBE before her principles and the Workers' Revolutionary party swung her off in other directions. The trouble arose with the award of MBEs to the four Beatles. Protests came thick and fast, especially from existing holders of the Queen's insignia. The words that Winston Churchill spoke in the House of Commons on 22 March 1944, were recalled: 'The object of giving medals, stars and ribbons is to give pride and pleasure to those who deserve them.' The Queen has no choice but to grant the honours submitted by her Prime Minister though she is not precluded from making the occasional observation. Some years later, when Cabinet secretary Robert Armstrong brought another Honours list for the Queen's approval, it included a peerage for the Prime

Minister's secretary Marcia Williams. The Queen merely raised an eyebrow and commented, 'Mr Wilson can always change his mind on any of these names, right up to the last minute, should he wish to do so.'[12]

In that summer of the Beatles' awards, nine people returned their medals and the first, Mr Hector Dupuis, a Canadian MP, said the whole awards system had been cheapened by giving honours to 'those four vulgar nincompoops'. Actually, John Lennon didn't want it in the first place; he tore up the letter offering them the honour and spoke furiously to his three comrades and manager Brian Epstein about the British class system. Epstein insisted that they accepted. It was seen as an attempt by Wilson to curry favour with the young and upwardly mobile but it rebounded when Lennon eventually returned his own medal as a political protest. At their investiture, the Queen asked the group how long they had been working together and Ringo Starr broke the stiff atmosphere of formality by reciting a line from an old music-hall song, 'We've been together now for forty years . . .' to which the Queen forced a smile. The band of the Grenadier Guards played 'The Teddy Bears Picnic' and 'We'll Gather Lilacs in the Spring' but no Beatles music. The scene that day was the same as it always was, repeated eight or nine times a year, with a line of hundreds with their families, waiting to see the Queen and receive their medals. The men wore uniforms or morning suits, the women formal dresses and they paraded forward, the knights first, going down on one knee to be dubbed with her sword, followed by the lesser medals. She spoke a few words to each one, and each award was timed to perfection – average twenty seconds. And thus, another royal day was done.

Recognition of the Beatles with the MBE was just one example of the new order of society at the beginning of what would be termed Swinging London. This was in fact showing itself in a variety of ways, and not least of them was in the rising hemlines which began in 1965 and moved on to the point where Jean Shrimpton, the David Bailey model, caused something of a sensation by wearing a mini-skirt at Melbourne races. As *Time* magazine pointed out a few months later in a special issue, 'In this century, every decade has its city . . . and for the sixties that city is London.' The Beatles, the

Rolling Stones, Twiggy, Mary Quant and Carnaby Street were suddenly the talk of the world. Britain was in fashion and it presented the royal house with a delicate problem of how it was going to react. Not least in the focus of the spotlight were the royals, whose four most attractive front-liners, as one American magazine described them, were the Queen, Princess Margaret, Princess Alexandra and the Duchess of Kent who were that era's equivalent to the Princess of Wales, Princess Anne and the Duchess of York in the eighties. The latter two additions to the family business were now taking on a considerable part of the royal workload.

To see them all side by side at their most glamorous was quite a sight. The Queen, however, was not far off her fortieth birthday and the prospect of rising hemlines for the Windsor wives filled her with some trepidation. During the coming months the discussions among them on fashion, which was such a major part of the British revolution, could not be avoided especially as Princess Margaret through her husband's association with the world of photographic arts and fashions was leading them all towards the modernistic look. It is not difficult to imagine the Queen's thoughts as she surveyed her vast wardrobes of dresses, frocks and coats all with their hemlines suitably pegged well below the knee.

If, as it seemed, the fashions were to dictate higher hemlines, she and her fashion advisers were to face something of a dilemma. Was she to have all her clothes altered? Or just have the new ones cut so that they were more in tune with the mood? In fact, as the length of women's dresses and skirts moved slowly upwards and above the knee, she made a tilt towards acknowledging the new style with a small selection of clothes which were cut so that the hemline hung just below the knee joint. Unquestionably she had moved with the times, as is now evident looking back on the photographs of the era, but reluctantly and briefly. Discussion in the royal household about dress lengths went on for months until the royal women, who were out every day of the week in the public eye, achieved a suitable balance between following fashion and not making a spectacle of themselves, which was a phrase the Queen is said to have used more than once when discussing the issue. 'It's a firm woman who can ignore fashion the way she does,' said one of her acquaintances. And generally speaking that has remained the Queen's attitude. She dismissed the higher hemlines, and kept to her own almost inimitable style.

If there were signs of slight rebelliousness amongst the youth of the nation, it was certainly matched in Harold Wilson's Cabinet by those who – now they had got over the novelty value – questioned the usefulness of the constitutional formalities that were the link between Parliament and the monarchy. There were rumblings again about disposing of the House of Lords. Richard Crossman, Wilson's housing minister, was not alone in sounding off expressions about the Privy Council meetings and other formalities at court as 'idiot flummery and I must admit that I feel morally superior to my colleagues in despising it'.[13] The Queen was soon to hear of the thoughts of Dick Crossman. One day over dinner with Lord Porchester, the Queen's racing manager and close friend, Crossman whose tongue was loosened by drink said he detested the mumbo-jumbo of monarchy, which was dreary and the court was filled with snobbery.

Porchester replied, 'I must tell you . . . the Queen is one of my greatest personal friends and I am an admirer.'

'Well maybe,' replied Crossman, 'but she finds me boring and I found her boring and I think it's a great relief that I don't have to see her that often.'[14]

Some time later, Crossman was at the palace for a reception for Cabinet ministers and the first signs that the Queen was winning him over began to show in his recollections. As she came towards him, the Queen said, 'Ah, Mr Crossman . . . Lord Porchester was telling me about you . . .'

Crossman recalled, 'It was very clever of her to mention it straightaway and let it be known that Lord Porchester had passed on the remarks . . . and I found it perfectly straightforward and simple to get on with her. Indeed, she puts one at ease immediately. And then in the actual reception George Brown took over and was familiar and cosy with her – "m'dear and such nonsense" – as anyone could possibly be.'

And so the Labour Party had talked her into giving away her medals to pop stars and its leading politicians went around calling her 'm'dear'. What were things coming to? Perhaps it wasn't all bad, not as bad as the Queen might have feared when Labour came to power. With a few adjustments to the system, they could have virtually ignored her altogether – which is what Crossman and others of the ilk would have initially been prepared to have done. Wilson got on well with the Queen and, as time wore on, he could see that she was seriously interested in his policies, not merely for a cursory view. She seemed to have a certain sympathy with his ideas and was probably the only member of the immediate royal family with a social conscience that veered naturally to the left, rather than the right where the Queen Mother and Prince Philip were to be found, firmly entrenched. She wanted to know the detail, the background and the prognosis of all situations. To Harold Wilson, this reaction from the monarch, who had become increasingly relaxed as the months went by, came as something of a surprise. He was also surprised by her knowledge and memory, as were most who came into contact with the Queen because it was only in the privacy of Buckingham Palace that she was able to demonstrate it. 'I had met the Queen formally on a number of occasions,' Wilson recalled 'and she had not seemed particularly formidable. So I thought my first meeting at Buckingham Palace would simply mean passing on what was happening in government. I was rapidly disillusioned. I returned to Downing Street and put my hand across my brow and said aloud, "I'm going to have to do my homework in future." It developed into a kind of competition as to who had read most of what was happening in the world that day. But her constant good humour and generosity meant we were able to joke about it as well.'[15]

Wilson was not averse to 'using' the Queen when it suited him. There was clear mischievousness, on 13 October which was the first day of the Conservative Party conference – and the first conference of its new leader, the 49 year-old Mr Edward Heath, the ex-grammar school boy who was the first Tory leader in history who was not the product of the 'magic circle' suggesting to the Queen where she might use her prerogative. At last, the Conservatives had taken George IV's advice and elected a leader by democratic vote. As Mr Heath made his opening address and launched into his tirade against Labour's first year in office, Harold Wilson stole the headlines by flying to Balmoral to see the Queen. Everyone believed he was going to the country, and was to tell her that he was calling a general election – thus setting off a few political fireworks. But as Crossman said, 'In sober truth he had no reason to go to Balmoral except to bitch at Heath's opening speech – a typical Harold trick.'[16] Wilson's 'use' of the monarchy caused much resentment among politicians. Cartoonists like Wally Fawkes, otherwise Trog of the *Observer*, lampooned him; typical was one captioned, 'Don't you feel the need to fly back each day to report, prime minister', while *Private Eye* carried them pictured together on page one with a bubble coming from the Queen's mouth with the words, 'We can't go on meeting like this . . .'

Though Wilson timed the visit to Balmoral exactly to hit the Tory Party Conference opening, there were other reasons for impromptu meetings. Mr Ian Smith, Prime Minister of Rhodesia, Britain's last colony in Africa, was on the verge of declaring UDI because of failure to agree terms over black representation in the charter for independence, following the granting of independence in 1964 to Northern Rhodesia, which took the new name of Zambia under the black rule of Dr Kenneth Kaunda. His senior Cabinet colleagues had discussed the developing situation and looked at the possibilities. If Smith did go for UDI, his government would be illegal and constitutionally the Queen should formally take over the running of the country through her representative in Rhodesia, the Governor Sir Humphrey Gibbs. Smith, conversely, claimed that he was the Queen's legal and correct link to the government of the colony and that she would continue to remain head of state; Rhodesia's dispute was not with her but with her government. What Wilson and his colleagues wanted to avoid at all costs was sending in troops; in that the Queen agreed. Neither she nor Wilson wanted another Suez. Wilson explained all the options to the Queen and then asked her if she would support him in a last-minute attempt he planned to make to halt a crisis of international proportions.

He would fly personally to Salisbury to try to talk Ian Smith out of it, and he would like to take a letter written by the Queen in her own hand, indicating that her feelings were identical with those of her Prime Minister and that any unilateral action would certainly not have her approval. It didn't help much and Wilson was criticised for involving the Queen. Wilson went to Rhodesia on 31 October carrying the letter and returned empty-handed. Smith rejected the Wilson government's proposals for an amicable settlement, declared UDI on 11 November and, in spite of worldwide sanctions and embargoes, Rhodesia survived as an outlaw nation for the next eleven years.

Afterwards, the Queen became a target for protest in the black world. As she set off in February for a long-planned tour of the Caribbean, her VC-10 airliner was held up for more than an hour at Heathrow after a call from a woman who said a bomb had been placed on board the plane. Nothing was found. Then she flew into controversy with a Jamaica firmly behind its black brothers in Rhodesia and she was met by placard-carrying demonstrators who insisted 'Rhodesia Sold Out by Britain'. She found herself confronting rows of glum faces as she read at the opening of the Jamaican Parliament the admonitory words written by her local Prime Minister, 'My Government in Jamaica deplores the actions of governments which deny the fundamental principles of human rights. It supports measures which may be used to put an end to the illegal government in Rhodesia.'

Ironically, the next port of call in the Caribbean was the Bahamas, where a white minority government ruled over an impoverished black colony. And straight from the black political stronghold, she had to temper her speeches at a reception by officials of the United Bahamian Party which had been kept in power by corrupt gerrymandering for years. Especially dubious was a new regime on the island of Grand Bahama where the new town of Freeport had been built on Crown land sold to private enterprise for £1 an acre – later being resold at 100 and then 1,000 times that figure which did little good for the native population, and was then run very much like the South African segregationalist towns. The author was working in the Bahamas at the time, and met a young black lawyer named Lynden Pindling who was protesting about corruption and the infiltration of numerous well-known figures of the American organised crime syndicates whom the author was investigating for *Life* magazine. As I gathered my material, eventually published in a major twelve-page article in *Life*, Pindling sent a letter to the Queen pleading for a Royal Commission of inquiry; he went to the United Nations and to Westminster and finally, at the end of 1966, forced a general election and became the first black premier since the Bahamas became a British colony. He went on to become the Queen's longest-serving Commonwealth prime minister, though unfortunately he did not manage to eliminate corruption.

So, there it was; the sun was setting on the last outposts of the empire and in the satirical, sarcastic and cynical Britain of the swinging sixties, no institution was safe from ridicule – least of all the monarchy, as the Queen's son and heir would discover quite soon. He was eighteen on 14 November. The question of his future, the final stages of his training for the task that lay ahead at some unknown point, was under discussion; the Queen was ready to involve others in the final choice. She had given a small dinner party at Buckingham Palace for the specific purpose of discussing it. Those invited were the Prime Minister, Harold Wilson, Earl Mountbatten as representative of the heads of all the defence services (and in a personal capacity as what he described as honorary grandfather to Charles), the Archbishop of Canterbury, the Dean of Windsor, Sir Charles Wilson, chairman of the committee of vice-chancellors, and Sir Michael Adeane. The views were so diverse as to his next move that the Queen invited them to form a committee with Sir Michael Adeane acting as secretary. To the outsider, this might have seemed like taking a sledgehammer to crack a nut – no offence intended – but at least it displayed the Queen as intent on giving the future King a suitable education, which no other monarch in history had received. A university education was something of a new custom in the royal family. Edward VII went to three, but was never permitted to indulge in undergraduate life, nor sit any examinations. Edward VIII had spent time at Oxford and Dartmouth Naval College while George VI had gone from palace schoolroom to the navy and then Cambridge. Prince Philip had gone straight from Gordonstoun to Dartmouth and, as he was ever ready to remind anyone who was interested, the lack of a degree never did him any harm. The committee met on a number of occasions, and finally recommended Trinity College Cambridge, after the Dean of Windsor had interviewed a number of heads of colleges and tested their views with some 'pretty searching questions'. Thereafter, Charles would take a naval course for a commission. In the end, they settled on virtually the route suggested by Mountbatten in the first place: 'Trinity, like his grandfather, Dartmouth like his father and grandfather and then to sea', to which Prince Philip merely added that there should be 'no absolute need for him to take a degree'.[17]

In the sardonic new world in which the National Anthem was no longer being played in cinemas so that audiences did not injure themselves in the rush to get out before it began, it seemed to be asking for trouble to expect the young man to take a university place under such circumstances. That, on top of the news that at eighteen, under his rights of heirdom to the estate of the Duchy of Cornwall, his income would be increased from the present £10,000 per annum to £30,000, might have been just too much for his campus colleagues to bear.

Chapter Ten

New Beginnings (1967–9)

The new year began badly, with a mass of messy press headlines about the Queen's cousin the Earl of Harewood who was then forty-three and being sued for divorce. The dreaded word, leading to the family upheaval that the Queen feared most, was about to become a reality. The scandal, for that is how it was certainly portrayed even in the 'swinging' sixties, mainly because he was who he was, had been bubbling just below the surface for some time and demonstrated how, as the central cog to the entire family around which all others circulated, the Queen had to be drawn into a situation she could not control whether she liked it or not. In this case, she certainly did not, especially as it would be she who, as a matter of course, would have to consult with her Prime Minister and the Church over the problem, and then finally commit herself to either giving consent or not. Lord Harewood was the elder son of the recently deceased Mary, Princess Royal, George V's only daughter. Like Princess Margaret, Lord Harewood, a charming man and an 'absolute gentleman',[1] mixed in artistic circles and had a great personal interest in music; in the course of his pursuit of this interest he met Miss Patricia Tuckwell, a former violinist with the Sydney Symphony Orchestra and sister of the famous horn player and conductor Barry Tuckwell. She was also a one-time fashion model during her marriage to an Australian photographer, with whom she had a son. Lord Harewood first met her in Milan in 1959 and their initial friendship soon blossomed into a full-blown affair. Miss Tuckwell was eventually installed in a house in St John's Wood, London, not fifteen minutes drive from the Harewoods' London home in Orme Square, Bayswater.

On 5 July 1964 Miss Tuckwell gave birth to the earl's illegitimate son, and since the youngster carried royal blood and his arrival on this earth would at some time or other become known, the earl obviously had to inform his family, and the Queen, of this new and unexpected twig to the tree. The sad irony was that the Princess Royal had been as firm as anyone in maintaining the rejection of her sister-in-law, the Duchess of Windsor. A few months before her death, she found herself signifying the same kind of disapproval of her son's tangled love life as her mother Queen Mary had faced over Edward VIII's, and indeed might well have been reminded of her mother's famous comment to Prime Minister Stanley Baldwin in 1936, describing Edward's romance as 'this pretty kettle of fish'.

In Harewood's case, the Princess Royal is said to have been so overcome with this news that she dropped down dead. For the royal family as a whole, however, the affair could not simply be brushed aside. The implications as far as the Queen was concerned – once again bringing in her position in the Church, and the requirement of the Royal Marriages Act – were made out to be considerable, and at the time they were. She called the Earl and Countess Harewood to her side but the countess, who got on well with the Queen and was shown considerable sympathy, was quite naturally rather offended by her husband's infidelity and there seemed no possibility of a reconciliation, even if it meant that the break-up of their marriage became publicly damaging to the monarchy.

It was pointed out that there had been no divorce at the heart of the British royal family since Henry VIII ended his marriage to his first wife Catherine of Aragon so that he could marry Anne Boleyn, which led to the rupture between the Church of England and Rome, and the fall of Cardinal Thomas Wolsey. At the King's behest, Parliament passed the changes which made him supreme head of the Church; thereafter, of course, Henry found that having them beheaded was a less troublesome way of disposing of unwanted wives. Although King George IV was married twice, the marriage to Mrs Fitzherbert was adjudged illegal and thus did not count, and though he was separated from Queen Caroline for twenty-five years before her death they were never divorced. There had been no other divorces connected with the family, apart from Queen Victoria's granddaughter Marie Louise of Schleswig-Holstein from Prince Aribert of Anhalt in 1900, but that was not a British divorce. Case histories were rather hypocritical, anyway, when the various affairs and marriages and illegitimate children of George III's sons were taken into account, not to mention Edward VII's famous dalliances. But these instances could not be used as precedent because no actual divorce was enacted; it was principle and the family's position within the Church, more than anything else, that mattered.

After being assured by the Harewoods that there was no alternative to divorce which even the earl himself 'initially looked upon with horror',[2] the Queen then had to decide whether she would give her consent to divorce and his remarriage. She could have withheld it, but under the Royal Marriages Act Harewood need only have waited a year before being able to inform the Privy Council of his intentions, and proceed. The Queen decided to allow the remarriage to go ahead and had to engage in various negotiations to complete the required formalities as they involved her. For this, she sought the advice of her Prime Minister, Harold Wilson, who promised that, as far as he was concerned, he could not envisage any problems other than the untoward publicity; the earl was only seventeenth in line to the throne, as compared to Princess Margaret being third when she wanted to marry Townsend and, anyway, public opinion had moved further down the road of acceptance. He would attempt to minimise the Queen's position as far as he was able. He then threw the task to his friend Arnold Goodman, the eminent lawyer who was made a life peer in 1965, asking him to produce a formula. Goodman's suggestion was the one adopted by Wilson for the record, that 'The Cabinet have advised the Queen to give her consent . . .' And so in the end, there was nothing the Queen could do to save the situation, except warn Sir Michael Adeane and press secretary Commander Colville to stand by for a barrage of press inquiries, since the newspapers were already known to be aware of the story and would undoubtedly respond with all due shock, horror and voyeurism when the divorce suit was filed on 3 January 1967. Lord Harewood issued a statement through his solicitors stating:

> Lady Harewood petitions for divorce on the grounds of her husband's adultery with Miss Patricia Tuckwell . . . Lord Harewood will not defend these proceedings and he and Miss Tuckwell would wish to marry if and when they are legally free to do so. Lord Harewood has lived separately from Lady Harewood for the last sixteen months at his house in St John's Wood. A son, Mark, was born there to Miss Tuckwell in July 1964, of whom Lord Harewood is the father.

So that was that. The divorce was granted in April and then Lord Harewood applied to the Queen as he was required to under the Royal Marriages Act, for permission to marry Miss Tuckwell. This she granted in July on condition that the wedding did not take place in England, and on the 31st of the month, Miss Tuckwell became the new Countess of Harewood in an out-of-the-way ceremony performed by a judge in Connecticut.*

What was perhaps lost in the welter of publicity that surrounded the Harewood marital collapse was the fact that a new precedent had been set and that divorce, though undesirable, was now possible within the royal family, and that was not merely a considerable step, but an important one for the future. It was unknown at the time, but the Harewood divorce became the written-down formula to chart the choppy seas of matrimony for both the Queen's sister and, possibly, her own daughter. Harold Wilson had assessed that, though certain sections of the press might kick up a row, there would be no large-scale public reaction. It was interesting, however, that when Peregrine Worsthorne wrote an article

*Marion, Countess of Harewood, remarried, in March 1973, to Mr Jeremy Thorpe, leader of the Liberal Party until he resigned on 10 May 1976, ahead of charges accusing him of conspiring to murder his former friend, the male model Norman Scott, of which he was eventually cleared.

for the *Sunday Telegraph* in the first week of the new year, effectively saying that in this new permissive society, divorce by a member of the Queen's family could hardly be taken as a threat to the security of the throne, the newspaper was inundated with letters from angry readers. The following week, the paper was forced to concede that perhaps 'Mr Worsthorne may have over-estimated the size of the "permissive" section of society'.[3] Yet the article posed a very valid point: whether the public had the right to exact from every member of the royal family the observance of standards and morals which it was manifestly unwilling to impose upon itself.

More immediately, the effect of the divorce was to neutralise to some degree the royal family's exclusion of the Duchess of Windsor from the family circle. The Queen seemed to have this in mind when she began drawing up a list of those to be invited to the unveiling of a plaque in memorial to Queen Mary, provisionally set for the end of May. 'I'm asking Uncle David to come,' the Queen told Mountbatten, and she added, 'Of course, he must bring his wife.'[4]

The Windsors received notification in March. 'Ha!' said the duke with apparent glee, yet with a touch of sarcasm which might have been expected, inasmuch as this was the first time ever that they had received a joint invitation to any family gathering and the first time they would be seen together at any public ceremony. 'Darling, you've been invited to meet the family at last. What d'you think of that!'[5] It was ironic too, that this first acknowledgement of the existence of the Duchess of Windsor was made for a memorial to Queen Mary, the woman who had so effectively maintained the vendetta against her daughter-in-law – for vendetta it was, and met with reciprocal feeling. For whatever reason, the Windsors decided they could not attend on that date; they apologised and said that they would be in New York for a pre-arranged engagement though this seemed a rather weak excuse in view of the importance to the family of the occasion. Under normal circumstances, the Queen would have accepted the refusal without comment. This time, however, it appears she genuinely wanted to make sure that Uncle David would attend, and bring his wife. And so the date was altered to suit the Windsors and set for 7 June 1967.

The Windsors arrived from New York on 5 June aboard the liner *United States*, on which they now preferred to travel. Wallis would not fly unless there was really no alternative, and the duke liked the liner because it held the blue riband for crossing the Atlantic in three days, ten hours and forty minutes. Mountbatten was waiting at Southampton to meet them as the Queen's official representative and went aboard as soon as she was alongside.*

Mountbatten drove them to his own home, Broadlands, where they stayed the night before travelling on to London the next day. It is not known whether or not they were invited to stay at Buckingham Palace; it appears not because they checked in immediately to Claridges and stayed there for the duration. The following morning, on the day of the ceremony, a small crowd had gathered outside of the hotel and cheered as the duke and duchess left for Marlborough House, Queen Mary's home for so many years, where the Queen was to unveil a plaque set in the wall in what was basically a family ceremony, though watched by a crowd of some 4,000. Every member of the royal family was to be present, with the exception of Princess Margaret and Princess Alexandra who both had prior engagements which they were unable to cancel. Lord Harewood was there alone, and on his arrival the Windsors noticeably went over and the two men shook hands. Harewood's brother, the Hon. Gerald Lascelles, was also there and was able to chat to Windsor about Fort Belvedere, the duke's first home which remained unoccupied for many years. Lascelles now lived there with his wife, the former actress Angela Dowding; incidentally, they were also heading for a marriage split. They were divorced ten years later.

The family chatted and waited and the air of expectancy

*Another echo: the last time they were on board a ship together was aboard Mountbatten's destroyer at Cherbourg where he had been sent to bring the Windsors home to England at the start of the war. They came aboard in high spirits with all their luggage and mistakenly thought they were going back to England for good. In fact, Windsor was furious when told that it would be preferred if they returned to Paris where he was to serve as a liaison officer with the British Military Mission.

was apparent as the Queen Mother arrived in her Rolls Royce to a cheer. The moment of reconciliation was upon them, and as she proceeded towards them, the duke nervously fiddled with his cuffs. He offered his hand and bowed; the Queen Mother leant forward enabling him to kiss her cheek. 'David,' she said, 'so nice to see you again.' Wallis was smiling and eyeing her sister-in-law's familiarly extravagant hat, with lace flowers and cherries, and her flimsy dress and lace overcoat about which Wallis joked to her friends when they returned to Paris. Wallis held out her hand and the Queen Mother took the tips of her fingers into hers, the signal at which the recipient is expected to curtsy. Wallis did not and the dozens of photographers whose editors had been instructed to 'capture the moment' were to be disappointed. There was no curtsy, just a few brief words as the Queen Mother moved along the line. The great moment passed quickly and Wallis would curtsy only to the Queen. The years of bitterness did not melt easily; if the Queen Mother, on the one hand, blamed Wallis Simpson for so much and especially, it was always said, for the early death of her husband, Wallis retorted privately to her friends, 'Without me she would have been nothing. She became Queen because of me, she became famous and popular, she has become the royal matriarch – I did that for her. And I certainly was not going to curtsy to her.'[6]

After the plaque had been unveiled the Queen and the Queen Mother chatted for some minutes to members of their family. There was a brief and seemingly light-hearted rejoinder to the Windsors and then they all prepared to leave. The Queen and Prince Philip and the Queen Mother were all off to the races; it was Derby Day, the great royal spectacular at Epsom. Was it possible that they had invited the Windsors to join them at this traditionally royal occasion? 'No,' said a Buckingham Palace spokesman. 'They have not been invited.'[7] Instead, the duke and duchess joined Princess Marina for lunch at Kensington Palace and in the afternoon they returned to Paris, half wishing they hadn't bothered to come. It was only partial acceptance back into the family, though to senior courtiers at Buckingham Palace it did not amount even to that; in the following day's newspapers the Court Circular published in *The Times* and the *Daily Telegraph* listed all of the royal dukes and duchesses present at the ceremony – except the Windsors. They were not even mentioned. Observers could only speculate that the causes of this vindictiveness must have been severe indeed for it to continue so obviously without either side being able heartily and publicly to bury their difference in a warm, familial manner instead of the rather restrained way demonstrated that day. However, privately it did signal more frequent contact between them and the younger royals, especially, and after their return to Paris, the Windsors began to receive regular visits from the Kents.

Canada was playing up again or at least the separatists were and the Queen was brought back into the world spotlight with threats against her safety during her forthcoming visit. General de Gaulle, who put the boot in a third time and voted *Non* to Harold Wilson's latest application to join the Common Market, intermittently fanned the flames of discontent in the Commonwealth by declaring that Quebec should control its own destiny, that Canada owed its origins to France and that it had suffered a 'century of oppression which followed the British conquest'.[8] These carefully chosen words were released to coincide with the centenary celebrations of the Canadian Confederation to which the Queen had naturally been invited and, once again disregarding the threats, she set off to Canada, though her schedule was pruned to avoid upsetting the French community; she was taken in and out of Montreal virtually by the back door and ordinary members of the public were not allowed into the Expo 67 exhibition area she was visiting until after she had left, which rather ruined the purpose of the visit. However, outside of Montreal, Canada gave her a rousing welcome, as ever, and her visit was billed as a very great personal triumph in the face of indifference. It was insufficient, however, to prevent some authoritative sections of the Canadian press suggesting that this might well be the last visit the Queen would make as Queen of Canada.

Obviously, the Canadian troubles, along with Rhodesia's illegal regime, the looming civil war in Nigeria and Harold Wilson's aspirations towards Europe had become a regular topic for discussion over the breakfast table at Buckingham

Palace, where not for the first time Prince Philip's views differed from those of the Queen. She still staunchly supported her Commonwealth family which she wanted to see grow further, in spite of all of its problems. Philip, who, it will be recalled, sailed around the world in 1956 as his personal contribution to the Commonwealth ideal, was remarkably, and perhaps unwisely, frank in his answers to some probing questions posed by the newly de-nobled Tony Benn, MP over lunch one day.

He was asked what his thoughts were on how the monarchy would work over the next twenty-five years. 'His answers were rather interesting,' Benn recalled. Philip said the first thing to be done was to get rid entirely of the 'Commonwealth angle . . . they (Canada) don't want us and they will have to have a republic or something'. He also wanted to connect the monarchy more directly to government, disposing of the Privy Council which he thought was 'an absolute waste of time' and extending the Prime Minister's audience with the Queen to include ministers 'who could explain things to her'. The monarchy appealed to certain sections, such the people in the East End of London where they 'still wave their little flags and are very keen on the monarchy'. But he admitted that when people got cars and became a bit more middle-class, they were not interested in or didn't want to show their affection for the monarchy. He made the remarkable suggestion that the Ombudsman who dealt with public complaints against officialdom should be placed within the royal household in order to make the monarchy seem closer to the people and represent the nation. Benn told him he thought the idea was 'nonsense', though later when reflecting on the conversation he admitted that the prince was a thoughtful and intelligent person, even 'if he did sound like a Tory MP'.[9]

The point is that Benn's conversation coming as it did before the Queen paid her visit to Canada that year demonstrated the continual thought and reappraisal that the Queen and Prince Philip gave to their position in British and Commonwealth life, their relationship with government and, above all, how the public saw them. Philip was always fearful that they would become, as he once put it, museum pieces and the time was right for another re-valuation of their lives and roles, especially now that there were more of them in the public eye with Charles about to be launched on to the public stage and Princess Anne not far behind him. It had been a decade since the last series of major changes following the attacks by Muggeridge, Osborne and Altrincham and another perhaps more drastic re-positioning of the family's public image was now necessary. The first clue to it went almost unnoticed but it was an important step.

That summer, the Queen gave personal permission for the *Observer* magazine to prepare a two-part article on her life and work which would be run in the autumn and she agreed to pose exclusively for photographs by David Montgomery. What the *Observer* wanted to do was to show the Queen in her relaxed off-duty moments, catching her laughing, resting, or at play with the family. When the article appeared, it was remarkable not especially for the words but for Montgomery's photographs which were dramatically different from any royal picture since the early days of Cecil Beaton. She was seen at her plainest, in cardigan and jumper, tartan skirt and heavy flat shoes. She wore virtually no make-up and minimal jewels. She was pictured out walking with the dogs, she was seen at a table doing the family jigsaw puzzle (there is always one on the go in each of their houses). But most striking of all, she was photographed sitting on the floor, resting against a sofa, with her two corgis apparently asleep at her feet, and in the background a tiny two bar electric fire glowing in the middle of a huge marble fireplace, towards which she was pointing her feet. And she had *no shoes on*. So there she was, sitting in front of a little electric fire, relaxing barefoot with her two favourite dogs – looking the picture of ordinariness. It would have been a charming study if it had not been too obviously posed, even down to the electric fire being switched on and clearly visible in the colour photograph.

The publication of these photographs did not raise too much comment but it marked the arrival first of a new phase in the way the Queen and her family should be presented and second of a startling new development in how the monarchy should actually attempt to harness the media more effectively to its own ends; and the clue to all of this lay buried in the *Observer* piece – it was the name of an assistant press secretary referred to rather familiarly for a palace spokesman as 'Bill' Heseltine. He had arrived at Buckingham Palace to understudy Commander Colville who was to retire in 1968, suitably rewarded with a knighthood. William Heseltine came highly recommended by the Queen's good friend and loyal devotee, Sir Robert Menzies, for whom he had worked as his private secretary. She first came across Heseltine in Australia, and remarked to Menzies that his new secretary seemed to 'find life a rich comedy'. Menzies took her aside and explained that the humour was something of a front. The man had just 'come through the darkest valley. The wife to whom he was devoted has recently died.' The Queen was impressed and sympathetic; not long afterwards, when there were discussions as to who should replace Colville, the Queen remembered Heseltine and very soon he was winging his way to London to begin a new life at Buckingham Palace, where he would remain for twenty years, become the Queen's most trusted adviser and retire with a knighthood.

In 1967, Heseltine brought with him some adventurous ideas which were music to the ears of Prince Philip, who had personally hired an American public relations man to massage his image prior to a visit to the United States in 1966. To Commander Richard Colville who had been sharpening pikestaffs to keep the media at bay these past two decades, the very thought of even cooperating with journalists, let alone actually persuading the Queen to pose in such a manner for photographs, was totally abhorrent. He believed that the day that monarchy needed a public relations department, the writing would be on the wall and the institution of monarchy would be in serious decline. The moment was almost upon them and the way in which the monarchy was about to be relaunched must have filled him with horror.

A number of things were happening which led the Queen to agreeing to plans to turn them all into film stars and finally break the mystique which Commander Colville had been trying to protect. First of all, Lord Mountbatten – having seen the film version of the Duke of Windsor's book, *A King's Story* – was now excitedly in the midst of having a film made about his own life. Lord Brabourne, his son-in-law, suggested it. Mountbatten wholeheartedly concurred and for two years had been engrossed in the making of his television biography, *The Life and Times of Lord Mountbatten*. He kept the royal family as a whole up to date with progress and would have the rushes of each section sent over to Buckingham Palace where they would all sit in the palace cinema to see the film of Uncle Dickie's latest interview.

Uncle Dickie and Prince Philip were completely taken by this medium as a way of reaching the people, though Philip thought it was killing the impact of the ceremonial. There were informal discussions with the Queen as to how it might be employed to launch Prince Charles in his new role as Prince of Wales come the investiture in 1969. The Queen was personally involved with every detail of what was viewed as a highly important event in the royal calendar, which would be only the second such ceremony in 300 years of monarchy. It was revived for Prince Edward in 1911 when Lloyd George, then Chancellor of the Exchequer and Constable of Caernarfon Castle, saw the occasion as an ideal opportunity to pander to Welsh national pride and win political support.[10]

The ceremony had to be virtually reinvented for the occasion and when Charles became Prince of Wales, it was necessary to amend it to modern-day requirements. The time of Edward's investiture also marked his progression into the world spotlight, as Lloyd George sent him off on the vast postwar tours of the Dominions which many felt had ruined him because he became intensely bored 'with all this princing'. When Charles adopted the role, there were high hopes that he would quickly reach the popular acclaim and esteem, and within the royal household it was *the* most important event to be focused upon. In early 1968 the Queen and Philip, through the new man William Heseltine, began to draw on the advice of a professional public relations consultant to 'launch' their son into his new life. The first move had already been completed, which was to have an authorised biography of Prince Charles published. Dermot Morrah, the author and journalist who was also the Queen's Arundel Herald appointed to serve her on state occasions, was commissioned to write 'the first authentic description of the upbringing of a future King of Great Britain and Head of the Commonwealth . . . a privileged account written with the approval of H.M. The Queen'.[11] It was entitled *To Be a King*, though naturally its pages were thinly spread with events since the story, for the purposes of the book, stopped when he reached the age of eighteen.

The publication of the book also marked the moment when the PR man entered the scenario: Nigel Neilson, who ran a firm called Neilson McCarthy Ltd, which represented a select band of international figures. Neilson was a former wartime colleague of David Checketts, Prince Charles's new young equerry who was by his side through his year in Australia, and through him, Neilson pointed out to the palace that Prince Charles was an excellent young man – 'a first-class product being criminally undersold . . . there's been far too much in the press about him being a chinless wonder and about his ears'.[12] In consultation with William Heseltine, it was agreed that Checketts should nominally enlist Neilson's aid, in spite of the protests from the more staid factions at the palace who moaned that their young prince was being classed as a 'product and sold like a tin of baked beans'. The Queen's son and heir was going to be given a solid grounding in public relations, and thorough rehearsal for the years that lay ahead in his speech-making and relationships with the press, though all the rehearsals in the world could not prepare him for the ambush that lay waiting from the latter. He was given mock interviews, sometimes roughly handled, all of which were taped and played back. He made mock speeches which were filmed and analysed; Neilson even arranged gatherings at his own flat which were to be attended by leading bankers and industrialists for 'discussions', often ending up with a sing-song around Neilson's piano, all aimed at strengthening the young prince's public performance. Neilson made himself available to the palace through Checketts to give advice and to reshape the whole approach of the royal family in their relationships with the press, even down to suggesting to Fleet Street that newspapers might like to consider appointing royal correspondents who could travel regularly on the tours of various members of the family. Discussions of press 'management' and 'cooperation' became commonplace, though all were held discreetly out of earshot of the Queen, to whom the eventual proposals would be finally submitted; she wanted to know every detail.

In the midst of this activity, Commander Colville retired

in February 1968 having made one final pronouncement on what was happening to the family he had served for so long; 'Royal lives have been progressively more exposed to public scrutiny and there is now a constant conflict of what may be termed in the public interest and what is private.'[13] As Colville despaired about the ever-increasing press coverage given to the trivia of royalty, and ignoring the constitutional and ceremonial and day-to-day workings, it was perhaps ironic that there were already moves in the background to break down the final barriers between public and monarchy. During the discussions over the launching of Prince Charles, it had been suggested that a filmed biography should be made to be shown on television, much like the Mountbatten 'life and times', but it soon became clear that there would be insufficient material to sustain such a programme; eventually from these initial ideas came the dramatic proposal to put the entire royal family on film – and call it just that, *Royal Family*.

Doubts were cast and everyone wondered whether it was the right move. Never in history had the monarch been heard talking 'normally' by anyone outside the royal circle, other than an official speech. Never had the royals been seen on film behaving like normal, ordinary people. In a recent television film based on the Queen's art possessions, not a moving soul was allowed to interrupt the landscapes or still life of the filmography. In all news events, for example, the microphones were kept well away from any member of the family – and still are – lest any accidental indiscretion be picked up, and certainly no cameras had ever been allowed more than the briefest glance at the royals *en masse*, off duty. There were great taboos about breaking the mystique, almost as if it were a superstition among the family that, once broken, they would all vanish. It hardly seemed feasible that a film crew of nine or ten men and women clad in their working uniform of jeans and sweaters would be allowed to follow them around the world, filming at the great state occasions, peering through lenses while the Queen worked at her desk and, briefly, recording her audience with Harold Wilson.

The Queen received the proposals with some caution and eventually met the man who would be in charge of the production, the BBC's Richard Cawston who was an expert in new techniques of cinema verité and hand-held 16 mm cameras most suitable for documentaries. She liked him, and they all came to trust him because the Queen agreed to give the film the go-ahead on condition that they could have sight of it before its final appearance. For the next twelve months, he followed the Queen and other members of the family around, through personal and private lives, through state functions and visits and through the ceremonial. Viewers saw a royal barbecue, with Philip cooking the steaks and sausages, a ballroom buffet for British Olympic athletes who included, incidentally, a young soldier named Lieutenant Mark Phillips. The final edited version ran for 105 minutes and the Queen and her family were given a private showing; she asked for no cuts to be made. Stills were passed out to the press, concentrating on the happy families' sequences and critical acclaim was lavished upon the film when it was premiered by the BBC. It was, everyone agreed, a milestone both in television broadcasting and royal history.

The film was finally shown a week before Prince Charles's investiture as Prince of Wales, around which so much planning centred and so much royal impetus had been built up, not merely for the projection of this event in terms of its constitutional function to launch the future king but also in its importance to the family itself. The television documentary, to which 23 million viewers sat glued in the first showing in Britain alone, presented the Queen and her family in an entirely new light, bringing the people into the parlour, as it were, to see them at first hand, talking and chatting and enjoying family occasions as well as the more formal events with which the public were more familiar.

Harold Wilson, whose fortunes and those of his party were slipping in those years of renewed financial crises, mounting unemployment and industrial strife, had already seen the possibilities of turning the spectacle of the investiture to his own advantage, just as Lloyd George had done fifty-eight years earlier with the last Prince of Wales. Indeed, he was as keen as any one to use the monarchy to further the aims of either the government or the country, as when in November 1968 the Queen went to South America to become the first monarch to visit Brazil and Chile, where not by mere chance a British trade delegation led by Lord Chalfont was trying to sell the nation's wares and the Queen was able to offer the hospitality of the royal yacht *Britannia* which had sailed ahead for the purpose.

Politically, Wilson's plight was far more desperate than the political scene of 1911 when the last Prince of Wales was installed and it seemed that he was prepared to clutch at any straw that would enhance his own and the government's standing. The power of monarchy could be tapped and the historian A. J. P. Taylor and the veteran politician Lord Butler were among those who were critical of Wilson's attempts to use the prince's investiture ceremony for political advantage.

Oddly enough, one of the threats to Wilson's personal position had recently involved Lord Mountbatten and, by association, the Queen herself. According to Harold Wilson's secretary Marcia Williams, Mountbatten was a 'prime mover' in a plot involving Cecil King, head of the Mirror Group, to oust Wilson and replace him with a national government, by military coup if necessary.[14] Cecil King gave this recollection of the highly disputed chronology of events:

> I had a message that Lord Mountbatten wanted to see Hugh Cudlipp and myself at his private flat and we got there having no idea what he wanted to see us about. Presently Sir Solly [later Lord] Zuckerman arrived. In the course of the discussion, Lord Mountbatten said the Queen had received more letters of complaint about the Government than any monarch ever before. She was worried by this because the letters had to be handed by protocol to the Home Secretary. The Queen was very disturbed by these letters and it was natural she should consult Lord Mountbatten. Obviously the Home Secretary was a member of the Government complained of and that wasn't very satisfactory – and he was wondering whether there was anything he should do. In my opinion, I think he was referring to making a critical speech in the House of Lords. I certainly dispute the idea that he was referring to anything like a military coup. I told him he should keep his hands clean and there might

> come a time when his position in the royal family and in the armed forces could make his intervention important.[15]

According to Hugh (later Lord) Cudlipp, King asked Mountbatten if he would be prepared to take over as head of government once Wilson was ousted. The conversation appears to have centred around the scenario of the collapse of the government, armed intervention, bloodshed on the streets and a rally of loyalty around the Queen. At this point, Sir Solly Zuckerman who was Wilson's chief scientific adviser stormed out of the meeting, 'The conversation was outrageous,' he said later. King, then a powerful voice in the land – or at least, he thought he was – through the medium of the *Daily Mirror*, where the author was one of his underlings, later maintained that Mountbatten indicated the 'great anxiety felt by the Queen at the parlous state of the nation . . . and said nothing to indicate that he would find the role unattractive'.[16] Mountbatten, though not entirely against the principle of a national government, was against the suggested means. Cecil King's colleagues at the *Mirror* felt his judgement and discretion had finally deserted him when two days after the meeting with Mountbatten, he ran the now famous leading article on the front page of the *Daily Mirror* under the headline 'Enough Is Enough'. The article suggested that Britain needed a new Prime Minister and the Labour Party a new leader. It claimed that Britain was threatened with 'the greatest financial crisis in our history . . . it is not to be removed by lies . . . but only a fresh start under a new leader'.[17] It was enough, for the Mirror group. King was sacked. What remained something of a mystery in the aftermath, however, was Mountbatten's own continued canvassing of opinions and soundings in Whitehall. Military commanders were apparently talking openly of the possibility of a 'coup' which some sources say emanated from Mountbatten's conversations. Sir Martin Furnival Jones, head of MI5, revealed to the *Sunday Times* that he carried out an investigation of such a plot in 1968 and reported his finding to the Home Secretary James Callaghan.

The Cecil King attack on Wilson, which he tried to revive eighteen months later, and which incidentally found favour with Harold Macmillan, faded into the past having further aided the decline of the pound in the process. The prospect of having the Queen and Uncle Dickie running the country in a monarchical-political alliance was never really a starter, but it made good copy when hints of it leaked out.

And presumably unaware of these noises off that could well have reshaped his entire future if they had come to anything, Prince Charles set forth on his ceremonial adventure to become the Prince of Wales. It was a day of pageantry and ritual for which the Duke of Norfolk, in his usual role as the Queen's Earl Marshal, had been preparing for almost a year. Half a million people thronged the streets of Caernarfon to see the procession and the presentation, with millions more watching on television. There were explosions, flour bombs and egg-throwing incidents as the Welsh Nationalists protested at this 'ridiculous charade', although it later turned out that two men who were killed in an explosion of gelignite were actually trying to blow the safe of the local national insurance office at the time. Nationalistic protests were drowned out by the fanfare of trumpets from the ancient battlements and deafening roars from the crowds as Prince Charles appeared. It was another great royal spectacular, which the Post Office said was watched by some 500 million viewers around the world. *The Times*, in its front page report of the proceedings, carried one inexplicable little sentence at the end, stating 'In Paris, the Duke of Windsor, who is 75 watched the investiture on television'. The report failed to mention that the duke was the only other living soul in the last three hundred years for whom such a ceremony had been arranged. Given that kind of history, it was extremely odd that the royal family did not do all in their power to have him there; he was still able enough to get about and only a year earlier had travelled from Paris alone for the funeral of his sister-in-law Princess Marina who died on 27 August 1968 from a brain tumour, aged sixty-one. Wallis, on that occasion, had deliberately stayed away for the sake of everyone's grief; Marina was a deeply loved member of the family. The investiture was different. It was a family celebration that happens so infrequently that every living member of the family could be expected to attend. The

Windsors did not. In August 1968, the Queen wrote to the duke to confirm that both he and Wallis could be buried at the family plot at Frogmore and added that she had agreed that Wallis should receive an annual allowance of £5,000 upon the death of the duke.*

One way or another, 1969 had been quite a year. Philip spiced it up a little further. In November, he was interviewed on American television; it was one of the last major interviews on the topic of family matters he gave live on tube and it was not difficult to understand why; he was asked about stories that the royal family was spending more than its £475,000 annual Civil List allowance from the taxpayer. His response started a hue and cry over royal money that still hadn't died down twenty-two years later: 'We go into the red next year, which is not bad housekeeping if you come to think of it. We've kept the thing going on a budget which was based upon costs of eighteen years ago . . . it's beginning to have its effects. Now inevitably, if nothing happens we shall either have to – I don't know, we may have to move to smaller premises, who knows? We've closed, well, for instance we had a small yacht which we had to sell and I shall probably have to give up polo fairly soon . . .'

*This, it will be recalled, was in consideration of his life's interest in the royal estates at Balmoral and Sandringham which he inherited from his father, George V, and which passed to George VI on his abdication – thus cutting by half the amount already paid to him. Almost as an aside, she added that she had hesitated to inquire whether he would like an invitation to the investiture 'considering the circumstances' but she hoped he would consider this an invitation and she looked forward to his reply in due course. He replied that he did not feel that the presence of an aged old uncle would add much to the colourful proceedings, though his official biographer Philip Ziegler maintained that if the Duchess of Windsor had also been specifically mentioned in the invitation, he might well have accepted.[18] The same applied soon afterwards when there was another family 'do' to dedicate some new windows at St George's, Windsor. The duke again refused, with a little reminder that although the Queen had not mentioned Wallis by name in the invitation, he assumed she was also expected . . . 'You see, after thirty years of happy married life, I do not attend such occasions alone.'[19]

The last sentence was sufficient to send the opponents of royalty into uproarious anguish in which the favourite word of the republicans – 'parasites' – was used with a spitting rage which enveloped the left of the government benches. Several members of Wilson's Cabinet were furious too, because the Queen and Prince Philip knew that discussions had been going on between ministerial departments and Buckingham Palace for months over the possible upgrading of the Civil List. He was clearly playing devil's advocate; his notes were prepared, and his selection of the time and place of the revelation that the monarchy was in financial difficulty appeared to have been well thought out to achieve maximum impact. Barbara Castle, at that moment erring towards the side of republicanism, thought that the government could make political capital out of Philip's 'outrageous' speech by setting up a Select Committee to inquire into the Queen's private fortune.[20] Wilson, Callaghan, Brown and other loyalists in the Cabinet who were all devoted to the Queen and thought Prince Philip was a thoroughly decent chap, took a more moderate tone. Though Wilson conceded that 'only royalty' could assume that private wealth was meant to be kept and accumulated and that they need not spend on such matters as seeing them through their public life, he would not publicly go against Prince Philip. In the Commons that day he made a restrained 'statesmanlike speech' on the Queen's finances,[21] though Edward Heath, the Opposition leader, was lying in wait to stir up some traditional rousing debate. Wilson would not give in to demands for an immediate Select Committee, though more, much more, would be heard on the subject later . . .

Chapter Eleven

Walking About (1970–72)

The new warm and cosy view of the royal family, as portrayed in the BBC film, and followed through with the togetherness of the investiture, had just a touch of fantasy about it. It was not so much that they had overplayed the 'happy family' angle, because they were and are generally a very happy family group who would fight and squabble amongst themselves privately, just like any other, but who support each other through thick and thin when necessary. The fantasy lay in that, because they were all highly individualistic people, togetherness came in very small bites, never for long, never continuous. There was always, too, the underlying suspicion that they were all acting out their roles for the purpose of the audience, that some of the jokes with each other were just a little too contrived and after years of well-practised appearances as the 'performing monarchy' they were also in danger of allowing themselves to enter the realms of the somewhat theatrical 'performing family'. Because this kind of exposure was so new, it was a very pertinent question that the renowned critic Milton Shulman asked: 'Is it in the long run wise for the Queen's advisers to set as a precedent this right of the television camera to act as an image-making apparatus for the monarchy? Every institution that has so far attempted to use TV to popularise or aggrandise itself, has been trivialised by it.' The film's purpose in launching Prince Charles and helping the revitalisation of the Crown had been a tremendous success, so much so that the Prince of Wales's aide David Checketts had been allowed to remain in the consultative employment of the public relations company which had advised on his coming out, while still continuing his full-time job. The interplay between the PR people and the palace continued – as did the further adjustment of the royals' working procedures to keep up the image. The homely, family style that was so commented upon was one that the Queen liked and which Lord Mountbatten complimented everyone on achieving, especially Charles upon whom he doted. He regarded it as his remaining task in life to help mould and build the young man's character for whatever the future held in store. He did it with kindness and practical advice, which came as a pleasant change from the years of naval-style bullying Charles had received from his father whenever the job at hand was discussed. Timed to precision, pulled up on every count of error or misdemeanour by Philip, Charles found his long talks with Mountbatten spiritually refreshing and the Queen appreciated his need for such older, wiser counsel.

Mountbatten was as glowing in his praise of their collective recent efforts as they were of his film but he took care to warn Charles against believing that his personal popularity was unassailable, though that seemed unlikely to happen to the quiet modest chap who was about to embark on the next stage of his training for kingship, which was to be a spell in naval service. 'Study the life and times of the Duke of Windsor,' Mountbatten told him. 'And don't imagine that because, like him, you have become some sort of a pop idol the British people will always support you. They will back you as long as you serve the country and do the job.'[1] And since they were all continually concerned with how they were being viewed by the public at large, the same principle could be applied presumably to all royals, young or old, and might well have been burnt into pieces of old oak and hung in strategic places for future reminders to all and sundry. Glamour and a shallow image were never enough.

Just as the Queen found to her cost after the Coronation, flimsy and near-hysterical adulation is quickly tempered by criticism which degenerates into cheap sneers at the monarchy as a whole. Princess Margaret had developed a see-saw relationship with her public and the media. She had nothing to complain about, really, because even after her marriage to Lord Snowdon, she continued to be seen in a high social whirl and was associated very much with what had become known as her jet-set, flitting off here and there to pleasurable spots, being pictured on faraway sandy beaches or rich people's yachts and returning to fulfil just sufficient public duties to justify her £35,000 a year Civil List income from which she could buy her beloved high fashion. Snowdon, meanwhile, was caught up in the jetstream. They seemed to be having a good time and the public does not like to see the royals enjoying themselves too much. Similarly, Princess Anne had not made quite the impression that might have been expected in her first year of public appearances either, though it was one which old hands at the palace might have completely anticipated. At seventeen, she was known to be the wild one of the family; even at that age she was not averse to a swear word or three; her temper was brisk; she quite insisted on getting her own way, and more than once the Queen was heard to employ a jaundiced plea to one of her closest friends, that phrase well used by mothers everywhere, 'Can you do anything with her? I can't.' She was known among some of those members of staff closest to her as not Madam but The Madam. Princess Anne's engagement book was filling up, and when she was not out on a public duty, she was off somewhere riding or with her group of zestful friends, notably the handsome if slightly irresponsible Sandy Harpur, her most frequent escort who she hoped would very soon ask for her hand in marriage, which she wanted almost as much as she wanted to be an ace on horseback.

Charles, meantime, was preparing for entry into the navy, while Prince Philip was constantly on the move, accepting far more engagements than might really be necessary and was hardly ever at home. Andrew and Edward had ample nursery and tutorial staff to take care of their everyday needs and, thus, all of the above combined to make the 'togetherness' ideal something of a misnomer and it left the Queen quite often a rather lonely figure at the end of her constitutional day, in spite of all that was going on around her. The image conjured up was one of her often eating alone or getting the young sons down for company, or telephoning her mother and asking her if she would like to pop over for dinner. The Queen Mother, at seventy, remained as busy as anyone and used the helicopter almost as often as Prince Philip, and so on many nights, company was sparse or evaporated completely. The Queen was left alone, shoes kicked off and corgis lying around her feet or barking at the slightest sound – 'those damned dogs' as the servants would say – with her reduced to eating a meal on a tray while sitting and watching the television. Once upon a time, she would get Patrick Plunket, her childhood friend and riding companion who was like a brother to her, to take her to the pictures if Philip was away. She'd put on a headscarf and they'd go to one of the local cinemas and slip in after the lights went down. But that was no longer possible now.

The 'humanised' image portrayed in the film was all very well but there was a very strong lobby which maintained that it undermined the symbols of unity, authority and majesty which the monarchy was supposed to represent. As Sir David Attenborough pointed out, primitive cultures became troublesome once 'tribesmen broke the old taboos and peered at the tribal mysteries inside the headman's hut'.[2]

This had already happened, to a degree, among the Queen's wider family of nations who came under the umbrella of the British Crown. Macmillan's 'wind of change' had long ago become storm force, and blown in trouble aplenty as the void left by colonial and imperial rule was filled by nationalist leaders of a variety of persuasions. An update of the situation for 1970 reveals that many parts of her Commonwealth had become no-go areas as far as the Queen was concerned and past triumphant and glorious visits to these parts were moved to the back-burner and in some cases would never be repeated. Ghana was still dangerous, through coup and counter-coup. Nigeria had been torn apart for three years by the genocide and slaughters of the civil war and on 12 January the breakaway state of Biafra capitulated. Throughout the war, Britain's response, as a nation which had reaped such commercial rewards from Nigeria, was remarkably sterile, almost to the point of letting the battle rage until it had blown itself out. Richard Crossman in 1969 had made an impassioned speech in cabinet about 'the birth of a nation'[3] but it turned out to be more like the American civil war, when no new nation emerged. Meanwhile, Milton Obote had nationalised everything that moved in Uganda – including many British concerns – and this garden of Africa which the British had ruled for seventy years until granted independence within the Commonwealth, was enveloped by political turmoil and uncertainty.

Another leader, more murderous and dictatorial than any before him; in the huge form of Idi Amin, was waiting in the wings, poised to make his coup – which he launched, incidentally, while Obote was attending the next Commonwealth Conference, in Singapore. South Africa, where Nelson Mandela had already been in prison for six years, was running its apartheid policy with ruthless rigidity and the sporting world was ready to make the final break and isolate the nation from international events, led by the MCC who cancelled the England team's tour, due for the summer. In Kenya, where 35,000 Asians were being expelled, many to Britain, the January 1970 cricket tour by England was called off because of the unrest and ill-feeling against Britain. Rhodesia was still under the control of its illegal regime and, short of sending in an invasion force to fight what amounted to its own kith and kin, there seemed little Harold Wilson could do to stop Ian Smith proceeding with his plans to declare the country a republic which no longer recognised the Queen's authority as head of state, from March 1970. Elsewhere in the Commonwealth, India and Pakistan remained at loggerheads and there was constant talk of hostilities, while in Pakistan itself, British intelligence was predicting a powder-keg, a possible civil war as leaders in the eastern province – once part of British India – prepared to declare the independent state of Bangladesh. And Borg Olivier, Prime Minister of Malta which used to welcome the royal family with open arms, had not long ago invited the British to 'get out'.

So where could the Queen go for her travels round the world, by which successive governments, and the Queen herself, had set such score? Like his predecessors, Harold Wilson had been no less punctilious in submitting for royal approval all proposals concerning Commonwealth countries, whether it was for the long and complicated series of negotiations for independence that stretched from Ghana in

1957 through to the Seychelles in 1976, down to discussions of her visits to leading member countries. While the Queen had no power, nor the wish, to intervene in internal affairs of those countries, it was her right to be informed of developments and, if she so desired, give her views and advice. Until the Commonwealth became more settled she had to become something of an armchair viewer of Commonwealth affairs, except in the older, more settled Commonwealth states. Meantime, New Zealand and Australia, then Canada and the United States were again selected for the 1970 venues.

Princess Anne was to accompany her parents down under, where they would be joined later by Prince Charles to continue the projection of the family group which had been so well received when the film *Royal Family* was shown there. A remarkable new development was in the offing which represented the next stage of the readjustment of the presentation of the royal family to a public which was not wholly without cynicism towards the monarchy. The new press secretary William Heseltine had obviously been a major influence on the way the tour was to be planned; it broke with all previous tradition and style and became famous as the one on which the Queen's 'walkabouts' were introduced.

For the first time, she came down off the platforms and the Land Rovers and began walking amongst the crowds. It seemed a spontaneous act but Heseltine admitted, 'The criticism of previous trips had always been that the Queen was too controlled in whom she met – she was always disappearing into town halls with officials. We are doing our best to change that this time.'[4] What he was not admitting, though it was implicit, was that the new-look royal visits had been carefully planned to counteract a predicted upsurge in republicanism as Britain continued its efforts to join the Common Market. In fact, the tour managers had been warned that the Queen should be advised in advance of possible anti-monarchist demonstrations. She was met by a few, carrying posters with inscriptions such as 'The Monarchy Is A Joke'; the students carrying them were immediately set upon by a gang of middle-aged women wielding umbrellas.

The first of the walkabouts was in Wellington, New Zealand, where, following a drive to the town hall, the royal personalities split up and went separately along the lines of people whose hands were stretched forward in the hopes of touching them. The effect was stunning and television commentators went into raptures about it. The royals stopped and chatted, shook hands now and again, received flowers and gifts. Philip looked relaxed, as an experienced campaigner in crowds. The Queen seemed a little tense while Charles was positively apprehensive. Though well used to seeing crowds at a distance, from the balcony at Buckingham Palace or from the comparative safety of a carriage, he found the close-up force of such a mass of faces quite daunting. Princess Anne seemed to go through a mixture of emotions, finding the whole experience pleasurable until it became a bit of a bore; during these latter moments of set-jaw expressions and sharpness of tongue the Australian newspapers were quick to brand her not just the youngest member of the royal family to visit them but the rudest, too. The walkabouts came thick and fast when the party travelled across to Australia. A national opinion poll had been prepared to coincide with their arrival and it was not half as bad as local pundits had been predicting. Amongst young people, 47 per cent were in favour of becoming a republic and dispensing with Elizabeth as Australia's Queen. Across all age groups, a mere 25 per cent went for abolition of the monarchy. And so with that vote of confidence, the Queen continued on her way, giving the security men a headache.

One aspect of the walkabouts that Heseltine had not taken into account was the crowd surges when the Queen came towards them; in Melbourne two people, a girl of seventeen and a man of thirty-five, died in the crush. The Queen later sent messages of sympathy to the relatives. However, in spite of the tragedy the tour had been the success that Heseltine and his employer had been hoping for and no better expressed than in the *Sydney Sunday Telegraph*: '. . . it has surprised the optimists and staggered the pessimists. No more will they appear remote figures removed from reality . . . they have been seen as warm and human . . . and intensely interested in and proud of Australia.'[5]

At the start of the tour, there was a sudden burst of contact between America and England, where the Queen Mother was left minding the shop, as a Counsellor of State for the nine weeks the Queen was away from home. The White House was in a flap. President Nixon had invited the Duke and Duchess of Windsor to dinner. The gala, in the duke's honour and planned for 4 April, was to be attended by more than a hundred guests for whom Mrs Pat Nixon had laid on a menu of Le Saumon Froid Windsor and Le Soufflé Duchess; it was all going to be sickeningly patronising. Anyway, when London heard about this, a 'flurry of telegrams'[6] surged forth instructing the British ambassador John Freeman to advise the Nixons that under no circumstances was the Duchess of Windsor to be addressed as Your Royal Highness, nor were the women amongst the guests to curtsy. In the White House Archives and embassies around the world where the duke and duchess had visited, there were similar memos dating back to the early 1940s. It did seem, that barely two months before the duke's seventy-sixth birthday, that the ruling expressly forbidding the use of the royal prefix for the duchess – first laid down by George VI and published in the *London Gazette* in June 1937 – might now be relaxed, ignored, or not pursued; it was not. Exactly who gave the order in London is not clear. It could have come directly from the Queen Mother; it could have come from the Queen to whom such matters would normally be referred.

Whoever it was, the deed was done and the ruling made, much to the embarrassment of the British officials who were expected to adopt the customary icy reception towards the duke and duchess in the face of American society – presumably to make the point that the ex-king's wife had not been forgiven even though most had forgotten what her crime had been. It was a pathetic sight, even to those who had no special love for the Windsors. Catherine Freeman said, 'Well, I curtsied anyway – and I called the duchess Your Royal Highness.'[7] She probably made history by becoming the first ever British ambassadorial wife to use the title. The duke, a frail and sick man barely capable of walking without assistance, noticed it instantly and was clearly delighted. President Nixon, carefully picking his way through the protocol, bearing in mind that he was to entertain the Queen and Philip later in the year, and make a reciprocal visit to London, toasted the duke in champagne and said nice things.

The duke responded and retold the love story: '. . . the good fortune to have had a wonderful American girl consent to marry me and have thirty years of loving care and devotion and companionship – something I have cherished above all else.' There were those in the audience who knew them well, and also knew that while the duke had remained deeply in love with Wallis, she had been shrewish and domineering for thirty years, although she had doubtless grown to love him which, according to Lady Alexandra Metcalfe, she did not on her wedding day.[8] Anyhow, the Nixons were gushing, everyone wanted to get close and be nice. There was something special about them as international celebrities, aged and lined though they were. And every time a British official was instructed by Buckingham Palace to cut the duchess, the question was asked, as it had been over and over, year after year in the past, and was unanswered once more: 'What was it they were guilty of that inspired such bitterness still, after all these years?'

The glowing press coverage of the duke and duchess in Washington was not enjoyed by the mainstream family, soon afterwards. The Queen, Prince Philip, Prince Charles and Princess Anne arrived for a 3 day visit at the end of a 10 day tour of Canada; reaction was mixed, largely because of Princess Anne's attitude to the pressing and demanding American media, whom she had never previously experienced. Coming as it did so soon after the nine weeks of touring the other side of the world – albeit with relaxation on the royal yacht *Britannia* in between – the princess looked tired and fed up, unlike the experienced Queen who was well used to the pressure and, as the American press reported, looked fresh and cheerful. Anne got it in the neck and for several days during and after their visit, she suffered the most vitriolic attack ever mounted against a member of the British royal family abroad. The *Washington Daily News* described her as 'snobbish, pouting, bored, sullen and disdainful' and Anne cried when she saw it. Her mother told her not to worry; she would experience much worse than that in her life, that was for sure, and in that prediction the Queen was entirely correct. Another writer suggested Anne should be 'limited to opening rhododendron shows in Kent' and never be unleashed on foreigners again. Anne was particularly moody in Washington because, following the quick and hard tour of Canada where there were more walkabouts, she was hoping for some fun on her first visit to the USA. None of this was permitted by American security who had thrown the proverbial ring of steel around the royals on Nixon's explicit instructions following the huge demonstrations in Washington recently triggered by the American invasion of Cambodia. The British Queen, seen by some as the epitome and symbol of imperialism, might well be a target. Thus, Anne and Charles were not permitted their interludes of socialising and Anne, especially, was very fed up. She wanted to be out of it all, and all the press people – 'There are twenty million reporters on my heels,' she screamed. It was a slight exaggeration, but it demonstrated her frustration. By the time they returned home, the British papers were also full of 'Anne's Antics' and 'What a spoiled brat'.

On the home front, the Queen received her new Prime Minister – the first Conservative Party leader in her reign whom she had not had to use her prerogative to appoint. Elected as party leader by a system of voting – much maligned as it was – and chosen democratically by the nation in a snap general election called by Harold Wilson, Edward Heath was also the first Conservative leader classed as a 'grammar school boy', going against the normal trend of leaders with roots in the public school system. Wilson, incidentally, was shocked by the outcome, as indeed were many of his colleagues who had been much heartened by the 4 per cent lead which Labour had in a pre-election Harris poll. The changeover came later in the day. The Queen had previously arranged to spend the day at the races; it was Ascot week and her private secretary contacted No. 10 Downing Street to delay Wilson's arrival. He went to Buckingham Palace at 6.30 p.m. several hours after conceding defeat, and handed in his resignation. The Queen was honestly sympathetic that he had lost. She was already well acquainted with Mr Heath, in his role for the past five years as leader of the Opposition and a member of the Privy Council. Compared to the cosiness of Wilson and the mischievous air of some of his Cabinet members, Heath was a pleasant but formal man whose reserved nature masked his shyness; there was already a reason for the slight uneasiness and distance which is said to have become the hallmark of their relationship. Heath was the original chief negotiator for Britain's entry into the Common Market. He was as convinced then as he is today that the government required total commitment to European unity in trade, defence and monetary policy. This, in turn, would undoubtedly have some effect on British sovereignty and he could not expect the Queen to fall in with his European proposals without some questioning as to the effects they would have on the Commonwealth. Heath lost no time.

Eleven days after winning the general election with a comfortable majority – won on a manifesto which included entry into the Market – talks began, to find a route for Britain's entry. However, Heath continued to have the Queen 'roped in' – as political commentator Terry Lancaster described it – for important issues and whereas Wilson had never managed to get royal guests to No. 10 whilst he was there, Heath very quickly secured two; Princess Margaret came to lunch for the anniversary of the Victoria League of Commonwealth Friendship and the Queen Mother went to a dinner party in honour of Leonard Bernstein. The Queen herself went down to Chequers, the Prime Minister's country home, for lunch. The occasion was to meet the visiting American President, Richard Nixon, whose support was being canvassed for Britain's arms policy to South Africa. And then Heath persuaded her at short notice to host a banquet for five-power defence talks over British policies east of Suez. It was, Lancaster told the author, 'a controversial and highly political occasion'.

Apart from the issue of the Common Market and the Commonwealth, Edward Heath also inherited another 'royal' problem from Harold Wilson – that of the monarch's money. It is interesting to note the chronology of events, from information now available, which occurred during the first half of 1971.

On 19 May, the Queen sent a 'most gracious message' to the House of Commons formally requesting an increase in her Civil List Allowance because of developments since 1952 when the allowance was first set. On 28 May, an unsigned article (but rumoured to be the work of Richard Crossman) appeared on the front page of the *New Statesman*. It began: 'What is the connection between the way in which we pay – and tax – Her Majesty the Queen and the Paris Commune which collapsed in bloody ruins a hundred years ago this week. The connection, one which Marx would instantly have perceived, is the effort established societies make to maintain the class structure . . . A pay claim from a dustman is an attempt to hold the nation to ransom. A pay claim from Her Majesty is termed as Her Majesty's most gracious message . . .' The *New Statesman* article went on to challenge her tax privileges: 'Anthony Barber (the Heath chancellor) has said the Queen's resources in her private capacity do not come into this. But the Queen is not private; nor is she treated as such. The bulk of her wealth is not subject to death duties. She pays no income tax or surtax. She is getting it both ways. One has to admire her truly regal cheek.'[9] In the ensuing uproar, the republican MP Willie Hamilton, a member of the Civil List Select Committee, added his own invective: 'It is the most insensitive, brazen pay claim made in the last 200 years.' He proposed that the Civil List should be abolished and the Queen and Philip should just get the rate for the job. All of those critics, of course, confused emotion with reality when they talked of 'pay rises'. As the royals are ever ready to point out, they spend the Civil List money on salaries and expenses connected with their public duties. The polo ponies, the yachts and the rest come out of their own money.

All this talk of the Queen's money worried Mountbatten. As he viewed the tide of ill-feeling, he was as always ready to venture a considered opinion on his forte of public relations – and how public opinion, swinging once again away from them, might be massaged.

On 5 June he advised Philip – after figures of between £5 million and £100 million began to appear, and this in 1971 – that unless they could get an informed reply published 'the image of monarchy will be gravely damaged'.[10] He suggested that they should try to get an authoritative article published in *The Times* on the subject; that would then be taken up by the popular press. 'So will you both please believe a loving old uncle and NOT your constitutional advisers and do it,' he wrote to Philip.[11]

On 9 June, Mr John Colville, former private secretary to the Queen (before she was married) and Winston Churchill, and by then a bank director, appeared in *The Times*, writing on the question of the Queen's wealth. He assessed that the true net worth of the Queen was 'probably not more than £2 million'[12] which in hindsight was something of an understatement, even for 1971.

It was not enough to quell the mood of resentment which was merely heightened when the Select Committee discovered the 'hidden extras' to the monarchy, services provided by various ministries who also footed the bill and which went under the heading of Departmental Votes. It seemed to come as something of a shock to some of them that the private airline, the Queen's Flight operated and paid for by the Ministry of Defence, was rather a costly item. The royal yacht *Britannia*, run by the Royal Navy, cost around £4.5 million a year to operate, in addition to the refits, almost once every two years. Then there was the royal train operated by the Ministry of Transport; the post and telephone services (including the 6,500 telegrams sent annually to centenarians and other anniversary celebrants), maintenance of twelve royal homes, palaces and castles, a contribution to the running expenses such as staffing (a total of 473 in royal employ), gas, electricity and fuel; operation of other royal cars, remuneration and pension contributions to the Queen's staff while on state business . . . it went on and on.

In 1971, the year the committee presented Parliament's one and only investigation into royal expenses, the additional costs amounted to £3 million over and above the Civil List payment. The scrutiny of the Select Committee learned only as much as the Queen and Philip allowed and, at the end of the day, the committee recommended that the Civil List allowance to the Queen should be doubled to £980,000. A further £255,000 was to be added to cover the expenses of her immediate family. Uproar followed, of course, and especially from the anti-royalists. It was all very obscene, observed Willie Hamilton who described Princess Margaret as this 'very expensive kept woman'. Even the Queen Mother came under attack; further would be heard on the subject later . . .

* * *

There had been little or no contact that year between the Queen and her uncle, the Duke of Windsor. She had not seen him since he and the duchess were in London for the unveiling of the plaque to Queen Mary. Other members of the family had called to see him, including Prince Charles who paid a visit during a tour of Paris, and found the duke's house 'full of noisy Americans'. Mountbatten also called but the duke and duchess got very angry at his constant references to the Windsors' personal possessions and what would become of them after their deaths. 'I find this topic exceedingly morbid,' Windsor told Mountbatten.[13] But Mountbatten persisted with his questions. 'Who will you leave that to . . .? What will happen to your papers . . .? Are you going to set up a trust fund for your relatives?' After he had gone, the duke fumed, 'How dare he . . . he's even telling me what he wants left to himself.'

The Queen had written in August 1970 confirming the final arrangements and location of the burial plot that had been allocated to the duke and his wife at Frogmore. The duke's appearances were becoming fewer. More than a year had elapsed since the Queen's note when she heard unofficially that he was ill. In November, it was confirmed that he had cancer of the throat which was so far advanced that it was inoperable. The duke began a course of cobalt treatment though it was clear, palpably even to himself, that his time was now limited. The duchess was not told of the seriousness of his condition, largely because of her own ill-health. Her mind wandered in and out of reality. The duke grew slowly weaker, and the pain more severe. Friends still called, but they were fewer now. One who came was the Dowager Lady Monckton who was so disturbed by the duke's condition that she immediately sent word to Buckingham Palace that he was dying; the duke's doctors had told her that he could go at any moment.

The Queen and Prince Philip were due to make a state visit to France in May as the advance party into Europe – just to show President Pompidou who had succeeded de Gaulle in June 1969 that Britain was well and truly behind the European ideal. In February, the duke's doctor Jean Thin was asked to call at the British embassy where he was interviewed by Sir Christopher Soames, the British ambassador, who told him of the forthcoming visit by the Queen and Prince Philip. Soames explained that it was an extremely delicate and important mission by the sovereign to improve the relationship between the two countries in advance of British membership of the EEC.

And so, the old Duke of Windsor, lying on his death-bed and growing weaker by the day, was a problem to the last. Soames sought almost impossible assurances from Dr Thin. He was blunt and to the point: it would be disastrous if the duke were to die during the course of the Queen's visit to France. Dr Thin could not, of course, state exactly when the duke would die; he could not say whether it would be before the visit, during it, or after it, and so it was arranged that the British embassy would telephone each evening for a bulletin prior to the Queen's arrival. By May, the duke had grown weaker. He could not eat, he could barely drink and was connected to an intravenous drip twenty-four hours a day. He saw no one except the nurse, his doctors, the duchess and his favourite pug dog who lay on the bed beside him. The day before they were expected, the duke had a serious haemorrhage; however, when the embassy rang that evening at 6.00 p.m. they were told that the duke would survive at least another twenty-four hours and the Queen's visit went ahead as planned. On the day they were to arrive, the duke insisted that he wanted to be dressed. 'Get me out of bed,' he instructed his medical staff, his butler Georges Sanegre and valet Sydney Johnson on the morning of the visit. 'I cannot receive the Queen in my bedroom.' Georges recalled that he was insistent that they should dress him; they put on a pair of slacks and a blue blazer that now swamped him. 'Take me downstairs,' the duke demanded, so that he could welcome his niece in the main reception salon. As they got him out of bed, it became clear even to the duke that he was too weak and tired to go out of his room. It was a painfully slow process, just preparing for the armchair. 'The effort of moving him just a few feet made him speechless,' Georges recalled. 'It was difficult to imagine the emotions he was going through. He did so want to be upright and dressed to meet the Queen but we managed to persuade him to sit in the chair, which he did.' The doctors had also insisted he should not become detached from the drip and it was rigged up so that a long tube, inserted into the duke's arm by needle, ran under his shirt and emerged at the back of his collar to the plastic containers hidden behind some curtains at the back of him.

The duchess was shakily nervous but calm when the Queen arrived with Prince Philip and Prince Charles. It was the first time that either the Queen or Philip had visited the house in which the Windsors had lived for twenty years. Butler Georges reported, 'The Queen came into the sitting room adjoining the bedroom and the duke struggled to his feet. The drip was still attached to his arm and the doctors were worried it would fall out. "My dear Lilibet," he said, "it is lovely to see you again," and he bowed forward slightly and kissed her.'[14] Then the duke slumped back into his chair as he shook hands with Philip and Charles who he said had grown into a fine young man. They chatted briefly and the duke began to cough and was clearly distressed. They remained for fifteen minutes. The royal party went downstairs to the salon where Georges served mint tea; they stayed for a few minutes longer, making polite conversation and in all the visit lasted under half an hour. The duchess was very tense, now being alone with them, and eventually they stood up and said it was time they had to leave. She went to the door with them, and curtsied as the Queen left.

Exactly one week later, the duke died. The end came at 2.00 a.m., and the Queen was informed by one of Windsor's aides by a telephone call to Buckingham Palace; she in turn telephoned the Queen Mother. And so ended the life of the man who had provided the monarchy with its most devastating blow, yet who in another way had brought to it a focus which highlighted the fact that those at the heart of the fierce white light are not placed there by divine right, to reign or rule like a deity; it reminded those who viewed the monarchy in such a way that its members are mere mortals, with human feelings – and failings.

The tributes that flowed from every part of the globe the following morning when the news became known were glowing in their praise, oddly so for a man who had reigned for only 326 days and from people who barely knew him or remembered his most glamorous adventures when he was Prince of Wales. President Nixon described him as a 'man of noble spirit and high ideals' which, along with others in similar vein, was a rather generous appreciation of a man who had achieved little in his life except to sustain a marriage and a love that cost him everything. Set against his brother's record, or his niece's, the duke left nothing but a fascinating life story.

The Queen sent a message to the duchess: 'I am so grieved . . .' And in the House of Commons there was something of a commotion over the government tribute to the duke which failed to make any mention of the duchess, or offer her any condolences. It was only on the inquiry of a back-bench MP that the omission was rectified. Meanwhile the annual Trooping the Colour for the Queen's official birthday was not cancelled, nor did Parliament adjourn on the day of Windsor's funeral, as it would have done for other members of the family, which to Tony Benn demonstrated 'the odious hypocrisy with which the royal family and the press and the establishment . . . really a lot of people are rediscovering how unattractive the monarchy is through the story of the Duke of Windsor'.[15]

The duchess arrived in England aboard an aircraft of the Queen's flight with Grace, Lady Dudley to accompany her. Mountbatten was at Heathrow Airport to meet her and they went straight to Buckingham Palace where she was to lunch with the Queen and Princess Anne. It was Anne's second meeting with her aunt, and the first time since 1936 that Wallis had been inside Buckingham Palace. In that day's newspapers, there was speculation that the royal family had at last buried the hatchet and was recognising the duchess as a member of the family by inviting her to stay at Buckingham Palace. The *Guardian* summed up several similar viewpoints: 'The Queen has apparently decided that with the passing of a generation since the abdication, it would be wrong to pursue the subtle ostracism which the royal family has hitherto practised.'[16] But a palace spokesman put them right: 'For obvious human reasons, protocol has been waived' and a plea from the *Evening Standard* that the Queen might now show the ending of the split by granting her the courtesy title of Her Royal Highness went unheeded.

The duchess had little memory of the last occasion she was inside the palace; she had suffered badly since her husband's death and was often confused, sometimes unable even to acknowledge that he was dead. She retired to her suite early and the next day declined the Queen's invitation to attend the Trooping of the Colour. The royal family all went to Windsor for the weekend; the duchess also declined the invitation to join them. It was, coincidentally, the thirty-fifth anniversary of her marriage to the duke and she decided to remain at the palace with Lady Dudley. In the evening, Prince Charles came back to the palace to drive the duchess to St George's Chapel, Windsor, to see the lying-in-state of her husband's body after the thousands who had queued to file past had gone. She asked to be returned to the palace immediately, and seemed occasionally to confuse it with Claridges where she and the duke had normally stayed on their visits to London in the past. The funeral service was a private one for members of the royal family, the government and only those friends whom the duke himself had listed. There was sherry and a light lunch at Windsor Castle followed by the last part of the duchess's ordeal which was to join the funeral cortège to Frogmore lawn for the burial. There, under the strain, she became disorientated and unlatched herself from Prince Philip who had been supporting her and wandered between groups of royal mourners, asking, 'Where is the duke? I've lost the duke,' until the Queen Mother strode forward and took her unresisting arm, gently, 'as if she were a lost child'.[17] The Queen Mother said, 'Come on, I know how you feel. I've been through it myself.'[18] Afterwards, the duchess stayed only briefly before returning to Paris. The entire royal family saw her off, but none accompanied her to Heathrow Airport. It was left to the Lord Chamberlain to represent the Queen in the departure lounge. Though she was to survive for a further fourteen years, for most of those who waved her off that day, it was the last time they would see her. She neither received nor sought an invitation to come back amongst them.

Perhaps the Queen felt she had done sufficient to show sympathy and regard for her aunt. But once she had recovered from the ordeal of the funeral, Wallis Windsor returned to her acid wit in describing the scene to her long-time friend Countess Romanones. 'How David would have laughed over Cookie (the Queen Mother). What did she look like? It was as if someone had opened an old trunk of clothes and draped them on, and that eternal bag hanging on her arm . . .' the duchess told the countess soon after her return. 'Yes, I remember, I wanted to burst out laughing when I saw her; then I remembered David was not there to share the joke. I smiled anyway; I wasn't going to let them show me up. I was next to the Duke of Edinburgh who I always imagined would be better, kinder, perhaps more human than the others. But you know, he is just a four-flusher. Not he, not any of them, offered me any real sympathy . . .'[19]

The years of bitterness could not be softened by a few days of kindness and in the public's eye the Queen did not come out of the Windsor funeral as well as she might have done. It wasn't merely the republicans and left-wingers who complained of humbug and hypocrisy and Willie Hamilton's observations received headline treatment: 'I hope that Prince Charles falls in love with a divorced hippy.'

But soon it faded, to be replaced by warm tributes to the Queen and Philip themselves on the occasion later that year of their twenty-fifth wedding anniversary. They basked in several days of photographic retrospectives of their lives together, and it was capped by a rather spectacular event – the bringing of 200 couples who were all married on the same day as the Queen to Westminster Abbey to join the Queen's ministers, officers of state, kings, queens and princes from overseas and other dignitaries giving thanks on the day of their silver wedding. It was something of a PR event, yet it meant well and *The Times* was among those newspapers which responded favourably: 'Within and without the Commonwealth, it has been continuous service that could only have been given by a tough, devoted and attractive Queen . . . we all acknowledge that these extended travels have meant long absences from her children. Today we can also declare that the Queen, the Duke and their children have set a standard of family life and family happiness that everyone must respect . . .' How times change.

Chapter Twelve

Divided Loyalties (1973–4)

At the time of Britain's entry into the Common Market, the Queen may well have been reflecting upon Hugh Gaitskell's warning that it 'will end a thousand years of British history'. Were a thousand years of monarchy and three centuries of imperial influence under the British Crown about to be cast adrift? Would there be a revolt among the Commonwealth nations, and her personal ties severed once and for all, leaving her the titular ruler of just her own backyard? There were supporters of this theory who saw, at the very least, Britain turning inward to the continent of Europe and that never again would the affairs of the Commonwealth loom large, though Edward Heath was always insistent that the Queen's position would not be assailed. In any event, though a total royalist, he never came anywhere near overstating the Queen's powers within the constitution as some had done, and were still doing.[1] To the Queen, the whole scenario must have seemed a problem of some magnitude; she must surely have pondered the possibilities of her losing status in at least three of her most important countries and, if that happened, the Commonwealth might reorganise itself under a new republican administration. It was by now, anyway, no longer the 'British' Commonwealth and there was a body of opinion which believed that it would take no great step to divorce it entirely from its imperial origins. It was no coincidence, therefore, that in the eighteen months following Britain's entry into the Common Market which became official on 1 January 1973* the Queen found herself thrust into one of the most frantic and exhausting sequences of overseas journeys since her succession. In 1973, she was scheduled to make two visits to Canada, and one to Australia. She was to visit Australia – and New Zealand – again early in 1974 and all within the space of seven months. Even as these tours were being arranged, there was talk that the oldest Commonwealth member-nations were upset by Britain's entry into Europe. The Queen, prompted by her government, attempted to allay their fears in her Christmas message to the Commonwealth, broadcast six days before Britain's entry became official: 'The new links with Europe will not replace those with the Commonwealth. They cannot alter our historical ties and personal attachments with kinsmen and friends overseas. Old friends will not be lost. Britain will take her Commonwealth links into Europe with her.'[2]

The latter sentence was quite rightly treated with some apprehension, especially in Australia, where Mr Gough Whitlam's newly elected Labour government had been in power only since 2 December 1972. As Whitlam came to power, there was a certain uneasiness in London; he was known to have voiced republican views, and while he admitted in response to a question by a journalist during his election campaign that the Queen would still be Queen of Australia during his lifetime, he thought that eventually the country would become a republic. It was extremely difficult to untie the Queen from the controversy; she had to tread a difficult path in which she veered neither to one side nor the other. Sometimes, that was made impossible. In the Queen's Speech at the opening of the new session of Parliament, for example, when she read out her government's intentions for the ensuing months, she had to speak the words written for her by Edward Heath on the 'great achievements' of the Common Market. And whether she herself believed them or not, and whether she was in favour or not, never entered the equation. She was the voice of her government on that day. She could make no diversion towards her normal

*The Treaty of Brussels when the six members of the European Economic Community became nine, with the addition of Britain, Ireland and Denmark was signed on 22 January 1972.

impartial stance and was forced to step into the ring of controversy. To the world outside, she appeared to be as enthusiastic as her ministers, though, as the Opposition members who criticised her speech well knew, she was merely the mouthpiece. If she was to be booed in her own country – as she was by a group of protesters when she arrived at Covent Garden for a celebration on Britain's joining the Market – then it could be expected that feelings might be running even higher in the Commonwealth.

So they were. When she and Prince Philip arrived in Canada for the first of their visits in July, the anti-royalist lobby had received unexpected support from an editorial in the *Toronto Star*, suggesting that the time had come for the nation to have its own head of state – not a surrogate one provided under outdated ties to another country.[3] It was a touchy time, especially since the Queen was there for the centennial celebrations of Prince Edward Island, the very cradle of the country's nationhood. The *Toronto Star*'s editorial had been noted, and when she arrived the Queen's speech-writers chose to break one of the monarchy's golden rules – never to reply to newspaper comment. 'The Crown,' said the Queen upon arrival, 'should be seen as a symbol of national sovereignty belonging to all . . . not only a link between Commonwealth countries but between Canadian citizens of every national origin and ancestry.' In choosing to point up the importance of the Commonwealth, the Queen also encompassed another delicate area, that of French-Canadian feelings towards their own breakaway movement. Canada's Prime Minister, Pierre Trudeau, himself a French Canadian, had been briefed on what the Queen intended to say – as is the normal custom when the sovereign is abroad – and when he joined her in Charlotteville for the Canadian National Day Celebrations, he added his own words of support to the Queen's message. His view was, 'Why change a system that works?' All Canadians should realise when they were well off, said Trudeau. The monarchy had served Canada well, and it had been the democratic authority over what was probably the only form of government acceptable to the Canadian people.[4] The Queen's rapid tour took on the tone of a general election in which she was the candidate, the one and only, running to secure the nation's vote to keep her as their Queen. Her speeches were pointed, punchy and awash with intent. She was there to serve them, the nation of Canada, and let no one dispute that.

Furthermore, and to make the point emphatic, Prime Minister Trudeau revealed that he had already invited the Queen to attend the next Commonwealth Conference of member-nations, to be held in Ottawa; it was another crucial 'first' – the first time she had attended such a conference outside Britain. It was especially poignant, not merely from the point of view of Britain's entry into Europe. So many other delicate matters were coming to a head, such as those already cited in previous chapters, with Africa in turmoil, the continued tense Indo-Pakistan relations after the 2-week war and Britain's recognition of the new state of Bangladesh which led to Pakistan's withdrawal from the Commonwealth.

Trudeau's invitation was not entirely without self-interest; these things never are. He saw the Commonwealth, and the Queen for that matter, as the route to encouraging Canadians to think of their global attachments and their historical connections, to preserve the Canadian identity and to halt its slide towards ever-increasing affiliations with the United States, a battle which eventually would be all but lost. The French Canadians were angry at Trudeau's support, as was best demonstrated in an editorial in *Le Devoir*, the Montreal newspaper, which asked, 'When shall we have a head for our crown?' It described as 'ineffective and useless' the system of retaining the Queen as head of state and said that the monarchy, apart from symbolising a state of political subjection for French Canadians, was simply not functional for Canada as a whole. 'She is not here to read an address from the throne in the latest parliament . . . she is not here to greet the Mexican president . . . it is in Edinburgh or Manchester, rather than Rimouski or Saskatoon that she cuts ribbons', the editorial concluded.[5] Regardless of the bitterness, the Queen flew into Ottawa for the Commonwealth conference and her very presence was described by royalist supporters as being of 'enormous significance', especially since she seemed to have a knack of calming and controlling politicians at times of overheating. It became another battle won and she flew home to England to continue the summer round of garden parties and a visit to Bath, before taking a brief holiday at Balmoral.

It was curtailed this year by the need to travel to Australia for a 6-day visit. Gough Whitlam had introduced the Royal Styles and Titles Act which would affect how the Queen would be described on all future visits to Australia. Under the new Act, she would henceforth be known as Queen of Australia as soon as she set foot on Australian soil, thus deleting the normal style of 'Queen of the United Kingdom and of Her Other Realms and Territories'. The Bill required royal assent, as usual, and to show her agreement she flew directly to Canberra so that she could personally sign the Bill after its approval by the Federal Parliament. While she was there, Whitlam got her to open the new £62 million Sydney Opera House and then she had to dash home to attend to some important family business . . . her daughter's wedding which had been arranged to slot in between her various globe-trotting activities.

'I fear,' said Willie Hamilton, 'there's a spate of bilge on the way.' Even *The Times* was moved to state: 'Months of speculation ended last night when . . .'[6] the engagement of Princess Anne to Captain Mark Phillips was announced by Buckingham Palace. For a couple who were said to be well matched and very much in love, it had taken a long time for them to come to the point of actually telling anyone officially. What was the delay? No one ever explained it. One thing was certain, for months Anne and Mark, with the complete cooperation of the Buckingham Palace press office, played cat and mouse with the newspapers and were denying their possible engagement almost up to the point of its being announced. The Queen obviously had to be involved, since her press secretary was the one who was making the denials. Weren't they sure they wanted to marry? They both seemed fairly relaxed about it all when they appeared in a succession of television interviews after the announcement. Mark, shy and monosyllabic, not knowing what he had let himself in for, and Anne honestly trying to explain what life would be like married to a member of the royal family. The difference was summed up in one simple statistic: Mark was earning £2,500 in the army while

Anne would get £35,000 a year from the Civil List upon her marriage. She couldn't spend her money on domestic matters – so they would have to live on Mark's fifty pounds a week. Even for a commoner in the higher bands of society, that was pretty common. Mark was petrified at the thought of it – and of asking the Queen and Prince Philip for their daughter's hand. The Queen, according to Anne, was not the slightest bit upset that her daughter had chosen to marry a commoner, though she became increasingly impatient when she heard that he did not care much about taking a title. He was going to be no pushover in that direction, not like Lord Snowdon. Philip thought he should have one; it was his daughter, after all, who should be kept in the same style, manner and title to which she had become accustomed. Philip was none too keen on the match. He thought Mark was dull and could talk only about horses and the army; nothing else. The point was, Anne seemed to have made up her mind she was going to marry Mark Phillips and, according to her, there was no discussion at the time that he was untitled. That may have been so, though privately the Queen and Philip would have preferred her to have at least married money, if not a title.

Mark had not a penny, but in that respect he matched Prince Philip when he married the Queen. 'I don't think there was ever any question as far as the family was concerned that one should marry anybody in particular,' said Anne. 'It isn't a duty because I am not a boy. That side of it doesn't apply to me. One's parents might possibly have said "we don't like him" or "we do like him" – but I think they trusted one enough to make up one's own mind.'[7] Like his prospective father-in-law, Mark often tended to try to joke his way out of difficult situations but he wasn't that funny, and the wit wasn't as acid as Philip's, honed by years of practice. Mark took a long time to become relaxed in the company of his future wife's parents. Being a military man himself, he initially felt the need to stand to attention when he was in Philip's company and the butterflies fluttered whenever he was about to meet the Queen, although she was better than Philip at making people feel at ease. Mark, it was said and hoped, would eventually settle to the royal life and if an example was needed as to how this could be done, some pointed towards Lord Snowdon. In the fullness of time neither would truly settle to it.

The wedding of Princess Anne and Mark Phillips on 14 November – Prince Charles's twenty-fourth birthday – had less of the royal spectacle about it, toned down slightly in the ceremonial because of the currently dire economic climate which gripped the nation like nothing had done since the thirties. Even so, it was still to be watched by half a billion people worldwide on television, and the newspapers gave it their all. Anne's image also had something to do with it; she was never in the fairytale mould, nor especially glamorous when compared to her mother and Princess Margaret at the same age. If anything, the wedding reflected the princess's own burning desire and ambition to live an 'ordinary' life.

She uses the word often, but then equally often says she realises it was virtually impossible, even though her definition of it may be rather different from those who actually *do* live such an existence. 'What some people don't realise,' she said in 1980, 'is that one thing you want to do is live what they laughingly call an ordinary life . . . I don't think we lead a particularly different life, insofar as there is an average life, a common denominator of life; we see a great deal of it.'[8] However, there were those who were immediately set to challenge the very concept of royalty leading an ordinary life, when it became known that Anne and Mark were to spend their honeymoon aboard the royal yacht *Britannia*. 'Well,' said Anne in angry response, 'it's none of their business and anyway the *Britannia* is going to New Zealand for the Queen's visit in February and it has to pass through the West Indies to get there.'[9] So off they went cruising in the West Indies – just the two of them, plus 21 officers and 256 crew with a huge flotilla of assorted small craft trailing behind, carrying the world's press who were all anxious to catch sight of the couple in their long-tom lenses.

The criticism over the cost of the wedding and the honeymoon and all the other trappings that go into the making of such a day hung like a cloud over the celebrations. How were the royal planners to know that the date they had chosen would fall in the middle of such dire social conditions? One attack on royal extravagances was only to be expected with the nation's industry on the brink of being forced on to a 3-day week by Mr Heath's resolution to fight the industrial disputes paralysing the coal mines, the power stations and the railways. It is also on these occasions that the choice of the word 'ordinary' as one which the royals would like to apply to themselves becomes defiantly unreasonable. My colleague Donald Zec cheekily summed up the whole scenario from his vantage point inside Westminster Abbey; that she had agreed to 'obey' in the service was, said Zec, 'the most loaded four-letter word of the year . . . and when Mark declared "With this ring I thee wed, with my body I thee worship, with all my worldly goods I thee endow" it was clearly no time to think of Anne's £35,000 a year stipend or the £8 a week mansion. Here in the sturdy masonry of centuries Anne has got her man and five hundred million viewers are permitted to share in the phenomenon of a slightly hard-up Britain laughing all the way to the Abbey.'

They sailed away from Britain, leaving the nation in a deep gloom, literally. Edward Heath, at his weekly audiences with the Queen, reported upon the worsening crisis, and on 17 December he announced that, because of the low coal stocks, industry and commerce would be restricted to just five days electricity consumption in the next two weeks and from the New Year, it would be limited to a 3-day week. All television programmes were to cease at 10.30 p.m. and a mini-budget announced by his Chancellor, Anthony Barber, brought down a huge clamp on public spending and hire purchase controls. These measures were taken not merely in response to the industrial crisis, but to meet the effects of the massive rise in oil prices announced by the OPEC countries.

The Queen tried to bring some cheer with a slightly different Christmas broadcast which showed some behind-the-scenes shots of Princess Anne's wedding, which were filmed by Richard Cawston whose earlier film *Royal Family* had won so many accolades. One scene showed members of the family urging Anne and Mark out on to the balcony to re-enact the ritual of all royal occasions and Anne turning to Prince Edward and saying, 'Well, all right then, but get off my dress first'. Another of the film sequences was of the royal reception in Ottawa for the Commonwealth prime ministers and showed, once again, how much the Queen personally had set by this event.

Although it was being widely rumoured that unless he could achieve a settlement to the strikes, Heath would have to call a general election early in the New Year, the Queen continued with the preparations for her overseas tour which would take in Australia, New Zealand, the Cook Islands, the New Hebrides, the Solomon Islands and Papua New Guinea. Now such a seasoned traveller, it was no longer necessary to get out the maps and plot their course as they used to do; there was still plenty of reading to be done for local customs.

She left Heathrow on 27 January with a small entourage, flying first to Ottawa where she met up with Princess Anne and Mark Phillips who had been on a weekend visit to Canada; they were to join the Queen for the remainder of the tour. Onwards, to the next stop in the Cook Islands where the Queen opened the new international airport at Raratonga, and from there they flew on to Christchurch, New Zealand where they were met by Prince Philip who had gone on ahead to open the Commonwealth Games, and Prince Charles from the Royal Navy frigate HMS *Jupiter*. Mountbatten was also in New Zealand, so as the Queen said, 'It's become quite a family gathering'. She arrived in time to see the last day of the Games and used the occasions to reinforce her Commonwealth message . . . 'When all barriers were forgotten in general friendship [no one] can doubt the real value of such a gathering.' Not all of the indigenous population agreed. With such a large contingent of royalty present, a group of New Zealand's Maoris staged a few demonstrations to record their feelings over the theft of their lands and were branded extremists, as were a larger group of Aborigines who booed and chanted outside the government headquarters in Canberra when the Queen arrived for her fifth visit to Australia. She just about had time to declare the Parliament open when she had to return home. Edward Heath had decided to let the nation vote on his fight against the unions and had called a general election, and under constitutional law the sovereign had to be in the country. The Queen left immediately for London with Princess Anne and Mark Phillips, leaving Prince Philip to continue the rest of the tour alone until after the election, when she said she would return immediately to resume her commitments. Things did not quite work out as planned.

Back home, Edward Heath was confident that the nation would vindicate his strategy and he fought on the slogan 'Who Runs Britain . . . the Government or the Miners?' Heath insisted that some of the miners' leaders wanted to change Britain's whole democratic way of life. But the election on 28 February gave Labour a slender lead of 301 seats against 297 for the Tories. With 14 Liberals and 9 Scottish and Welsh nationalists holding the balance of power, Heath clung to a life-line of trying to form a coalition government. Far from being able to slip in and out of the country to complete the formalities of receiving her newly elected Prime Minister – as it appears she had expected – it soon became clear that the Queen might yet become a key player in a constitutional crisis. On the evening of 1 March, Heath told the Queen, who was tired and heavily jet-lagged from her dash across the globe, that under his constitutional rights as outgoing Prime Minister, he would attempt to negotiate an alliance with the Liberal leader Jeremy Thorpe during the weekend. Thorpe, whose party had secured a far greater number of votes than was reflected in the number of seats won, was seeking reforms to accommodate proportional representation at the next election. The Scottish and Welsh nationalists were both naturally pushing their plate forward for their own parliament. The Queen's prerogative came into play in a manner she had not anticipated, though her advisers were well versed in the constitutional procedure should it become necessary for the Queen to make her views known. With no working majority available to either party, the Queen had to consider the situation from both points of view. Heath was within his rights in attempting to stay in power, in spite of the fact that his party had fewer seats than Labour. The Queen, however, was under no liability to accept or approve his tactics, especially if they became protracted and could be seen to be putting party and power above the good of the country. Sir Martin Charteris, who had taken over from Sir Michael Adeane as the Queen's private secretary, was in no doubt that the Queen had 'absolute rights' to consult whom she wished and 'absolute rights' to make a decision on who should be called to form an administration, should her intervention become necessary in a stalemate. In the end, her judgement would only be tested by events – but 'there has to be some risk attached in order to provide excitement for the monarchy,' Sir Martin once told Tony Benn.[10] It was an interesting word to use – 'excitement' – as if the Queen actually looked forward to a bit of constitutional controversy in which she could take a hand, although it is known that she was pleased when the Tories adopted a new system of electing their leader so that she did not have to become involved. The occasion which now presented itself could be seen as an exciting one from her point of view, and a risky one, too. If she had been called upon to exercise her prerogative in a stalemate situation, there would undoubtedly have been uproar afterwards because, in such a finely balanced situation, she was bound to receive a vigorous response from the losing side. Her rights in doing so were confirmed by the view of constitutional specialist and devout royalist Norman St John Stevas (later Lord St John of Fawsley) who said:

> You could get a situation where she would be right to refuse a dissolution if it were against the national interest but, of course, that right has to be sparingly used. She also has the right in certain circumstances to pick a prime minister when there is no clear leader of a governing party. In the last resort – and I don't think it too fanciful – suppose there were a nuclear war or some disaster and the whole fabric of the state destroyed; as long as you have the Queen or her successor, there's always a focus of loyalty around which things can be rebuilt.[11]*

*The last comparable situation this century was in 1923, when Prime Minister Stanley Baldwin called a snap election – just as Heath had done – expecting to be returned with a comfortable majority. However, although the Tories secured more seats than Labour or the Liberals, they did not command an overall majority, not by a long chalk. Baldwin, in talks with George V, decided to test the situation when parliament reassembled. He was immediately defeated on a vote of 'No confidence' and the King was forced to send for the Labour leader Ramsay MacDonald who had patched together a tenuous deal with the Liberals and avoided calling a second general election.

In the event, the Queen's immediate involvement did not become necessary. Heath had two meetings with Jeremy Thorpe during the weekend, while others in the Tory hierarchy spoke to the Scottish and Welsh nationalists. Thorpe continued to press for a firm commitment to proportional representation which, had it been in effect at this election, would have secured for the Liberals 123 seats, as opposed to the 14 they won. Heath could not give that assurance and Thorpe came out of the meeting to say, 'No deal'. By Monday evening, Heath had pursued all his possible options and was unable to form a coalition with a sufficient working majority to beat Labour. At 6.30, he drove to Buckingham Palace to resign. The meeting was a short one; he left at 7.12 p.m. and at 7.19 Harold Wilson arrived. The Queen poured him a whisky and formally invited him to form an administration for the second time. She asked him what he intended to do about the miners' strike, and he told her that his Cabinet would give the National Coal Board permission to begin negotiating a wage settlement at a figure well above what his predecessor's government had been prepared to accept and thus he expected to have a full return to work within a matters of days. (This he succeeded in doing. The strike ended two days later, with a £100 million pay award, twice what Heath had offered.)

Though, in the end, the situation resolved itself without the Queen being called upon, her prerogative was very much in the minds of both sides then – and for the next few months when there was an uneasy cat-and-mouse game played in the Commons, with neither side yet willing to test themselves with either the expense of or possible humiliation in another general election. Furthermore, national interest would not have been best served by another election so soon and this is what the Queen and her advisers had to consider. The prospect of a dissolution of Parliament was clearly on the agenda for discussion at the palace. If, in the face of a Commons defeat on some issue, Wilson had decided to ask the Queen for a dissolution, she would be have been within her rights to refuse if she felt that another prime minister might form an administration without dissolution. This, presumably, would have meant recalling Edward Heath, or even another political figure to form a government of national unity; Cecil King, the sacked *Mirror* boss, had by no means given up his soundings for such a move. It is also interesting to discover, now, that a number of political figures of the era had boned up on the Queen's rights during a dissolution.

Edward Heath did not attach such great importance to the royal prerogative as his predecessors, because the mechanics were in place to resolve any difficult political situations before reaching the Queen. And as the year wore on, the political scene stabilised. Heath's day had come and gone; for him it was a time for reflection and, like his predecessors, he was not unimpressed by the Queen. 'She is one of the most informed people in the world. I used to look forward to my weekly audiences with her, which often lasted up to two hours.' Heath was never called by his first name, always 'Prime Minister'. During his period of office, he had had a different system of initiating discussion, whereby his secretary and the Queen's agreed an agenda in advance; she was particularly interested in foreign affairs and the Commonwealth. During the Queen's holiday at Balmoral, it was practice for the Prime Minister to join her for a week in September. There were usually about twenty other guests, for whom the Queen would personally arrange picnics and outings, often cooking meat and vegetables over an open fire. 'A lot of business was also done,' Heath recalled, 'and we would discuss plans for the next session of parliament.'[12]

Far from making her expected prompt return to Australia after the general election in Britain, she was obliged to stay in London for the opening of Parliament under the new administration of Harold Wilson. She also had to receive her new ministers in the Cabinet who included Eric Heffer, the staunch left-winger whose visit to Buckingham Palace left him somewhat bemused; he felt pleased, on the one hand, to go and kneel before the Queen but on the other, he felt he was 'betraying the working-class movement . . . the Queen sucks you away from your supporters and makes you feel that you are only there because she has appointed you'.[13]

And so she read her speech to Parliament, announcing her new and tenuously appointed government's proposals for the coming session, and then flew off the next day to link up with Prince Philip to continue the rest of her tour, from which she had now been absent for fourteen days. On the way, her plane flew directly into the path of a NATO military exercise in Germany and it later transpired that the aircraft was wrongly identified as a 'dummy' target by four US fighters and was within minutes of being brought down. An immediate full-scale inquiry was ordered, as the Queen flew on.

Philip had left Australia and was in Bali ready for the Indonesian segment. Already somewhat shell-shocked by the events of the past two weeks, she would find Indonesia no rest cure. The country's relationship with Britain was as tenuous as Harold Wilson's working majority in the House of Commons, almost non-existent. In the past decade, the British embassy at Jakarta had been attacked and looted, though the visit by the Queen was intended to establish reconciliation. Even so, the unrest that continued in the capital had caused the Foreign Office to raise the question of cancelling the visit altogether. In January, the Prime Minister of Japan, on a similar state visit of friendship, had been kept a virtual prisoner for several days by riots. The authorities assured Britain that the same would not occur on the Queen's arrival, and she had herself once again waved aside any personal danger. However, the security was intense and 5,000 extra police and military guards were positioned on the streets of Jakarta during her tours, which were enthusiastically greeted by the Indonesian crowds. She remained there for six full days of activity and at the end of the penultimate day of the visit, exhausted and pleased with the outcome, she was looking forward to the final round of activities. At five o'clock in the morning of the last day, she was awakened by Prince Philip who himself had been awakened in his own room by the Queen's private secretary Sir Martin Charteris. It was one of the benefits of separate bedrooms that, on this occasion, difficult tidings were first relayed to Philip. Princess Anne was on the telephone and had the most incredible story to tell. That evening in London a lone gunman had attempted to kidnap Princess Anne and hold her to ransom, demanding a payment of £3 million from the Queen. The meticulously planned attempt almost succeeded and in the process, Anne's chauffeur, her detective, a policeman and a journalist who tried to rescue them, were all shot and seriously wounded.

It happened after Anne and Mark had attended a special showing of a film for the Riding for the Disabled Association of which Anne was patron. As they were driving back to Buckingham Palace along the Mall, the would-be kidnapper, armed with four revolvers and driving an old Ford Escort, had forced the royal limousine to a halt and attempted to drag Princess Anne from her car, threatening to shoot Mark who was holding on to her other arm. The kidnap attempt ended only when the shot policeman managed to radio for help, while lying injured by Anne's car. The drama of the event, sensational in its audacity, left the Queen and Prince Philip shocked, as was the House of Commons when business was interrupted that evening for a statement by the Home Secretary Roy Jenkins. Assured by Anne that she and Mark were safe and unharmed, the Queen decided to remain in Indonesia to complete the last day of her tour, carrying on regardless as if nothing untoward had happened. At the end of the day, however, she appeared to feel the need to talk about her daughter's experience, which suggested that she had been thinking about it herself for most of the day. With a group of aides and British staff, she talked frankly over a rare alcoholic drink, a large whisky; barely a day went by, she told them, when she did not fear for the safety of her children and members of her family, as indeed the whole security of those in exposed public positions was becoming more difficult.[14]

She said she was scared on occasions herself but she could never let it show; she had learned to read a crowd, in the same way that her detective had and, it would appear, had taken his advice and hints. The masses were cheerful and jolly and in their midst a tense person of evil intent stood out. But the dangers that were always there might not come in a crowd. They could come from a bomb, or as in Princess Anne's case, some lone, mentally disturbed person for whom there could be no accounting.

It was yet another example of the one great, unremitting aspect of her reign – event upon event, again.

Towards the end of the year of 1974, there was an unsuccessful conclusion to negotiations that had been going on unofficially with the Duchess of Windsor over the duke's estate and his large cache of papers and letters dating back to the thirties. Presumably with the Queen's approval and knowledge, Mountbatten had taken it upon himself first to attempt to ensure that the duke's money and valuables eventually came back into the royal fold and second to retrieve the papers and documents, which contained many of considerable historical significance, along with many more of a highly personal and confidential nature and which the royal family would have preferred to have deposited in the royal archives. Soon after the duke's funeral in 1972, Mountbatten had contacted the duchess to arrange to visit her; his purpose was to discuss the duke's will. The Windsor butler Georges Sanegre remembered the visit well.

> Mountbatten swept into the house and I could tell it was going to be difficult for the duchess. She was not at all keen on seeing him. She said it brought back too many memories. She was still in black mourning when she received him, in the shuttered library of the house in the Bois de Boulogne and I could sense immediately that there was an atmosphere between them. If she was broken by emotions, there was none on his part. I showed him into the library and closed the doors behind him. They were closeted for about twenty minutes and when the doors finally opened, I knew there was something wrong. He again swept out of the room without a backward glance and when he had gone, the duchess said to me 'Georges, he only came for the money. He wanted me to write my will so that all that David had given me would pass to members of the royal family in a charitable trust. I told him I would think about it . . . but I wasn't really interested.'[15]

Mountbatten returned to the subject again in 1973 but discovered to his horror that the duchess had ended her long association with her husband's English solicitors, who had drawn up the duke's original will leaving everything to his wife. In their place, she had appointed Maitre Suzanne Blum, the French lawyer who had been a friend for many years. Mountbatten persisted with his efforts on behalf of the Queen. He offered to act as an intermediary, with himself acting as executor, and again suggested the formation of a foundation with Prince Charles as its chairman. Neither the duchess nor Maitre Blum seemed enthusiastic and indeed when he visited the duchess in June 1973, he was unable to see Wallis. Maitre Blum insisted that she had no authority to divulge any information to him about the estate, other than that it would 'honour the duke's memory'.[16] Mountbatten tried again to reopen negotiations the following year, and received what was to be the final rebuttal of his attempts to secure the duke's money and papers. He received a note from the duchess in December 1974, stating that while she was always pleased to see him, she had to say that she was always left terribly depressed by his reminding her 'of David's death and my own'.[17] She added that the estate had been dealt with in accordance with her husband's wishes. The royal family did not allow the matter to rest. The matter of the duke's private papers became the topic of particular controversy. Certain documents were, the author understands, released following a direct appeal from Buckingham Palace, with an emissary calling personally to take them away, along with ceremonial items of dress. However, over a period of a number of years, the private correspondence and letters of the duke and duchess were widely used as source material for a series of books which would reveal intimate detail that the Queen would rather had remained untold, and better still locked away in the royal archives where, at least, she could have a measure of control of it. Some were indeed retrieved, though there remains to this day a discrepancy as to how these documents found their way back to Windsor. For her part, Maitre Blum complained of underhand methods in a letter to the Windsors' old friend, the Duke de Grantmesnil, who gave a copy of it to the author:

> The duchess has not handed over the duke's documents. Someone took them without her knowledge; she did not realise until later when I was there, she opened the duke's safe in his office and files containing his confidential papers were empty. She agreed only to give back the historical archive material, such as his papers concerning his activities as Prince of Wales, his letters to his family and so on, in exchange for some of her personal files,

> her divorce papers etc. Naturally, at the heart of this operation we found Mountbatten. I have a report signed by three of the duchess's closest confidantes, confirming that the files were taken in her absence. It all happened immediately after the duke's death. Secondly, Mountbatten came to see the duchess, who was ill, to try to make her sign a paper by which she would put all of her belongings into a trust which the Prince of Wales would administer. He harassed her so much that she revoked all her pledges and the powers she gave the duke's English advocate. She was so exasperated that at each visit Mountbatten spoke only about her death and her will. The whole thing made a real police thriller that would be too long to be written here. Finally, Mountbatten was banned from the house. He thinks I am responsible for that and attacks have begun against me in the papers. About the Prince of Wales – he is controlled by Mountbatten. The duchess never heard anything else from him since there is no question of the Foundation. I trust you will destroy this letter, which is intended for your personal information . . . Suzanne Blum.[18]

It must surely have been a matter for the Queen's personal interest that many of her uncle's private possessions should be recovered, not least the magnificent jewellery he gave to Wallis, some of which came from the family collection before his abdication. In the event, the British House of Windsor would get none of it . . .

Chapter Thirteen

Nothing Personal (1975–6)

The machine was ticking over nicely and Prince Charles was already thinking about plans for his mother's Silver Jubilee in 1977. It seemed a long way off but big celebrations were to be organised, including extensive tours at home and abroad. The circle had just about been completed since the mid-fifties and early sixties when people had been telling her she was priggish. We have seen what had passed since and in all the centuries of British monarchy, never had there been such a highly professional approach to what had become a global enterprise, to such a degree that it was almost too methodical – and there were still many detractors. Some Labour MPs, for example, wanted to have all the monarchy's expenditure channelled into one government department so that it could be seen at a glance exactly what it was costing. It might have clarified the situation under which the costs were met from a diversity of sources, ranging from the Foreign Office to the Defence Ministry and, perhaps quite deliberately, it is not always easy to pull these figures together to establish the true cost.

To see it in one bottom-line figure might have given the opponents such ammunition as to bring those costs under more severe attack. In that respect the Queen was already a rose in a bed of thorns. The whole issue came before the Commons again in 1975, when proposals for a further increase in the Civil List allowance to the royal family came up for review, accompanied by a mêlée of protest, which was slightly unjustified in view of the economic climate. Buckingham Palace made it known through the channels that reach the newspapers that the Queen had already dipped into her own pocket to make good deficits of £60,000 in 1971, £32,000 in 1974 and the expected shortfall of £150,000 for 1975.[1] Costs had risen dramatically at the palace, just as they had across the whole of the economic spectrum in the wake of oil price rises of the early seventies and the resultant rampant inflation which reached 21 per cent by May 1975. To meet the bill, the Queen's Keeper of the Privy Purse and her accountants had calculated they would need a Civil List allowance of £1.4 million to stay afloat in 1975, even after the Queen's own contribution. The pressures of inflation meant that it was virtually impossible to set a figure at which the Civil List could remain indefinitely, with increases at infrequent intervals as had been the case in the past. Until 1975, there had been only one increase in the Civil List since the Queen's accession; now the government planned to make an annual review in view of inflation. There were howls of protest in a lively Commons debate and the Queen's former Foreign Secretary Michael Stewart made the very sensible point that, in all the discussion, it was difficult to assess the Queen's true needs without knowing her true wealth, how much tax she would normally have to pay on her income, and how much the nation was spending to make such subsidies to the royal family. 'The example of the Head of State who is immune from that part of the law which requires us to pay taxes is unfortunate,' said Stewart.[2] His words continued to ring bells in the eighties, and it remained one of the most controversial issues of her reign as she headed for her fortieth anniversary in 1992.

Still, for all the rows over the Queen's Civil List, she and Prince Philip had managed a pretty tight ship, especially when compared with numerous government departments and nationalised industries, top-heavy with officials and staff who would have done better to copy than be critical. The Queen's personal wealth continued to be a subject of intrigue and when the rows descended into a discussion about the future of the monarchy, Prince Philip always had a ready answer: 'If we are no longer wanted let's get it over with amicably.' Well, there was little fear of that now. In spite of a newspaper poll that alleged 39 per cent of the population would like to dispose of the free-spending and costly royal family, it was more than likely a freak result. Willie Hamilton spoke for probably less than half a dozen anti-monarchists and a very small number of others who were in the closet; he made much of it, and spoke often of the parasitical band, sucking their lifeblood – money – from the long-suffering British taxpayer. Republicanism remained a frail body in England and Northern Ireland, and only slightly sturdier in Wales and Scotland.

There were very few, even in those days of hyper-inflation, who would not agree that the Queen gave very good value for money. She had largely risen above criticism; when it came she would take note and, if necessary, act upon it. Experience. That's what it all came down to and by the mid-seventies she had pretty well covered every eventuality and most of them several times. The fear of actually being there, staying there, doing the job and wondering if and when some unctuous politicians would turn nasty and pull down the curtains on the performing monarchy had long passed. Her whole well-oiled machine just clicked into gear and purred along. Her team of aides and helpers knew her style and exactly what she wanted. 'How is your wife?' she would ask an astonished mayor of some shire borough she had never visited before, and everyone wondered how she knew the poor woman had been in hospital. Her researchers always did a good job. Often she relied upon her own memory. 'You won't remember . . . but we met in 1962?' was a greeting she often received. 'Oh yes . . .' and then she goes off into a complete recall of the incident. She remembered staff birthdays and always wanted to be kept informed of the health of members of staff or their relatives, and when Patrick Plunket, the deputy Master of her Household, was dying of cancer, she went to see him nearly every day, although, in his case, he was more of a friend than an employee. At a reception not long after his death, she said to one of his friends, 'I know how to throw a good party, Patrick taught me.' Sir John Betjeman, poet laureate, described her as 'strong, brave; tough and sympathetic', while Alistair Forbes, the memoirist and family friend, likened her to 'the head of General Motors running the corner shop'.[3] This was not sycophantic praise, either; it was the view offered to the author from several sources who were in the corridors of Westminster at the time, and showed the respect which recognised that the Queen was exceedingly good news for Britain in the most difficult of economic circumstances; the stabilising factor while the politicians were scratching each other's eyes out.

There were still the predictable jibes but just as it had once been smart to criticise, it had also become smart to talk about the failure of the second Elizabethan Age. There was some evidence to support the complaint that the royals were philistines, especially when compared to the renaissance of the first Elizabeth Age. The much-quoted fact that *Dad's Army* was one of her favourite television programmes of the age and that she preferred Agatha Christie to Trollope did not inspire the confidence of the artistic or literary intelligentsia. She could recognise a name of a writer in the racing pages, but not one in *The Times Literary Supplement* and that rankled with the so-called establishment. But who cared about them, anyway, when she could claim to have similar tastes to 80 per cent or more of her subjects? The establishment was made up of an incestuous bunch at the best of times, though they did have a point that she could have done more to support the arts. The Queen's personal contribution was the extension of her own personal collection but the arts were very much in the shade when set alongside the family's more overt interests, such as horses and sports, and because of this high profile on whatever field of endeavour they were competing, with the Queen egging her husband or children on from the sidelines, they appeared to be an extravagant lot, viewed over a period of days and weeks when it was possible to assess their changes of clothes, for example, and their liberal usage of the now extensive variety of boats, planes, trains and motorcars are their disposal. There was still plenty to complain about but less to criticise. Staff numbers at the palace had fallen. Salaries had improved, though not greatly, and new systems and modernisation of the old practices had rationalised even more of the Victoriana. There was in operation as the Queen approached her twenty-five years on the throne, a royal system which was pretty well unbeatable.

Some things had suffered; the magic and the mystique

which had been so long preserved and for so long protected by those who felt it was the integral secret that kept the monarchy aloof and in place, was now beginning to disappear. If there was some invisible aura remaining, it perhaps applied only to the Queen herself who remained to all intents and purposes on the pedestal. Lesser royal mortals had long since become the daily fodder of the gossip columns and the cut-throat competitive spirit that existed between the popular daily and Sunday newspapers which seemed to become more strident as each year passed, especially now that Rupert Murdoch's new *Sun* had gained such a huge foothold in the market against the *Daily Mirror*. Similarly, the *Daily Mail* and the *Daily Express* were locked in their own circulation battle, in which the royal element was always to be a common denominator.

It seemed, by the mid-seventies, quite fatuous even to contemplate a future without the monarchy. Some tried, of course, but George Orwell's prediction in 1940 that after the war 'an English socialist government will transform the nation from top to bottom but quite probably will NOT abolish the monarchy' seemed correct in only the latter. H. G. Wells, who wrote in a letter to *The Times* 'the time has come to rid Britain of the ancient trappings of throne and sceptre'[4], had fewer supporters sixty years later than when he made the original appeal. Willie Hamilton, the reincarnation of Victorian republicanism, quoted Tom Paine, 'Royalty is as repugnant to common sense as to common right', yet coyly called himself a wayward subject. He made, by the way, a lot of money from his lectures and writings on 'My Queen and I . . .' and apart from giving the popular press some startling adjectives in his description of various members of the family, notably Princess Margaret and Prince Philip who were by their own actions quite often deserving of the headlines they received, his words were never taken too seriously. In the Commons, however, he did serve a very useful purpose in reminding the House that royalty was never above scrutiny, though his repeated attempts at obtaining full disclosure of the Queen's wealth met with a defiant 'No'.

Otherwise, her relationship with the government was fairly smooth. Harold Wilson had long ago dispelled any prospect, once harboured, that a Labour government might curtail the activities of the royal family and restrict their budget and finances by way of cuts and even taxation on the Queen's personal income. Wilson made no secret of his admiration for the Queen and soon after he retired from office, he made one of his classic little observations, 'If a Constitutional Monarchy had not existed, it would by AD 1977 have been necessary to invent it.'[5] He found his weekly audiences with her almost therapeutic. And after his re-election, the relationship between them was more of the same, only perhaps even more of the cosy informality that was Wilson's style and which the Queen apparently enjoyed, punctuated as it was by the serious issues of the day about which he always found the Queen well versed. He would arrive in the ante-room where traditionally the Prime Minister is kept waiting for a few moments to collect his thoughts before an equerry opens the door to say 'The Queen will receive you now, Prime Minister.' He would be shown as always into the Audience Chamber, a fairly small room in the family's private suite, where two armchairs were placed before a black and white marble fireplace, and Gainsborough and Canaletto paintings peered down. Although topics for discussion were more or less pre-arranged, the Queen would often lead the conversation into other areas, bringing up subjects she might have read about in the official government papers in the boxes or perhaps an item in the newspapers.

The Audience Chamber keeps its secrets; no minutes are taken and the Prime Minister could speak freely about current problems with 'someone who knows her stuff' without fear of it leaking out. She liked, especially, to hear the political gossip which Wilson also liked to impart. When, in November 1974, the famous case of 'The Spanking Colonel' – Lieutenant Colonel John Brooks – became public, a rivalry developed between Wilson and the Queen as to who had the latest information on the case, which involved the colonel's alleged penchant for spanking nubile young ladies aboard his boat on the Thames. Wilson beat her to the news one day, having seen a later edition of the *Evening Standard* than the one the Queen had read. 'Why didn't I have that edition?' she said in mock admonishment to her private secretary.[6] Not long afterwards, Wilson began his audience with the question, 'Have you seen the story about Giscard d'Estaing?' She had not and he explained that the French President currently featured in allegations of his involvement with young ladies in the back of his car.

'Ho-ho, Mr Wilson,' said the Queen with a grin. At the time, Wilson had to go to Paris for a conference and when he returned the Queen asked him how the trip had gone and he replied that they had settled some very important matters. 'No, I don't mean that,' said the Queen. 'I meant what about the Ho-ho?'

Wilson replied, 'Ma'am, I am able to report that the French Prime Minister and I attended a very large dinner after which I was violently sick. There was definitely no "Ho-ho".'[7]

Wilson often stayed longer than normal for a Prime Minister's audience. Positioned on either side of the fireplace, he and the Queen chatted about life and politics while the Queen poured him a liberal quantity of whisky. According to Joe Haines, his press secretary, Wilson often returned to No. 10 Downing Street in a warm and friendly mood, grinning and occasionally slightly tipsy.

Like Edward Heath and other former prime ministers, Wilson also had fond memories of his visit to Balmoral during the Queen's holidays. 'She seemed far more relaxed up there,' said Wilson, 'much more so than in the palace. I don't think she liked the palace very much. In those Highland surroundings, she is one of the most natural women and I have this strong image of her and my wife Mary doing the washing-up in a holiday chalet they have on the Balmoral estate during our weekend stay.'[8] On one occasion, she said to him 'Let's go over and see Mother,' and they got into her Land Rover – 'We don't need the detectives, do we,' she said – and drove to the Queen Mother's house at Birkhall. Like Wilson, many other visitors to Balmoral have been impressed by the personal attention they receive from members of the royal family, and perhaps were not aware that it was all carefully calculated to 'keep the guests amused'. Each member of the family shares the task during the period when there are guests present.

Back to business; and in February the Queen came face to face with the reminder of the new scourge of British life, the threat of IRA bombs which had become increasingly devastating since the first in 1973. The Queen met members of the emergency services and of the bomb squad who had to deal with the recent wave of bombings in London, Guildford and Birmingham, killing 30 people and injuring more than 300. Her own safety from attack was under constant review, and in spite of her insistence that 'we must be seen or there is no point to it' it became necessary to step up security at all royal buildings and at all events which members of the royal family would be attending. Special facilities were always to be made available; routes were to be checked and double checked; all buildings were to be thoroughly searched, and transport looked over; an ambulance should be on hand and parked unobtrusively near to where the Queen or other senior members of the family would be attending. These were some of the initial steps which were taken to protect her, though as the Queen was more experienced in meeting crowds and observing security measures in varying degrees of effectiveness at cities anywhere in the world, she knew very well that terrorist attacks were almost impossible either to predict or to deter.

And, coincidentally that very week, one other woman to whom that fact would become so painfully apparent stepped firmly and confidently into the public limelight. Mrs Margaret Thatcher, housewife and mother of twins, became the front-runner for leadership of Her Majesty's Opposition on 4 February 1975, at the age of forty-nine. She sent Edward Heath into the wilderness, but not obscurity, when she defeated him 130-119 in the leadership ballot. A week later, she came through the second round of the Conservatives' election process by winning an overall majority against four male contenders.

The security alert was not merely a British problem, of course, and there were tight precautions made when the Queen travelled to Bermuda on 16 February 1975 for her first visit to the island since 1954. At the time, Hamilton was in the grip of a general strike and only a few months earlier the Governor Sir Richard Sharples had been assassinated. When she arrived, she was met by a picket line of strikers at the dockyard who were singing 'We shall not be moved . . .' to a calypso beat. As the Queen later observed, 'They were very good-humoured, and just moved back as we approached.'

The men's bitterness was temporarily set aside and one of them called out, 'It's not you, Your Majesty – it's the government'. The Bermudan stopover, followed by visits to Barbados and the Bahamas, was made on her way to her first state visit to Mexico at the invitation of President Echeverria; it was timed to coincide with a trade convention from Britain which used the royal yacht *Britannia* as a reception and conference centre for meetings with local businessmen who were, in the main, suitably impressed by Britain's courtship of their trade. As to the Queen's own reception in Mexico, royal observers were positive that it ranked amongst the most spectacular of all royal visits to date.

It was estimated that a million or more Mexicans lined the streets to watch her arrival in the central square of Mexico City, by the cathedral, festooned with flags and banners, and 5,000 children held up cards which, when turned over, compiled an elaborate design of giant portraits of the Queen and the President, linked by an heraldic symbol to show this new spirit of friendship between the countries. Storms and torrential rain marred the visit. The *Britannia* had to be moved from her mooring to seek calmer waters during gale force winds, and a helicopter called in to airlift the Queen's luggage ashore broke down and a special boat had to be sent to bring her dresses back to the mainland for the remaining celebrations. The inclemency did not dampen the Mexican spirit. The welcome at each port of call was far greater than anyone had imagined, and there was a joke going around at the time when a million people turned up to watch her arrival which alleged that the President commented, 'I only ordered half a million.' The whole tour clocked another 16,000 on the Queen's travel mileometer. And a further 26,000 mile journey was already in sight.

The Queen returned to London in early March, while Philip continued on alone, visiting other South American countries. He arrived back at Buckingham Palace to join the final preparations for the next overseas jaunt – this time to Hong Kong and Japan, in support of another 'Buy British' campaign to help the cause of Britain's daunting balance of payments deficit.

In between arrival home and departure on 25 April the Queen managed to fit in numerous engagements on the home front, and then she flew off with Philip to Jamaica where she was to open the 1975 Commonwealth Conference before flying on to Hong Kong via Honolulu for the first visit to the island community in its 134 year history as a British colony. Similarly, when she landed in Japan on 7 May, she was the first British ruler in history to make a state visit. It was a sign of the times that the personal bodyguard of Prince Akihito had been sent to England the previous year to watch a royal visit to Norwich and study the methods of British police in protecting the Queen. There was barely a strand of comparison between Norwich and Tokyo, and the Japanese detectives' recommendations for security precautions in the current international climate of terrorism hardly reflected the scenario in the heart of sleepy Norfolk. The Japanese were determined that nothing should happen to her while she was on their soil and 50,000 men were given the task of protecting her. The British entourage that surrounded the Queen's visit was all aimed at promoting trade and cultural exchange. A 'Made in Britain' display was staged at virtually every major shopping centre; there were British trade and cultural exhibitions in seventy-five different locations and as well as the strong contingent of businessmen, there were performances by the Royal Ballet and the Royal Shakespeare Company. The Queen loaned twenty-three paintings from her private collection for an exhibition of British art. Meantime, she plugged British industry at every opportunity. 'I hope trade between our two countries will flourish,' she said, 'because it is and will be the mainspring of Anglo-Japanese relations.' She in turn became dubbed by Japanese newspapers as 'Britain's most elegant saleswoman' which must have pleased Harold Wilson and the British politicians no end, desperate as they were by the end of May for any contribution towards the appalling state of the home economy.

Not long after she returned to England, her Prime Minister was being forced into the most draconian of peacetime measures to combat inflation which reached a horrific 25 per cent by June and unemployment which had gone above the 1.2 million mark for the first time since the war. With rail workers demanding a 30 per cent pay increase, doctors asking for 38 per cent and pay awards generally running at an average of 32 per cent, Chancellor Denis Healey pleaded the case for a pay freeze by saying, 'Something has got to be done to bring this madman's merry-go-round of inflation to a stop'. It did not, for the time being, succeed and once again the Queen showed her concern for women and children, seeking information on the effect the proposed government action would have on families. Wilson was unrelenting; if the unions did not accept a voluntary pay freeze it would have to be enforced by law.*

Still, it wasn't all gloomy news. The Queen was about to open the pipeline that would bring the first North Sea oil ashore and Harold Wilson said optimistically, 'We shall be self-sufficient in oil by 1980'. But for the time being, restraint from the workers was needed, and who better to plead the case than the Sovereign herself. Her Christmas broadcast that year was noteworthy for its content and its unusual production techniques, so far removed from the normal situation of the Queen seated at her desk or relaxing in an armchair. It was clearly aimed at supporting the government's stand against higher wages. With half the nation glued to her speech after Christmas lunch, it was a good time to offer them a little subliminal advice: 'So much of the time we feel that our lives are dominated by great impersonal forces beyond our control. The scale of things and organisations seems to get bigger and more inhuman. We are horrified by brutal and senseless violence, and above all the whole fabric of our lives is threatened by inflation, the frightening sickness of the world today.' Now the camera switched to a prerecorded moment where the Queen was standing on a small stone bridge by a lake, from which she threw a stone in the water and the camera zoomed in on the ripples it caused and she continued, '. . . if you throw a stone into a pool, the ripples go on spreading outwards . . . a big stone can cause waves but even the smallest pebble can change the whole pattern

*On 3 September, the TUC voted by a majority of two to one in favour of a voluntary £6 a week pay rise limit with immediate effect; such a commitment was a prerequisite before Chancellor Denis Healey made his famous application to the International Monetary Fund for Britain to borrow £1,000 million to tide it over the current financial difficulties.

of the water. Our daily lives are like ripples, each one makes a difference, even the smallest . . .'

There were ripples elsewhere; history was repeating itself again. Just at the very time when the Queen's personal standing was at a peak, something, some problem or trouble, from within her own sphere darts out to reveal itself and cause unwanted vibrations around the throne. These vibrations were particularly disturbing. The activities – some preferred the word 'antics' – of Princess Margaret had been a matter of concern among the royal circle for some time; she and Lord Snowdon appeared to have drifted irretrievably apart and it was worrying the Queen, not merely from the point of view of the situation becoming public. Those close to Margaret knew that the marriage had been a shell and a sham for some time; if she had not been the Queen's sister and controlled still by sub-sections of that dreaded Royal Marriages Act, Margaret would have been separated from Lord Snowdon months, if not years earlier, and a whole chorus of people who said she'd married on the rebound would sing out 'Told you so!' It would have come as no surprise to the Queen or the Queen Mother, if at any time the balloon finally went up. There were allegations in the gossip columns of rows and long periods of not talking to her sister, to which was later added the astonishing claim by Willie Hamilton that the Queen would actually welcome 'the full glare of public criticism' switched to her sister because of her behaviour.[9] He claimed he was asked by a Tory MP with 'connections' when he was going to raise the question of Princess Margaret in the Commons, as if it were an invitation to do so. The Queen was still deeply attached to Margaret – and very fond of Lord Snowdon – there had been some heated exchanges on the state of the Snowdons' marriage which appeared to be in the process of public disintegration.

Princess Margaret had been ridiculed quite damagingly during the past three years or so, at first through her own demeanour and the company she kept, aided by the extravagance of adjectives used by the MPs when attacking the rises through inflation of her Civil List allowance which went up to £55,000 in 1975. With Lord Snowdon often abroad or tied up on long photographic assignments, Princess

Margaret had been seen and photographed with several unattached men accompanying her to some nightspot or other, including an old flame from the fifties, Dominic Elliot, and a tragically ended friendship with pianist Robin Douglas-Home who committed suicide.

Later revelations concerning the princess included a batch of letters allegedly written by her which came to light in New York; talk of a blackmail attempt was rampant. The gardening socialite Roderick Llewellyn came into the princess's life the year after Douglas-Home's death. He was invited to make up the numbers at a weekend party thrown by Margaret's old friend Colin Tennant, at his Scottish estate. Thereafter, they were to be discovered by the paparazzi in each other's company on occasions too numerous to quantify. Perhaps the most famous, however, was when Margaret went alone to a communal farm, described in the newspapers as an upper-class hippie commune, at Surrendell in Wiltshire, which had some titled inmates, including Sarah Ponsonby, the niece of the Earl of Bessborough, who was not at all taken with the photograph which appeared in the *Sun*, of her doing the weeding in just a pair of jeans. Roddy Llewellyn was a member and he invited Margaret down to spend a weekend at the commune farmhouse, set in 47 acres near Malmesbury. It would be noted that she stayed the night and joined Roddy in leading a sing-song after dinner. The free-thinking, free-speaking members of the group who had dashed around to find a clean bed for her to sleep in, eventually provided ample copy for the morning papers by telling all to reporters who came bearing gifts of money in brown paper bags and chequebooks for photographs.

Typically uninterrupted by the attendant publicity of the 'vile and common newspapers', Princess Margaret proceeded to get on with her life, with apparent disregard for any embarrassment that she might cause her family. Could she really have imagined that she could slip away from the family holiday soon after Christmas and fly away to her holiday island with Roddy in tow and not have the news front-paged all over the world? Well, perhaps so, because she had done it before and had succeeded in avoiding any hint in the press. Her paradise island of Mustique had been her hideaway and recuperation zone every January for the past five years. Colin

Tennant bought the island in 1952 for £25,000 and then made a fortune subdividing it into plots which he sold for up to £40,000 a piece. One of them he gave to Princess Margaret free of charge, perhaps not altogether an unwise move in view of the tourists she might attract. He built her a house which was completed in 1970 and she named it Les Jolies Eaux. Lord Snowdon was never too keen on the place, and only ever visited it twice. Roddy visited it too; the first time was 'almost a honeymoon', according to Nigel Dempster.[10] And now they were going again.

In January 1976, cutting short her stay at Sandringham with the rest of the family, she flew to Mustique with Roddy, intending to have three quiet weeks away from the world and the fierce white light and the vulgar gossip. If the Queen had shown any signs of disapproval of her sister's plans, then they were disregarded; Margaret and her unwealthy paramour carried on with their tryst and succeeded in slipping away from Norfolk and into Mustique without any sign of problems, or so they thought. Unknown to them, a New Zealand journalist named Ross Waby who worked for the New York bureau of Rupert Murdoch's News International had booked into the island's hotel, describing himself as a schoolteacher. Before long, he captured Margaret and Roddy in casual beach attire dining with a group of friends. It made the perfect picture of a couple happily enjoying their holiday which under normal circumstances would not have caused a ripple of concern, even if it was adulterous, except that this was the Queen's sister – and by Saturday night, that ever-ready guardian of royal morals, the *News of the World*, was printing its 5.5 million copies with the photograph on the front page to appear on tomorrow's breakfast tables; the rest of the party with whom they had been dining was cut out of the photograph, leaving it to appear an intimate twosome, which in truth it was not, though the latter was a hair-splitting point. The fan was whirring and the revelations hit it in a furore. Headlines and embarrassment reigned over Buckingham Palace where the press office, for once, was quite justified with 'No comment'. There was simply nothing to be said. That evening, with every possible character and location in the plot staked out by whole armies of reporters and photographers, Princess Margaret was contacted in

Mustique and was told that her husband was very angry; he had already been in touch with the Queen, apologised for the mess and accepted at least some portion of the blame but this time, he said, he had been made to look a fool once too often. It was a total humiliation. The indignation was sufficient to pass the public focus entirely over to Princess Margaret who would be seen as the guilty party, though she and a few other close friends knew that Lord Snowdon, having knowledge of his wife's flirtations when their marriage ran into trouble, had decided what was good for the goose was good for the gander too. For the past fourteen months, he had been seeing a lot of Lucy Lindsay-Hogg. Anyway, the headlines were either the last straw for a humiliated man, or the moment he had been waiting for to escape from the marriage; probably, it was a bit of both. He told the Queen his position was untenable; and now it had arrived – another scandal. DIVORCE.

The Queen could see it, at that moment, hanging like a great cloud over what should have been the most happy and successful months ahead since the Coronation – the celebrations for her own fiftieth birthday and the twenty-fifth anniversary of her succession. And it was ironic that the last great headline-inspiring royal romance of this age was Princess Margaret's love for Group Captain Peter Townsend. That, it will be recalled, all blew up on the day of the Queen's Coronation – and now, as the Coronation was about to be revisited, it was a supreme irony that the princess who was stopped from marrying a divorced man was herself facing the prospect of divorce. This time, it really was the greatest internal crisis within the royal family since the Abdication and it was perhaps fortunate indeed for them that Harold Wilson was still Prime Minister. It was Wilson who 'fixed' the formal procedure for the divorce of the Earl of Harewood and the Queen would seek his advice again, not merely because of the requirement to do so under the Royal Marriages Act, but also to get Wilson's personal counsel on how it should be handled. Margaret cut short her holiday and returned to London to face the gathering storm, only to discover that her husband had left the royal household and had moved in with his mother, Lady Rosse. The media worldwide were still camping on everybody's doorstep and the headlines ran for days; to those involved it must have seemed endless. No story in recent history had contained all the ingredients that captivated public interest so avidly: royalty, church, sex, scandal, divorce, love nests and goodness knows what else, to be followed with yards of hollow compassion for the two unfortunate children caught in the middle of the crossfire. In another impeccably timed piece of ironic coincidence, the Queen and Prince Philip had a long-standing engagement to make a tour of Fleet Street on 27 February to discover the mysteries of newspaper production. The Queen pressed the buttons which set the presses rolling for the lunchtime edition of the *Evening Standard* and the only royal photograph it contained was one of herself arriving at the building an hour earlier. 'Good gracious, that's me,' she said as one of the production executives handed her a copy hot off the presses. The tour continued with visits to the London *Evening News*, the *Daily Mail*, the *Daily Telegraph*, the *Daily Mirror* and one of her favourite newspapers, the *Sporting Life*.

Behind the scenes, events moved quickly, and Snowdon seemed to be forcing the pace. He wanted a divorce and the Queen finally had to accept the fact, reluctant though she was to have her sister given the historic distinction of being the first member of the immediate family – discounting cousins – to be divorced since Henry VIII. The Queen's personal solicitor Matthew Farrer was called in to negotiate a legal separation. He was instructed to offer Lord Snowdon a settlement of £100,000 from Princess Margaret's personal fortune and asked the disgruntled earl earnestly to consider saving the royal family from the wholly unwanted publicity that would surround divorce proceedings at a time when the great national celebrations which Prince Charles was supervising and with which Lord Snowdon himself would be involved, were almost upon them. Snowdon agreed and put his signature to a set of documents before flying off to Australia on a photographic assignment, having been shown the wording of a statement that he expected would be put out to the newspapers the following day.

There was a sudden and incredible interruption to the sequence of events concerning Princess Margaret which was as dramatic as the stroke Churchill suffered after the Coronation; and it was not entirely accidental. On 16 March Harold Wilson announced he had decided to retire. He had already told the Queen of his intentions some time earlier. One who was present at a private dinner at No. 10 on 9 December 1975 with Wilson and Lord Goodman, the lawyer, would recall to the author that, in his almost manic desperation to show that he had not just 'cut and run' to get out before the 'balloon went up', Wilson made the then mysterious comment to Goodman, 'I told her this evening about that topic which we were discussing earlier.'[11] Nothing more was said, but it was a Tuesday evening and Wilson had, it later transpired, reminded the Queen of what he had told her when he became Prime Minister for the second time, that it was his intention to retire in two years. The two years were almost up, and when the time came for him to make his announcement, it coincided with the current situation involving Margaret.

When the Queen sought Wilson's advice on how the announcement of the separation of her sister and brother-in-law should be handled, Wilson came up with 'one of his typical and memorable acts of egotism'.[12] It was his own 'ingenious idea' that the separation should be revealed to the press immediately following the announcement of his own resignation; thus, he said, the unfortunate news of Margaret's marital break-up would be blanketed by the bombshell of his own decision. What followed was a carefully planned and deliberate ploy to lessen the impact upon the royal family. On the morning of 6 March, the normal Cabinet meeting was held at 11.00 a.m. No one in the room apparently had any idea what Wilson was going to say when he shuffled up some papers and addressed his colleagues, 'Before we come to business, I would like to make a statement.'[13] He then read a prepared eight-page speech announcing his intention to go to Buckingham Palace that day to offer his resignation to the Queen. He said it had always been his intention to quit after two years and he insisted that it was his desire to retire and no other reason that had led him to his decision. His colleagues were stunned, some even tearful, and senior members of his government began making their little speeches of tribute, and how they could never thank him enough for what he had done for the party and the country. Joe Haines, Wilson's press secretary, made the announcement and very soon Downing Street was under siege from an army of photographers, reporters and television cameras. The entire world of international politics was baffled that he should go just as the economy was beginning to show signs of recovery, yet many expressed the fear that he had left the door open for the dreaded coalition or national government that had been talked of for so long. Other darker rumours and conspiracy theorists suggested other more sinister reasons, later linked to MI5 and the theft of some of Wilson's private papers the previous year. The Queen was one of the few who knew the truth. The following morning and for the next two weeks in fact, the newspapers were full of it, first with the resignation news and secondly with the speculation over his successor.

With Wilson's resignation statement sending the newspapers into a state of prolific industry, the next stage of the operation came into play; this would, Buckingham Palace believed, take the focus off what was then considered to be quite shattering news the palace press office was about to release. A brief statement announced: 'Her Royal Highness the Princess Margaret, Countess of Snowdon and the Earl of Snowdon have mutually agreed to live apart. The princess will carry out her public duties unaccompanied by Lord Snowdon. There are no plans for any divorce proceedings.'[14] The scene in Fleet Street, as the author well recalls, was one of frenzied high drama and almost disbelief, not at the facts but that another story of such great public interest should land so quickly after the first. The plot between Wilson and the Queen did not, however, go quite according to plan. 'The trouble was,' Joe Haines recalled, 'the Buckingham palace story was not eclipsed by Wilson's resignation – it went the other way.'[15]

Lord Snowdon, meantime, had reached Sydney where, in response to the posse of journalists waiting for his arrival, he read a polished little statement. 'I am naturally desperately sad in every way that this has had to come. I would just like to say three things: first to pray for the understanding of our two children; secondly to wish Princess Margaret every happiness for her future; and thirdly to express with utmost humility the love, admiration and respect I will always have for her sister, her mother and her entire family.'

To the close friends of Margaret and Tony, the resignation of Harold Wilson came as more of a surprise than their separation. As Lord Lichfield recalled, 'They used to trade insults like machine-gun fire', while another of their friends said that they were too much alike, almost the same person in so many respects, which sometimes worked in a relationship and sometimes did not. In their case, it was the latter. Up until this moment, both had apparently tolerated each other's liaisons and friendships until eventually bitterness replaced jealousy and resentment followed infidelities. Blazing rows and 2-day reconciliations provided the classic ingredients for a marriage which had run its course, and there was no point in it continuing, princess or no princess. If the three parties prominently involved believed for one moment – and on the strength of past experience Princess Margaret probably did not believe it – that the press would now leave them alone, they were to be mistaken. More, much more, was still to be written on the subject when Princess Margaret surprisingly threw another log on the fire . . .

The diversion to the royal drama was one that also affected the Queen but this time only as an observer to the election of the new Prime Minister. In the meantime, she attended a farewell dinner party for Harold Wilson and gave a 'highly amusing and very impressive speech'[16] which she made without notes – thus contradicting Tony Benn's assessment that she could not utter a word without a script. She joked with Wilson about the fact that they had one thing in common, that they both lived in a tied cottage and now, unfortunately, he would have to leave his in favour of the next incumbent.

In fact, the next man in arrived with the minimum of fuss which required no more than the formality of appointment by the Queen after the Labour Party's swift election procedure nominated James Callaghan as the party's new leader, and in consequence, Prime Minister. Michael Foot and Denis Healey were the other two leading contenders. Healey was eliminated on the first ballot and on 5 April the

Queen received Callaghan at Buckingham Palace after he had defeated Foot in the final ballot, 176 votes to 137.

Mr Callaghan was jubilant but characteristically low-key; his beaming smile, like that of a benevolent uncle, which could turn instantly to iron-hard and angry response to unwanted questioning became the hallmark of his leadership. He got on well with the Queen, but at the start there were reports that it would not be an easy relationship. He turned down an invitation for himself and his wife to attend the Queen's official fiftieth birthday party at Windsor on 20 April and became the only leading member of the British political scene absent.

In the resultant stories which were written in some quarters as 'Callaghan's snub to the Queen', Buckingham Palace explained that 'the Prime Minister was invited but was unable to come'. Instead, he stayed at his Sussex farm, reading himself in to the mass of papers that portrayed in fullest detail the problems he had inherited as the nation's new leader. The Queen, we learned later, 'quite understood' and instead invited Callaghan and his wife Audrey to dinner at Windsor the following week, where in less frenetic surroundings they were able to indulge in long conversations. He missed quite a party. Before a grand ball to be attended by some 500 guests, there was a dinner party for some 60 family and friends; Lord Snowdon was conspicuous by his presence, thus dismissing gossip-column stories that he had been cut off from the royal family because of animosity between himself and the Queen; the reports were quite wrong. Ex-Prime Minister Edward Heath flew back from Spain especially for the party; Liberal leader Jeremy Thorpe and his wife Marion, the former Countess of Harewood, were also there. Mrs Thatcher and Denis were much in evidence though Vincent Mulchrone, witnessing the occasion, observed, 'If this lady [the Queen] was in politics she would make Mrs Margaret Thatcher look like Little Bo Peep'.[17] The party was destined to end at 3.00 a.m. and none could leave before the Queen – and she was determined to stay to the end for a very special reason. At 2.40 a.m., the precise time she was born, she and Prince Philip took to the floor to dance in her fiftieth birthday to the minute.

The birthday marked another outpouring of respect and

admiration for the Queen, sycophantic and over the top in many cases, by the same newspapers and leader-writers who had, just a month before, portrayed the Princess Margaret affair as a national scandal. The *Mirror* was typical: 'Happy and glorious birthday, Ma'am . . . the *Mirror* toasts your half-century with affection, warmth and pride. We haven't always seen eye to eye . . . but our criticism has never been personal . . . Today we would like to be very personal indeed. We think you are the tops. And damned good at your job . . . the status of the monarchy has gone from strength to strength.'[18] This latter statement was confirmed by a Gallup opinion poll the following month which showed that, in spite of Margaret, 81 per cent of the nation was in favour of the monarchy. And the Queen herself could do no wrong . . .

Nor could she in America which was gripped by bicentennial fever when she and Prince Philip crossed the Atlantic for a magnificent welcome. This odd mixture of soap and pomp which rolls up into one unique package which constitutes the royal roadshow, continues to fascinate in ever-increasing amounts. President Gerald Ford's invitation for the Queen to take part in the actual 4 July celebrations was quietly declined; it might not be fitting for the great-great-great-great-granddaughter of George III who lost the American colonies to be present on the day. She flew to Bermuda and then sailed aboard the royal yacht *Britannia* into Philadelphia, the city where the Liberty Bell was originally sounded to proclaim independence from Britain; it was at this point she planned to participate. The new Foreign Secretary in the Callaghan Cabinet, Tony Crosland, and his wife Susan were experiencing the royal command for the first time – whereby the Foreign Secretary 'is commanded to join Her Majesty . . .' Crosland was uneasy about being away at such a crucial time with the crises in Rhodesia and Uganda both on the boil. However, Callaghan told him there was nothing to be done except go; it would be a very useful trip as far as British trade and foreign relations were concerned.

The royal entourage was not a large one, just ten in all including the Queen's lady in attendance, her lady in waiting, her private secretary, her deputy private secretary, her doctor, her equerry in waiting and Prince Philip's private secretary.

The purpose of the *Britannia*'s presence was to provide the Queen with a place to rest between a hectic round of engagements and to double up as reception centre for her own private inner party. Ciphered messages came regularly to the *Britannia*, to be delivered to Tony Crosland; some were urgent, and required ciphered replies. Susan Crosland, whose account of the trip provides a fascinating insight into life in the royal circle, observed that aboard the *Britannia* it was hardly a 'hugger-mugger' existence. They seldom saw anyone except footmen, except one day when Tony wanted a haircut and his wife was trimming it for him on deck. At that moment, there was a 'Ha-hah . . .' from an upper deck. They glanced up and discovered Prince Philip watching.

A gale was beginning to rise and by evening *Britannia* was being hauled up over the crests of great waves and heaving to the side at a 45 degree angle. Everyone was supposed to assemble in the drawing room for pre-dinner drinks and because of the conditions it was uncertain if the Queen would be present, because it was said she was a poor sailor in bad weather. The Queen appeared, looking philosophical, almost merry, twenty yards of chiffon scarf flung over her shoulder. Half a pace behind her was Philip, his face 'less fresh than usual, ashen and drawn, in fact'.[19] They didn't spend long at the table that evening and soon after returning to the drawing room for coffee the Queen came to say goodnight, resting one hand against the handle of the sliding door which at that moment began sliding shut. The Queen gripped the handle and moved with it as it slid slowly shut, the chiffon scarf flying in the opposite direction. 'Wheeeeee,' said the Queen. *Britannia* shuddered, reeled again. The chiffon scarf flew the other way. 'Wheeeeee,' said the Queen. *Britannia* hesitated before the next heave. 'Goodnight,' said the Queen, slipping through the door with Prince Philip half a pace behind her. During the night the force 9 gale abated to a mere 6 and in the morning Susan Crosland went out to sunbathe on the immaculately scrubbed deck. Later, when they gathered for lunch, the Queen observed that she had never seen so many grey faces at dinner. 'Philip is not at all well . . .' she paused, giggled and added, 'I'm glad to say,' offering her pointed jibe at her own Admiral of the Fleet.

The ciphered messages came thick and fast. The Israelis

had made an airborne raid on Entebbe to free 100 hostages aboard a hijacked airliner whose captors were being aided by Idi Amin. On Monday 5 July before the Queen's arrival at Philadelphia, she gave Susan Crosland a lesson in standing to relieve the pressure on the feet. 'One plants one's feet apart like this,' she said demonstrating. 'Always keep them parallel. Make sure your weight is evenly distributed.' Everyone agreed, Susan Crosland observed, that the Queen's schedule was 'murderous'. 'I have never experienced anything so arduous,' said Mrs Crosland. The Queen had brought to the city of Philadelphia a new bell as a gift to replace the old one which was cracked in 1835 and could no longer be rung. Well, that caused a spot of bother. The Queen's bell bore the inscription 'Let Freedom Ring' whereas the old bell read 'Proclaim liberty throughout the land unto all inhabitants thereof', and though Buckingham Palace had already pointed out that it was not intended as a replica, protesters paraded with banners demanding that the 'counterfeit' bell should be sent back to England. No one took them too seriously and the Queen and Philip began a whistle-stop tour of the city in between which Tony Crosland received more urgent messages and was directing the Foreign Office's response to the situation in Uganda concerning Mrs Dora Bloch who had been missing since the night of the raid on Entebbe; she was of dual English and Israeli nationality.* In the evening, there was a special banquet for them arranged by the mayor of Philadelphia. The royal party was allowed ten minutes between the banquet and a reception afterwards to freshen up. Susan Crosland noted another humorous exchange. The Queen had gone into the Ladies room and at the door of this her own lady in waiting was 'wrestling' with a woman dressed in an emerald green satin gown. There appeared to be an argument going on, that the woman in the satin gown wanted to follow the Queen. 'You won't,' her lady in waiting insisted. 'I must,' came the reply. It turned out that she was an FBI agent whose orders were never to let the Queen out of her sight. At that moment the Queen reappeared, unflustered,

*Mrs Bloch was separated from the main block of the hostages when she was taken to hospital before the Israeli raid. She was never seen again.

and calmly observed, 'Frightfully hot in Philadelphia. Is it always like this in July?'

From Philadelphia, they moved on to Washington where more engagements kept the Queen on the go, twelve to fourteen hours a day. President Ford's banquet for the royals proved to be the most eventful. His wife Betty was unable to attend, because she had a cold, and Susan Crosland also felt unwell. Half way through the soup, she thought she was going to faint. The Queen's footman, eagle-eyed and always on the look-out for trouble, noticed Mrs Crosland's distress and brought her some water. It was no good; she had to leave before she fainted. She dashed towards the swing doors and collapsed before getting through them. The door swung back and hit her face, splitting it open and fracturing her jaw. A small crowd of unidentified dignitaries came to assist her, including the Queen's own doctor, ever-present, and President Ford's personal physician. Susan was removed to her room in the British embassy where the two eminent medical men agreed that some plastic surgery might be necessary on her face, and was later taken to the President's Suite at the Bethesda Hospital, Maryland for further treatment. 'An interesting couple,' observed Henry Kissinger of his British counterpart and his wife. Next day, the royal tour headed eastward, to New York and Boston for more of the same. The crowds were delighted; the officials were occasionally slightly cool about her visit, especially in Boston where two centuries earlier Paul Revere hung his lantern to warn of the approaching redcoats. But it had been among the most hectic six days ever recorded on a royal tour. Although Susan Crosland was the only one actually to suffer injury through her collapse, two experienced royal attendants were admitted to hospital immediately their duty was completed, suffering from exhaustion. As Mrs Crosland said, 'Only the Queen showed no signs of wear and tear!'[10]

French Canadians were not merely cool about her arrival in Montreal for the opening of the 1976 Olympics; they would have preferred her not to have been present at all, and the crowds for her opening speeches were noticeably small. She put on a brave and optimistic note in predicting that the French and English fractions were finding a new *entente cordiale*, recognising 'a human diversity and an acceptance of the rights of others'. Such appeals for unity in Canada had become commonplace, just as the protests and controversy surrounding her visit seemed to have become a permanency. The arrival of the family group, with Princess Anne competing as a member of Britain's 3-day eventing team and husband Mark listed as reserve, Prince Charles flying over to join them, and Prince Andrew, sturdy and handsome at sixteen becoming a new focus of attention, was not unnaturally presented as a mirror in which all Canadians might perceive their own ideals of life. This perception was already outdated in Britain, and before long it would be to the Canadians. She did not know it yet, but Prime Minister Pierre Trudeau was already secretly considering amendments to the constitution which would affect the Queen's standing, leading eventually of course to the final severing of the colonial ties first set in place when Queen Victoria approved the British North American Act.

One by one, the royal prerogatives were diminishing in their importance, the real influence vanishing. Change which she herself had predicted had to come was affecting her standing – but not her popularity; as one leader-writer had put it: 'Nothing Personal'.

Chapter Fourteen
Jubilee
(1977)

Royal Jubilees seem to have a habit of falling during hard times and the twenty-fifth anniversary of the accession of Elizabeth II was no exception. Of the few comparable events, that of King George III in 1809 was notable for its arrival during a dire economic crisis and one historian of the day accused the King's government of using the occasion to divert attention from the nation's plight. Similarly, King George V was apprehensive about his own jubilee celebrations in 1935: 'all this fuss . . . what will people think of it in these hard and anxious times?' Later, the King remarked upon the 'never to be forgotten day . . . the greatest number of people in the streets I have ever seen.'[1] After touring the slums and tenements of north and southwest London, he said how fascinated he was by the decorations 'all put up by the poor'.

This time, Britain was not quite so desperately impoverished, though similar quotations about the cost of it all were certainly applicable at the start of 1977, and neither would it have been completely without foundation to assume that a year of royal-linked activity would divert attention from the nation's economic ills. As the year dawned, cold and grey, unemployment had reached 1.3 million and on 12 January inflation was still running at 16 per cent. Chancellor Denis Healey announced that he had just managed to borrow $3,000 million from the International Monetary Fund to halt the nose-dive in the value of sterling. The IRA attempted to set fire to Oxford Street, with seven fire bombs, and the Queen's old friend and former Prime Minister, Lord Avon (formerly Sir Anthony Eden), died on 14 January. Added to that was Rhodesia's rejection of the latest proposals to end UDI and the embarrassment of the announcement from Idi Amin that he planned to travel to Britain with an entourage of 250 to pay homage to the Queen – who he said was his 'Commander-in-Chief' – and the Foreign Office was forced to admit that there was nothing they could do to stop him. It was not an auspicious start, and the year had all the hallmarks of becoming a memorable one for the wrong reasons.

Prince Philip, outspoken as ever, strongly deprecated the state of his wife's nation, writing, 'The economic situation in Britain is rather like dry rot in a building. You don't know when it starts, you don't know when the crisis is, but gradually the place becomes uninhabitable.'[2] Another sentence written by Philip seemed almost deliberately provocative: 'People are slowly coming round to the feeling that we have been driven too far along one road; that we have got to come back a little and not concentrate so heavily on the unfortunate, the underprivileged but try to create a situation whereby the enterprising can make their contribution . . .'[3] With the focus on the monarchy just building to the greatest outpouring since the Coronation, this unexpected interjection by Philip brought the kind of response that he presumably knew it would; fury from many quarters. It was a considered essay which sounded like the plans of the advance party for Thatcherism, and with all his experience of controversy and sensational press headlines, he could not, surely, have imagined that it would cause any other reaction than furore at the very beginning of the year of celebrations for his wife.

That reaction was not long in coming. In the House of Commons, he was immediately branded impudent and ill-advised. Left-winger Tom Litterick was perhaps the most vitriolic in his attack, stating that 'as one of the best kept social security claimants in the country, he ought to have spoken with a better sense of responsibility'.[4] The Speaker interrupted the debate to reprimand members of the House, saying that it was normal to speak with respect of the royal family, while Prime Minister Callaghan, pressed to reply to

Philip's words, cautiously stated that he had no intention of assuming ministerial responsibility for any such comments, whoever made them. This was fodder for the columnists in the following day's papers, and especially for Keith Waterhouse who wrote, 'What I find refreshing about the Duke of Edinburgh's speeches is that no one any longer takes much notice of them . . . as a theme for serious (even frivolous) national debate, the duke's latest outburst is a non-starter.'[5]

These exchanges were soon to be followed by more general misgivings about Jubilee year; several local councils were discovered to have put the block on any spending at all in connection with the event and were warmly congratulated by Tom Litterick, who denounced the royal family as 'useless layabouts'. Barking Borough Council, for example, stated ominously that it had not celebrated the Festival of Britain, nor the Coronation, and it had no intention of celebrating the Jubilee. There were other unwelcome suggestions in the London boroughs as to how the event might be marked – such as the councillor in Tower Hamlets who thought it might be appropriate to hold a torchlight procession down Jack the Ripper's Walk. Elsewhere, celebrations were more welcome, and in towns and cities throughout the country street parties and special events were already being organised, and in the capital itself the 80-strong London Celebrations Committee for the Queen's Silver Jubilee, made up of numerous lords, ladies and gentlemen plus a goodly number of sporting and artistic personalities, were determined to ensure there would be celebration aplenty all summer long.

The Queen remained silent, of course, and left it to her son to become involved in the arrangements and fund-raising and her husband to respond to the attacks of the kill-joys. By 6 February when they were all back at Windsor after their Christmas holidays at Sandringham, the papers were full of praise. The actual anniversary day fell upon a Sunday, thus giving the royal family the opportunity for a peaceful remembrance of the death of George VI with a service at the Royal Chapel; as peaceful, that is, as a large posse of photographers would allow. The Sunday papers all published their 'specials', examining the Queen's first twenty-five years as Sovereign in depth. These were, in general, laudatory pieces . . . 'whereas Great Britain has experienced national decline since 1952, the Queen's own reputation and the institution she embodies has gone from strength to strength'.[6]

Prince Philip was allowed his say, too, with a two-page article written especially for the *Sunday Mirror*, in which he ranged across business and politics as well as the monarchy's role in the changing state of British society. It was another hard-hitting assessment which he presumably allowed the Queen sight of before his private secretary had it delivered to the newspaper's offices. There were 'many worms in the fruit', he wrote. Poor output and productivity and industrial unrest were the origins of many of the nation's troubles. He went on to say that high unemployment, falling living standards, falling exports and frightening increases in government spending hardly gave the most auspicious start to the Queen's Silver Jubilee . . . 'yet it may well be that this experience is needed to bring us all back to a greater sense of reality.' Apparently answering those critics who had said nasty things about his family when the new increases in the Civil List allowances were announced, he said Buckingham Palace had already recognised the need for savings and reduced costs. The royal family had had to distinguish between those things which were traditions and customs worth preserving and those which were out of touch with modern attitudes. In the end, though, said Philip, the nation continued to have emotions of pride and attachment to its homeland and he advanced support for the continuation of the monarchy. 'People still respond more easily to symbolism than reason; the idea of chieftainship in its representative rather than its governing function is still just as clearly and even instinctively understood. From the point of view of national identity, this function is perhaps more important than ever.'

Meanwhile, Her Majesty's Cabinet was locked in discussion as to what they should buy the Queen for an anniversary present. 'A token gift of some kind,' said James Callaghan at a meeting of the Cabinet on 10 February. 'Any suggestions?' Shirley Williams, Secretary of State for Education, suggested a saddle, knowing that horses and riding were one of the Queen's few passions. She was reminded by another member that Charles I had been given a saddle by his government, whom he promptly dismissed, ruling without a parliament for eleven years until overthrown and beheaded. Laughter ensued. Mr Callaghan did not think that was a good idea. Tony Benn suggested a leather-bound copy of the constitution, perhaps to prove that Britain was a democracy and a constitutional monarchy; and when that idea was ruled out, he said, 'Well, I think we should give something that comes out of the Labour movement . . . I have a vase given me by the Polish Minister of Mines, carved out of coal. What about that?'[7] Elwyn Jones, the Lord Chancellor, said that in Wales there were some very nice clocks set in carved coal. But no one seemed impressed with those ideas either. Callaghan said he would think about it and a month later, at a Cabinet meeting on 10 March, he reported that he had resolved the problem. He had asked the Queen at audience if there was anything special she would like and she said she would like something to use personally – a coffee pot. A silver coffee pot. The Cabinet chuckled in unison, noting that of all the presents which might be available, silverware of that nature must already lie in considerable abundance in every single royal palace or household; indeed it did, several hundredweight of it. Anyway, Callaghan had sent his wife Audrey out shopping and she had found a good second-hand one, a Victorian solid silver coffee pot, which cost £350, and each member of Cabinet would be required to contribute £15. It would be formally presented later in the year.

As to the Queen herself, the year ahead was more crowded with engagements, tours, banquets and lunches than it had ever been. If Susan Crosland, who witnessed the American bicentennial visit, found the demands of the Queen's schedule on that occasion 'merciless',[8] then for an adjective to describe the touring plans for Jubilee year, the *Thesaurus* gives us the following selection: 'barbarous, callous, cruel, harsh, relentless, severe, unpitying'. It began at 10.25 on the morning of 9 February when she and Prince Philip flew from Heathrow aboard a British Airways 707, on which she discovered a surprise servant – her steward was Kenneth 'Nobby' Clark who had been the steward on the flight which brought the Queen back from Africa twenty-five years earlier.

They flew first to Western Samoa in the Pacific where almost the entire population of 170,000 islanders turned out to see the Queen. They were getting quite used to welcoming VIPs; only recently they had entertained – separately – the heads of other wooing nations, including China and Russia. The Queen could cap those earlier callers – she invited the Samoan President Malietoa Tanumafili aboard the royal yacht which was parked there waiting for her arrival and knighted him. He responded by accompanying the Queen and Philip to a huge banquet of roasted sucking-pig, and local bands serenaded the Queen with a song which, roughly translated, said 'You are the flower behind my ear and the necklace around my neck.'

From Samoa, they sailed on to Tonga where a substantial welcome awaited them from the King of Tonga who had grown into a strapping likeness of his famous mother whom he succeeded; she was the Queen who won the hearts of the British during the Coronation. Her son, now tipping the scales at 34 stones, revealed the reason for his obesity when the Tongans rolled out their food for their welcoming festivities. Though the royal couple were there for only a day, there were enough sucking-pigs, turkeys, lobsters, water-melons and yams to last the average eater a week and minute-samplers like the Queen rather longer. Food is the centre of all Tongan occasions, since there is little else to offer, and it was with great ceremony that the Queen was presented with her own sucking-pig as well as two lobsters, a turkey and a coconut. The surrounding activity was such that she did not have time to eat much of it. In the tropical midday sun, they were fanned by Tongan girls dressed in white, while the footmen from the *Britannia* sweated in their more formal attire.

Fiji was the next port of call, and the fourth time since her accession that the Queen had called there; an advance party of traditional dancers came aboard the *Britannia* where the Queen and Prince Philip sat on two dining chairs placed on deck while the painted Fijians in full native dress performed their welcomes just a few paces in front of them. A rousing and spectacular reception was always ready in these islands where tourism was a staple industry, especially from the Waimaro tribe which is famous for its ritual to ensure fine weather. On this occasion, it didn't work – and heavy rain dampened the celebrations but not the spirit. The Queen and Philip were presented with a table and six chairs made by local craftsmen which would doubtless come in handy in one of the Queen's several hundred rooms back home.

New Zealand was reached on 22 February and before lunch she had completed one of her walkabouts in Auckland where an estimated 10,000 people were able to get a close-at-hand look at the Queen. Thereafter, they visited twenty New Zealand cities and towns and went roaming the streets in walkabout style on nineteen separate occasions. It was later estimated that one third of the population of New Zealand had turned out at some point or other to see the Queen on her Jubilee Tour of the country. There were protesters, too; as always, none of these visits would seem quite right without them and the banners which read 'Anarchy not Monarchy'.

Australia was rather more vociferous in its protest than normal, with the memory of Gough Whitlam's sacking still fresh in the memory. Many wrongly blamed the Queen for the decision to oust the Labour Prime Minister, but in truth the Queen had had nothing to do with it. Her local Governor-General was controlled by the Australian Parliament, not by the British Crown, and though Whitlam had been sacked in the Queen's name it was purely an internal matter. However, Gough Whitlam's dismissal had aroused further support for the republican movement and as the Queen headed towards Australia from New Zealand, a national opinion poll claimed that 58 per cent now felt that there was no longer any need for a monarchy in Australia. Whitlam was still around, of course, as were many of his followers; 300 demonstrators booed the Queen when she opened the second session of the Australian Parliament while Whitlam himself, in a deliberate slip of the tongue, referred to the arrival of the Queen of Sheba. The Queen managed a smile. He was rather more bitter in his assessment that Great Britain had become a lonely outpost of the Commonwealth, indicating that the founder of the movement and the Queen who headed it were no longer its leaders. Prime Minister Fraser, taking account of these views, had provided Australians with the opportunity of dumping the British National Anthem, having decreed that there was a choice of three they could use: 'God Save the

Queen', 'Waltzing Matilda' and 'Advance Australia Fair'. The first was the least popular.

Still, in spite of this undercurrent of ill-feeling, the crowds turned out in fair numbers, and that is always the measure of the Queen's pulling power. They were no less enthusiastic in Papua New Guinea which was the last stop on the tour. Newly independent and seeking its own way in the world, Papua was question-marked initially by the royal tour organisers. But the crowds were huge and the welcome good-hearted. The Queen was still their head of state and they made sure she was aware of it. Afterwards, the royal party returned to Australia for five more days before flying home to England at the end of March. Highlights of the tour made good television, and what was especially apparent so far in this Jubilee year was that, while politics and politicians have their ups and downs, and while causes which favoured republicanism or total independence from the mother of parliaments seemed to be increasing, the Queen's popularity by and large remained unaffected. It was a good point, one admitted by Harold Wilson after involving her in the Rhodesian fiasco, that if she became too closely linked to the political manoeuvres of her various governments, she would also be drawn too deeply into conflicting political arguments. Thus, when governments or politicians fell from favour, so she would follow them down in the public's opinion. By keeping herself above it all, she ensured that her position would not be affected. This was perhaps never more apparent than in Australia; the divisions had cut deep locally, but the Queen managed to ride above them, even though the greatest upheaval in Australian political life had been carried out in her name.

They had been away for almost eight weeks and back home the Queen's diary was pretty well filled up for the remainder of the year and included an extensive tour of towns and cities across the length and breadth of Britain, before going back overseas in October, to visit Canada and four Caribbean countries. In May, for example, there were full 12-hour days of engagements booked on eighteen of the thirty-one days, and in June nineteen days were earmarked for touring. That pattern was to be repeated for pretty well the rest of the year.

After a couple of weeks off to recover from the Australian schedules, and performing some local engagements around London, the Queen began her tour of Scotland on 17 May with lots of pomp, although it seemed as if she was going to walk straight into stormier political waters. The devolution issue was being promoted by Scottish and Welsh nationalists at every opportunity. The Queen stepped into it in a surprisingly frank Jubilee speech to Parliament on 4 May when she made it known that she was against the break-up of the United Kingdom:

> I number kings and queens of England and of Scotland and princes of Wales among my ancestors and so I can readily understand these aspirations. But I cannot forget that I was crowned Queen of the United Kingdom of Great Britain and Northern Ireland. Perhaps this Jubilee is a time to remind ourselves of the benefits which union has conferred at home and in our international dealings, on inhabitants of all parts of this United Kingdom.

To Scottish nationalists, those were strong words but surprisingly there were few demonstrations of disaffection. In fact, it was quite the opposite. She drove through wildly cheering crowds in an open landau through the streets of Glasgow, attended a service in Glasgow Cathedral and went to that hot-bed of nationalist spirit, Hampden Park, where a team of Scots footballers beat an English select eleven. There was a royal variety performance at the King's Theatre where local stars of show business were joined by the likes of David Soul, Dolly Parton and the royal favourite Frankie Howerd – in kilt. The tour progressed over the next few days, and enthusiasm bubbled over in Dundee where a crowd of several thousand broke through a flimsy rope barrier and surrounded the Queen and Prince Philip, or the Duke of Edinburgh as he is always described north of the border. For a few moments, the Queen was cut off from her aides and separated from Philip and, though she might well have been in danger, she pressed on, looking slightly apprehensive until the police fought their way through to bring the crowd back to a more controlled fashion. It was a frightening moment for all concerned.

The most spectacular ceremonies were saved for Edinburgh where the Scottish State Coach was brought out for the ride through the city streets to the General Assembly of the Church of Scotland. They were joined by Prince Charles, who was installed as a royal knight of the Thistle in St Giles Cathedral; he was in good humour, retorting to a shout from the crowd to give them a smile, 'What do you think I am bloody well doing?' The media coverage of the Scottish tour seemed to jolt the rest of the United Kingdom into the realisation that this was Jubilee year, and the strength of feeling was best demonstrated at the General Assembly when a lone voice called out 'Will ye no' come back again?' and instantly and spontaneously, every person in the hall started singing.

The zealous reaction of the Scots inspired other feelings in London, too. A hasty police conference was called to discuss the Queen's security as it became apparent that no amount of pleading would stop her from the walkabouts and reaching out to the crowds. On 20 May, questions in the House of Commons were voiced on the same subject and, with the tenseness over IRA attacks still running high, Scotland Yard's Special Branch was detailed to carry out a programme of systematic checks and double-checks along all routes which were to be passed by the royal entourage.

But one thing had seriously resulted from the Queen's visits so far. Apathy and criticism of the Jubilee celebrations had suddenly turned into a wave of enthusiasm. Where once the London *Evening Standard* was bemoaning 'the ceaseless barrage of Jubilee propaganda, nostalgia and exploitation', it had by the end of May begun to respond to the London committee's plans with enthusiasm. The then editor of the *New Statesman*, Anthony Howard, took an anti-royalist stance and spent numerous column inches deprecating the time and money which he suggested were being wasted upon Jubilee celebrations, but he returned to the office one day from giving a broadcast interview on the subject to find that members of his staff had put up Jubilee decorations. Even the council at Barking, which had earlier decided that on no account would it be spending ratepayers' money on such extravagance, had a change of heart and produced a pageant entitled *Merrie England* on the steps of the town hall. At the end of the day, the London boroughs alone had more than 3,000 people involved in organising Jubilee events with more than 650,000 taking part, either performing, putting up street decorations, making food and cakes, or joining other events. By June, the nation had become enthralled by what the newspapers were now calling Jubilee fever. The royals were out in force. Street parties and events were planned in virtually every city, town and village and the signal for it all to begin was the lighting of a chain of bonfires, or beacons, which were lit on the eve of Jubilee Day – 6 June – after the Queen was escorted through the Long Walk at Windsor Great park by young people bearing flaming torches; at 10.00 p.m. she torched the first bonfire and within an hour, 102 other fires were lit, stretching from the south coast to the Shetland Isles. The whole was a re-enactment of the lighting of the beacons ordered by Elizabeth I to warn the nation of the imminent arrival of the Spanish Armada in 1588. Another gas-burning torch, also lit by the Queen, was carried aboard a jet and flown to Sydney, to be used to set off a chain of 3,000 bonfires all over Australia.

By now, the streets of London were filling up. Some ardent royalists and lovers of the spectacle had been in position for twenty-four hours, camping at their chosen spots on the route along which the great Jubilee Procession would take place on the 7th. It was later thought that 5 million visitors crowded into London that day, 2 million of them from abroad. Every hotel and guest-house was full and by midnight hundreds of small groups were setting up camp on the pavements from the Mall to St Paul's Cathedral. A great roar went up when the royal family returned to Buckingham Palace from Windsor Castle just after midnight. There, they discovered that messages of congratulations to the Queen had been arriving from all over the world at the rate of 1,000 an hour. And while this detail of the run-up to Jubilee day would test the patience of those who deplore and detest these events which surround a great royal occasion in Britain, it none the less serves to remind us, from a distance further along the road, just how great was the expression of enthusiasm.

Jubilee Day itself, which was a national holiday, was one of mixed scenes and emotions for the Queen and the crowds. There was the great ceremonial occasion of the huge procession with every single member of the royal family, arranged in order of precedence, leaving from Buckingham Palace in six open carriages to travel along the route through London, with the Queen and Prince Philip travelling in the Gold State Coach, and there were no ponderings this time (as in 1953) whether the prince should ride with the Queen or whether he should travel behind. They drove through crowds twenty and thirty deep, cheering and good-humoured. There was not a hint of trouble of any kind, though from special vantage points and hidden from view were the ever-watchful eyes of specially trained police. There were 2,700 guests inside St Paul's awaiting their arrival, and the countless millions watching on television played the usual game of personality-spotting, and noting what was being worn. It was rather odd that in the tenseness of all such occasions, and even though this one had great underlying good cheer about it, the Queen had one of her 'set' expressions for part of the service. It was picked up by the newspaper cameramen and the television cameras whose lenses kept zooming in and out of the main centre of activity in front of the Archbishop of Canterbury, Dr Donald Coggan. One writer who noticed and chose to interpret it as showing that the Queen looked 'cheesed off' was Clive James. The *Observer* newspaper, which published his observations, was immediately besieged by hundreds of angry letter-writers protesting that the Queen felt nothing of the sort. Another explanation came by way of a lip-reader; this was a new trick first thought of by the *Daily Mail* for Princess Anne's wedding to eavesdrop on those intimate, but unheard, little royal conversations while walking down the aisle or standing in groups to have their photographs taken. The lip-reader watching the proceedings on television later claimed to have seen the Queen saying to Prince Philip during the service, 'I feel sick'.

The solemnity soon vanished, however, once they all came out of the cathedral. 'Get ready,' shouted a voice over the walkie-talkies to alert the police and guards, 'she's coming.' The Queen was off on one of her walkabouts, with both herself and Philip dashing forward to greet the crowds fearless and perhaps not even considering that at any moment someone might turn nasty. The walk from St Paul's to the Guildhall for a reception by the Lord Mayor of London was supposed to take only twenty minutes. It took almost forty-five, with the royals all mingling along the way; nothing quite like it had been seen before on the streets of London – nor since, because sadly the need for tighter security eventually made it simply impossible. At the end of the day, the traditional balcony appearance was greeted by rapturous cheers from 100,000 people around the palace and as far as the eye could see down into the Mall.

The week of events in London culminated in a 30-minute firework display which cost £50,000 and brought howls of protest from the anti-Jubilee lobby, yet the whole captured the imagination of the world's television viewers daily, especially in America where audience figures were higher than for their own bicentennial celebrations. In a way, these celebrations, the like of which would not be seen again for many years, gave Britain a bit of a boost, not merely in spirit. Virginia Wade, for example, won the Women's Singles Title at Wimbledon; Liverpool won the European Cup final; James Hunt won the British Grand Prix; and Princess Anne announced she was expecting the Queen's first grandchild. British industry put on an extra surge, especially those in the areas of making souvenirs of pottery, T-shirts, magazines and booklets. A panel headed by Prince Charles selected 63 out of 250 souvenirs officially submitted for approval, but the Queen's Lord Chamberlain finally had to admit that there was little he could do to control the mass of other unapproved material that sped its way into the system as the fever gripped the nation. North Sea oil was also flowing and cheering up the balance of payments as the year wore on, though the underlying ills – by then widely termed the British disease – were still around.

The navy also mustered its best show, of around 100 ships, for the Jubilee Review of the Royal Navy; in addition to the navy's vessels there were thousands of smaller craft. The rest of the summer was taken up with a provincial tour of the country, with the Queen and Prince Philip visiting virtually every region before leaving for a royal visit to Canada, the Bahamas, the Virgin Islands, Antigua and Barbados before returning to London for the state opening of Parliament on 3 November. The aura was positively glowing and for the moment, though not for long, the ever-present debate over the value of the monarchy, the usefulness of royalty and the cost of the whole shooting match was temporarily silenced. Everyone celebrating in Britain knew that, during the Queen's 25-year reign, her country had suffered unprecedented decline in power, influence, wealth and status. Perhaps all that was good in 1977 was best portrayed by the nation's democracy and its ability to look good, even in the face of occasional humiliation, by the show it puts on around its royal family. Churchill's former private secretary Sir John Colville perhaps best summed up this peculiarly British scenario when he said:

> It would have been easy for the British monarchy to degenerate into a meaningless pantomime in which magnificent scenery was no more than an alternative to a night at the opera or a Hollywood extravaganza. It has not done so. The Queen's tireless visits abroad have done more to remind people that Britain still exists . . . to build goodwill in foreign and Commonwealth countries alike and to stimulate British exports than any number of ministerial conferences and diplomatic protocols. To almost the entire world, the image of Britain is linked with one of the Queen.[9]

Prince Charles was also a star of Jubilee year. Apart from being deeply involved in many of the organisational aspects of the celebrations, and especially the setting-up of a charitable trust, he also made his own tours of Africa and Canada. In fact, the Jubilee year seemed to be a starting point for quite widespread speculation that the Queen was preparing Charles for her own imminent retirement. A number of articles began to appear and it looked, for a time, as if their frequency was part of one of those secretly orchestrated campaigns that occasionally occur to prepare the media and the nation for a forthcoming announcement. It was suggested in some quarters that Mountbatten was pressing for such a move, or at least to see Charles, over whom he had great personal sway and influence, given a more demanding royal job as soon as he left naval service. It was one of Mountbatten's greatest fears, that unless there was a clearly defined role, a path to follow and a distinct goal at the end of it, Charles could become bored and unsure of himself, just as his great-uncle David had become. Worse, he might go off the rails as his great-great-grandfather Edward VII had done while waiting to succeed his long-serving mother who also precluded him in every way from government business. Charles had gained confidence in the navy, but Mountbatten said that it could slip away very quickly without a positive direction. Some carefully placed articles about the possibility of the Queen's retirement were heavily supported by comments from an undisclosed source close to or at the heart of the family. There were quotations such as this: 'The future of the monarchy is now in the most stable hands and part of that stability is based upon the Queen's remarkable ability to look ahead. There is no suggestion that she is planning to take dramatic action soon . . .'[10] but the situation might arise, the article continued, where she might consider retiring. The prospect seemed unlikely in the near future but at least there were some valid points about Charles's own role in life.

The Queen seemed to answer it herself when, at an elite gathering at London's Guildhall on Jubilee Day, she requoted parts of her speech of dedication to service, which she made in South Africa in 1947: 'When I was twenty-one, I pledged my life to the service of our people and I asked for God's help to make good that vow. Although that vow was made in my salad days when I was green in judgement, I do not regret one word of it.'[11]

At moments like that she was capable of bringing a lump to the throats of the most sceptical of her audience and indeed it is difficult not to make the above report of her Jubilee year sound too laudatory for words; that is the effect of some things which the Queen does or inspires. It can be tempered by examining the lasting effects of this year of unadulterated sentimentality, and saying that really there is no evidence that the cost of it all could be justified and only in a year such as this are all aspects of royalty challenged and re-examined but, in the main, applauded. The debate continues, the speculation abounds and the mysteries remain.

Chapter Fifteen
Bad Tidings (1978–9)

The characterisation of individual members of the extended royal family seemed to have crystallised during the previous year, forming the basis for the more personalised, even intrusive, presentation of their lives through the media that was to follow in the eighties. The Queen was the most discussed woman and potent symbol of the time. There was the husband, always controversial, hectoring and lecturing the nation regardless of the paradoxes in his own life. There was the bachelor son and heir, shy, caring, apprehensive, for whom the newspapers were in the process of selecting a bride. There was the slightly spoilt and bad-tempered daughter who had married beneath her station, produced a Jubilee infant, liked galloping around on horses and playing in tanks. There was the adored mother, approaching eighty, and people were now asking how much longer she would go on flitting around in her helicopter? There were the attractive cousins of the Kent and Gloucester factions, ever ready to adorn the balcony scene, a Wimbledon tennis final, or a hospital opening. There was the succession of births and marriages, and the occasional death, which kept the nation riveted . . . and there was the wayward matronly sister, carrying on regardless.

The continuing saga could not be complete without the incidents and events that reminded us that they were real people, and not television creations, and that they suffered from the same human frailties, the same yearnings and the same infidelities that occur in every family. These flaws had

ıt home, the new young royal family of the sixties was becoming far more high-
rofile than ever it had been under George VI. Sunday wasn't Sunday without
hilip galloping around the polo field with stick swirling in the air, and the Queen
ı animated enthusiasm shouting, 'Go on, go on!' from the sidelines and then
resenting the trophy to the winners, as here in June 1959.

The Queen also used her enthusiasm for riding to help blow away the cares of State and relax between the intense pressure of public engagements. Here, she took part in a family race at Ascot in June 1961, finishing sixth out of eleven runners.

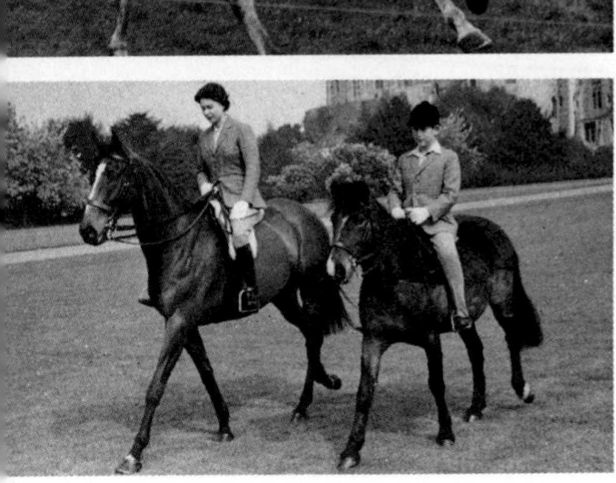

Prince Charles, meantime, still preferred a more sedate ride and his mother bought him this calm pony named Mayflower. Much later, of course, he became the daredevil of the polo field, like his father.

The Queen's mix and match jewellery has provided royal observers with an interesting task: spotting what has come from where. The tiara in the two pictures above is the same one: it was once owned by the Grand Duchess Vladimir of Russia and smuggled to safety after the Revolution. Queen Mary bought it at a knock-down price. Originally it was hung with the pendant pearls (above right) but it is also interchangeable with the huge stones (left) known as the Cambridge emeralds, with matching necklace, which were clawed back by Mary from the mistress of her dead brother. Right is the famous George IV diamond diadem, one of the few valuable items inherited from his reign, which was filled with rented stones many of which eventually had been replaced and is now worth millions.

'his is 'granny's tiara', nother piece given to the)ueen by her randmother. It consists of iamond festoons, scrolls nd twenty-seven collet pikes, all set with nagnificent and delicate tones.

nother famous tiara is his one, known as the Russian tiara and passed n from Queen Alexandra or whom it was bought in 888 as a twenty-fifth vedding anniversary resent by the Ladies of ociety. Ironically, its solid iamond bars are shapped the form of a Russian easant's head-dress.

'he balcony scene has become part of royal life, both for the family itself and vid observers of them. Queen Victoria did not especially enjoy being 'gawped at' ut since then – and especially during Elizabeth II's reign – it has become a raditional focal point for national and royal occasions, such as Trooping the Colour (left), Coronations (the Queen's, top) and royal weddings (Princess Anne's, bove) and even such occasions as VE Day and the ending of the Falklands War.

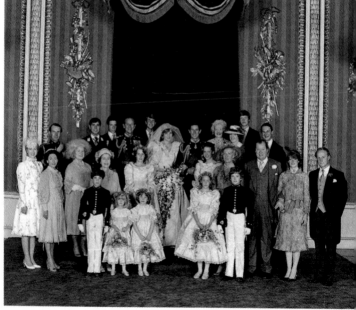

Tradition still rules inside Buckingham Palace and a classic example is the spot at which all the relatives are gathered together for the traditional wedding group picture, in front of the red velvet drapes. The decor remains the same, only the faces change in these three pictures of the Queen's own wedding in 1947, Prince Charles's in 1981 and Prince Andrew's in 1986 (see also the wedding of George, Duke of Kent in first picture section).

World leaders, and even other monarchs, come and go, while the Queen has reigned for forty years: nine British prime ministers, eight US presidents, eight Russian leaders, countless Commonwealth statesmen. Here are a few she has known but not necessarily liked:

1976, with Pierre Trudeau, former Prime Minister of Canada who pushed through constitutional chang ending colonial status.

1977: President Giscard d'Estaing whose alleged exploits involving young women intrigued the Queen in gossip with Harold Wilson.

1976: President Gerald Ford, well known accident prone, managed to step on the Queen's foot.

1986: With two of her longest serving Prime Ministers, Mrs Thatcher and Sir Lynden Pindling, Bahamas leader since 1966.

1980: An historic meeting with Pope John Paul II, with the Queen in black full-length gown, attracted world-wide attention.

'82: Nancy Reagan istook statesmanship for endship when she and esident Reagan stayed at 'indsor. The Queen asn't much pleased either hen, while out riding, he opped to talk to the ess.

1991: New Prime Minister John Major makes a command appearance to welcome a visiting dignitary, accompanied by Foreign Secretary Douglas Hurd.

olish leader Lech Walesa ade an astute observation ıring his first State visit hen he stayed at 'indsor, describing the ueen as the 'mother of e nation'.

A classic family portrait, by a family photographer – Lord Snowdon was asked take the formal and album shots at the christening of the Wales's second son, Prince Henry, in December 1984.

Another unique family moment was the first and last visit of the Queen, Prince Philip and Prince Charles to the home of her uncle the Duke of Windsor in Par where they were pictured with the Duchess. The Duke died soon afterwards.

Off duty, the Queen reverts to her role as the countrified lady, which she would have chosen had she not been Queen. Typical was this study captured at a horse show in 1968.

The Queen leads Prince Charles forward in the grounds of Caernarfon Castle after his investiture as Prince of Wales in what was, for the royal family, a supremely important event; it marked the launching of the Queen's heir apparent into full public life, marked also by the appearance of an especially commissioned biography. The prince's crown was too big and during rehearsals for the big day it slipped over his eyes. Although the crown was reduced in size, the Queen later admitted she almost burst into laughter when placing it on his head at the ceremony.

ıe Queen's twenty-fifth Jubilee celebrations provided the opportunity for the eatest reaffirmation of public affection for the monarchy since the Coronation. ter a slow start, Jubilee fever gripped the nation. A moving service at St Paul's ıs televised, the Queen later went on many walkabouts (right) and among other bilee events was Virginia Wade's success, winning the Women's Singles at imbledon.

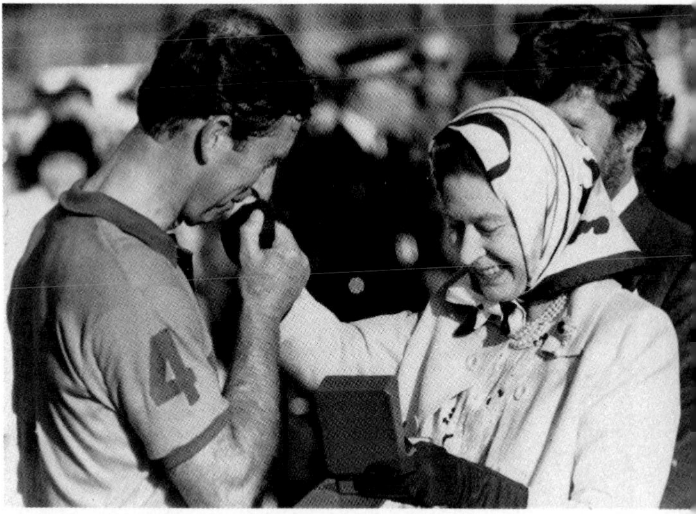

Once it was her husband who collected the polo prizes, now it is her son – as he when he receives an award in the Silver Jubilee Cup at Windsor Great Park in July 1988.

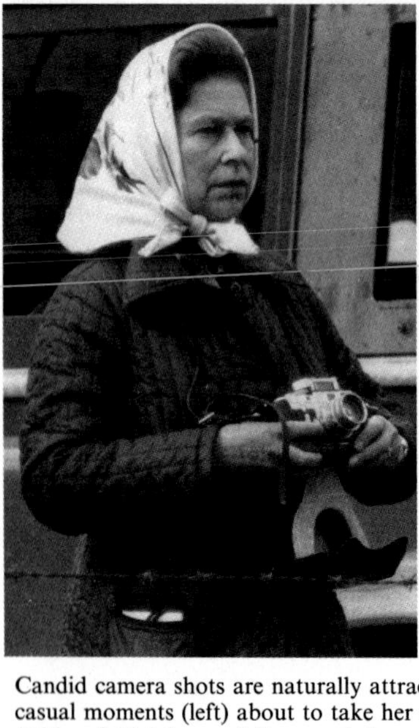

Candid camera shots are naturally attractive to the paparazzi, as were these less casual moments (left) about to take her own snaps at Sandringham horse trials 1984 and (right) gracefully negotiating a fence at Windsor in 1982.

'She's never happier,' Lord Mountbatten once said, 'than when she can dress down, in casual clothes and flat shoes.' This, then must have been a happy day – with her new daughter-in-law too, at Windsor Horse Show in 1987.

The four generations: The Queen'
children, pictured above, lively,
extrovert and attractive – qualitie
guaranteed to attract over exposu
in the media. Now, the next
generation, the Queen's
grandchildren, are reluctantly
taking their places in the
newspapers so that the family
group – 'us four' as King George
once said – is providing at least
fourteen front-line members of th
royal family. They gathered for th
Queen Mother's ninetieth – a tim
for reflection, especially for Princ
Charles.

to come out, like an inbuilt, subconscious self-destruct mechanism. What other reason than basic human error could have inspired Princess Margaret to go trotting off to Mustique with Roddy Llewellyn again? Was it just a wanton disregard for what the public (or more correctly, the newspapers) felt, or for how the press would pounce as she surely knew it would? Was it a couldn't-care-less attitude that her private life was her own affair, regardless of whether it was to be shared with the 13 million readers of the *News of the World*? Could she really have believed that her flight to Mustique with Llewellyn would become any less sensationally reported than it was the last time? She was, after all, still married in the eyes of the Church, though legally separated, and still sixth in line of succession.

Only she could answer the riddle; it would be worse than last time and the Queen, more than anyone, would feel the grief. The Queen had never met Roddy Llewellyn, nor did she intend to; he was not on the invitation list to any of the family gatherings nor had he been invited to tend the rose-beds at Windsor. Roddy had become famous since the last bout of publicity he received when Margaret separated from Snowdon. He had been signed up by Claude Wolff, Petula Clark's husband and manager who was one of several opportunists who realised the value of Roddy's alleged singing ability. To launch him, Petula arranged for Roddy to sing a duet with her on a French television show; they sang a number called '*Venez Donc Chez Moi*' ('Come Around to My Place'). He was then rushed straight into a recording studio to begin rehearsals for an album. All this for a young man whose only claim to fame prior to his association with Margaret was that his father had ridden a famous horse called Foxhunter. He was suddenly under a bright spotlight and surrounded by an entourage of managers and agents whose expertise in the music business taught them to take advantage of every opportunity.

It would, ultimately, be the royal family who would suffer. The Queen is quite happy to lend her family to charitable causes, and to give awards to industry or to recognise those suppliers who are in receipt of royal patronage. In so far as commercial ventures are concerned, there has always been a fairly strict adherence to a policy of non-cooperation. Lord

Snowdon's career had undoubtedly benefited from the association. The City connections of Princess Alexandra's husband Angus Ogilvy broadened considerably because of who he was, and became all the more financially damaging to him personally when things went wrong and he was virtually forced to quit certain of his directorships during Edward Heath's onslaught against 'the unacceptable face of capitalism'. Captain Mark Phillips became an instant candidate for sponsorship deals for which the Queen gave her approval. The first he struck was with British Leyland to help finance the eventing stables of himself and his wife and it brought equally instant furore. Later, the commercial ventures became his driving force, as he strove to cut his ties with the royal purse. So, in the spring of 1978 Roddy Llewellyn became the singing gardener by royal appointment and, after cutting his first disc, went to Mustique with Princess Margaret on 25 February hoping that the publicity would not be long in dying out.

But Roddy was a 'star' now and the record people would welcome any publicity, good or bad. It was bad . . . and dramatic. The day after arriving in Mustique, Roddy collapsed with a gastric ulcer which burst and he was flown off the holiday island to hospital in Barbados. Princess Margaret followed, and much was made of 'her fussing at his bedside'. She returned home when she was sure he was on the mend and ran straight into trouble herself. She too collapsed and was so ill she was unable to attend her own daughter's confirmation. Subsequently, she was admitted to hospital and was found to be suffering from alcoholic hepatitis. The publicity surrounding Princess Margaret was as tragic as it was appalling – 'Will the agony never end?' was a typical plaintive plea – and it was indeed a very valid question. Ought she to retire from public life? It ran for days; huge headlines not merely questioning her position, but once again using her to attack the Crown. There were plenty who were ready to put the knife in, and Margaret's plummeting popularity became a real worry to the Queen. In fact, the whole family was concerned, and they had to rally round to talk Margaret through her recovery. The Queen was not without sympathy for Lord Snowdon through all of this high drama, and with a fairly typical gesture which also contained a fairly typical loaded clue to her feelings, she invited her brother-in-law to take the official fifty-second birthday photographs of herself in April.

The rhetoric came from the usual sources who made much of the fiasco and complained once again that the princess's personal excesses were a drain on public funds at a time when everyone else was being asked to tighten their belts. The fact that under the 1978 readjustment of the Civil List her allowance had risen to £59,000 a year in line with inflation, merely fuelled the insults that were being flung from several quarters. Presumably on the basis that it is always best to get the bad news out of the way at once, the Queen gave approval for the announcement from Buckingham Palace that Princess Margaret and Lord Snowdon had decided to seek a divorce.

On 10 May, it became known that they were seeking a 'quickie' divorce on the grounds that they had lived apart for two years, and at the end of the month their case, number 5684/78, came before Judge Roger Blenkiron Wills of the Family Division, who became the instrument of British history by granting the mutual application. The effect that this single act had on the Queen personally was never fully appreciated at the time. It cut deeply and the words of one of her favourite churchmen, Dr Mervyn Stockwood, then Bishop of Southwark, explained why:

> The Queen is an out and out supporter of the Church in its insistence upon the importance of the family unit. She has an understanding attitude towards the weaknesses of human nature but this does not shake her conviction – that a nation runs into troubled water when the family unit disintegrates. She is not just a believer; she practises what she preaches. Anyone who has had anything to do with her family circle knows what a precious thing it is to her.[1]

Stockwood also made the point that the Queen quite understood that her family was taken as an example to others, and she appreciated the need for Christian stewardship as an essential part of their lives.

In the spring of 1978 Princess Margaret was a very sick

woman and cancelled a number of engagements – though she could not give up her cigarettes of which she smoked more than thirty a day. One of her close friends said he believed she was going through a period of intense emotional turmoil and that her judgement was impaired to such a degree that she could not see the difficulties she was actually creating for herself. She also became the victim and the innocent tool of the publicity machine surrounding Roddy Llewellyn's singing career. They used every trick in the book to keep his name in front of the public, and Margaret was dragged into it. Llewellyn personally was enjoying wealth he had never previously known, with payment for his recording and cabaret contracts being supplemented by offers of considerable money for 'exclusive' interviews. One American publisher was following him around with a blank cheque, which eventually became a firm offer of £150,000 to tell the tale of his association with the Queen's sister. Llewellyn did not take it up. The temptation of such offers, plus an expensive heroin habit, was too much for Charles Tennant, the son of Margaret's good friend Colin Tennant. He stole some photographs taken by his mother of Princess Margaret doing a raunchy impersonation of Sophie Tucker, which he gave to a friend to sell to a newspaper for £7,000.

Through all of this, the Queen could see that her sister was suffering, and as speculation began to increase on whether or not she would allow Margaret to marry Llewellyn, two things happened. Margaret was asked by the Queen to say what she intended to do. The Queen was certainly not in favour of her marrying Llewellyn; if she insisted then it would be necessary for the marriage to take place abroad and she would certainly have to give up her Civil List income and live abroad herself for a while. Margaret said it was not likely to come to that. Their friendship was not a prelude to marriage at that stage, though the Queen could see that Margaret was obviously very fond of him. And so would it not be better for the friendship to discontinue, at least for the time being? the Queen suggested to her sister. It was a cautious ultimatum that either she gave up Roddy or gave up the royal life, much the same as Margaret had been told when she wanted to marry Peter Townsend twenty years earlier.

Pressure was brought to bear upon Llewellyn and he voluntarily accepted the same treatment that Townsend had received – banishment. He went off to North Africa for three months using the alias of Mr Johnson, until he was spotted by reporters and had to flee again to Portugal. In London, as the divorce hearing approached, Princess Margaret announced that she would be continuing her royal engagements and this was taken to mean that she was not intending to follow her friend abroad or considering leading any other sort of life. Llewellyn promptly responded with an emotional statement from somewhere on the continent that 'for personal reasons' he could never marry Princess Margaret. All of this was a deliberate attempt to cool the publicity, which worried not just the Queen but also her advisers; yet when Roddy returned from his travels, they continued to meet privately, often at drinks parties given quietly for them by friends, including Bryan Forbes and Nanette Newman.

In the meantime, another delicate family romance had been maturing for the previous nine months or so until it too, finally, had to be brought to the Queen's attention. Her cousin Prince Michael of Kent, who was thirty-six years old and who many feared would become a confirmed bachelor, had fallen in love. In any other family, the fact that his bride-to-be was a divorcee, would not have presented any problem. For the Queen, it was a double blow because Marie-Christine, Baroness von Reibnitz and lately Mrs Tom Troubridge, was also a Roman Catholic. That presented an even greater problem than the first, and one which eventually she would have to report to her Prime Minister. Prince Michael, of whom she was extremely fond, was the silent man of the British royal family, often called the 'invisible prince' because he had deliberately kept a low profile compared with his brother the Duke of Kent. It was another of those supreme ironies that seem ever destined to clamp themselves to the Queen and her relations, that the woman with whom he had fallen in love would catapult him instantly into front-page stardom. It was also ironic that his relationship had reached the point where they desperately wanted to get married at exactly the time that the Queen's own sister was in the process of getting a divorce, and thus she could hardly raise any objection to what, not many years earlier, would have been ruled out of court as a totally unsuitable royal marriage.

Divorce and Roman Catholicism would have been sufficient to rule it out; the third element remained a secret though it must at some point have been revealed to the royal family before the engagement, since, as a matter of course, the antecedent history of all spouses would be vetted. Marie-Christine had a history as well as a past, one which any courtier at Buckingham Palace could have guessed in an instant would make fascinating reading in any of the nation's popular newspapers – as indeed it did, eventually. It was that her father, Baron Gunther von Reibnitz was, in his day, an officer in Hitler's Nazi storm-troopers, the SS. At the end of the war, a 4-inch thick dossier on von Reibnitz was on file at the Berlin Documents Centre. Gunther met Marie-Christine's mother, the Countess Marianna Szapary, in 1941. At the time, she was twenty-seven, very beautiful and rich, and being questioned by the Gestapo. They had discovered that just before the war she had entertained two Englishmen – one of them was William Douglas-Home, brother of the former Prime Minister Lord Home – who were at the time trying to persuade Unity Mitford to return home to England. A postcard written by the countess which referred to 'Unity being silly to stay with her boyfriend', meaning Hitler[2], was read by Gestapo censors. Gunther von Reibnitz, twenty years older than the countess, rescued her from suspicion by divorcing his own wife and marrying her. Marie-Christine was born in January 1945, shortly before von Reibnitz abandoned his property and fled from Germany with his wife and children and a few possessions on a handcart, to Czechoslovakia. At the end of the war, he learned that he was on the Allied wanted list as an SS officer and decided to seek refuge in South-West Africa, along with numerous other German expatriates. The countess did not enjoy this prospect and refused to join him. Instead, she divorced Gunther in 1946, and subsequently settled in Australia with her daughter.

Twenty years later, Marie-Christine left Australia, which had been her home since 1949, to try her luck in London. She let it be known that she was a baroness, that her grandmother was Her Serene Highness Princess zu Windisch-Graetz and her grandfather had been Austrian ambassador to the Tsar of Russia at St Petersburg. Before long, she met wealthy young banker Tom Troubridge whose family had connections with Kleinwort Benson and they were married in 1971. At the wedding, Marie-Christine first came into contact with a member of the royal family. One of her husband's best friends was Prince William of Gloucester; they had been at Eton together. William was the most handsome and extrovert young man in the entire royal family; the author often came into contact with him first in youth and again during the late sixties and early seventies. He had just returned from Tokyo when I met him again; he had come home to take over the running of the family estate in Barnwell, Northamptonshire from his father who was paralysed after a stroke. He had with him a startling girl, Zsuzui Starkloff, who was of Hungarian origin and eight years older than William. They were sharing an apartment together in 1969 and Princess Margaret even visited them once. Perhaps she warned Zsuzui of the trauma that lay ahead – because Zsuzui was also a divorcee; not long afterwards Zsuzui took off to America, and never saw William again. Prince William was taken by a mixture of anger and sadness. 'In many ways, I love being a member of the royal family,' he told me quite frankly one evening in 1971. 'But there are also many things I hate. The goldfish bowl . . . it's a pain. The church is forever breathing down your neck. It is a very restrictive life we lead, especially for those of us who actually believe there is life outside of the royal circle.' He was heir to the Duke of Gloucester and would have been a dashing successor, had he lived. In the last few months of his life, he saw a lot of Troubridge and his wife Marie-Christine, to whom he also introduced his cousin Prince Michael. They dined together often in London, and William was obviously quite taken with her; sometimes they went out as a foursome and William dropped by often for tea or a drink at the Troubridge home. Those close to them thought William had fallen in love with his friend's wife.

However, on Bank Holiday Monday, 28 August 1972, Prince William was killed in a flying accident while taking part in the Goodyear Air Race at Halfpenny Green, near

Wolverhampton. Thereafter Prince Michael saw Marie-Christine infrequently for the next few months, until Tom Troubridge was posted to Bahrain on business. His wife decided she did not want to leave England. Not long afterwards, she was heard cancelling an evening engagement with a girlfriend, giving the excuse that 'I have a very big fish on the hook at the moment and I don't want to let him off'.

Prince Michael had fallen in love with Marie-Christine while she was still married to Troubridge and in 1977, anxious to try to avert a scandal of Princess Margaret proportions, she applied to the Roman Catholic Church courts to annul her marriage to Troubridge, which was eventually granted on the flimsiest of grounds, apparently with the help of Mountbatten who had connections in the Vatican. Meanwhile she and Troubridge also filed for a civil divorce.

Marie-Christine von Reibnitz had by now reverted to her maiden name, just as the Duchess of Windsor did after she obtained a divorce from Ernest Simpson in 1936. She was of no significance yet, and her name was linked to Prince Michael's only by their closest friends. Secretly, Prince Michael had already been down to Broadlands to see Uncle Dickie Mountbatten, who had been the Kent brothers' adopted 'uncle' since their own father, Prince George, Duke of Kent was killed in 1942. Michael took Marie-Christine with him, explained the position and asked what they should do about it. Her cosy version of events later was that Mountbatten said to Michael, 'You'd better marry the girl – she's obviously madly in love with you'. The interview was far from light-hearted, nor was Mountbatten in the least frivolous. He must have thought, but did not say as much, that he had been down this road before, except now there was the added complication of the Roman Catholic Church, and the Pope would have to become involved. Calm but stern, his immediate thoughts went to the Queen and the implications for the monarchy, especially the additional worry it would give to the Queen who already had enough on her plate with Princess Margaret's messy affair. It was a pity, he said, because otherwise Marie-Christine was an ideal candidate to become a royal princess. But if they were sure they could not live without each other, there were really only two options, that they could live quietly in sin which would rule out having a family, or they could seek the Queen's permission to marry. Michael said that above all else, he and Marie-Christine wanted to marry and start a family as quickly as possible.

Mountbatten was quite taken with Marie-Christine. She was a strong and confident girl, he said later[3], and when he realised how determined the couple were and that they would not be dissuaded, he warmed to their plight and did everything possible to help. He said he would have a word with the Queen, but first Prince Michael must write to her, setting out the position in detail and requesting her permission to marry. He should then go to see his brother the Duke of Kent and his sister Princess Alexandra – who both knew he had been seeing Marie-Christine but had no idea it had reached this stage. 'One other thing might help,' Mountbatten told Marie-Christine. 'If you were to change your religion it might ward off possible trouble in the Queen's Church.' Marie-Christine refused point blank; the women of her family had been devout Roman Catholics and she did not intend to desert her faith, even though she had married her first husband in an Anglican church. Mountbatten then suggested they should go to see Dr Donald Coggan, the Archbishop of Canterbury, and Marie-Christine should write confidentially to the Pope asking for his guidance. The interview with Coggan was strained; Coggan was understanding, but could not give his blessing. In April, the Troubridges' divorce came through, exactly a month before Princess Margaret's. And one week after Margaret's, the Queen, apparently wishing to dispose of all the publicity which she knew would result from these two events, announced that she had given her permission for Prince Michael to marry Marie-Christine. The Queen naturally had to inform the Prime Minister, James Callaghan.

Permission for the marriage was granted on 31 May by a meeting of the Privy Council, which must approve all royal marriages; four men approved the Queen's request: Michael Foot, Merlyn Rees, Lord Goronwy-Roberts and Robert Sheldon, the Financial Secretary to the Treasury. Three conditions were attached to the permission and the Queen stipulated that unless Prince Michael agreed to them, it would be withheld: first that he should forfeit his right of succession to the throne; second, he must guarantee that any children of the marriage should be brought up as Anglicans and not Roman Catholics; third, they should be married abroad. The latter condition was necessary because, first of all, the prince could not be married in the Church of England; Dr Coggan had already made that clear and anyway, it would be too much of an embarrassment to the Queen. Neither was it possible under the Royal Marriages Act for any member of the royal family to be married in a register office or any other form of civil ceremony in Great Britain. Oddly enough, however, Marie-Christine, who was to be known as Princess Michael of Kent after her marriage, was granted royal status by the Queen – thus giving her the style and title of Her Royal Highness, which had been denied to the Duchess of Windsor for the past forty-one years.

After that, it should have been plain sailing. Marie-Christine said she wanted to be married in the church in Vienna in which her grandmother had been married; it was a Roman Catholic Church, of course. Mountbatten said he would fix it with Pope Paul VI and he telephoned the Apostolic Delegate, Bruno Heim, personally. He assured the couple that there ought not to be any problems. And so they went gaily on, with Marie-Christine planning her white wedding as the born-again virgin surrounded by the young choristers of the Vienna Boys Choir, booked in its entirety. In the meantime, the affairs of the heart of Prince Michael and Princess Margaret had actually cast a gloomy shadow over Buckingham Palace and the Church of England alike. What was happening to the royal family? Was it disintegrating, or what? The Queen had made a bold decision to allow the announcement to be made so quickly, but she had not expected it would lead to a direct confrontation with the Pope himself. In spite of assurances given to Mountbatten, Marie-Christine's plans were suddenly cast adrift. The Pope, having been made aware of the conditions imposed upon Michael before the Queen would agree to the wedding, now had something to say on the matter. In view of them, His Holiness had no alternative but to forbid the wedding taking place in a Roman Catholic church; it was made quite clear that the religious upbringing and baptism of the children of the marriage was the central issue. The fact that the bridegroom happened to be a member of the British royal family had no bearing whatsoever on the case, other than to aggravate it by attempts at 'diplomatic pressure' – i.e. from Mountbatten. The whole issue had erupted into bitterness which encompassed senior figures in both Churches and the royal family, always a touchy subject to the Romans at the best of times. So Marie-Christine, so used to getting her own way, saw her wedding plans crumble. In the end, they had to settle for just the civil ceremony, in German, at Vienna Town Hall; no white dress, no Vienna Boys Choir, and no recognition of the wedding by either Church. It was a sorry affair, and with only a small number of royals present – including Princess Anne, Mountbatten and the Kent contingent.

There was one final twist to this first instalment of the Princess Michael story which also surely gave the Queen and the Queen Mother a tinge of heartburn. The newly styled princess wrote to the Duchess of Windsor to introduce herself, and to say how much she had admired the duke and duchess, and now here she found herself niece by marriage to 'Aunt Wallis' whose traumas she had just experienced in a rather minor way. Some of her friends said that Marie-Christine believed she was the second Wallis Simpson. At the end of their honeymoon which took them to India, Iran and Paris, Prince Michael and his new bride called to see the duchess at the Bois de Boulogne which was a rather odd thing to do, considering what had immediately gone before.

It was almost as if they had deliberately tried to pass themselves off as the new Windsor story. The duchess's butler, Georges Sanegre, was one of the three remaining staff in the empty, decaying house and showed the newlyweds to the duchess's salon where she was to receive them. Marie-Christine handed the duchess a bouquet of flowers. 'Thank you, darling,' said the duchess whose mind now frequently drifted in and out of lucidity, 'it is wonderful to have such a beautiful woman in the house again.'[4] Turning to Prince Michael, the duchess said, 'Your father was David's favourite, you know. He loved him and he was also the only one who showed any sympathy to me.' Thereafter, Marie-Christine visited the duchess twice more alone, and later said quite openly, 'The duchess is a great lady. History will show she was unfairly treated.' This was not the kind of remark to endear herself to her new relatives in London. When she turned up wearing a pair of earrings given to her by the duchess, the Queen noticed them. 'Aunt Wallis gave them to me,' Marie-Christine admitted. Later the Queen made it known that she would prefer it if Princess Michael did not wear the earrings in her presence.

If change in attitudes and realities within the family was forced upon the Queen by the events of the early months of 1978, it was also showing itself elsewhere. Britain's European partners looked on with dismay as it became increasingly possessed by its self-destructive battle with the trade unions. The tenuous consensus between the Labour Party and the unions which had survived the past decade, was nearing its end and Prime Minister James Callaghan clung to power by compromise. In spite of his vague threats to resign, industrial action became the bane of Callaghan's life. Five years of price rises, especially in food, had become synonymous with the Common Market as Britain readjusted to the policies of Europe, and the unions, along with a fair number of MPs of all persuasions, wanted out. It fell to the Queen, in her few visits to Common Market countries, to speak with a unifying voice and reaffirm her government's commitment, as she did in her second state visit to Germany in May 1978. Her speeches were notably political, and obviously not written by her own hand. She was, according to one Cabinet minister the author consulted, as unenthusiastic about Europe as the Labour left, for different reasons. In that, she had a supporter in the wings in Mrs Margaret Thatcher, who had a definite dislike of the persistent demands the Market had made on Britain, especially the Common Agricultural Policy which she regarded as legitimised theft.

As far as the Queen was concerned, she could see little role for the British monarchy in Europe. Apart from making these occasional state visits and being the reciprocal hostess when they came to London, there was no other way in which she could be involved. National sovereignty was devolved around the central administration of the EEC, and it did not include any contact with the Queen. There was no machinery through which she could have any direct contact with the European politicians. She could not command the presence of any one of them, as she could with her Prime Minister, nor, for example, request a European minister, as she had her Foreign Secretary, to accompany her on an overseas visit. As far as the Community was concerned, she was relegated to the same status as the lesser crowned heads of Europe, a colourful adornment of a member-nation. Nor was she especially fond of some of the European politicians with whom she came into contact. She once described Chancellor Helmut Schmidt, who welcomed her on the state visit in 1978, as 'so rude and unfriendly' and she spoke of other Common Market heads whom she had entertained to dinner at Buckingham Palace in July 1977, as 'cynical and disillusioned'.[5]

However, whatever her personal view of the men who were in charge of the countries with which her nation was allied in trade, she discovered that enthusiasm for the British Crown among the German people transcended politics just as it did wherever she went. Thousands turned out to see her and she responded by brushing aside the massive security guard that had been thrown around the royal party, expressing in advance a wish to meet the people. The cheers were long and loud when she spoke of her government's continued support for West Germany's front-line stand against the eastern bloc: 'My soldiers and airmen stationed in Berlin embody the British commitment to defend your freedom for as long as needed, until the divisions in Europe and your city can be healed.' As she spoke, she may have pondered for a moment her own freedom of movement, glancing as she did to the buildings surrounding the dais in front of the Blue Church in Berlin from which she made her speech. On every rooftop, and in every overlooking window, armed marksmen peered through the sights of their guns. Terrorism was a fact of life throughout Europe and the Germans were determined that no harm should come to the British Queen while she was on their soil.

In Canada two months later, when she was making her third visit in two years – which in itself spoke volumes about the concern felt in Britain over Canada's continued loyalties – there was rudeness from one of her own prime ministers. Pierre Trudeau, soon to face a general election, was clearly not wishing to show too much favour towards the Queen for fear of upsetting the republican and separatist factions. Much was made of the fact that he was not even in the country when the Queen arrived with Prince Philip and her sons Andrew and Edward for a packed 12-day tour, which would include the opening of the Commonwealth Games in Edmonton. Trudeau was still sunning himself on a holiday beach in Morocco, and a spokesman said he did not plan to return just to greet the Queen on her arrival. In England, the Prime Minister is invariably on hand to greet the Queen on her arrival from an overseas trip or to see her off when she leaves for one; headlines thus raged that Trudeau had deliberately 'snubbed' her arrival as a forerunner to the further constitutional reforms he was planning to reduce the Queen's role. Former Prime Minister John Diefenbaker said he personally would campaign against Trudeau's moves all over Canada, and so controversy continued to rage in what should have been one of the Queen's most comfortable visits. The welcomes were always loud, of course, because the monarchists invariably outnumbered the rest.

The Queen returned to Britain to an aura of gloom and doom, the like of which had not been experienced for years. 'Sunny Jim' Callaghan was lurching from crisis to crisis, though he denied that one even existed. He travelled up to Balmoral for a brief holiday with the Queen. He could be a most charming man, yet had a habit of being condescending to women and patronising to men. Meanwhile, the Labour Party's annual conference loomed and in the backroom he papered over the cracks which came apart again almost as quickly. The TUC rounded on him with a massive No to the flagship of his government's economic policy, a 5 per cent pay-rise ceiling to check inflation, and the unions contemptuously ignored the warning at conference that to go against the pay policy would lose Labour the next general election. The winter of discontent had arrived and over the coming two or three months, the nation was put on the rack – with stinking, uncollected rubbish piling high in the streets; mortuaries and funeral halls were full because the grave-diggers and crematorium workers were on strike; hospitals turned away patients. Hundreds of thousands of workers were laid off and union leaders warned it would get worse unless the government relented on its pay policy. Callaghan continued to insist that there was no crisis, while urgent cancer patients were being turned away from hospitals and meals-on-wheels intended for a blockaded old folks' home were overturned.

On 28 March, the inevitable happened and Callaghan's government was forced out of office – not because of pay and economic conditions, but by the government's refusal to meet its earlier promises to nationalist MPs to go ahead with home rule for Scotland. When Margaret Thatcher, scenting Callaghan's blood, launched a vote of No Confidence, the Liberals decided to vote with the Conservatives and the Scottish Nationalists and Ulster Unionists decided to put Callaghan's discredited government to the test of a general election. The government was defeated by one vote, and the following morning, Callaghan went to see the Queen to request dissolution of Parliament for a general election. His day had come and gone. On 4 May Mrs Margaret Thatcher became the first woman Prime Minister and the first woman to rule Britain since Queen Elizabeth I. She stood on the threshold of No. 10 Downing Street and said, 'Where there is discord may we bring harmony; where there is despair may we bring hope.' She went to Buckingham Palace to be received by the Queen in the Audience Chamber. Scarcely able to hide her jubilation, she went down in a deep curtsy before the Queen who congratulated her on her victory. The interview did not last long; Mrs Thatcher was anxious to get on with what she had promised would be a complete transformation of the British economic, domestic and social climate. And thus began, formal and cool, what was to become the longest prime ministerial relationship of the Queen's reign.

They did not share an immediate rapport and the Queen could be excused for commenting, as she may have done over breakfast to Prince Philip, 'I wonder what this one's going to be like?' It was going to be tougher, that was for sure; though a follower of protocol, could it really be expected that the woman who was going to face a Commons full of hard-bitten politicians would allow herself to be 'advised, encouraged or warned' in the Audience Chamber of

Buckingham Palace? Her style had been virtually forced upon her, overcompensating for her sex, and barely a month passed before there was a disagreement. Mrs Thatcher had inherited arrangements for the Queen to make an extended tour of Africa to coincide with the Commonwealth Conference in Lusaka. From the Queen's personal point of view, it was an important undertaking. First of all, she had no intention of missing the Commonwealth Conference at which she regarded her presence as vital if she was to maintain respect for her position as its head. Secondly, apart from a stopover in Kenya in 1972, she had not visited a single African country for fourteen years.

Much had happened since then and in 1979, after years of turmoil, some of the more extreme black leaders and despots like Idi Amin had been deposed and regimes toppled. She had remained the Commonwealth leader of these countries and provided a valuable continuity that no politician could ever have succeeded in doing. She forged her own links in this male-dominated club and though she took no formal part in any of the Commonwealth conferences and regardless of the strength of the anti-British feeling that may have pervaded any one of the countries at the time, she was the unifying bond. It mattered not to her whether one of those prime ministers could not get on with Edward Heath – as many did not – or Harold Wilson, or now Mrs Margaret Thatcher, about whom there was great foreboding. The Queen would still give audience to whoever came to call. Apart from occasional lectures she was forced to deliver on behalf of her government when on state visits, she managed to remain above politics. It would not, for example, have gone unnoticed in the rest of Africa that the new Prime Minister's husband Denis had substantial business contacts inside South Africa and that one of the companies he was associated with was paying its black workers virtual slave wages. Furthermore, Mrs Thatcher was personally seen as a sympathiser with the Rhodesian lobby in the British Parliament, a group of back-bench Conservative MPs who wanted to end the sanctions against the illegal regime of Ian Smith.

When Mrs Thatcher came to power, Rhodesia was in the throes of civil war. Ian Smith had grudgingly acknowledged that he must sooner or later respond to world opinion and had ordered a general election which had produced Rhodesia's first black Prime Minister in Bishop Abel Muzorewa, a Smith puppet. Mrs Thatcher had sent out a team to assess the elections and they came back to report that it was held 'fairly'. Indeed, she was sorely tempted to recognise the new government, in spite of the fact that the election had precluded the true opponents to the Smith regime, black nationalists Robert Mugabe and Joshua Nkomo. The Commonwealth Conference was fixed for 1 August and Mrs Thatcher, along with her Foreign Secretary Lord Carrington, viewed it as an opportunity for talks to begin on the future of Rhodesia. In the meantime, the civil war raged on and the venue of Lusaka was perilously close to some of the cross-border skirmishes between Rhodesian troops and the black nationalist supporters of the Mugabe-Nkomo alliance. As the time approached for the conference, Mrs Thatcher suggested the Queen should cancel her plans to go to Africa; it was far too dangerous, she said, and in that she had the support of the Foreign Secretary and her Cabinet.

As usual on such issues, the Queen remained firm. Through her aides, the Prime Minister's office was informed that as this was a Commonwealth matter, the Queen did not feel bound by the advice of her Prime Minister, and unless the situation in Lusaka became more serious – in which case the Commonwealth Conference itself might be moved – then she felt she should go. In the meantime, one of her secretaries contacted the President of Zambia, Dr Kenneth Kaunda, one of the Queen's closest African advisers and givers of counsel. Through his office a ceasefire between the African nationalists and the Rhodesians was arranged to come into effect for the duration of the Queen's visit. And so the Queen set off on her tour, going first to Tanzania, and just to make sure that everyone was aware that she did not fear the possibility of attack, she took Prince Andrew and Prince Philip with her.

President of Botswana and another friend of the Queen's, Sir Seretse Khama commented that he expected nothing less from her because he understood implicitly her reasons for taking the action she did, showing 'great personal courage and commitment in visiting southern Africa at this most difficult period in the history of the area'. Even so, while in

Tanzania, she learned that there had been a further clash between the opposing Rhodesian forces 200 miles from Lusaka. Added to that was trouble in Nigeria, where the military regime seized British Petroleum assets in that country in protest at the British government's policy towards South Africa. The Queen pre-empted the possibility of being requested by Mrs Thatcher to return home immediately by letting it be known that she did not regard the new fighting as a breach of the agreement. The ceasefire would, as she understood the agreement, come into effect the moment she set foot in Zambia. As for Nigeria, that was a political matter.

Courageous though she was, there were some risky moments for the Queen once she arrived in Lusaka. She had to listen to the city's mayor ranting angrily about the racist government of Rhodesia, for which Kenneth Kaunda later apologised. Security was so intense that each of the royals was surrounded by their own assigned guards to the extent that they were cut off from each other and the whole mêlée was a confusing mess that allowed the crowds virtually no vision of the Queen. 'Now they're arresting each other,' Prince Philip commented angrily as they were jostled along. However, Kaunda provided a relaxing and safe house where they spent five days until Mrs Thatcher and the British contingent arrived for the Commonwealth Conference. Unsmiling and taut, Mrs Thatcher walked into a hostile camp. Kaunda accused her of prejudging the issue and said she was obsessed with the idea that the Soviets would gain the initiative in Rhodesia if Mugabe, a confirmed Marxist, and Nkomo achieved power.[6] In Lusaka Mrs Thatcher had already been labelled a 'racist bigot',[7] and was compared unfavourably with the 'extraordinary loving heart of the Queen'.

It was now that the Queen's personal diplomacy was seen at its best. By her meetings with her Commonwealth prime ministers, she had already defused many of the tensions, and averted what might have been a crisis through her own Prime Minister's earlier tactless comments. She also cooled the atmosphere by talking to Kaunda about the newspaper hostility to Mrs Thatcher, which then ceased overnight. It was an historic performance by the Queen, for which she was given little public credit. Mrs Thatcher and Lord Carrington were given a tough time initially. But Mrs Thatcher reacted strongly against any attempts at bullying her, especially by Kaunda and Julius Nyerere, President of Tanzania. She impressed them by her directness, 'sweeping fearlessly through the crowds . . . and sailing into the other prime ministers; she cut out all subtlety'.[8] However, she eventually did what amounted to a U-turn and accepted most of the demands the Africans had asked for; and so it became her deal and her success in resolving the Rhodesian crisis which had been a thorn in Britain's side for fifteen years.

The reaction of the two women was notable. As she left Lusaka amid cheering crowds, the Queen was apparently close to tears. Mrs Thatcher swept away, handbag on arm, followed rapidly by her little entourage and, after accepting defeat at the hands of the Africans, she held her head up, and turned it into victory by declaring that it would be her goal to see Rhodesia genuinely independent, as indeed it became on 17 April 1980. Even Kaunda was moved to comment that the 'Iron Lady has brought a ray of hope to a dark horizon'. But he, more than anyone else present, also knew that the Queen had played an 'indispensable role'.

The cross-border shoot-outs between the Rhodesians and the Mugabe soldiers resumed where they had left off pending the Queen's visit, and she returned home to safer climes. Safer? The royals seemed to have accepted with resignation that it was now necessary for them to be surrounded by members of the security forces and allow themselves and their property, their cars and their destinations to be thoroughly checked for terrorist attack. Princess Anne had already experienced it at first hand, but fortunately it was an amateur who attempted it. Mountbatten had also been threatened with kidnap by a terrorist group who had kidnapped his cousin Prince Moritz a year earlier. But the IRA with their continued campaign of mainland bomb atrocities were considered by Scotland Yard to be the main threat to the British royal family. There were constant reappraisals of the security arrangements, yet it was the Queen herself who observed that if someone was determined enough to attempt to kill any of them, they might well succeed. The threat would not, however, drive her behind bullet-proof shields or stop her from meeting the people, although it was only when on holiday at Balmoral that she was allowed to wander to the village without a detective immediately by her side.

Mountbatten had annual discussions with Scotland Yard about the number of police posted to his own holiday home of Classiebawn Castle, near the village of Mullaghmore, County Sligo. The protection had been increased from a 12 man guard in 1972 to a team of twenty-eight highly trained anti-terrorist marksmen by 1974; each year he would write confidentially to Scotland Yard and let them know when he and his family would be arriving at Classiebawn and 1979 was no exception. Mountbatten himself viewed it increasingly as a formality since he was now so far removed from the power he once wielded that 'no one is interested in an old man like me'. Unfortunately, IRA chieftains had chosen him, to demonstrate to the people of England that they could strike at the heart of the royal family with utmost ease – and simultaneously murder eighteen soldiers on the other side of Ireland. The bomb that killed Mountbatten consisted of 50 pounds of explosives planted on board his fishing boat *Shadow V*, in which he went out most days while on holiday. Aboard were his daughter and son-in-law Lord and Lady Brabourne, Lord Brabourne's mother, their 14-year-old twin sons and a young man from the village, Paul Maxwell, who helped Mountbatten with the boat. A police car was on hand to escort them to the harbour and to keep surveillance from the coast. As the boat veered off past the harbour wall, the explosion could be heard for miles. The bomb was planted below Mountbatten's feet, where some observer must have known he always stood. It was probably detonated by remote control from the shore; he would have been killed instantly. One of his grandsons, Nicholas Knatchbull, was also killed, as was Paul Maxwell; Lady Doreen Brabourne died later. The remaining three were badly injured, but survived. This was a warning to the English ruling classes, said the IRA . . . 'We will tear out their sentimental imperialist heart.'[9]

The Queen led the world in mourning and Prince Charles made sure that they buried Mountbatten with all the pomp and ceremony that he desired, exactly as he had instructed in his will. The Queen had lost one of her staunchest supporters and advisers, and a man who had influenced the development of the royal family and the institution of monarchy like no other for more than three decades – to such a degree that many felt his power, balanced between the throne, the government and the military, to be sinister. Had he really been a leading figure, if not the head, of an elite Secret Service group who operated on a level above the SIS, and out of reach of the government? Was he really the prime mover of the plot to get rid of Wilson backed by military coup, while posing as his good and loyal supporter?

As his biographer Philip Ziegler wrote, 'He sought to rewrite history with cavalier indifference to the facts to magnify his own achievement . . . yet he possessed virtues which outweighed his defects.'[10] Whatever the defects, and we know of many, the Queen considered Mountbatten's passing a great loss to her court – and the last remaining male link she had with her father's day.

Chapter Sixteen

The New Star (1980–81)

The Anthony Blunt affair would not go away and for once it looked as if the Queen had been drawn into a political and security cover-up which has never been properly explained. As the new year began, the publicity surrounding the Blunt affair was still being discussed in the newspapers six weeks after Mrs Thatcher revealed in the House of Commons on 15 November 1979 that the Queen's former Surveyor of Pictures was a Russian spy and a traitor who confessed and was given immunity from prosecution in April 1964. It will be recalled from earlier references to this story that the discovery of Blunt's treachery was revealed to the Queen during the short premiership of Sir Alec Douglas-Home, who now vaguely denied knowing anything about the matter. It seems distinctly odd that Home would not have been informed, yet the Queen's private secretary Sir Michael Adeane was told. From a variety of documents in the Public Records Office and elsewhere, it can be shown that in all such cases it would be the Prime Minister who would be told first – not the Queen's private secretary. It would be the Prime Minister, effectively head of the Secret Service, who would normally make any kind of decision relating to matters of security, especially when public exposure – of which there was always a threat – would embarrass the Queen. It would be inconceivable that MI5 was ever likely to contact Buckingham Palace for permission to have a chat with the Queen's Surveyor of Pictures without first clearing it with the Prime Minister. It had all the hallmarks of government departmental arrogance – permeating from the top downwards – which existed through the confident years of Tory Party rule in the fifties and early sixties, when certain people thought they could actually prevent scandalous embarrassments from reaching the ears of the outside world by organised cover-up or extensive use of censorship. Often they succeeded and as far as the royal family was concerned, the Prime Minister's office simply slapped on top of the file 'Closed for 100 years'.

In the first eight years of the Queen's reign, numerous files containing documents concerning the Queen or the royal family which were either discussed in cabinet or which were brought to the attention of the Prime Minister confidentially, now lay sealed in the Public Records Office at Kew. Most may not be opened for 100 years from the date of closure, and two are sealed for fifty years; both terms, excessive though they may seem compared with the normal 30 years closure rule, can only indicate the serious or embarrassing nature of the subject matter.[1] Sealing the files for 100 years was a simple solution which went unchallenged – and still is today, for that matter. Occasionally, it is possible by long and delicate research to get an idea of what the files contain and occasionally too, as in this instance, it is possible to obtain more detail than is available in England from American security files under their Freedom of Information Act. Far from having to wait 100 years, much historical matter can now be gleaned from American State Department and FBI files within ten months of making an application for declassification.[2]

But it is unlikely that we shall ever know exactly how much *she* knew at the time. In the wake of the exposure of Blunt's treachery, certain members of the establishment have attempted to downplay his importance, and have even tried to discredit reports that he brought back from Nazi Germany certain documents for King George VI, some of which related to the activities of the Duke of Windsor. There is still, however, evidence which supports the view that Blunt's errand for the King could not be dismissed that easily; he brought back material which in postwar Britain would have caused a furore.[3] The importance of Blunt as a spy, or even the value of his mission to Germany for the King, is not the real issue. Nor is the suggestion by John Costello that Blunt in some way held sway because of his connections with a prewar homosexual ring which included members of the royal family.[4] It is the principle of keeping hidden a matter of supreme public interest through devious means. In 1979–80 when the issue was being discussed, it was stressed that it was not known whether or not the Queen had been told of Blunt's treachery. In fact, the author discovered that Buckingham Palace had long ago become aware of suspicions about him, but he was a trusted servant of the King. When Sir Michael Adeane informed the Queen of MI5's interest in 1964, she is purported to have said 'It is something I do not want to know too much about'.

Adeane certainly knew what was involved; he was aware that Blunt first came under suspicion in 1951 when King George VI learned that it was thought Blunt might have been involved in the defection of Burgess and Maclean. The King was told that the security people were anxious to talk to Blunt and he naturally gave his permission. Between then and 1964, Blunt was interviewed on eleven separate occasions by MI5 and each time he denied that he was a Russian agent. The Americans seemingly had more on Blunt that their British Intelligence counterparts but were prevented from pursuing their inquiries in England. Declassified FBI documents[5] reveal that Blunt was identified as a source of information to Guy Burgess as early as 1951. By 1953, the FBI was considering informing the British that they wanted to interview Blunt, who was planning a trip to America. They were apparently talked out of it by British Intelligence and the reasons are still censored, obscured by the thick black pen marks on the declassified papers.[6] However, in early 1964, certain new information was received via America which directly implicated Blunt. The new information was corroborated by an FBI agent in Louisville, Kentucky.[7] He investigated claims that a coded letter found in a library book in the British embassy in Cairo had a Louisville postmark. Blunt, it was discovered, was in Louisville at that time on a lecture tour. Results of the investigation, completed in 1964, were passed to the British. Blunt was interviewed again, and this time he confessed and on the promise of immunity from prosecution, he made a full statement.

Blunt, who worked for British Intelligence during the war and, as we have seen, on some specific duties for King George VI, was passing classified information to the Russians throughout the war until early 1946. If he had been caught during the war, he could have been hanged for treason. If he had been caught after the war, at the very least he would have been given a long prison sentence. Unperturbed, he helped his friends Burgess and Maclean to escape to Russia in 1951, while he continued to have regular contact with the Russians and the central villain of the spy scandal, Kim Philby. All of this, Blunt included in his confession, and in April 1964 the Queen's private secretary was told that Blunt's case would go no further. He was also told, and presumably passed it on to the Queen, that as part of the arrangements under which Blunt was granted immunity from prosecution 'Blunt would not be required to resign his appointment within the Royal Household'. Whether the wording of this notation was meant as an instruction to Buckingham Palace to keep Blunt on the staff, or whether it was to accommodate Buckingham Palace's request to do so – or perhaps even a compromise between the two – cannot be confirmed. Thus, the public was asked to believe that the then Prime Minister did not have any discussion whatsoever with his Sovereign as to the continued employment at the palace of a man who had been a Russian spy and talent scout since the thirties and a key figure in one of the greatest spy intrigues in British history.

The questions remain unanswered to this day: Why did the Queen continue to allow Blunt to operate as her Surveyor of Pictures for the next twelve years until he retired (even allowing herself to be photographed with him), when it would have been a simple matter quietly to dispose of his services through early retirement at any time? It was, after all, an unpaid task which he continued to carry out as if nothing had ever happened; nor was he excluded from the palace or Clarence House. And why was it decided to grant him immunity from prosecution? Was the suggestion that Blunt blackmailed the Queen's advisers by saying that he would reveal too many embarrassing secrets if he ever went to court, so 'picaresque', as one of the authorised royal biographers put it?[8] Furthermore, if Mrs Thatcher had not been forced to make a public statement on Blunt in the House of Commons in November 1979, we must assume that his treachery would have remained a secret until the day he died and beyond. If that was so, it also follows that the Queen would not have been forced to strip Blunt of his knighthood in his lifetime, which she did on the day of the Commons statement, and he would have died a knight, saved from exposure by conspirators inside Buckingham Palace, Westminster and MI5. If Blunt's actions were so dastardly as to require him to be shorn of the Queen's honour in 1979, then surely the same must have applied when they were discovered in 1964; numerous wrongdoers in the following three decades have been relieved of their medals far more quickly. The excuse that he was never publicly exposed because of 'continuing investigations' and lack of evidence simply did not hold water when we now know how much evidence the Americans had obtained.

One other aspect is also mysterious. Mrs Thatcher's plans to reveal the Blunt story in the House of Commons were relayed to Buckingham Palace in advance, and they made all the necessary arrangements to follow up Mrs Thatcher's statement by announcing that the Queen had that day stripped Blunt of his knighthood. This certainly seemed to give the impression that Buckingham Palace had been unaware of his wrongdoings and that now they had been exposed the palace had acted instantly – which was not of course the case. Buckingham Palace was not the only recipient of advance warning of the Prime Minister's intentions. Two days beforehand Blunt packed two suitcases of clothes and left for foreign parts where he remained until the furore had died down. Just who tipped him off about the Prime Minister's intentions remains open to speculation, as does the unresolved question of the extent of Buckingham Palace's involvement. It is the author's understanding that the Queen knew in 1964 that Blunt was a spy, and so did members of the Cabinet. And whoever advised the Queen on the course of action which was taken then, and pursued in secrecy, put at risk one of the fundamental elements that makes the monarchy secure in British democracy, that the sovereign remains above such conspiratorial entanglements. Shenanigans of this nature are expected of the Secret Service, and to some extent among politicians; it is dangerous for the monarchy to get within a mile of them. It was indeed a shoddy business.

Apart from the Blunt scandal which only marginally touched the Queen in terms of criticism, there was an unnaturally quiet malaise overhanging the House of Windsor at the start of the new decade. The afterglow of the Jubilee had disappeared from view, overtaken by the impact of the nation's social and economic ills. But each new decade seems to have imposed elements of change which were once again to affect the whole perception of the monarchy. This time, they were going to be projected as world stars, as opposed to a little group of wealthy, historical eccentrics, and this would first show itself in how the Queen was to be 'used', as Walter Bagehot wrote in his Victorian constitutional thesis.

The year 1980 was going to be busier than most, with tours of Switzerland, Italy, Algeria and Morocco, Belgium, Germany and another 5-day flying trip to Australia, which presented the prospect of an alarming number of handshakes. The personal impact of these increasingly gruelling tours had been facilitated by the ease of travel, carrying her fast around the world from one country to the next by jetliners; gone were the days when sea travel allowed an intervening rest period to catch up on sleep. However, there must be a counterbalancing mention of the fact that, in spite of the Queen's greater overseas commitments, she had still spent more days on holiday on her Balmoral estate alone in the last ten years than she had on foreign trips. But it was probably necessary, otherwise she would not have survived. Fast travel brought the new hazard of jet-lag and though the royal yacht more often than not travelled separately to wherever the Queen might be going, it was used more as a floating hotel and conference centre.

The new Thatcher government began to place greater emphasis on the Queen's role as a promoter of British trade and industry and a fillip for tourism. 'What else is left?' Mrs Thatcher once observed to a Cabinet minister who questioned her on how the Queen could best be used. 'She is the best saleswoman we have got.' Her tour planners were being asked to accommodate a far greater number of engagements, blatantly aimed at buttering up the prospective purchasers of British goods and services. The result of these new overtly promotional ventures, once covered by the excuse of allowing the Queen to be seen by all her people wherever in the world they might be, was that she was being forced to meet a good number of people who were never going to be so subservient and adoring as the old colonialists of the past. There was a big difference, her aides were discovering, in sending the Queen to a country with historic affiliations where she would be warmly welcomed and sending her to one where her main object was to encourage trade. This was never more obvious than on what one royal aide described as 'that bloody trip' to Morocco, which provided the Queen with a lasting memory of a man she would not wish to meet again in a hurry, even if he did present her with a gift of four Arab horses.

Princess Margaret had already warned her sister that going to Morocco and driving in a motorcade of King Hassan's was rather like being kidnapped – 'You never know where you are going and with whom.' As far as the Queen was concerned, he seemed intent on showing her that he did not regard the Queen of England as his equal. First of all he ducked out of a welcoming lunch for her in Marrakesh in favour of a round of golf, and left two of his children to perform the welcoming ceremonies. Later, when she arrived at a banquet she was left hanging about for some time before discovering that the King had decided not to attend that function either. The following day, he joined them on a tour of the mountain regions but because of his obsession with security and the constant fear that at any given time someone was planning to assassinate him – which was probably true – he kept changing cars and made the whole carefully planned schedule meaningless.

The final humiliation came when the Queen was ushered into a tent to take tea from a silver urn and was left there for an hour while the ill-mannered Moroccan King disappeared into another tent for a rest. She was angry, very angry, and tapping her foot impatiently when he finally turned up. When headlines the following day reported the Queen's fury at this appalling behaviour, he did it again by arriving an hour late for a banquet on the royal yacht. The Queen bit her lip, as she had throughout, because the goodwill of King Hassan was important. On it rested the possibility of British industry being awarded a multi-million engineering contract on which Mrs Thatcher had personally set great store.

The Queen's tours are full of silly incidents, but more often it is the laughable ones that are most noticeable; like the time in Italy when the women she was meeting heard she did not like them to wear red or black dresses, which caused a panic; then there was the time in Australia when it went around that she only liked to eat from biscuit-coloured table-cloths, not white ones, and so every hostess ditched her best table-cloth and bought new ones. There was an occasion when a railway station manager took all the 'Gents' signs down so that she would not be offended, and the town council who had all the dustbins on a housing estate emptied and cleaned immediately prior to her visit; or the visit to a new children's park where three boys were demonstrating the art of fishing. 'There's no fish in there, surely,' asked Philip. 'Yes there is,' said one of the boys, 'they came and put five hundred in there today so I could catch one for you.' That was the kind of silliness they were used to; but nowhere had she experienced the kind of rudeness displayed by King Hassan.

The Queen's ambassadorial role in smoothing the way for traders, engineers and politicians, seemed to be extending to new heights. By 1980, she reigned over what the historian A. J. P. Taylor had described as the greatest peacetime decline of a nation's power, wealth and influence in history.[9] Taylor blamed successive governments for a series of obsessions, such as the balance of payments which kept the nation's destiny at the mercy of the Bank of England. He blamed them for their obsession with Europe. And he reckoned that Britain's influence in the Commonwealth had dwindled to vanishing point. 'When we kept in the Commonwealth people who felt no British sentiment, we did not strengthen the Commonwealth, we weakened it . . . we have tried to keep a pretence alive by the distribution of economic aid which earned no gratitude and brought little benefit to those for whom it was intended.'

Whereas at the start of her reign, the tours – like the travels of previous monarchs – inspired those spectacular demonstrations of native welcome, where she would sit through hours of local pageants, or be scared half to death by fully fledged warriors galloping towards her, or lifted aboard an elephant to join a colourful procession in India – that had all passed. As the eighties turned, the receptions were quieter, less colourful and the trading element had become more important than the Queen's original object in travelling, which was to allow herself to be seen by as many of her people as possible. 'Let my people see me,' was her statement of intent in 1953.

Unfortunately, there was a diminishing requirement for that aim. The tours, though still reported by newspapers and the other media, were taking a backward place in terms of column inches or television time devoted to them. Interest in the monarchy as an institution was flagging and whereas once anything that the Queen did was immediately put into news bulletins and newspaper schedules, she was disappearing fast from even the smallest headlines, largely because of the repetitive nature of her appearances. Apart from the one-off family highlights that seem to occur naturally and provide the monarchy with a sudden boost, the whole business seemed to have taken on a touch of sameness.

The Queen had been doing the job for thirty years and the same photocalls came around each year with monotonous regularity – such as the distribution of Maundy money, the drive down the course at Royal Ascot, Trooping the Colour, the arrival at Balmoral for the summer, the state opening of Parliament, the arrival at Sandringham for Christmas. It was always the same. The spectacle of ceremony was making less impact as each year went past; frankly, the nation had seen it all before. Short daily news items of 3 minute 'bites' in television news coverage seemed to be able to satisfy what Malcolm Muggeridge once said was a need to be sated like a religion. The sorry fact was that the monarchy's edge had been dulled; only the trivia was becoming reportable. Even Princess Margaret's affair with Roddy Llewellyn was over, so there was only an occasional swearword from Princess Anne to spice up the headlines.

But help was at hand and even the Queen, who never appeared especially surprised about anything these days, would be totally bowled over by the extent of public interest that was about to be unleashed, for good or bad, around her and her family.

The first clue for those students of royal undercurrents was Prince Charles's decision in the summer of 1980 to buy himself a house. Not just any old house; no bachelor pad. Highgrove was a family home, the sort of place a man settled into when he was thinking long-term of filling the rooms with servants and children. According to Mountbatten's secretary John Barratt, if Mountbatten had lived, he would have talked Prince Charles into marrying his granddaughter Amanda Knatchbull, so that the Mountbatten bloodline was totally secure in the succession of future kings and queens of England, even if his name might never be that of the reigning house. Mountbatten had planned to take Charles on an extensive tour of India, and Amanda was going along too, as Mountbatten's 'secretary'. But the IRA put paid to that, and afterwards Amanda announced she was going off around the world for a year.

There were plenty of other suggested names, too, but these appeared to be just part of what Mountbatten had advised – 'sowing your wild oats' before you settle down. As an object of intense curiosity, every move the Queen's son made was noted and yet his circle of friends were loyally devoted, as were his mother's, and sworn to help keep what bit of private life he had out of the gossip columns. Charles had been very fortunate in that respect, as the Queen once observed. In 1980, he was thirty-two years old and had enjoyed several good years of a relatively trouble-free bachelorhood during which he thankfully demonstrated a healthy interest in the opposite sex, unlike some of his ancestors. There had been no serious kiss-and-tells, and yet he was seldom without a pretty girl on his arm. He was a creature of habit; he would get up early, exercise and bathe. He had a good staff who cared for his every need and there were always interesting places for him to go. He sometimes bemoaned the fact that his life tended to be uneventful, but that apart he had a pretty good social life, with lots of dinner invitations and plenty of girls, married and single, to advise him or accompany him on his various excursions. The purchase of a house for £750,000 was an indication that he was at last ready to settle down. By chance – or was it? – that month, when the royal family, as always, took the yacht down to Cowes, Lady Diana Spencer, nineteen years old, slightly shy, two O-level daughter of the Queen's old friend Johnnie Spencer, was among the guests. Friends reckoned that Charles was still obsessed with Anna Wallace, but Anna, impetuous and strong-willed, had recently walked out on him because she was fed up with coming second to royal duties, which was a fairly good indication that, had she married him, she might not have stayed the course, anyway. Thus, when Charles spotted Diana that summer, he was without a girlfriend and the clamouring for him to find a bride was at its peak. Out of the blue he sent Diana a dozen red roses and made sure that she received an invitation to Balmoral when she went to Scotland that summer for a short holiday with her sister Jane.

Much royal courting has been done at Balmoral and since it has figured so often in our story, it is perhaps worth at this point discovering the type of routine so enjoyed by the Queen, which Lady Diana, as the Princess of Wales, would have to get used to; she did not like it much at all. Balmoral was described by one visitor as an open prison and Diana, in future years, would be inclined to agree with that assessment. Every year since Victoria's time, the royal family have moved north with a large number of servants to complement those already in residence, along with a large amount of luggage, numerous corgis, plus the summer guests; traditionally the current Prime Minister makes a brief stay in September. The Queen loves the seclusion of Balmoral and here, more than in any other of her family homes, guards against intruders of any kind. The routine is firmly established and has hardly varied in years and the decor of the place is a reflection of the type of holiday home that it has become, with antlers from deer shot by members of the family hanging from the walls, and the halls littered with fishing rods and Wellington boots. There are the relaxing sports, for which most of them have been criticised at some time or another. They go deerstalking, grouse-shooting, fishing for trout and salmon and there is plenty of horse-riding. They go for long walks among the scented heathers of the estate where it is quite easy to get lost. Many have, since Queen Victoria began inviting her relatives and members of her government there, after she bought it from the inheritor of the previous owner who choked to death on a fish-bone. She had the old house demolished and built the baronial-style castle in its place. A weekend at Balmoral for guests has traditionally begun on a Thursday; they usually arrive after lunch and stay until Sunday. The mornings are generally relaxed, unless there is a fishing or shooting expedition planned. Old-fashioned breakfasts may be taken in bed, especially for the ladies, or in the main dining hall. Usually, the Queen will take breakfast in her bedroom if there are guests present, otherwise, she may wander down in casual clothes. All the newspapers are available to guests, as if they were at an hotel, and the dinners can be formal and dressy but more often are relaxed and casual. There is a pipe major invariably in attendance to entertain. Guests are expected to join in their famous after-dinner games, like charades, which the Queen Mother is especially keen on.

Lady Diana's introduction to these quaint royal holiday customs that summer of 1980 was a mere taste of what was to come for years hence, when she would be expected to join the Queen and Prince Philip, come what may, and enjoy their summer arrangements. The royal family have ways of making their guests 'enjoy' themselves.

The Queen and the Queen Mother were pleased, if not pleasantly surprised that Charles had invited Diana over. He was, after all, nearly thirteen years her senior. It was a trifle unexpected that after all the years of the royal family's close association with the Spencer family when the latter were neighbours to the royal estate at Sandringham, Charles should end up sending roses to the youngest daughter. There had been talk that he might marry the eldest, Sarah, with whom he went skiing in 1978, but she was married earlier in the summer of 1980. What no one knew then was the Queen's concern and kindness to Sarah when she had emotional problems and anorexia nervosa; her weight had gone below 6 stone. The Queen took an active part in getting Sarah to have treatment, inviting her to Balmoral, personally taking her riding and talking to her as much as she could, before finally persuading her to book into a nursing home where she was cured. The Spencers were always thankful, afterwards, to the Queen because they felt she, above all, had helped out.

The second of the Spencer daughters, Jane, was also a friend of Charles's, and she married the Queen's future assistant private secretary Robert Fellowes in 1978; even so, when Charles's relationship with the glamorous woman of the world Anna Wallace ended, Diana, shy, unknown and unworldly, could hardly have been an anticipated choice. Though well used to the royal circle, she was unsophisticated and untroubled by the demands of the elitist band of young people with whom Charles had been spending his free time since leaving the navy.

However, that summer at Balmoral she fell unwittingly into the unstinting gaze of that species of summertime birdwatchers known as tabloid journalists, notably the portly frame of James Whitaker, who became so familiar to the royals that most now call him by his first name. He was hiding in the bracken with his binoculars and before long had identified the pretty young girl walking with Charles and featured her strongly in the following day's paper.

Even the Queen was surprised at the speed with which Charles's new friend had been spotted and for the rest of the year there was no peace for her, although it was still too early to predict any serious involvement. Fifty years earlier, she too would have been ruled out of court as a suitable bride for a future king because her parents were divorced. In 1980, it didn't matter. Even so, Diana's childhood, paradoxically in the shadow of royalty, had not been happy after her mother and father split; the thing that was most appealing about Diana to the royal family was that she was a girl without a past. There was not a single stain or blemish on her life that might be dredged up and used in evidence against her as the newspapers began to build up their picture of the unsophisticated young girl who had captured the heart of the Queen's heir.

'She'll have to get used to that,' the Queen observed when Charles spoke of the 'bloody press' and Philip hit at the 'bloody vultures', and she would, in her own way. And so in the space of four or five months, Diana had progressed from being an unnoticed little sister of one of Charles's earlier girlfriends to becoming his fiancée. First of all, there were certain formalities to be completed. The heir to the throne had formally to seek his mother's permission to marry, which she gave gladly, and she had to place before the Privy Council a formal request which they granted. Someone, probably a member of Mrs Thatcher's Cabinet which was told of the impending engagement some days before it was announced, leaked the news to *The Times* who subsequently beat Buckingham Palace to the announcement of the expected engagement on 24 February. When it was confirmed, Diana mania broke out; it was a kind of hysteria whipped up partly by the newspapers, who in turn were reacting to quite a massive ground-swell of public interest in Charles's chosen girl.

The public had been waiting so long for the news that Charles was getting married, and had been teased with false information so often, that when it finally came, they went into raptures – as did most of the royal photographers who doubled in number overnight. The Queen became angry and for the first time anyone could remember actually spoke angrily to the photographers who were surrounding Diana. 'Why don't you go away?' she said. They would not, of course, because editors had just discovered the biggest circulation-booster for years – a good front-page picture of Lady Di could sell 50,000 extra copies. After the engagement was announced, Diana was promptly taken into the protective custody of the Queen Mother away from the baying hounds. From that moment, she had joined the royal circle and her life would never be the same again. Her personality, her past, her future, her family, even her virginity were discussed. Her uncle Lord Fermoy attested that 'Diana has never had a lover', while the Queen's gynaecologist confirmed her ability to reproduce heirs to her husband-to-be, who would themselves be heirs to the throne.

What Charles had managed to do by selecting Lady Diana was, at a stroke, to restore the flagging interest in the British monarchy. He had produced the true fairytale princess whose only equal in the past fifty years had been the Queen herself. She was innocent and ordinary, like the classic girl next door with whom a million and one other girls next door could identify and in whom a similar number of mothers of girls next door could see aspirations for their own daughters.

Comparable only with the Queen's Coronation, the wedding of the heir apparent, set for July 1981, was going to provide the pageant and the magic which, in spite of the grandiose spectacular that it would undoubtedly prove to be, would none the less portray the royal family as a down-to-earth, middle-class family. The family's great wealth and the Queen's huge landed estates are dismissed by the masses at times like this. A royal wedding of this nature, probably accidentally, brought about a reaffirmation of traditional loyalties to the Crown. The wedding itself was the climax of what Professor Edmund Leach described as 'the irrational theatre of monarchy'[10] because it combined the power of ritual with a contemporary love story *and*, more importantly it came at the very moment when the people themselves needed an escape valve.

What endeared them even more to the 500 or 600 million viewers who watched the wedding on television was their apparent disregard of the dangers from a terrorist attack. In the months prior to it, there were attempts to assassinate President Ronald Reagan and the Pope. On 5 May, a parcel bomb addressed to Prince Charles was intercepted before it could do any damage. There were fears of counter-attacks from the IRA which was in a mood of high tension after the death from hunger strike of Bobby Sands in the Maze prison in May; in the weeks following, up to the time of the wedding, ten more hunger strikers died. And then on 30 June, an unemployed youth from Folkestone fired six blank shots at the Queen as she rode down the Mall for the Trooping of the Colour. Her face, for a fleeting moment, was captured with a look of horror and then she bent forward to pat and reassure her horse, the black mare Burmese. The incident demonstrated again just how simple it would be for a more determined assassin to murder a member of the royal family.

There was also a burning desire for the wedding of Prince Charles and Lady Diana Spencer to become a focal point, not only of the nation's fondness for the royal family, but also a means of evading the realities of life in Britain at that moment in time. Apart from the threats of an IRA bombing campaign, there were real and unpleasant problems facing the government and the nation. The recession was deepening, and unemployment was edging towards its highest levels in history. The effects of Thatcherism were carving deep into the 'lame ducks' of British industry. The 'lady's not for turning', Mrs Thatcher declared defiantly in October 1980, but very soon even those who were not personally affected knew someone or had a relative who had lost their job. The royal wedding also coincided with the outbreaks of rioting in Brixton and Toxteth, first in April and then spreading to cities throughout the nation; 10 July was what became known as Britain's night of anarchy as youths black and white rampaged through the town centres of Bristol, Liverpool, Luton, Reading, Chester – almost every major city suffered some kind of outbreak. In the space of the three weeks prior to Charles's wedding, communities were set ablaze and whole areas of inner cities took on the appearance of having suffered a recent blitz. If an event was ever more welcomed by a government in power as a diversionary interlude, then only the accession of Elizabeth II was comparable, when Winston Churchill sought the utmost pomp and ceremonial glamour to surround the throne in that year, and divert the nation from its downhearted state.

Britain, by that summer of 1981, was a nation locked into a unique political, social and economic experiment and was even more ill-at-ease than it had been during Callaghan's winter of discontent. The Queen, not unnaturally, raised the issues of street violence at her audiences with Mrs Thatcher. It is known that she was deeply concerned and shocked by recurring television images of looters walking away with armfuls of stolen goods from broken shop-windows, while the mobs hurling stones and Molotov cocktails kept the police at bay. 'Those poor shopkeepers,' Mrs Thatcher cried on first seeing them.[11]

There were many of the nation's social thinkers – not to mention members of the Cabinet – who seriously believed that what was happening that summer was merely the foretaste of a massive breakdown of civil order, which would surely follow the epidemic of high unemployment and anti-union policies. With the nation in flames, right-wingers, inaccurately blaming black activists, demanded more and more police to deal with them. As a woman well known for her social conscience and a natural instinct for concern about her people on the lower echelons of the social spectrum, the

Queen might well have thought that there must be a better way, just as several of the so-called Tory 'wets' did but were incapable of doing anything to curb the Thatcher experiment. One of them, James Prior, the Minister of Employment, thought the Prime Minister was gripped by a Joan of Arc complex at the time and would have risked bringing the whole government crashing down around her if she was not allowed to proceed with her policies in the way that she and her monetarist advisers had perceived them.

Privately the Queen may well have agreed with the 'wets' but realistically she could only question Mrs Thatcher as to her intentions. The tone of her relationship with her Prime Minister is said to have become cooler by the week; Mrs Thatcher was the least popular Prime Minister with the nation since polling began, and the Queen undoubtedly shared her people's view. 'Mrs Thatcher appeared more like a second Queen, surrounded by her courtiers, than a Prime Minister,' said Shirley Williams, the former Labour Cabinet minister and founder member of the Social Democrats. 'And the contrast between her and the real Queen became more marked.'[12]

The rioting may have seemed endless but it did stop, eventually, and when the nation turned its weary eye towards the royal celebrations, the Home Office breathed a sigh of relief that the diversion had arrived at last. Riots beget publicity which begets riots; a change of mood and temperament could do no harm at all. In the meantime, the Queen's security advisers were themselves worried, convinced that the royal wedding could become a target of extremism in these volatile times and it was suggested that both the Queen and Charles should consider driving in their procession in bullet-proof cars. As usual, the Queen would not hear of it, and they all went in their open-topped landaus.

The success of the wedding, which the Archbishop of Canterbury Dr Robert Runcie himself decided was the 'stuff that fairytales are made of', captured the hearts of not just Britain, but the world. No amount of theorising, and no smart references to political science, the constitutional system, or the unhappy state of the nation could provide explanations for the tumultuous and hysterical celebration which cut across all divisions of class, party, or country. Prince Charles wanted a big do – and he got one. 'I can't wait for the whole thing,' he said in an interview beforehand. 'I want everybody to come out, you know, having a marvellous and musical and emotional experience.' It was he who personally insisted that the wedding should be in St Paul's and not Westminster Abbey, where most royal weddings take place. Eyebrows were raised; the cathedral is at a three times greater distance from the palace than Westminster, providing greater security risks, and there weren't enough soldiers and police to stretch along the route. 'Well, stand them further apart,' said Charles. And they did. The usual critics came out to play, of course, especially about the £150,000 spent on fireworks, and all the other attendant expense of providing the richest pageant Britain can stage; it went almost unnoticed, though, that the subsidiary events surrounding the wedding which Charles had put into operation raised £750,000 for charity.

The media coverage around the world was unprecedented and far more extensive than even for the Queen's own Coronation; she was taken by a mixture of pleasure and shock at the reaction to her son's wedding day. It hardly seemed credible or natural that so much attention should be focused on the marriage of a very privileged young couple. Front pages and numerous pages inside the popular newspapers were eclipsed by the wedding for days; events such as the election of a government or the selection of an American President looked insignificant in terms of column inches devoted to the newlyweds. The massive crowds who surged down the Mall at the end of the day to watch them all appear on the balcony of Buckingham Palace made a scene reminiscent of the ending of the Second World War; there was simply no logical explanation for these displays of devotion and support, except perhaps that, out of those tense summer months, a new royal star was born who would carry with her the popularity and survival of the British monarchy into the next century.

The star was truly born in those dark post-riot days, just as Queen Elizabeth the Queen Mother had won national approval in the East End during the war. The Queen not only recognised the Diana phenomenon, she actually took steps to try to curtail it, not simply for the effect it would have on the girl herself, but also on the monarchy as a whole.

Throughout the honeymoon on *Britannia*, the long and sometimes incredibly boring summer holiday at Balmoral, the autumn when she had her introduction into public engagements, the Princess of Wales was given a slow acclimatisation to royal life. The photographers and reporters were still hanging from trees and hiding under the hedgerows of the countryside, or bobbing up whenever the princess appeared at a window or a doorway. Barely a day passed without her photograph appearing on the front page of one, if not all, of the popular newspapers and she peered down repeatedly in the bookstalls from the covers of endless glossy magazines. Virtually since the engagement, Diana had eclipsed the rest of the royal family in terms of media coverage; especially put out was Princess Anne whose charity work received nowhere near the attention it deserved.

The publicity was descending into the most banal trivia; a balance had to be struck, the Queen told her new press secretary Michael Shea, and following their conversation, to which her private secretary Sir William Heseltine was party, it was decided to call all Fleet Street editors to the palace for a drink and a chat. Nothing quite like it had ever happened before. Twenty-one editors from all the national newspapers, news agencies and television news services were invited to the palace. All but one – Kelvin MacKenzie, editor of the *Sun* – came crunching across the frozen forecourt on 4 December 1981, to be shown into a room inside Buckingham Palace known as the 1844 Room, so named because Tsar Nicholas, Emperor of All Russia slept there in that year. Mr Shea assured the assembled company that the Queen would be joining them for a drink shortly, but in the meantime he wished to state the reason for requesting the editors' attention. The Queen and other members of the royal family, he said, were becoming increasingly alarmed about the invasion of privacy by some enthusiastic members of the newspaper profession. While the royal family always went out of its way to cooperate with the needs of the press, he said, things were getting rather out of hand. And now the crunch of the matter . . . the Princess of Wales was, in particular, feeling under pressure and the strain on her was beginning to tell, especially now that she was in the early stages of pregnancy and suffering morning sickness. On that morning there had been ten separate 'royal' stories in one newspaper – *The Times*. The Prince and Princess of Wales, said Shea, considered themselves to be under siege at Highgrove House and the Queen, through him, wished to make an earnest appeal for this situation to halt. The last straw was when the princess went into the village shop to buy wine gums and was promptly surrounded by a posse of cameramen. Prince Charles was getting angry, and it wasn't as if the princess was going to vanish off the face of the earth at any moment; she was going to be around for a very long time, become part of British history and it 'will be a real tragedy if worries about the media continue into her mature life'.

So what could be done? How could the Prince and Princess of Wales be assured their privacy? How could the Queen obtain seclusion when she retired privately to Sandringham? These were the questions Shea posed to the assembled editors and hoped they would come up with their own self-policing suggestions. It was an interesting proposition. Among the editors was Robert Edwards, of the *Sunday Mirror*, which had carried a story before the wedding that Charles and Diana had met secretly one night aboard the royal train parked in a siding. Shea had issued a vehement denial and demanded a retraction, which the *Sunday Mirror* did not give; instead it complained that Shea should challenge the 'professional reputation of its journalists'. There was John Junor, editor of the *Sunday Express*, whose newspaper had, in its day, used many of the paparazzi photographs that Shea was complaining about; there was Michael Molloy, editor of the *Daily Mirror*, whose standing instruction to his night editor (the present author) was to provide his readers with their 'daily dose of Di' – a large photograph invariably published over three or four columns on the front page; and there was Barry Askew, then editor of the *News of the World*, who made his own views known to Shea by saying that if 'the next Queen of England walked into a sweet shop to buy wine gums' then she could more or less expect to be besieged by photographers, upon which statement other editors present pounced and made it known he wasn't speaking for the rest of them. There was a sort of gentlemen's agreement about cooling down the royal coverage by Fleet Street and thus having been saved from any more sinister punishment, the party moved into the

Carnarvon Room, hung with paintings of Spanish battles against Napoleon's armies; the Queen and Prince Andrew came in and began circulating.

Most of the editors were sympathetic and, for a time, at least there would be some acquiescence. But Barry Askew, the other Rupert Murdoch editor present, seemed unlikely to show any mercy in his newspaper.

'If Lady Di,' he said to the Queen, failing to accord her the correct title which she had acquired since marriage, 'wants to buy wine gums without being photographed, why doesn't she send a servant?'[13]

The frozen-with-horror look on the faces of his editor colleagues cracked in united, thankful laughter when the Queen replied, 'What an extremely pompous man you are . . .'

Chapter Seventeen

Where It All Began (1982–4)

Apart from her unswerving loyalty to the Commonwealth, the Queen has shown similar dedication to members of Her Majesty's armed forces. Neither of these were fashionable causes. Her favourite regiments are the Life Guards, the Blues and Royals (Royal Horse Guards and 1st Dragoons) and the Royal Scots Dragoon Guards of which she is colonel-in-chief – the rank she holds in a long list of regiments at home and overseas. She would not have believed it beyond her constitutional rights, for example, to remind Mrs Thatcher of the need to recognise any individual or collective acts of bravery by serving men, especially those who faced the continued troubles in Northern Ireland. She has also always shown a special interest in naval activities; her father, her husband, Prince Charles and now her second son, Prince Andrew, were all serving officers. But she could never have imagined during the winter of 1981–2 that the reports she was reading in her top secret Foreign Office boxes signalled the start of events that would very soon force her to sign a declaration that would send her son to war, along with thousands of his military and naval brethren. Or that, hard on the heels of this event, troopers of her personal guards from the Blues and Royals would be slaughtered by an IRA bomb. Those were just two of the dramatic and devastating events which 1982 held in store . . .

The Queen was already familiar with the detail of the Falklands crisis that had its beginnings a year or so earlier, when the Thatcher monetarist policies were being pursued with increasing vigour and, apart from the closing factories and disappearing hospitals, the Ministry of Defence was among those whose budgets were to be drastically pruned. Mrs Thatcher had appointed her loyal supporter John Nott to succeed her first Defence Minister Francis Pym and exert a tougher line, and the Queen had received him at Buckingham Palace a year earlier when she granted him his seals of office.

The Queen would also have noticed, as her avid readership of the daily boxes continued with unstinting scrutiny, that there was a bit of a to-do over a seemingly unimportant naval vessel called HMS *Endurance*, a hydrographic survey ship which also carried a small number of guns, helicopters and twenty-five Royal Marines and was employed permanently sailing the waters of the South Atlantic, around those remote British islands called the Falklands. Though it cost only £3 million a year to operate and was very small fry indeed compared to the overall defence budget, the *Endurance* was included in Nott's 1981 Defence Review as a candidate for the axe. The Nott strategy called for a re-evaluation of the role of the surface fleet, and a reduction in the size of the navy accordingly. The withdrawal of *Endurance* was almost penny-pinching in comparison to the major cuts, but go it must said Nott and he proceeded to ensure that it went, in spite of protests from the Foreign Office. Though she had never been there (but Philip had, in 1956), the Queen's attention would have been drawn to this far-flung and tiniest outpost of what remained of her colonial empire, by a series of Foreign Office papers in the past few months on what to do with the islands, whose future had been a thorn in the side of successive governments. Nicholas Ridley, then a junior minister at the Foreign Office, had been down to the South Atlantic and returned with the suggestion that sovereignty of the Falklands should be granted to the Argentinians, then leased back to Britain, rather like Hong Kong. This, he wrote, was the only way of halting the sabre-rattling of the Argentinians, yet retaining British protection for the islanders themselves. Lord Carrington thought the idea was right but rash.[2]

Mrs Thatcher did not; she fumed that it was giving away

more territory and that was a sensitive issue, coming as it did at the time of the official transfer of Rhodesia to black nationalist rule. Ridley was, however, given the opportunity of paying a further visit to the Falklands to canvass local opinion. There was resignation to the idea on the part of the islanders, who had for so long been a low priority; at least someone had bothered to come up with what seemed a workable solution. Back in Britain, Mrs Thatcher's reaction of 'fury' was matched by her back-benchers; the leaseback idea was put on ice but, in the meantime, it was publicly announced that the *Endurance* was being withdrawn from the South Atlantic, a move which Mrs Thatcher herself defended when she was forced to answer a parliamentary question on the subject put by Mr James Callaghan, the former Prime Minister.[3]

The Queen may well have noticed from the telegrams and diplomatic messages in Foreign Office boxes the flurry of reaction which followed. Intelligence reports indicated the interest shown in these developments by General Leopoldo Galtieri, who had recently taken control of the military junta which ruled Argentina. Mrs Thatcher's dubious insistence on the *Endurance* being withdrawn was duly noted by Galtieri, just as it was by the Queen. Too late, the Prime Minister realised that Galtieri took it as a signal that Britain was no longer interested in the Falklands and when, on 3 March, the Foreign Office boxes which went to the Queen contained a telegram from the British ambassador in Buenos Aires indicating the threat of invasion, Mrs Thatcher had written at the side 'We must make some contingency plans'.[4]

The rest is history; Argentina invaded the Falklands on 2 April and captured the Queen's only representative there, the island's Governor Rex Hunt, and the contingent of Her Majesty's forces on the island – the hopelessly outnumbered single company of Royal Marines. Lord Carrington took the can and 'resigned as a matter of honour' and went to Buckingham Palace to return his seals. The same day, HMS *Hermes* and HMS *Invincible*, on which Prince Andrew, now twenty-two, served as a helicopter pilot, sailed from Portsmouth, crammed with Harrier jumpjets and Sea King helicopters, as the first instalment of a 40 warship task force and 1,000 commandos setting off in the next few days. Thus the Queen's involvement was seen immediately as a personal one. Hers was a mother's-eye view of the impending hostilities, and her family experienced the same kind of apprehension shared by ordinary families throughout the country, only more so in as much as she had the complete knowledge of developments in a conflict filled with the new hazards which changed the shape of war at sea – the deadly Exocet missiles. Like the rest of the nation, she was glued to the television day after day as the families and sweethearts lined the embarkation ports to watch the ships carry the sailors and troops away to the theatre of war; and she shared the anguish of thousands who waited for news of the casualties . . .

Two weeks after the Argentinian troops invaded, the Queen had to deal with another pressing matter – a flying visit to Canada to witness the severing of the country's last colonial ties with Britain. Exactly 115 years after Queen Victoria put her signature to the British North American Act which made Canada a colonial protectorate of Great Britain, her great-great-granddaughter signed a proclamation handing all remaining constitutional powers back to the Canadian Parliament which until that time still needed to seek British approval for new laws.

While she was away, a special hot-line and scrambler was installed in her suite in the Governor-General's residence in Ottawa linking her directly to the Prime Minister's office in No. 10 Downing Street so that she could be kept in touch with developments concerning the Falklands. Coincidentally, on the same day that Canada's constitution was patriated, another former British colony put the finishing touch to its own new nationalist constitution; once it was Southern Rhodesia, now it was Zimbabwe, and on 17 April the capital, Salisbury, was formally renamed Harare, the last link with the colonial past obliterated. To Mrs Thatcher, this was the formation of another Marxist-inclined Third World country which would be ranged against her; to the Queen, it was confirmation of the seat of government of a new republican state with whom her relationship would be restored through the Commonwealth. The two viewpoints taken by Queen and Prime Minister had never been so evident, nor so far apart.

A week after her return, on 24 April, the first Briton to die in the Falklands conflict was a Royal Navy helicopter pilot, killed when his Sea King crashed. From then onwards to the end of the campaign, the casualties mounted. Several British ships were hit, including destroyer HMS *Sheffield* which was sunk with the loss of twenty-one lives. On 25 May another twenty-four died when HMS *Coventry* took a direct hit and the supply ship *Atlantic Conveyor* was sunk as the Argentinian aircraft bombarded the task force. The Queen would have known from the intelligence reports what everyone in the British task force around the Falklands knew, that 25 May was the day marked down by the Argentinians for a major attack on British ships. It was their National Day and Galtieri had instructed his forces to chalk up some spectacular successes to bolster the flagging enthusiasm of his own supporters. The Queen was preparing to go to Northumberland the following day, when she received details of the attacks; they were initially sketchy and there was a strong rumour that the *Invincible* had been hit. Later, two Argentinian news agencies – well aware of the Queen's interest – reported that the *Invincible* had taken a direct hit from an Exocet missile. Mrs Thatcher recalled the difficulties of confirmation:

> This was one of our worst moments . . . when John Nott came to my room at the House of Commons and said, 'I'm afraid I've bad news'. HMS *Coventry* had been sunk. Later that night, when I got back to No. 10, I was told that the *Atlantic Conveyor* had been hit and there was a rumour that the *Invincible* had been hit, too. That, gladly, wasn't true although we weren't always able to confirm quickly.[5]

So the Queen, like a thousand other mothers, was waiting to hear the news, and eventually learned that Prince Andrew was safe. As she opened a new water conservation scheme near Alnwick Castle, she said, 'Before I begin here today, I want to say one thing . . . Our thoughts are with those in the South Atlantic, and our prayers are for their safe return to their homes and loved ones.' Then after saying a prayer and standing for a minute's silence, she added, 'Ordinary life must go on'; she smiled and got back to the task at hand. 'I would have thought it more appropriate to declare this dam closed . . . but it gives me great pleasure to declare it open.'[6]

She returned to London to greet the Pope on his first visit to Britain, on 28 May, when she welcomed him with a 35 minute audience at Buckingham Palace. And only later that day, after continued rumours about the *Invincible*, was it confirmed that her son's ship had not been hit. Later the same week, President Ronald Reagan arrived for a visit to reciprocate that of Mrs Thatcher to Washington shortly after his inauguration; somehow the Queen seemed to be a mere ceremonial adjunct to this mutual admiration society. True she entertained the Reagans at Windsor, where she invited the President to join her for an early morning ride through the Home Park, and he incurred her wrath by actually stopping to talk to journalists while riding with her. He was royally welcomed, for a real purpose of continued Falklands backing; Nancy Reagan seemed to believe that the invitation to stay with the Queen was out of friendship, perhaps not realising that visiting statesmen and diplomats are quite often invited to stay. 'Our relationship with the royal family began when Ronnie and I met Charles in Palm Springs when Ronnie was governor and it continued when I attended Charles's wedding in 1981.'[7] And to show how much they meant to him, Ronnie had lots of photographs of famous people in his study; virtually every surface was covered with them – including the Queen, Prince Philip, the Queen Mother, Prince Charles, the Princess of Wales, the Princess Royal and Mark Phillips, Princess Alexandra and Angus Ogilvy and Princess Margaret. But obsessed as they were by their 'relationship' with British royalty, Reagan's purpose on this occasion was to offer his moral and verbal support to his friend Margaret Thatcher at a time when, as victory neared, voices were being raised and she was coming under attack from those who believed the war should never have started in the first place.

She pressed on until victory was hers: 'Despite these grievous losses neither our resolve nor our confidence is weakened.' It was her war; anything but a crushing defeat of the Argentinians would have put her position as Prime

Minister in jeopardy and she could have gone the same way as Eden over Suez. But on 14 June, the 1,900 residents of the Falklands, whose sovereignty could have been successfully and peacefully negotiated a year earlier, were liberated at a cost of some 260 British and 652 Argentinian lives. Prince Andrew flew into Port Stanley in his Sea King bearing a message from his mother: 'The Queen is proud of you,' he said.

Exactly one week later, the nation was given added cause for celebration and did so accordingly: a new royal child was born. On 21 June, the Princess of Wales gave birth to her first child, a boy weighing 7 pounds 1 ounce, in a hospital room in Paddington – William Arthur Philip Louis – and the Queen was overjoyed. The special significance, of course, was that the child was born to be king, to continue the line after the Prince of Wales, presumably to assume the mantle some time in his mid-life in the next century, barring unforeseen events. But, then, unforeseen events continue to bear down relentlessly . . .

As she had already said, life goes on through all adversity and the summery weeks of June and July saw her engagement book crowded with the usual kind of events designed to take advantage of the expected fine weather, such as open air visits, garden parties and walkabouts. On 1 July, she visited Scotland; she was welcomed by, among others, the Honourable Member for Fife, Mr William Hamilton, the most vociferous of critics of the royal family for the past two decades or more. She smiled, and Prince Philip congratulated the MP on his recent second marriage which did not stop him from taking a customary swipe after they had left, complaining that the Queen's handshake was rather frigid. But perhaps people who call members of her family 'parasites' could expect no more.

Back in London, one of the most startling events in the annals of royal history began to unfold. The morning of 9 July was already warm and sunny when one of the palace housemaids, doing her rounds, threw open a window in the office of the Master of the Queen's Household, Vice-Admiral Sir Peter Ashmore. A half an hour later, a 31-year-old unemployed labourer, Michael Fagan, scaled a wall on the perimeter of the palace, hid momentarily behind a canvas awning near the Ambassadors' Entrance and then climbed into the palace through a window which he discovered was not locked. The window led into a room which housed one of the Queen's valuable stamp collections. Fagan discovered, however, that his route into the palace was blocked; the door leading out was locked. He climbed back out of the window and saw another one open – the window to Sir Peter Ashmore's office – and so, scrambling up a drainpipe and through this office, he found his route into the palace. Taking off his shoes and socks, he wandered through the corridors for almost half an hour 'following the pictures' until he came more by luck than judgement to the private suite of the Queen, who was still sleeping. So far, he had proceeded through the palace unchallenged and with ease, through a lax comedy of errors which highlighted the appalling security systems operating inside the palace at the time. Fagan had actually set off an alarm, twice, which an officer in the security control room switched off, assuming that it had gone off accidentally. Fagan was also seen by a palace servant, who assumed he was a workman arriving early. There was no guard outside the Queen's apartment, because the armed police sergeant normally posted in the corridor went off duty at 6.00 a.m., when his shift ended and he was not replaced. The one further warning device – the Queen's own corgis – had been taken out into the grounds for their morning walk.

Thus, Fagan proceeded to an ante-room adjoining the Queen's bedroom; there he smashed an ashtray with which he later claimed he intended to slash his wrists in front of the Queen. He entered the Queen's bedroom, presumably not knowing for certain whether it was hers or indeed if she was inside. She was, and awoke with a start when the door slammed behind him and her eyes met the intruder who had reached her bedside. If he had been a violent man or a terrorist, he could have murdered her in her own bed, there and then.

'I knew immediately that it wasn't a servant,' she said later, 'because the servants do not slam doors. Our eyes met and both of us looked dumbfounded.' Recovering her composure, she shouted, 'Get out of here at once' in a tone that would have sent her bravest courtier dashing for the exit; Fagan sat down on the end of her bed, with blood from a cut finger dripping down on to the bedclothes. He was clearly not going to be moved by a stern voice, and the Queen instantly resorted to her 'conversation mode' which is used instinctively from years of practice to engage those who meet her who are too nervous to speak. They chatted for a moment, the Queen using small talk, and mentioning her family and that the man sitting before her was about Prince Charles's age. She had already pressed an alarm bell which had so far brought no response and now courageously decided to risk calling her security guards, dialling 222 on the internal telephone system and telling the palace operator on the other end to send a police officer to her suite. The call to the police lodge was made at 7.18 a.m. and a further five minutes elapsed before the Queen telephoned again; where was the policeman? None, apparently, was immediately to hand and when Fagan asked if he could have a cigarette, the Queen then managed to attract the attention of a chambermaid, Elizabeth Andrew, a young Middlesborough girl who, startled by the Queen's bedside visitor, forgot her place and blurted, 'Oh, bloody 'ell, Ma'am, what's 'e doing 'ere?' which the Queen later retold in her well-known talent for mimicry.

Still no policeman had arrived when the Queen and her chambermaid managed to persuade Fagan to go outside, where they could get some cigarettes from a pantry, at which point a sturdy young footman Paul Wybrew appeared, grabbed Fagan firmly by the arm and detained him in a pantry where he gave him a cigarette. Finally, three policemen arrived at the top of the stairs and seeing the Queen there in her nightclothes, one young officer stopped to adjust his tie. 'Oh, come on,' she said, 'get a bloody move on.'[8] Fagan was led away and arrested and only then did it emerge that this was the second time he had broken into the palace, the first occasion being five weeks earlier. On that occasion, he admitted, he had wandered around the palace and had taken a bottle of wine from the cellars.

With security of VIPs and the royal family especially under review following the IRA bomb outrages, the Fagan incident revealed the remarkable inadequacies in the protection of the Queen. Her famous walkabouts and policy of letting herself be seen were one thing; to have an intruder virtually walk into Buckingham Palace unhindered and actually get inside the Queen's bedroom was simply incredible – so much so that one Sunday newspaper editor who was offered the story exclusively by a freelance journalist the following day later treated it with a caution verging on disbelief.

The Fagan story also had a rather odd conclusion; he was charged with stealing a bottle of wine whilst trespassing in Buckingham Palace on the first occasion, 7 June. Mr Stephen Wooler, for the office of the Director of Public Prosecutions, said that there would be no charges arising out of the second incident relating to the intrusion into the Queen's bedroom, since there was no evidence to suggest that Fagan was in a state of mind 'to convert trespass into a criminal offence'.[9] He was sent for trial by jury – and cleared. He was, however, taken into custody over other offences unrelated to the palace break-in. He told the court that he had done the Queen a favour by revealing that her security system was 'no good'.[10] This, indeed, was true. A police sergeant who had twice failed to respond to the Queen's telephone messages for help was suspended, and two police constables were moved to other duties.

Prime Minister Margaret Thatcher received an interim report from Scotland Yard on the break-in and went to the palace on the following Monday for an audience, and to apologise personally for this amazing lapse which had naturally put the Queen under a great deal of stress. 'No one is more shocked and staggered by the Queen's ordeal than I,' said the Home Secretary William Whitelaw in the House of Commons[11], but no amount of apology could erase the incident from the Queen's memory; she was angry and shocked and did not take too kindly to the very obvious scramble for scapegoats among the lower ranks of the royal protection squad which ensued.

Nor was she pleased with the prurient 'follow-up' discussion in the newspapers and elsewhere on the whereabouts of Prince Philip at the time of Fagan's break-in. The explanation that he had left the palace early on that morning to take part in carriage-driving trials in Scotland developed into a debate on the sleeping arrangements of the Queen and Prince Philip, culminating in the *Sun* demanding in its boldest of front-page headlines: 'Give Her a Cuddle, Philip.'

It was also the *Sun* which came to the Queen's assistance barely a fortnight later, by revealing that a 32 year-old male prostitute named Michael Rauch was claiming that he had had a casual relationship with Commander Michael Trestrail, the Queen's personal bodyguard. Trestrail, a homosexual, had been at the Queen's side incessantly for nine years, stewarding royal activities as if his own life depended upon it. He was well liked at the palace and especially well thought of by the Queen for his total devotion to duty; the fact that he was homosexual was probably known but that was not unusual in palace service. Bachelor staff are often found to be more dedicated to their duty and prepared to work long hours without complaint about the unsocial aspect or the pay. However, likeable though he was, Trestrail's position in the current climate, or indeed any climate, was untenable. Any risk to the Queen's security had to be eliminated immediately, and Trestrail was called to Scotland Yard the morning Rauch's story appeared. Though the association with Rauch had ended three years earlier, Trestrail admitted that it had taken place and further revealed that he had received blackmail letters demanding sums of money for the information to be kept quiet. Though the Queen was personally saddened by these latest revelations to strike at the palace, she agreed that he had to go. The following day, the Home Secretary gave the full details of Trestrail's indiscretions to a packed House of Commons, and the commander was ignominiously evicted from the service of Her Majesty, a broken man.

In the midst of these events came more shattering news. On 20 July, the day after Trestrail's resignation, two IRA bomb attacks killed eleven of the Queen's men and seven of her horses. The first explosion occurred in Hyde Park as a detachment of the Blues and Royals trotted along South Carriage Road on their way to the changing of the guard at Horseguards' Parade; two hours later, as the band of the Royal Green Jackets was playing a selection from *Oliver!* another bomb exploded under the bandstand in Regent's Park. Apart from the eleven deaths, fifty-four people were seriously injured.

Yet more bad news was to come. The Queen then learned of the sudden death of Lord Rupert Nevill, one of her closest friends since childhood; he and his wife Lady Anne had been her most trusted and supportive courtiers. Lord Rupert was also private secretary to Prince Philip. At this, the Queen burst into tears. The strain of these events, one after the other, interspersed as they were with her normal engagements, plus a brief spell in hospital herself – on 17 July two days before the Trestrail affair – to have a painful wisdom tooth removed, proved too much. She was ordered to rest.

Outwardly, the Fagan intrusion into her bedroom had left no apparent scar and she made light of it in conversations during the garden party season. But it was quite clear to those closest to her that she had been deeply affected by the experience and could not wait for Princess Anne to return home from her trip to America. She wanted her daughter close at hand, to confide in; although she had joked about the incident in public she had actually had difficulty in discussing it in detail with anyone until Anne came home. In the remaining days before the royals began their holiday at Balmoral, Anne spent as much time with her mother as she could and then joined her at Balmoral. Anne's presence helped a great deal. Theirs was now a very close mother and daughter relationship, and had altered a lot from a couple of years earlier when Anne was supposedly at the peak of her awkwardness. She was asked some time later if she found it difficult to retain a close relationship with a mother who was also Queen, and replied, 'I think you have got the question the wrong way round. It's much more difficult to remember that she is the Queen, rather than my mother. After all, I've known her longer as a mother than as Queen and that's the way I regard her. Only the formalities of our work bring us down to earth.'[12] But it took Prince Andrew's arrival back from the Falklands on 17 September to really cheer her up.

In the Falklands aftermath of welcome-home parties and thanksgiving services, there was a quite dramatic comparison between the responses of the Queen and her Prime Minister. The Queen's will surely be well remembered; she adopted a restrained, almost pensive, stance throughout, as if to say '. . . yes we should be happy for those returning home, but let us remember the anguish of the families of those who did not, and the suffering of the many who were so severely injured or burned'. This restraint merely tended to exaggerate the jingoistic celebratory noises coming from the office of the Prime Minister who, in her front-line participation in the revelry, was said by some to be 'Queening it'.

John Grigg, the historian and journalist and formerly Lord Altrincham, gave the Queen a few words of advice, it will be recalled, when she had been Sovereign for a mere five years. The words still jar at Buckingham Palace. He offered further advice to those around the monarchy in 1982, when the Queen had completed her thirty years. While paying tribute to her personal achievements, he attacked the royal household as a whole for failing 'to illustrate vividly and dramatically, what the monarchy represents here in Britain and still less what it represents in the world at large'.[13] He suggested a more diversified court which would enhance the quality of advice the Queen received. 'For instance, it is unthinkable that senior aides not drawn from the British establishment would have advised her to keep Sir Anthony Blunt on her staff after she had been told the truth about him,' Grigg wrote. It was a very valid point and he went further in criticising the rising tendency to treat the monarchy with servility and gush, where normally serious writers seemed to lose their power of discrimination when addressing themselves to the subject.

In comparison to his earlier writings, Grigg's words raised hardly a flicker of protest. He wrote his new assessment of the monarchy before the great morass of events and headlines which encircled the Queen's activities that year, but it was a topical moment, as she entered her thirty-first year on the throne, to contemplate the changes, yet again, in the way the collective family went about their public duties. In many ways, it reflected the massive publicity impact brought on by the Queen's new daughter-in-law, the Princess of Wales. Though some politicians and constitutionalists remained mindful that it was around the monarchy that the system of British democracy and government continued to flourish, elsewhere the Queen and her family were unfortunately heading towards a position in which they were identified as travelling salespersons for Mrs Thatcher's new Great Britain Ltd, or as tourist attractions, or the continuing soap opera in which the Princess of Wales had become the megastar.

In between those dramatic reports and photographs from the Falklands conflict, the coverage of the Queen's bedroom intruder and her homosexual bodyguard, the Diana mania continued unabated to the extent that the Queen's earlier fears were confirmed that the more serious elements of the family's work were being overshadowed to the point of obliteration. It was during these early stages of the Princess of Wales's huge press coverage that the Queen suggested that Princess Anne ought to be projected in a different light; her work for charity was hardly ever mentioned and whatever publicity she got tended to be of the sort they did not want. Her long-running battle with the press was a real problem, and the sensational headlines about the state of her marriage dominated the coverage she received. The image had to be massaged to bring it into line with what the Queen described as one more reflective of the work she was doing. And so her first major tour of Save the Children field centres in various part of the world was organised for 1982. It was the most extensive and dangerous tour ever tackled by a member of the royal family; a 14,000 mile trip taking her to Swaziland, Zimbabwe, Malawi, Kenya, Somalia and North Yemen, and a secondary trip to one of the world's danger zones, Beirut. Within a few months, this was followed up by a tour to the remotest regions of Pakistan, and then on straightaway into plans for even worse hazards by going into some of the disaster areas of North Africa. She set a new standard for royal achievement which was quickly reflected by the newspapers, and even one of her most frequent adversaries, Jean Rook, had to admit 'she is like a latter day Florence Nightingale, Curie, Queen Victoria or member of the SAS'. Insect-bitten, slimmed down through weight-loss in extremes of temperatures, suffering the pain of countless injections against such things as meningitis, hepatitis and rabies, travelling miles on dangerous, dusty, dirt-track roads, flying in and out of danger zones and coming face to face with leprosy and other disease-stricken colonies, she at least was seen to be earning her keep. She became the 'blossoming princess', going to parts that the rest of the royal family could never reach and putting herself at some risk. It did not stop the headlines about her personal life, but at least it provided the whole of the family business with a counterbalance of high profile aid work; she provided something tangible to see and read about – the Queen's daughter out there, in the field of endeavour. It was an important development because, without that kind of substantial background of real service, she might well have been washed away in the ground-swell of personal publicity which followed in later years; a 'cotton wool' princess – her words – would not have survived. As former Prime Minister Edward Heath correctly assessed for the author: 'She has become one of the most active royal patrons of all time, tireless in travel, fearless in facing hazards in countries overseas which are often starved by drought or riddled with disease, and uninhibited in showing understanding of children's problems wherever she finds them.'[14]

Even if the Queen had wanted to take a rest after that year which had again been packed with events, she could not; more travels were planned for the months immediately ahead. Soon after seeing Andrew back home, she was heading back to Australia where her visits were receiving increasingly mixed reactions. The response to her 5 week tour down under, calling at the Commonwealth islands in the Pacific on the way home, was soured by some dismissive comments. 'The monarchy is in decline,' said Labour Party leader Robert Hawke, 'I don't believe it will last in Australia beyond the end of the century.' Since he was soon to be elected Prime Minister, and future host to the Queen, he might well later wish to revise that statement. She heard the same kind of prediction when visiting Jamaica early in the new year when another of her former Prime Ministers, Michael Manley, said on American television, 'We have the greatest respect for Queen Elizabeth as Queen of England and Head of the Commonwealth and as a distinguished woman in her own right, but when she comes here we do not now regard her as the Queen of Jamaica'. In both places, the cheering crowds provided no evidence to support such a change of heart among the people.

Jamaica was the first leg of her trip across the Atlantic on which she embarked eight weeks after returning from Australia. The tour also gave the Cayman Islands their first visit from a reigning British monarch in the 300 years since colonisation. The wealthy tax-haven, whose capital, Grand Cayman, has more banks and registered companies than it does people, gave the Queen a cheque for £500,000 towards the South Atlantic Fund set up as an appeal after the Falklands War, which represented a donation of £28 by every member of the population of the Caymans. Her next port of call was less well off.

Mexico was teetering on the brink of bankruptcy and the Queen went to have a look at the new steel mill which was being built with a £200 million investment from Britain, including a £35 million grant from the government. In view of Mexico's precarious state, some newspapers queried whether the Queen had come to pay a courtesy call or to inspect the real estate which secured so many debts to British banks. 'We in Britain have made our contribution,' said the Queen at a state banquet in the courtyard of a fort in Acapulco, referring to Britain's part in the international $10 billion rescue plan to save Mexico from even deeper crisis. Yet there, in the midst of the poverty and the misery gripping the great underclass of Mexican society, the Queen received a reception which can only be compared to that of the Pope. Photographers fought each other to get close and the streets were lined with people as if some spiritual presence was about to descend upon them. It is in these areas, where basic, ordinary life means dire straits for many millions of people, that a certain divinity sets in, and the Queen is seen more as a messenger from the almighty than the crowned head from some distant land whose connection with the host country was merely the financial link created by her nation's bankers and industrialists. The motive for her visit was undoubtedly to ensure the well-being of the latter; in the process it was and is still something of a phenomenon that she can inspire such reaction from the mass of the people, and perhaps goes a long way to explain the affection she holds for the Third World countries of her Commonwealth, and vice versa.

The contrast of perception was never more evident as the Queen moved on out of Mexico and up to the west coast of America, where the razzmatazz of Los Angeles lay waiting to be roused. When they knew she was coming to America, the Reagans arranged to put on a wild west coast show of celebrities and stars, including Frank Sinatra who was going to sing for them.*

A star-studded banquet welcomed her to Hollywood, where there was fortunately a good contingent of British expatriates to join them, including director Tony Richardson who sat next to the Queen, and Julie Andrews who was placed beside Prince Philip. 'Nice to see you again, dook,' said Sinatra casually as if he was addressing his old bandleader.

The Reagans had invited them up to the ranch, at Santa Barbara. As they set out, the worst weather to hit California in years brought a tornado and torrential rain; it was so bad that it seemed they might have to cancel, especially as the road to the Reagan place was suddenly engulfed by a sea of mud. However, as Nancy Reagan explained, 'The Queen was dying to go riding with Ronnie,'[15] so the Queen and Philip drove up the mountainside in a four-wheel-drive truck. Nancy apologised for the weather. 'Don't be silly,' said the Queen. 'This is an adventure.'

Nancy noted her feelings at the time: the Queen was wonderful. 'And she really endeared herself to me by the spirit she showed that day. I ended up leaving the ranch with them and continuing our visit on the royal yacht. I spent that evening with the Queen, sitting on a sofa in the large living room talking about our children like old friends.'[16] The yacht sailed on to San Francisco but, because of the bad weather, the Queen and Philip flew on ahead, and were accommodated at the St Francis Hotel, with their entourage of forty-three until the *Britannia* arrived two days later. It was not part of the original plan, but Nancy had joined the tour and while in San Francisco she suggested that they should all go to dinner at Trader Vic's, the Polynesian restaurant.

*Things had moved on a touch since Prince Philip's first meeting with Sinatra in 1948. Then, in London with his wife Ava Gardner, Sinatra raised £14,000 for the prince's National Playing Fields Association. In spite of that, Philip was strongly criticised for hobnobbing with film stars by the snobbish courtiers who were in situ at the time.

'You'll feel like you're on a Pacific island,' Nancy said to the Queen, as if she'd never been on a Pacific island before, though a little research would have shown she had been on several but a few weeks ago. Very chic, very commercial and just the place for a high-class tourist. Or was it? They had to have privacy from the locals and so were shown into a private dining room, which did not look anything like a Pacific island, but was like the private dining room to be found in any smart place anywhere in the world. Not only that, it needed a motorcade of fourteen vehicles to carry the Queen and Philip and Mrs Reagan and guests through the streets of San Francisco because ever since her arrival in the city – with its huge Irish population accounting for 25 per cent of residents – she had been surrounded by 200 security men. Later in the week, someone dropped a hint that it was the Reagan wedding anniversary. So the Queen invited them back on board *Britannia* for a dinner, to which they were able to bring some friends. It was, said Nancy, an unforgettable evening. One of the friends Nancy brought along, Mike Deaver, happened to play the piano. No one quite remembers how it happened, but before long Mike was playing the piano in the Queen's sitting room on the *Britannia*, and Nancy was singing 'Our love is here to stay . . .', giving her Ronnie the romantic treatment in front of their royal hosts.

Mr Reagan was extremely cheerful and got up to make a little speech. 'Well, Nancy . . . I know I promised you a lot thirty-one years ago but I never promised you this . . .'

On the way home, they called in for a quick look around Canada, which meant that, in twenty-nine days since they left London, they had visited six countries before the end of March – and another four state visits were already planned for the remainder of the year, to Sweden, Kenya, Bangladesh and India. It is worth reminding ourselves that interspersed between the foreign travel were the visits to towns and cities in the British Isles as well as the affairs of state to contend with; the daily audiences with ambassadors and other VIPS, plus the boxes, twice a day every day, wherever she was in the world. Palace life had become routine; overseas travel, as we have seen, accounted for a third of her public duties – so much had changed since she became Queen.

In November she made one of the most remarkable

journeys of those thirty-one years, with a pilgrimage back to where it all began, at the Sagana Lodge, Nyeri, which the people of Kenya had given her as a wedding present. She arrived back in Kenya to a sober and restrained official welcome that was not mirrored by the enthusiasm of the vast sea of black faces who came out to see her; after the ceremonies and the welcomes by native drummers in the capital, she set off on her journey down memory lane. She had undoubtedly retained visions of Treetops where she spent her last night in Kenya as Princess Elizabeth and where at some time unknown she became Queen. The crowds were the same in number. Word travelled through the bush and several thousands lined her routes across the dusty plain, by the roadside and the rail tracks; her carriage had an open side so that she could wave to the crowds as she passed by. Union Jacks were suddenly fluttering everywhere. 'This is going to be one of the happiest times of her life, revisiting the Kenyan heartlands,' said one of her aides.

Sadly, it was not the case. Though they were aware of changes, the Queen and Prince Philip were shocked. When they came in 1952, the Sagana Lodge and the Treetops Hotel were in dense jungle. Now as they approached, they were surprised to find no jungle, just a huge clearing; the trees had all but disappeared and Philip seemed disbelieving of the explanation that the elephants had done the damage. Treetops, the famous house in a giant fig tree where at some unknown time she became Queen, was no longer there. The Mau Mau burned it down in 1954 to wipe out this symbol of colonialism. Later it was replaced by a modern 38 bedroom hotel. Sagana Lodge was barely recognisable.[17] Since the Queen was unable to return to it because of the troubles, and then independence, it had been enlarged by adding five bedrooms to serve as a country retreat for the President, which was perhaps another indelible sign to mark independence – the Queen's place becomes the President's. However, she and Philip stood in the corner of the lounge where he had asked her to accompany him outside to receive some bad news; now she looked 'thoughtful rather than sad'. The Queen went outside again. 'Is this really where it was?' asked the Queen. 'It all looks so different now.'[18] And it did. Even the wild animals who came in such plentiful numbers last time had virtually vanished, scared off by all the photographers and television crews who came there to record the visit, leaving just a few buffaloes and warthogs. In all, it was a disappointment.

A lot had changed since she was last in Bangladesh and India too. Bangladesh was then still part of Pakistan, and her first task on arrival from Kenya was to lay a wreath at the tomb to commemorate the estimated 3 million who died in the fighting with Pakistan forces in the battle for independence in 1971. These were more sad moments of reflection for the Queen, because what had happened in Bangladesh was typical of the scenes of suffering that had occurred in so many former colonial protectorates. The poverty and squalor and the misery of the children were pitiful sights. She was very impressed by a Save the Children Fund malnutrition unit, which she later described to Princess Anne who visited it herself a year later. Nevertheless, the people of one village clubbed together, each donating a day's pay to buy the Queen a silver box.

She travelled on to India where she made it known she wished to make a personal award to Mother Teresa, who had been awarded the Nobel Peace Prize for her work with the poor in Calcutta; the Queen presented her with the Order of Merit, which is in the Queen's personal gift in recognition of public service. The changes were evident here too, and there must have been a debate among the local elders as to the wisdom of staging a re-creation of the splendiferous decor of the British Raj at the Viceregal Palace – now the presidential mansion – which had once been Mountbatten's as the last Viceroy of India. Old furniture was brought from the cellars, their suite had been specially redecorated in the style of that era, uniforms of the lancers dating from the days when her grandfather was crowned Emperor of all India in 1911 were cleaned and pressed into service by their attending officers.

If, for a moment, the Queen discovered what it would have been like if she was Empress, the business of the later twentieth century soon whisked her back to reality. The Commonwealth Conference for which her visit had been arranged, was being hosted by Mrs Indira Gandhi. While the Queen was attending to conference business, Philip piloted an aircraft of the Queen's Flight on which they had been travelling, up to Kanha Safari Park, 300 miles away. He came to observe at first hand the success of Project Tiger, financed in part by the World Wildlife Fund International, of which he became president in 1981. The tiger population had dropped from an estimated 100,000 at the time when King George V's party shot 37 in one day in 1911, to a mere 1,800 in 1972. After an appeal from Mrs Gandhi, the WWF had invested $100,000 in a project to get the tiger re-established in India, and far from causing the huge row that developed the last time he was here with the Queen, when he shot one between the eyes and was photographed with it, this time Philip could see how well the WWF's money was being spent.

Philip returned to find his wife angry over Mrs Thatcher. Christopher Buckland, the political writer who observed the tour, said:

> There were definite signs of icicles when Mrs T and the monarch got together. At the royal banquet for heads of state, everything had been arranged for a photograph to be taken of Her Majesty with India's Prime Minister Mrs Gandhi and Mrs Thatcher – you know, the three most powerful women in the world. It was arranged apparently without consultation with the Queen who dismissed the idea with a flick of the wrist and Mrs Thatcher looked at her as black as thunder.[19]

It was not that the Queen did not especially want the photograph taken; she was angry over the number of complaints she had received from Caribbean prime ministers about Britain's lack of support for their protests against the Americans' invasion of Grenada a month earlier. The Queen was, according to reports from Delhi, already 'fuming' over the incident herself. As Grenada's head of state, she was entitled to be told of America's plans. So was Mrs Thatcher, who flew into a blinding rage when told the Americans had invaded the British colony to rid the nation of its Marxist leader without asking her permission. The Queen was equally unhappy with Mrs Thatcher's rapid public acceptance of the fact that the 'people of Grenada will be glad to be free of this oppressive rule', while giving her friend Ronald Reagan a slap over the wrist for his invasion of British soil. She had to deal with a flow of Commonwealth prime ministers seeking a one-to-one audience with her and according to her press secretary Michael Shea she had performed a 'feat of mental gymnastics' in her conversations with them on a variety of issues, but most predominantly the situation in Grenada.

It was, constitutionally, one of the most difficult situations the Queen had been forced into, in as much as those Commonwealth leaders who sought both her sympathy and her advice were often at variance with the views of Mrs Thatcher. The lack of any kind of statutory foundation in her Commonwealth role placed her in a sort of no man's land – listening to the views from both sides and offering what advice and understanding she was able, given the limitations of the constitutional character of her role. It did not help matters when, around this time, it was noted that Mrs Thatcher had begun speaking of 'My government . . .' which was, of course, a phrase normally reserved for usage by the Queen. The discord between Mrs Thatcher and certain Commonwealth nations would become ever more severe, leaving the Queen caught in the crossfire.

Chapter Eighteen

The Queen and the Queen Bee (1984–6)

In the three years since the arrival of Lady Diana Spencer into the royal realm, the Queen, along with other members of the royal family, had continued to be relegated to a back-seat role in terms of front-page publicity. The newspapers had eyes only for Diana, especially when it was announced in the spring of 1984 that she was expecting her second child, and thus it could be assured that the camera lenses would be focused even more incessantly, if that were possible, on the expectant mother – the expectant mother looking glamorous in maternity wear, the expectant mother in bikini on holiday – followed by the glorification of the post-natal scene. Was she some kind of mystical goddess? A visitor from Mars might well have thought so. The Queen's public appearances were quite ignored for the sake of a snatched picture of her daughter-in-law. Princess Anne managed to claw back a few column inches with another arduous trek into the wilds of deprivation or through a television interview with Terry Wogan or Michael Parkinson. Only Koo Stark, the American actress whose main claim to fame, as far as could be seen, was a role in a film slightly pornographic in nature, continued to compete for the front covers over her association with the Queen's second son, dubbed 'Randy Andy'.* Prince Andrew was obviously intent on having a

*It was a source of extreme irritation to publisher Robert Maxwell that on the day he took over the *Daily Mirror* a story about Koo Stark

good time before settling down to dukedom and made no secret of his affair with Koo; later his seaside frolics on a Caribbean sunshine island with Koo – and later still with others, including the sixties model Vicki Hodge – similarly confirmed that he too had healthy interests for a young man of his age. That he should continue to draw a healthy Civil List income while doing so was a debatable point for which the kind of adjectives once reserved for Princess Margaret were being drawn upon. But all of this had become part of the 'human face', hadn't it? Queen Mary-style moralising simply did not apply any longer – except in the area of the monarch and heir who could do no wrong and should not be seen to do any wrong. As long as the monarchy was never too seriously devalued and continued to be represented in a good light overall, then they could live with the trivialising publicity of Diana's fashions, Anne and Mark's rows and Randy Andy's latest girlfriend.

The trouble was that the monarchy *was* being devalued; it did not stop at an acceptable level. Andrew's romantic liaisons became the topic of numerous front pages, culminating with the *Sun*'s 'World Exclusive: Astonishing Inside Secrets of the Fun-Loving Royals'. These were based on the revelations of a palace servant who sold the *Sun* his story. The *Sun* was in the process of telling all about Prince Andrew's 'sexy romps at the palace with Koo', complete with 'do not disturb' signs on the bedroom door, when the Queen's solicitors served a High Court writ on the newspaper for damages for the breach of contract by the servant, one Kieran Kenny.

It was one of a series of similar actions brought by the Queen to stop this sudden impetus of palace employees selling their stories. Prince Charles's homosexual valet Stephen Barry collected more than £500,000 in newspaper fees and royalties on a book which he succeeded in getting published in America after the palace threatened him with legal action in Britain. He did not, however, survive to enjoy his money – he died of AIDS not long after his second book was published. Once

---

*dominated the top half of the newspaper's front page while the news of the day – in his eyes – was carried at the bottom under the headline 'Maxwell Buys the Mirror'.[1]

again the material found its way into the *Sun*. At the same time, Princess Anne's former butler was in the process of selling his story to the continental press when the palace served him with a writ; one of the Queen's maids was offering her story to the *News of the World* until she too received an injunction. Some photographs which came from the Queen's own family album, taken soon after the birth of Prince Edward, showing the Queen in bed with her newborn and Prince Andrew, appeared on the front page of the *Sun* with 'more amazing palace pictures on pages 15, 16 and 17'. The same pictures, which had been taken by Prince Philip, appeared in a German magazine to which they had originally been sold and a palace inquiry failed to discover how they were removed from the palace. It was almost a full-time effort by palace lawyers to keep the lid on life at the palace. The Press Council made rumbling noises about a gross intrusion of privacy, but for many months the relentless pursuit of royal stories continued without any sign of flagging interest, either from newspaper editors or the readers of the mass-selling dailies.

Underneath this mass of tabloid headlines, however, the Queen was still concerned about image, and that is why she insisted on trying to stop any of her servants who broke the rules. These things *do* matter; though the royals have denied that they are bothered by the 'ratings' and the polls that are run in newspapers and magazines as to their popularity and public perception, it would not be true to say that they paid no attention to them. Polls might not especially interest them but the right sort of publicity was still important. Prince Charles once said in an aside to the press corps who followed him around, 'It's when you characters don't want to photograph me that I have to worry'. He would probably now wish to retract that statement, having experienced the sheer weight of press attention that has focused upon his wife since the day they were engaged.

Apart from Diana's overwhelming command of the news columns there was, however, another, more disconcerting challenge to the Queen's unrivalled position as the world's most famous woman. Emanating from around the corner, it had not, apparently, gone unnoticed back at the palace. The idea that there were currently two Queens of England was propagated out of Margaret Thatcher's own general demeanour as the Queen Bee, especially after her landslide re-election in 1983. Her global travels, in the early eighties, matched those of the Queen. It was, according to some sources, a matter of concern at the palace that, in many ways, the Queen's position was being usurped by her Prime Minister as Mrs Thatcher threw herself into the forefront of international politics, especially in her aspirations for trade and political influence in the Middle East, where, incidentally, the activities of businesses with which Denis and Mark Thatcher were involved had inspired a considerable amount of press attention – and embarrassing questions in the Commons for Mrs Thatcher. It was also being said that a noticeable friction was occurring in the Audience Chamber when Mrs Thatcher arrived for her regular Tuesday meetings because, it would be alleged, the Queen felt her government's current policies were 'uncaring and socially divisive' at home and destructive within the Commonwealth. The scenes of pitched battles between the striking miners and the police which became almost a daily occurrence could not fail to have moved the Queen's thoughts towards sympathy for the families of all concerned. She undoubtedly held quite definite opinions on this and other burning issues of the day, but the trouble which followed eventually forced the Queen, through her private secretary, to make a quite unprecedented intervention over the 'preposterous suggestion' that she was going to depart from the constitutional principles by which she was bound and let her private thoughts become known. The suggestions of the Queen's disquiet over the Thatcherite policies bubbled below the surface for a year or two, and we will return to them later in this chapter. In the meantime, the Queen was scheduled to return to the Middle East for another state visit at the start of 1984. She had, incidentally, carried out nine overseas trips in the previous twelve months as well as 341 engagements at home. The current journey was one which caused the Cabinet to agonise over whether the visit should proceed or not, because of the imminent terrorist dangers in the Middle East following the eviction of the PLO supporters from Lebanon, and the latest assassination attempt upon her host, King Hussein of Jordan.

The Queen had long been a supporter of King Hussein.

They had much in common in the early years, both accepting the burden of monarchy at an early age. Hussein invited the Queen to come for a state visit shortly after Mrs Thatcher visited him in 1981. Now, he was seeking reassurance of Britain's support for his moderation in attempts to find a solution to the Palestinian question; Mrs Thatcher was anxious to provide it. Two days before the Queen was due to arrive in Amman, the Abu Nidal group planted three huge bombs, and made it clear that they were intended as a warning to the British Queen that this was a protest over the imprisonment in Britain of three members of the group who were serving long prison sentences for trying to murder the Israeli ambassador. That weekend, Mrs Thatcher was due at a Conservative Party rally in Birmingham, and when she received news of the bomb attacks in Amman, she called a meeting of those of her ministers directly involved – Foreign Secretary Sir Geoffrey Howe, Defence Secretary Michael Heseltine and Foreign Office Minister Richard Luce.

Mrs Thatcher's view was that, though she was wary of the visit going ahead, she agreed with the Queen's stance, that she should not be seen to be bowing to terrorists. The Prime Minister also spoke on the telephone to King Hussein who asked that the visit should continue, although, as Heseltine said, he was perhaps a touch blasé about assassination attempts, having survived seventeen during his own reign. By this time, the Queen had reached Cyprus and had landed at the sovereign airbase at Akrotiri, and she was requested to wait there overnight until Mrs Thatcher's emergency Cabinet could be assured of absolute security. Elaborate measures were already being set in place. A unit of the elite SAS was hurriedly sent to Amman to await Her Majesty's arrival and give her clandestine protection at all times. Her plane was re-routed so that it would not fly through any potentially dangerous airspace and she was flown directly to a military airbase, patrolled by Jordanian troops and with an armoured car surrounded by a heavily armed combat unit standing by to meet her. The Queen and Prince Philip were whisked away at high speed to Basman Palace – travelling so fast that the British expatriates who lined the streets barely caught sight of her car, let alone her person. The troops were very much in evidence throughout the five days, and it seemed hardly worthwhile to have risked the Queen's safety to make a speech so clumsily loaded with political rhetoric that it might just as well have come from the mouth of a member of the government, or from Mrs Thatcher herself: 'My government will continue to work to achieve a peaceful, just and lasting solution . . .' But when a queen's visit to a foreign land is so evidently controlled and so obviously surrounded by every kind of available quick-reaction weaponry to ward off a possible terrorist attack then the purpose of the visit, to foster friendship and encourage trading ties, has already become a fatuous exercise. It would be seen quite clearly for what it was, a political mission, and though the Queen had deliberately and repeatedly refused to be put off by these threats on her life, the belief that these stage-managed visits to hostile climes were really not worth the risk must surely have been worthy of at least consideration. As has been seen so often when the Queen is placed into a political arena, it invariably follows that she is drawn into controversy. There was considerable debate on her return home that the highly successful visit made in the face of grave danger was marred by the fact that 'she had become a political pawn'[2] in one of the world's most sensitive political areas.

The potential danger facing the Queen – and all world leaders, for that matter – was bad enough under normal circumstances without walking into the open mouth of the lion to score political points. This chilling fact of life came very close to home before the year was out. It will be remembered that in Delhi, when the Queen last met the Indian leader Mrs Indira Gandhi, there was an attempt to get the 'three most powerful women in the world' together in one photograph. On 12 October, Mrs Thatcher came within an ace of being murdered by the IRA in the bomb attack on the Grand Hotel at Brighton where she was staying for the Tory Party Conference; just over two weeks later, assassins elected to murder Mrs Gandhi were from her own guard; and the three became two, and very nearly one.

At the time of the Brighton attack, the Queen was out of the country, having decided to do what she had never done in her entire reign – to go abroad, unofficially, with no fanfare, and without Prince Philip. She flew to America with her racing manager Lord Porchester to spend eight days visiting two stud farms, the first in Kentucky and the second in Wyoming on the eastern foothills of the Rockies. She had long been sending some of her best mares to America to be covered by stallions in the Kentucky stud, and was able to see some of her mares and foals which would eventually come back to her own stables in England as potential classic winners. Porchester told Audrey Whiting, 'I am hoping to give the Queen a relaxed holiday – she certainly deserves one. She will ride and walk and look at horses. It's going to be a 100 per cent no fuss holiday.'[3] She was staying at the vast Big Horn Ranch at Sheridan, Wyoming, owned by Lord Porchester's brother-in-law Senator Malcolm Wallop, when she received the news of the bomb attack in Brighton. Though not directly involved, the event was no less shocking for the Queen; that a terrorist bomb should come so close to wiping out her Cabinet brought home to the nation just how exposed British politicians and members of the royal family were to the attacks by the IRA. 'It was an attempt to cripple Her Majesty's democratically elected government,' said Mrs Thatcher as she moved among the crowds of reporters in the aftermath, showing an impressive composure which masked her private fear. As she watched those horrific scenes of the rescue broadcast live throughout the world, the Queen might well have observed to herself, 'I know how you feel . . .'; the reverse of that sentence would also have been applicable: 'Now you know how I feel . . .'

But, as Mrs Thatcher said after Brighton, 'Life goes on', which was the same sentiment expressed by the Queen so many times as to be countless, but never after a experience quite so serious.

'A monarch,' said Clement Attlee, 'is a kind of referee. Although the occasions when he or she has to blow the whistle are nowadays few.' Another such occasion was on the horizon; it had been rumbling away for a year and finally arrived with such force that the Queen's lifelong ideal seemed as if it might crumble. The same thing had been said on occasions in the past, that the Commonwealth was so fragile a concept that it could collapse and fizzle out at any moment, and no one would particularly notice. Well, as the 1985

Commonwealth Conference neared, the head count of member countries had reached forty-nine, compared with nine when the Queen came to the throne. She had visited most of them and in the four weeks before the conference, which was being staged in Nassau, she was to visit a dozen or more of the remaining smaller countries which had most recently gained independence, most of them scattered around the Caribbean and West Indies, and even down to Belize, which had been granted independence only four years earlier but still relied on a contingent from the British military to ward off any possible takeover ambitions from Guatemala. By the time she sailed into Nassau harbour aboard the royal yacht, the row was in full flight and threatened to ruin the conference, and possibly the Commonwealth. It was, of course, the issue of sanctions against South Africa, which a majority of the Commonwealth nations were insisting upon and to which Mrs Thatcher was adamantly opposed. As the black African leaders bitterly attacked Britain's policy of opposing their call for a complete imposition of wide-ranging economic sanctions, Mrs Thatcher countered that such a policy would be self-destructive, since it would cause thousands of blacks in South Africa to be thrown out of work. The argument raged back and forth and the Queen once again found herself in the middle of it. She was reported in Canada to have sought the help of the Canadian Prime Minister Brian Mulroney in trying to establish some common ground, while stormy headlines raged outside alleging that Mrs Thatcher's intransigence threatened to break up the alliance – or even to have Britain thrown out, just as the Commonwealth had done to South Africa twenty-five years earlier. Apart from her presence at the opening, the Queen remained on board the *Britannia* where, as usual, she received requests from an endless stream of anguished prime ministers desiring an audience. What passed between them remains, as it always does, a matter of supreme confidentiality. It can hardly be doubted, however, that she found herself in any other stance than trying to calm a very volatile situation; in fact, that was all she could do. Even if one of her Commonwealth leaders was indiscreet enough to call for her intervention, it was an impossibility, other than to employ her usual tact with those who pleaded: 'Will you talk to her?' While normally the pressure does not show, she was noticed on this occasion to be nervy and even irritable. When she had to marshal her prime ministers for the annual group photograph, for instance, she was tetchy and impatient. Prince Philip, on these occasions, usually helped with some humour, though some had never quite forgiven him for the remark they overheard on a similar Commonwealth gathering when they were being assembled for the photograph. He looked at them, turned to the Queen and said within their hearing, 'Fancy looking at this lot, and realising that the peace of the world depends on them.'[4]

Mrs Thatcher barely budged an inch in her stance on the sanctions issue. Privately she was furious over the attitude of the Commonwealth which she regarded as flawed and filled with hypocrisy, especially by those African nations who were themselves trading with South Africa. The Commonwealth was also being used as a Trojan horse, which was stacked with the ANC demanding the release of Nelson Mandela. Thatcher kept to her position, stating that she firmly believed diplomatic pressure from the western world on South Africa would in the end bring reforms; she gave the merest inch of ground, agreeing to a final communiqué banning the import of gold Krugerrands and ending government assistance to the British trade mission to South Africa. She also agreed to the setting-up of an Eminent Persons Group to visit the republic, meet its leaders and report back. Mrs Thatcher gave no quarter at the television press conference either. 'Tiny,' she said, holding up the forefinger and thumb of her right hand to demonstrate the amount. 'Tiny,' she repeated, to describe the effect upon South Africa of the Commonwealth's actions. And, as someone wrote back to London, oh, to have been a fly on the wall when some of the black prime ministers trooped in and out of the Queen's sitting room.

The South African question picked up steam and became a major political issue, even a platform from which Mrs Thatcher could begin her own revival after local reverses with such issues as the miners' strike and unemployment still cutting deep. She undoubtedly recognised it herself; the television interviews and the mass of press coverage swung into place and, like the Falklands, it was a debate which inspired her to her passionate best. 'Apartheid will not end by creating unemployment . . . apartheid is not the root cause of violence.'[5] When the Eminent Persons Group reported back, it recommended urgent economic sanctions against South Africa and Britain's partners in the European Community agreed to some form of blockade. But Mrs Thatcher, standing alone, continued to oppose, drawing on what she believed to be the view of Britain – that the Commonwealth demands were humbug. Commonwealth leaders called her names and Rajiv Gandhi, the Indian leader, warned the Queen that Britain was in danger of losing its position as head of the Commonwealth. Britain's relationship with the Commonwealth had reached rock bottom. No other issue had stirred such emotion, nor brought this group of forty-nine nations to the brink of collapse and the cutting of its ties with what was basically the mother country. The events catalogued so far in this book alone, illustrate what a deeply wounding time it was for the Queen, to witness this discord and come within an ace of seeing thirty-three years' work come to nought. But that wasn't the issue; many political pundits believed that the Commonwealth had had its day – 'a pretentious international grouping of no significance, taken seriously by no one except its secretariat, representing neither interest nor cause and embracing liberal democracies and corrupt dictatorships,' George Gale had written earlier.[6]

There were also those under Mrs Thatcher's wing who would have gladly cut the Commonwealth loose. Why continue to put up with the insults of a group of predominantly Third World nations throwing their weight around? The Commonwealth, and the Queen, had become something of a political football, even being kicked by some member-nations. The above did not augur well for the Commonwealth Games which the Queen was to declare open in Edinburgh in July. Two weeks before the opening Mrs Thatcher gave a series of newspaper interviews which offered no break in the deadlock, quite the reverse. She told Hugo Young of the *Guardian* that she could see nothing moral in calling for economic sanctions. 'To me that is immoral,' she insisted. 'To me that is repugnant.' In the week prior to the opening, eighteen nations who would have sent 600 competitors declared their boycott of the games in protest at Mrs Thatcher's refusal to declare sanctions. Chaos reigned, and Edinburgh Council even passed a resolution demanding that Mrs Thatcher should be barred from attending.

Throughout, the Queen's advisers – if advice on this subject was needed by the monarch – would have confirmed her right to offer advice and warning on any issue if she felt so inclined. The reaffirmation that she was able to do so came from Buckingham Palace itself, in anger, prompted by a lead story in the *Sunday Times* on 20 July 1986, shortly before the Commonwealth was due to meet for another summit on the South African issue. The story began in dramatic fashion:

> Sources close to the Queen let it be known to The Sunday Times yesterday that she is dismayed by many of Mrs Thatcher's policies. This dismay goes well beyond the current crisis in the Commonwealth over South Africa. In an unprecedented disclosure of the monarch's views, it was said that the Queen considers the prime minister's approach to be uncaring, confrontational and divisive.

It was stressed immediately in the story that Downing Street had remained silent to the newspaper's approaches and that none of the information came from sources in the Prime Minister's department, nor was any assistance given. This put the ball firmly in the palace's court, suggesting that someone 'close to the Queen' had spilled the beans to the *Sunday Times* with full knowledge that they would be printed, and cause an almighty row. The article went on to allege that the Queen believed the Thatcher government lacked compassion, that she feared the miners' strike had caused long-term damage to the fabric of society and that she was angry that Mrs Thatcher had allowed the Americans to use British bases to bomb Libya. It claimed: 'The new criticisms have surfaced as a result of the Queen's fear for the possible break-up of the Commonwealth . . . she feels duty-bound to do everything she can – short of speaking in public – to save it.' Inside the newspaper, a whole page was devoted to what was said to be the view from the palace, set against the view from Downing Street. It lacked both weight and substance; the detail was both repetitive and speculative and although there was an underlying ring of truth, much of it would be obvious to close observers of relationships between the palace and Downing Street. Everyone in that circle knew it was in the Queen's nature to be concerned about these issues. In fact a letter declaring as much to one of her subjects had already been made public. Her private secretary Sir William Heseltine wrote:

> I am commanded by Her Majesty to acknowledge your letter about the miners' strike. Her Majesty profoundly hopes that a way to settle this dispute will soon be found. The Queen is constitutional head of state, but Her Majesty takes advantage of her weekly meeting with the Prime Minister to follow closely the developments in this and other matters of current interest and to discuss these with the Prime Minister.[7]

Privately the Queen probably worried about Thatcher's confrontational stance, her intransigence which was becoming legendary, and that her social policies were indeed divisive. It seemed most unlikely, however, that the Queen would choose to allow one of her aides to reveal her feelings to the *Sunday Times* since this would go against everything she stood for, in her meticulous regard for the constitution. The palace denied that there had been an unofficial placing of the Queen's views – as suggested the following day by James Naughtie, chief political correspondent of the *Guardian*[8] – and said that the very idea put forward in the *Sunday Times* represented a totally unjustified slur on the impartiality and discretion of senior members of the royal household. In the subsequent uproar, the *Sunday Times* stuck to its guns and went further, the following week, to describe it as the 'story they could not kill', although no one, it appeared, had attempted to do so. The Queen, as a matter of course, seldom replies to newspaper allegations. On this occasion, Buckingham Palace came back with the most strongly worded letter of reply in living memory. The letter, signed by Sir William Heseltine, but undoubtedly written with the Queen at his side, demolished the reports purporting to be the Queen's opinions of government policies as 'entirely without foundation', though naturally it did not deny specifically that the Queen felt Thatcher was uncaring, confrontational and divisive since that would have revealed the Queen's views, anyway. Amid overheated talk of a grave constitutional crisis, the row rumbled on for weeks, and has continued to crop up every so often ever since. Although in the first instance the palace dismissed the story as rubbish, it later conceded that the Queen's press secretary Michael Shea – he who had been forgiven by the Queen for revealing to reporters in San Francisco in 1983 that palace staff referred to their employer as Miss Piggy – had given his own observations to the newspaper. What he had said, however, remained a matter of severe dispute. The rights and wrongs of the *Sunday Times* allegations, serious as they seemed at the time, were not the main issue, however. Heseltine's letter was revealing in one most important aspect and that was his (or more correctly his employer's) reaffirmation of the monarch's constitutional rights which, taken against the current political climate bearing down upon Buckingham Palace just as oppressively as it did elsewhere, could easily have been written as a memo to the Prime Minister. Sir William wrote:

> In the debate about the supposed revelations of the Queen's opinions about Government policies, I take three points to be axiomatic:
>
> 1) The Sovereign has the right – indeed a duty – to counsel, encourage and warn her government. She is thus entitled to have opinions on Government policy and express them to her chief ministers.
>
> 2) Whatever personal opinions the Sovereign may hold or may have expressed to her Government, she is bound to accept and act on the advice of her ministers.
>
> 3) The Sovereign is obliged to treat her communications with the Prime Minister as entirely confidential between the two of them . . . after 34 years of unvarying adherence to these constitutional principles, it is preposterous to suggest that Her Majesty might suddenly depart from them. No sensible person would give a moment's credence to such a proposition.[9]

Strong stuff from the palace, it was, and underlined the strength of feeling the Queen still holds about her constitutional role. The prerogative that was called upon for the selection of three prime ministers in her reign is now obviously kept safely for emergency use only – such as dissolution or a hung parliament – but she made it quite clear that she considers her position a very active one in relationship to the government, and that it does not preclude her telling her Prime Minister exactly what she thinks about issues of the day, and specially where they concern the Commonwealth. As successive former prime ministers have testified, they have been struck by her combination of warmth, sagacity, experience and detached advice on matters of state. And it seems safe to assume from the Heseltine statement that she did indeed give Mrs Thatcher the benefit of her thoughts; and as several of her recently departed or about to depart Cabinet ministers would also testify, Mrs Thatcher did not take kindly to such advice. However, though the tone of the discussions which took place between the Queen and the Prime Minister during these traumatic months will never be known because the meetings go unrecorded, it seemed that the Queen might well have helped her Prime Minister see the light over her attitude to the Commonwealth. Mrs Thatcher's position would remain unbowed until, almost at the last minute, the ultimate crisis was avoided. She accepted a modified version of the Eminent Persons Group proposals, calling for a ban on coal and steel exports to South Africa, and a voluntary reduction in British and European investment and tourism. Even so, the Commonwealth's view of her was not enhanced a jot, nor hers of it. At least the Queen had provided the power to go on talking, and it is these kinds of political involvements and crises that supply a very acceptable reminder, every now and again, that she is not just an amiable rubber stamp whose life revolves around the trivia of her family's adventures as portrayed daily in the popular newspapers to the avid readership of the eighties.

There was that, too. And through it all . . . another death, another marriage, a special birthday for the Queen (at sixty) and a landmark birthday for the Queen Mother who celebrated her eighty-fifth by flying around Britain in Concord . . . the mixture which keeps the populace happily sated with royal deeds, brought to their breakfast tables and on their television screens daily, between these bouts of heavy political infighting about the Commonwealth in which interest to the public at large was, sad to say, somewhat overestimated by Mrs Thatcher.

In February, the Queen took off to Nepal, Australia and New Zealand. The royal yacht had gone on ahead and was passing through the Arabian Sea when civil war broke out in South Yemen; hasty communication diverted the yacht to Aden where more than 300 Britons and other nationalities were waiting on the beaches to be evacuated and were already under fire when the *Britannia* sailed in as close as she could to the shore. As the evacuees were being brought aboard, *Britannia*'s captain, Rear-Admiral John Garnier, had to send in an armed contingent to cover them against rebel troops heading towards them. The *Britannia* ferried the rescued expatriates to the frigate HMS *Jupiter* and continued its rescue operations for several more days.

Nepal provided a spectacular welcome, especially from the Gurkhas, who had been part of the British armed forces for almost two centuries. Philip went off into the wilds on the back of an elephant and saw a rare rhinoceros being shot – but this time, not for its feet to be cut up to be made into waste-paper baskets. It was tranquillised so that a monitoring device could be fitted around its neck. How times had changed, as indeed they had in Australia and New Zealand. The Maoris were still protesting, and rightfully so, over their land rights; one bared his buttocks and was arrested and in Auckland there was a security scare when two girls threw two eggs at the Queen, one of which smashed on her pink coat. Otherwise, the welcomes were more in keeping with the enthusiasm of the fifties, especially in Australia where the mood of republicanism had been quelled, some said, because of the new interest in the monarchy generated by the recent visit of the Prince and Princess of Wales. A poll conducted shortly before her arrival showed that only 28 per cent were in favour of ditching the Queen. Even Bob Hawke's Labour Party officially declared that the monarchy would last well into the next century and it would be 'a brave man who tried to say otherwise'.

Their return to England was marked with an

announcement which would send the newspapers into another flurry of high industry and provide them with a new royal star. On 19 March, after several weeks of speculation, the Queen confirmed the engagement of Prince Andrew to the previously unheard-of Miss Sarah Ferguson, whose father Major Ronald Ferguson was Prince Charles's polo manager; he was also divorced from her mother who had remarried an Argentinian polo player and it seemed an odd coincidence that, of the last few royal spouses, Lady Diana, Princess Michael, Lord Snowdon and now Sarah Ferguson all had divorced parents. She immediately became 'Fergie'; they had known each other since they were four but only recently had rediscovered each other after Miss Ferguson's earlier romance had ended. She was given a huge press welcome, of course, and the Princess of Wales had a new starring partner to join her on the front covers, especially when it was discovered that, unlike Diana, she had a past as well as a history, the former being a live-in relationship with a racing driver and the latter a family relationship to Princess Alice, Duchess of Gloucester, who was Major Ferguson's cousin.

The engagement was announced just four weeks before the Queen's sixtieth birthday which was marked by a week of various pageantry and family celebrations, accompanied by a very considerable media accolade of tributes, that she had breathed new life into the House of Windsor and guided the family on a journey in which they had encountered hazards undreamed of by her predecessors.

The swings swing and the roundabouts turn – there had to be a third element. Three days after the Queen's birthday, Buckingham Palace was informed of the death of the Duchess of Windsor, long expected because of her declining health, though no one in the family had seen her for some years. She had become a bedroom recluse, tended by Suzanne Blum and her aides behind the closed curtains of the Windsors' house which declined in its appearance along with its tenant. When Lady Diana Mosley published her book on the duchess in 1980, she said she had not seen her old friend for three years, apparently having been discouraged from visiting. Countess Romanones, another of the duchess's old friends, was, with persistence, allowed into the house and shown up to her friend's boudoir, still exquisitely furnished. There were flickers of recognition, but on a later visit, she was unable to get the duchess to speak a single word. Not long afterwards, Dr Thomas Hewes of the American Hospital in Neuilly said, 'The duchess is a vegetable and is in a pitiable state. I don't believe she suffers anything at all any more.'[10] And so by 1986, the duchess had spent almost nine years in the seclusion of her boudoir, latterly not recognising anyone, sometimes wheeled out into the sunshine by her nurses and listening occasionally to a pianist whom Maitre Blum hired to come in and play the duchess's favourite old tunes. Wild and exaggerated stories began to circulate about her condition, likening her state to that of Howard Hughes, but they were largely untrue, except for the enforced seclusion, born out of Suzanne Blum's wish that no one should see the duchess in her last years of physical decline. The rest of the staff drifted away, one by one, save for the butler and housekeeper Georges and Ophelia Sanegre. Only in death was the Duchess of Windsor afforded the recognition of the British royal family who all gathered for her funeral. The Queen naturally stood by her promise to her Uncle David in 1972, and sent her Lord Chamberlain to Paris to accompany the duchess's coffin aboard an RAF aircraft and bring her body back to Windsor to be laid to rest in the plot reserved for her beside the duke. Sixteen members of the royal family were present, and among those who mourned was the duchess's friend Lady Diana Mosley. Only Georges and Ophelia who had been in the Windsors' service for forty years came to the funeral from the household. Afterwards, the Queen came over to them and said, 'This is very sad. It must be a great loss to you both. I am so very sorry . . .'[11]

All that remained was the disposal of her estate in which the Queen and the Queen Mother were naturally interested, since it contained items which originated from the royal vault in London. A discreet inquiry revealed to them the intentions of Maitre Blum who was acting 'in accordance with the wishes of the duke and duchess'. Maitre Blum replied that every item of jewellery was to be auctioned, and that every penny of the proceeds should go to a trust which would be administered by herself and benefit the Pasteur Institute in Paris, initially for research into AIDS; though the will reflected the duchess's intentions, she would not have known either the value of her estate or its eventual destination. The royal family got nothing. The Queen would have hoped that there might have been some mention of any remaining documents belonging to the duke and duchess which could be repatriated to the royal archives. That prospect evaporated when it was revealed to the Queen that a third book containing love letters and very personal extracts from the couple's private papers was about to be published. The author, Michael Bloch, a barrister born in 1953 and a graduate of St John's College Cambridge, first went to Paris to seek assistance from Maitre Blum on a writing project. He became her assistant in 1979, editing and collating the Windsor papers. According to Maitre Blum, the duchess had signed over to her all rights concerning the Windsor papers. Bloch's first book, *The Duke of Windsor's War*, which carried an inscription 'To Maitre Suzanne Blum, guide, pupil, master, friend', was published in 1982. He wrote four more Windsor books, largely based upon their papers and letters they wrote to each other and to Wallis's Aunt Bessie. Combining this documentation with his own historical research proved to be a successful formula, and they all became best-sellers. Meanwhile, the Windsors' clothes, furniture and possessions, even their photograph albums, were still inside the house and none was to find its way back to London. There they were to remain, to become part of a shrine, a private Windsor memorial established by Mohammed al-Fayed, the owner of Harrods, who acquired the lease of their house in the Bois de Boulogne on condition he restored it to its former glory.

There were 230 lots of jewellery and other items of silverware, such as a splendid cigar box presented to the duke when he was Prince of Wales in 1915 while he was on military service in France. And so it was dispersed, by international auction, with the Hollywood crowd, led by Elizabeth Taylor, bidding in force along with a mad scramble of others seeking trinkets and mementoes of the most famous couple in the world, for which they paid in total £32 million. The highest-priced item was a Royal Navy sword presented by King George V to the Prince of Wales which went for over £1 million, vastly more than its worth. The buyer remained anonymous. It is not known whether the Queen was a bidder, though it was rumoured that she had covertly arranged to buy back pieces which she and her mother particularly wished to see restored to family ownership. These did not include a small gold-framed illuminated manuscript, containing a small verse with a coronet over the top and which read:

My friend to live with thee alone
I think 'twere better than to own
A crown a sceptre or a throne.

The wedding of the year seemed to be upon them very quickly. With the ongoing Commonwealth saga and an extensive list of engagements at home the Queen had barely had time to think about it; the publicity and resultant outcry over the *Sunday Times* article was also tiresome, coming as it did just three days before the wedding. It made no difference to the interest but, even so, it did seem that this young couple, who had been elevated to the station of duke and duchess, had been given a start in life slightly more than was merited by their prospective contribution to the family business. The wedding, with all the usual pageantry and followed by the balcony appearance, was an extravagant display for two as yet unimportant members of royalty. There was no deep significance in the wedding, nor importance. Andrew, an arrogant young man, was not especially well liked and interest centred on his bride who had been plucked from common obscurity to take her place amongst this elite band, and it really did seem that on the occasion of this 'royal wedding' the royal family was playing to the crowd, milking it for all it was worth and using this religious expression of family unity to inspire some additional warming to the House of Windsor itself. It went badly wrong very quickly. The 'fun-loving Fergie', as she became in every newspaper story, soon found that her honeymoon with the press was shortlived and she very quickly took over as the butt of criticism and nasty jokes, that uncomfortable position in the royal family once held by Princess Margaret, who was succeeded by Princess Anne. But in this case, the attacks were not entirely unwarranted. The Duchess of York, whose very title brought a smirk to the faces of some of her sarcastic Sloane Ranger friends, caused the Queen some early anguish over her new daughter-in-law's personal appearances: her choice of clothes, her jet-setting ambitions and her inability to extract herself from any kind of motorcar without showing the waiting, drooling photographers, who could number 100 at any one time, the colour of her underwear, combined to make her entry into royal life both spectacular and difficult. If the Queen was any judge, and she surely was, she might well have predicted a bumpy ride ahead for the latest duchess.

It had already been a year packed with events and pressure and overseas travel, and there was still one more major trip to complete, which was so important that it had taken almost two years to plan. The Queen's tour of China was viewed by Buckingham Palace as one of the greatest challenges of her reign, and much the same was thought by the Foreign Office who were in the throes of delicate negotiations for the return of Hong Kong to Chinese administration in 1997. It was similarly treated by the media. Both ITN and the BBC set up satellite stations on the Great Wall of China, and more than 200 western journalists followed the tour which was filled with superb sights of Chinese history, ritual and spectacle. Prince Philip made it all worthwhile for the reporters with his comment to a Scottish student that if he stayed there much longer he would go home with slitty eyes. And when someone asked him what he thought of the Forbidden City, he replied, 'Ghastly.'

The Queen, correcting him, said it was fascinating.

'The Forbidden City? Oh yes,' said Philip. 'Fascinating. But Beijing was ghastly.'

Tactful as ever, he found himself branded the Great Wally of China in the following day's tabloids, in headlines of a size normally reserved for the declaration of war or some other catastrophe. The newspapers had spent a small fortune sending reporters and photographers to Peking and they wanted value for money. Philip's comment was better copy than a description of the Queen climbing 118 steps to the Buddhist Temple of Kinming. It made their day.

Chapter Nineteen

Just the Fourteen of Us (1987–9)

On the evening before Princess Elizabeth married Prince Philip in 1947, her father wrote her a slightly melancholy letter expressing his feelings about the family and the family business: 'Our family, us four, the "royal family" must remain together with additions of course at suitable moments!' The additions had come thick and fast during the past few years and by the mid-eighties there were at least fourteen front-line members of the royal family available for duty, and a small battalion of reserves following on behind. This was good news for the recipients of visits by royalty, both at home and overseas, and having more of them in action gave Princess Anne, for example, the opportunity to give specialist attention to two or three worthwhile causes and interests, while still maintaining contact with and patronage of a wide range of other organisations. She, like the Queen, has become the epitome of service, the ideal that her great-grandmother Queen Mary, and eventually Anne's great-aunt Edwina Mountbatten, inspired as role models for all royal women; service above all else. Anne, with the Queen's help and encouragement, has done exactly that, and it *has* stood above all else, including, even contributing to, the difficulties in her personal life. Edward Heath recalls that he attended a lecture given by the Princess Royal in Salisbury Cathedral and observed that she had

> a packed audience spellbound . . . with such a mastery of her subject that everyone was full of admiration of her

> grasp of the issues and her detailed knowledge of the situation in so many countries. I fully appreciate the immense contribution the Princess Royal is making to increasing public understanding of worldwide problems and mustering support for the underprivileged. She maintains a personal elegance and quiet dignity worthy of the Queen and acknowledged by those who meet her the world over.[1]

The Queen would like to see that kind of tribute paid to all of her family; unfortunately Anne's example was, in 1987, the best on offer, and it was not typical of the rest of the Queen's children, cousins, nieces and nephews. The royals admit that much of their time and energies are devoted to turning up at a great many unremarkable events, most allied to charity and service organisations, and they readily admit that their presence is required as one of the best guarantees of raising money that exists today. Between them, they travel hundreds of thousands of miles a year, and share an annual workload of more than 3,000 engagements within the United Kingdom and another 1,000 abroad, but a third of those engagements are often undemanding 'hellos and goodbyes', and another third are shared by the Queen and Princess Anne. But before looking at the division of labour between the various members of the royal family in its enlarged form, it is worth examining for a moment another phenomenon which occurred as a sort of side-effect to the enlargement of the working family. With the Queen's husband, mother, sister, sons, daughter, son-in-law and daughters-in-law all actively participating in the family business, plus the Kents, the Ogilvys and the Gloucesters, it meant there were many more occasions and opportunities for them to receive coverage in the newspapers and many more opportunities for one or other of them to attract the wrong sort of publicity; in fact more than half this coverage is not the sort the Queen would have preferred for her family. Glamour photographs, humorous photographs, sad photographs, action photographs, posed photographs, serious stories, funny stories, scandalous stories, fictitious stories had begun to appear with – in the Queen's view – alarming frequency. Press coverage had always been there and has been encouraged by the palace, but never had it been such a problem; the Queen and her advisers regularly reflect upon it and try to control it. Where once they could expect a newspaper item about themselves once or twice a week, it was now *every* day; sometimes there would be pages devoted to them and very little of the coverage concerned their work. With the Duchess of York's controversial entry now added to the equation, along with the coverage given to anything that the Princess of Wales did and anything that Princess Michael said, there was, going into 1987, another explosion of royal 'stories'.

So what was new in that? Nothing much, except the sheer volume of it; even King George VI used to keep a clippings scrapbook on 'the things my daughters never did'. The extent of media coverage and the inventiveness of some of the writing had quite suddenly taken on gargantuan proportions, and the fact that there were so many of them in the public eye merely contributed to what can now be seen, reflectively, as a period of the most intense royal coverage ever witnessed. The problem for the royals was exaggerated by the most cut-throat circulation battle between the popular newspapers in recent memory, which gave rise to some of the worst excesses of tabloid journalism. If the Queen had ever needed the services of a good public relations firm, the time had arrived, and in many ways her own staff was simply overwhelmed by the volume of material upon which they were being asked to comment. The Queen was already concerned about the press attention given to the Princess of Wales, worried about the effect it would have on Diana's health and that her continual appearance in the newspapers would trivialise her own position as well as the family's. The Princess Royal was worried for her own reasons. She more than any member of the family had suffered the brunt of personal attacks about her demeanour, often well deserved in the early days before she became a born-again Florence Nightingale; lately, while the press recognised her good works, she had suffered regularly from inferential headlines about the state of her marriage and the friendships which she and her husband Mark Phillips had enjoyed. She chose a meeting of media people in London to vent her feelings, and her speech was so strong that it would have needed the Queen's clearance before she made it:

> I suffered severe aggravation from the amount of unadulterated trivia, rubbish and gratuitous trouble-making that appeared in all sections of the so-called media in response to a perfectly normal family occasion . . . I try not to let this colour my objective assessment of the serious 'news' as portrayed by the media but I don't care what anybody says about the average newspaper reader or television watcher not believing what they read or see. They do. And the sheer volume of repeated stories, half truths and lies has its effects on the subject concerned.[2]

The fact that she chose to deliver that speech at a dinner attended by the cream of Britain's newspaper establishment, as well as newspaper moguls Robert Maxwell and Rupert Murdoch, showed the sense of anger she, and the Queen, felt at the time.

They had very good cause and a brief scan of some of the huge headlines in the tabloids at the time explained the anger the Queen and her children felt: 'Fergie in Tears in Bust-up over Koo', 'Diana the Dictator', 'I Snorted Coke at Palace Party', '20 Things You Didn't Know About Charles's Bald Spot', 'I Feel So Trapped Says Di', 'Charles Is Not My Wife's Lover'. These were a few of the less offensive headlines which were appearing day after day. Soon after Anne's attack on the media, Harold Wilson's former press secretary Joe Haines wrote an article complaining that the royal family had become The Westenders, the only global soap opera in existence, seven days a week, year in and year out, and though blaming the royals in part, recognised that the newspapers themselves were on a self-feeding spiral. 'It is too much and time to give the show a rest,' said Haines, 'it is time for the royal family's sake, for the newspapers' sake and the country's sake, to start backing off.'[3] Haines recalled for the author that he was once asked by Harold Wilson, when he was Prime Minister, to draft a definition of privacy to protect people in public life from the intrusive camera and notebook. His answer was 'That every citizen should be accorded the same right to privacy as is accorded the families of newspaper proprietors'. Haines also made reference to the *Sunday Times* article alleging a rift between the Queen and Mrs Thatcher which had the makings of a constitutional crisis, if it had been true. He suggested that Michael Shea, the Queen's press secretary, and Andrew Neil, editor of the *Sunday Times*, should 'do the decent thing' and resign.

Soon afterwards, Shea, who had been the Queen's press secretary for the past nine years, did in fact quit but not, he insisted, because of the *Sunday Times* article. He had been offered twice the money to perform an ambassadorial role for Lord Hanson and the Hanson Trust. Shea had admitted he was a source for the article but denied he had asserted that the Queen was worried about government economic and social strategy. 'No, it was nothing to do with the *Sunday Times*,' Shea said. 'Nine years is quite enough in that job. I feel a sense of relief and although I enjoyed my time in the Queen's service, I don't want to have to deal with the media in that sort of way ever again.'[4] Shea was highly critical of the tabloid newspapers in Britain at the time and more so of the continental journals that had long been disregarded by the Queen. 'Page after page of it is fairy story writing,' said Shea. 'It's a case of find a fact inside and win a million pounds.'

He had been charged with the thankless task of performing an almost impossible balancing act ensuring that the Queen's mystique was protected and that her work received the public acclaim and recognition it deserved, and at the same time trying to offset the worldwide obsession with the House of Windsor which the media exploited to their own commercial ends, virtually obliterating the serious, constitutional and ceremonial side of the monarchy. Again, there was nothing new in that, because the serious side of coverage had been in decline since the beginning of the Queen's reign. It was itself almost a product of the 'Isn't she loverly . . .' brigade who wrote about her dresses, hair, lipstick and waistline first and the task at hand last. There was nothing new in revelatory stories and scandals which had always been there, nothing new in criticism or insults. There was a sardonic irony in the fact that it came to a head in 1987, the year of the fortieth anniversary of the Queen's own marriage which was widely pronounced to be on the rocks in 1957. It also mirrored the great torrent of critical comment the Queen faced through the likes of Malcolm Muggeridge, Lord Altrincham and John

Osborne in the late fifties. The difference was that, then, there was only the Queen, Prince Philip and Princess Margaret to write about, with occasional interventions from the Duke and Duchess of Windsor.

Now the stage was full of attractive, extrovert, wealthy players who were going about their high-profile lives at a time when the likes of Joan Collins, Larry Hagman, Linda Evans and company were topping all the television ratings playing the mythical characters who populated series like *Dallas* and *Dynasty*. The available comparisons were so remarkably evident that – just as Malcolm Muggeridge had predicted in 1956, and Joe Haines in 1986 – the adventures of the real-life characters in the Royal Soap Opera became an indispensable fetish. *Today* newspaper, then owned by Eddie Shah, produced a very good analysis of the situation, under the headline 'How do the Royals Stay Sane?' and published a cartoon showing the Queen and Prince Philip staging a rooftop protest at Buckingham Palace, adorned with a banner which read 'Leave us alone!'

The problem was, of course, that while everyone knew that the press and magazine coverage was going well over the top and eventually some curbing measures would be necessary,* one of the underlying causes actually came from within the family itself, first by their numbers and secondly by their own human weaknesses and actions. On very few occasions is the Queen moved to take action. We have seen that she had already called in editors to try to curb their enthusiasm over the Princess of Wales, and took legal action to stop palace servants selling their stories. She took legal action again in 1987 when the *Sun* got hold of a very private and personal letter Prince Philip had written to the Commandant General of the Royal Marines. It detailed how he and the Queen had tried to counsel Prince Edward on his actions in leaving the Marines and outlined the difficult decisions his son had to make about the future. Within two weeks of its being written, the letter appeared on the front page of the *Sun*. The Queen

*They eventually came into effect with the new Press Complaints Commission which replaced the old Press Council following Mrs Thatcher's warning to newspapers that unless they cleaned up their act she would do it for them!

was astonished that such a leak could occur; her husband was furious. He contacted the Queen's solicitors Farrer & Co and within twenty-four hours, the newspaper agreed to make a £25,000 donation to charity for breach of copyright.

This by no means dampened the press ardour or the public appetite. The unfortunate plight of Prince Edward, who had been virtually forced into a career he did not want, was one which evoked great sympathy from many readers; the other side of the coin was that his father erupted into a 'volcanic fit of fury' when he learned his son wanted to quit. But that was just one story; pretty well all of the young royals figured in one way or another, culminating with their collective participation in a rather undignified *It's a Royal Knock-Out* which was shown on television. By June 1987, months of unrelenting headlines about the royal lives prompted the editor of the *Sunday Times*, Andrew Neil, now the established guardian against any royal indiscretion or indolence, to remind the Queen that she was the key figure in an overdue reappraisal of the way her family went about their lives and duties. An editorial in the newspaper said bluntly:

> The royal family has become so used to being treated like a soap opera by large sections of the media that some of its members are beginning to act as if they are in one. Many may see this . . . as good, harmless grist to the tabloid mills. But there are grave dangers . . . They need to be reminded that the public's appetite for soap operas eventually wanes. Ratings dip, producers put their characters through even more ludicrous plots in an attempt to revive audience interest and when that fails they are replaced in the schedules with something else. Those who do not wish the monarch to go the same way sometime early in the next century must realise that casting the royal family as soap opera contains the seeds of its own destruction.

Lack of direction and meaningful roles for the emerging young royals was clearly an important issue. The Queen had a real problem with her three sons, none of whom had been able to put together a working schedule which compared with the international spectrum of Princess Anne's charitable and sporting associations. And the kind of engagements Buckingham Palace was laying before the three princes offered no career for grown men. Prince Charles, basically a very caring, sensitive man, who seemed quite desperate to do *something*, filled his time with a dull routine forced upon him by the palace which tested neither his ability nor his stamina. He was approaching forty, and had no responsibilities outside of managing his own estates, and none in sight. A Cabinet minister once suggested that he should be given a governor-generalship. 'No, no, we can't possibly do that,' came the reply from the Foreign Office. 'Too political.' He had grown thoughtful and introspective, and that meant 'eccentric' in newspaper jargon. He liked horticulture, farming, getting close to the land. He became putty in the hands of intellectual manipulators, pushing him down certain avenues of controversy. The only way he could make a serious contribution to the nation was through his charitable causes such as his Inner City Aid Trust and his Prince's Trust, and even this did not account for a third of his available time. He dodged in and out of self-motivated campaigns, such as his views on architecture, the environment and inner city deprivation; he spoke with genuine sensibility which brought admiration from the environmentally minded and stirred the minds of those in authority. Outside of these campaigns, it was an unfortunate truth that there was little to do except wander through undemanding and unrewarding engagements, part salesman, part ambassador.

Prince Andrew, fresh from his carefully catalogued love life and surprise marriage, was spending less time than he ought on his career in the navy, and had begun undertaking various public engagements in the wake of his marriage so that he and his wife could be seen to be taking an active role in the family business. It did not work; he did not move easily into the royal world in which he had to wear a permanent smile and be polite to the bowers and scrapers from whom he and his brother Prince Edward had been shielded until a remarkably late stage in their lives. Like his father, Andrew could not shake off that arrogant air and could easily upset those who were trying only to please. Before long his father suggested he should go back to naval duties; he did, and we have barely seen him in action in public life since. He is a straightforward man who speaks his mind, and is very conscious of his position and status, except when he is in the company of his naval colleagues who ignore it. He has his father's energetic approach to life, but lacks the same clarity of thought, has no intellectual ability and little experience of meeting people at government level.

Prince Edward drifted rudderless and seemed naive and immature for his age. While on the one hand he was deprecating cynical journalists who couldn't understand him, he gave an interview to *Woman's Own* and discussed his reasons for leaving the Marines, and was then surprised to find it splashed over everywhere. 'It was an agonising decision to make,' said Edward. 'Four years ago, I wanted to be a Marine but having got there I changed my mind and decided that the services generally, not just the Royal Marines, was not the career I wanted.'[5] He chose instead a career in show business – 'You're going to do what?' raged Philip when he was told.

The Queen could see their problem. She sympathised with Charles but he, conversely, supported her unwillingness to consider abdication in his favour; there is, on close inspection, surprisingly little of her work that she can delegate. The Sovereign is the Sovereign, and her own devotion to that duty leaves little to hand over to the heir.

Philip was impatient with all of them, especially when they did something daft that the press picked up, and his aides would say, 'He can talk!' As one close to the sons told the author:

> What does Philip expect? He has been an absolute shit to those boys. That's why Charles always went to Mountbatten for advice, rather than him. Philip was hard and pushing all the time; he was hell bent on building their characters and doesn't know the meaning of compassion or kindness. It all came from his own upbringing, and he's been inflicting his bullying tactics, which are a cover for his own insecurities, on everyone around him ever since.

Meanwhile, Princess Diana and the Duchess of York had been cast as light-hearted and lightweight Sloane Ranger girls with no other function than to be decorative, while the 'new' Princess Michael had attracted some especially bad press with her pushiness and friendships abroad. The Princess of Wales, admired and loved everywhere, was, however, seen to be rather shallow in her work, nothing much more than a royal clothes-horse, and the later moves towards deeper, even courageous, commitment had their beginnings in 1987 until, as was seen in the early nineties, she began to devote herself to causes dealing with handicapped and deprived children and, more especially, those of all age groups afflicted by AIDS.

But in 1987, the problems confronting the Queen over her family and family relationships were very real indeed. With all the resultant publicity the dignity of the monarchy was severely in jeopardy, and in its old-fashioned way the establishment panics whenever that happens. Scandal and trivia damage the Crown, and so the state is in danger. Well, perhaps that's the way it was once, but if Britain's constitution could withstand the philanderings of Edward VII and the absurdity of Edward VIII's abdication, it could withstand a few relatively unimportant happenings related to the children of the Crown. It could be damaging to the family long-term, however, and the *Sunday Times* and Joe Haines were certainly correct in suggesting that the nation might just begin to tire of some of the royal performers; contempt follows familiarity and signs of public indifference were already apparent. And it must have been with some considerable discomfort that the Queen and Prince Philip retired to Balmoral that summer, knowing that there was obviously a need for some heart-searching self-examination after this deluge of headlines and advice from newspaper leader-writers.

Worse was to come.

The marriage of Charles and Diana had been turned into the second greatest love story of the century. So when their 6-year itch came along, the fierceness of the speculation which surrounded them was, and always would be, so much greater. There had been rumblings already, after they had failed to celebrate their wedding anniversary together, and then during the summer holidays the Princess of Wales returned to London from Balmoral early. For the next five and a half weeks, they saw each other for only six hours when they joined forces to offer consolation to storm-damage victims of the 16 October hurricane, before Charles flew back to Scotland to continue his reclusive meditation and heart-searching, advisory chats with his grandmother, the Queen Mother, and Diana caught the next helicopter to Highgrove. Fever-pitch speculation followed, and even ITN, which is normally respectably restrained on such matters, was moved to record this brief reunion and immediate separation. The plight of the hurricane victims was totally overshadowed by the speculation on the state of the royal marriage, and that story rumbled on for weeks.

The Queen had just flown to Canada, to a summit meeting of the Commonwealth in Vancouver. More trouble. Mrs Thatcher, spurred on by her overwhelming general election victory in June, was in a bossy mood about the South African problem and other difficulties on which she could not see eye to eye with her opposite numbers who had already noted her remarks, 'It's their club, their Commonwealth. If they wish to break it up, I think it's absurd.' On the Queen's arrival Canadian Prime Minister Brian Mulroney lost no time in complaining to her about Mrs Thatcher's autocratic approach to the troubled summit, while Zimbabwe's Robert Mugabe insisted once again that 'Britain has lost its traditional role as leader of the Commonwealth – Canada has taken over'.[6] So once again, the Queen was faced with the task of smoothing over the ruffled prime ministers as best she could. The tour of Canada did not go well either. Former Prime Minister Pierre Trudeau failed to turn up at a banquet in the Queen's honour, which was widely taken as a 'snub', and her walkabout tour planned for Quebec was cancelled after she was booed on arrival by a large and unruly crowd.

She arrived home on 24 October to be informed the following morning by the *News of the World* that her son had finally flown home from his Scottish retreat for a 'High Noon Showdown at Highgrove' to discuss his wife's 'girl-about-town' activities and his own tea-and-sympathy meetings with his friend, Lady Dale Tryon. But if it was a showdown, it solved nothing and certainly did not stop the abundance of headlines. They went together to the wedding of the Marquess of Worcester. Diana danced a lot with her friend

Philip Dunne, the merchant banker who is more adept at the modern dance than Charles; Charles danced a few waltzes with women friends more his age and at 2.00 a.m. wandered across the dance floor and said he was leaving and he did – alone. The most remarkable incident in this rather pathetic spectacle occurred two weeks later when Diana fell into the hands of a waiting photographer late one night after a dinner party. Diana broke down in tears when she was photographed leaving the home of her close friend, Kate Menzies. There were some playful high jinks outside the house with another of the guests, a young Guards officer named Major David Waterhouse, which were photographed. Diana pleaded for the film and her detective confronted the paparazzi cameraman who duly reported to the *News of the World* her alleged words, 'No one has to know this has happened, do they? You just don't know what I go through. I must have that film.' The cameraman gave it to her, and arrangements were made for it to be returned the following day, which it was, minus the negatives of Diana. Now, Scotland Yard became involved, apparently having been told of the incident and made aware that Buckingham Palace was increasingly concerned by the 'persecution' of the Princess of Wales by the activities of the paparazzi, mostly financed by continental journals, who were following her everywhere on their motorbikes equipped with two-way radios to make the pursuit easy. There were literally dozens of them operating in London, and there was a ready worldwide market for their wares. A 'good picture' could get between £1,000 and £5,000; a series of snatched photographs of senior members of royalty could go as high as £25,000, depending on the circumstances, more if there was also a 'good story'. The *Daily Mail* attacked the Murdoch press, which it claimed was breaking the compact between Fleet Street and Buckingham Palace, whereby the royals provided regular picture opportunities in exchange for respect of their privacy.

'Can the marriage be saved?' asked the *Daily Express*. 'And if it can't who gets what . . .?'

The storm raged on, fuelled by the paparazzi and a growing attendant press corps assigned to the story who were racing around following every move they made and talking to alleged 'close friends' and mysterious 'insiders' who were supposedly giving the low-down on the royal marriage. Next, it gained added impetus from a surprising source – the House of Commons, where Conservative MP Tony Marlow raised the remarkable question of whether Prince Charles was fit to rule, should the need arise through some dramatic event? In spite of the rules of protocol he asked, 'Isn't it a bit strange that in a modern society the succession to the Throne is by the eldest male heir rather than the most suitable heir?' And in what was a guarded reference to Princess Anne being the most suitable heir, he continued, 'Would it not be better if it were either male or female?' The Speaker of the House immediately intervened and rebuked Marlow for breaking the rules of silence over royalty; 'I don't think the question is appropriate.'[7] Later Marlow was unrepentant outside the House when he pursued his line, urging that in view of the current situation it might be wise to reconsider the whole question of the line of succession.

The Queen was worried; her family was engulfed by this mass of unattributed speculation. Charles was at his wits' end, Diana verging on a nervous affliction, and Philip raging about the palace in a furious temper. These were no mere left-wing insults of the type her old sparring partner Willie Hamilton used to throw, nor easily discarded tabloid sensation-mongering. Even the *Daily Telegraph* came in with criticism of a speech Charles made during a visit that week to Germany; the newspaper described as 'unhelpful' the Prince's endorsement of Nato's nuclear defence strategy, said he was normally thoughtful and intelligent but should not involve himself in politics and wasn't it about time the Queen found him a real job with real responsibilities?[8] During that week, also, the Conservative Party's 1922 Committee had held a special meeting to discuss a two-page report on the background to the current controversy surrounding members of the royal family. Several members expressed their dismay at the way the royal family had become the subject of continuous press and public criticism and speculation. The whole was so damaging to the monarchy that the Queen ought to enlist better advisers. The latter was supported by a Mori poll which suggested that the monarchy had lost twice as much support during 1987 as it had the previous three years put together. The poll was said to reflect the growing public indifference to the royal family in the wake of this year of intense coverage, with 29 per cent of the nation believing that the country would be no worse off without them. Sixty-three per cent still believed, however, that they should stay.[9]

The Queen could not let it pass; she called her son and daughter-in-law to her side that month, sympathetic and caring as always and ready with calming words and good advice. She had, after all, been through it all before, several times. But they had to find a way of curbing the publicity surrounding their marriage. A period of public togetherness was firmly recommended. The marriage was strained, of that there is no question. It was bound to happen, once Diana's initial excitement and awe had subsided, giving way to acceptance of her royal life as the norm and making that of her friends on the outside marvellously tempting, like a great, red juicy apple hanging on the next-door neighbour's tree. She wanted it, but it wasn't hers; and also, as he approached forty, Charles had frankly become a little boring. It was made worse by the endless attention they received and life, for Diana especially, became so unbearable that she felt she had to resort to the companionship of friends to help with the therapy of warding off a breakdown in her health. A temporary diversion was at hand, although it was merely a transference of the focus from one royal another. Princess Anne went to an equestrian conference in Paris with her father in December. While they were there, actor Anthony Andrews who was making a television film on the life of the Duke of Windsor – he starring as the duke – came to Anne's hotel. He and his wife Georgina were old friends of the Phillipses. The *News of the World* heard of this and immediately sent two reporters to the French capital to report back on the following Sunday's front page: 'Anne and Anthony's Three Nights in Paris'. With each new story came a new follow-up and so Anne was once more in the spotlight and when she and Mark Phillips took her two children off skiing in the New Year, she discovered that the Ratpack were now trailing her; at least Charles and Diana had the luxury of a more peaceful Christmas.

The Queen was planning another trip. They were going back to Australia again, for the bicentenary celebrations, visiting

Western Australia, Tasmania, Victoria, Queensland and Australian Capital Territory from 19 April for almost four weeks; state visits to the Netherlands and Spain were planned for later in the year. Before she left, the Duke and Duchess of York called round and brought good tidings. They were expecting a child, which was as good a diversionary measure as one could hope for. The duchess then proceeded to be photographed almost daily to record her progression from her normal fulsome figure to an even more fulsome one several months later; pages and pages, week after week, were devoted to the forthcoming infant. When the baby was born, every popular newspaper devoted most of the front page to the event as well as several inside. It was quite an amazing array of coverage: *Today* newspaper, by then owned by Rupert Murdoch, showed how to exploit the good royal news as well as the bad by devoting ten of its thirty-two pages to the arrival of the Yorks' baby, compared with eight in the *Sun*, six in the *Mail* and *Mirror*, and three in the *Express*. As Jean Rook said, 'Since the first coming, no infant's birth has been so prophesied, heralded and all but starred in the East.' She was right; in thirty years in newspapers, I had never seen anything quite like it. One baby of no particular significance other than being the Queen's granddaughter commanded more coverage in some newspapers than the death of King George VI and the Coronation put together; had more on-the-day pages devoted to it than the death of Stalin or the assassination attempt on the Pope, and an equal amount to the assassination of John F. Kennedy. Those were the perspectives and it was not over yet. On the day Fergie came out of hospital, there were over 200 cameramen and eight television crews waiting for her to arrive at the hospital door carrying the baby and to photograph her walking to the waiting car with her husband; even she was so overwhelmed she almost tripped and fell. And what followed when those pictures were developed and printed? Why, doesn't Fergie look fat? The bitchy fashion writers could be expected to focus on her shape – the *Sun* did under the headlines 'Return to Slender', advising the duchess to lose at least 56 pounds.

The Queen, to be sure, viewed all of these months of feverish newspaper coverage with considerable disdain. She was moved to personal anger when a family photograph of herself with her new granddaughter Princess Beatrice suddenly appeared on the front page of the *Sun*. It had been removed from Buckingham Palace without her permission and reprinted in breach of copyright. Once again, she had to contact her solicitors, Farrer & Co, who sent a hand-delivered message to Kelvin MacKenzie, the newspaper's editor, demanding an explanation as to how he came to have possession of the photograph, a front-page apology to the Queen and a donation of a suitable amount to charity for breach of copyright. The following day, the *Sun* devoted the whole of its front page to the apology and donated £100,000 to a worthwhile cause.

When next a small parcel arrived for the attention of the editor from an anonymous source at Buckingham Palace, the *Sun*'s executive opened it and read the contents with amazement; MacKenzie must have been sorely tempted to splash the letters across the front pages of his next several issues and ensure for himself an instant and considerable increase in circulation. Instead, the contents were noted and the letters were then despatched promptly to Scotland Yard. The following day's paper recorded its discretion yet still managed to produce what was a sensational story: 'Palace Thief Steals Anne's Letters: Sun to the Rescue'. It merely revealed that some very personal correspondence had been stolen from Princess Anne and delivered to the *Sun*; the letters had now been returned. The story did not identify the author or the contents of the letters but gave a pretty good idea. The ensuing speculation was such that the Queen eventually gave permission for the palace press office to make a statement because it was causing embarrassment to the wrong person; the letters to Anne were from Commander Timothy Laurence, the Queen's equerry for the past four years. This revelation was naturally taken as the cause of the announcement in the summer that Princess Anne and Captain Mark Phillips were to separate. The marriage, in truth, had been one of convenience for several years. Love had unfortunately evaporated and was replaced by a work relationship that proved to be unworkable because of the volatile nature of the couple. Both needed affection and attention and Anne especially had suffered years of comparative loneliness, with only staff and a detective for companionship and a very small number of friends.

Long before the letters from Timothy Laurence were stolen and posted to the *Sun*, Anne had asked the Queen for permission to separate from Mark Phillips. Publicly, it was Princess Anne who took the brunt of the blame for the break-up of her marriage to Captain Mark Phillips when the bombshell announcement of their separation came in August 1989.

The assumption everywhere was that the over-friendly letters she had received from Laurence became the straw which broke the camel's back and Mark wanted out as quickly as possible. It was he who was given the sympathy. It was he who was portrayed to some degree as the victim of Anne's demanding royal lifestyle, her friendships and her legendary temper. And the royal family closed ranks, as it always does, to protect its own.

In fact, even before the existence of the letters became known Anne herself had discussed, if not pleaded, with the Queen to consider the possibility of her calling a halt to what had become a sham of a marriage. Anne wanted a divorce; the Queen, sympathetic as ever, did not especially want another one so close to the heart of the family, but eventually accepted that a legal separation which would lead to divorce after a suitable lapse of time was unavoidable. The modern family had to deal with a modern situation in the modern way. Unknown to the media and the public then, as all of this came spilling out, was a royal secret about which Anne was certainly aware, and undoubtedly the Queen, too: a young woman in New Zealand was claiming that Mark was the father of her daughter, born on 10 August 1985. Miss Heather Tonkin's revelations were revealed in the *Daily Express* which serialised her story for eight days, surrounded by follow-up stories in virtually every other newspaper. This, surely, must have been the cause of the separation announced in 1989 and not, as was widely thought, the letters from Laurence to Anne. At best, it was a combination of both events.

The news of Miss Tonkin's claims put into perspective the reasons why Mark Phillips had quickly been ostracised from the royal circle, unlike Lord Snowdon who remained a close friend to all after his divorce from Princess Margaret. The clues were there to see. When the discovery of Commander Laurence's intimate letters to Anne became known, the Queen's private secretary Sir William Heseltine called Laurence to his office and gave him a dressing-down of considerable proportions. That a royal servant should presume to make such familiar contact with a member of *the* family could not be tolerated.

Yet, the Queen saw it rather differently, possessed – we could assume – of other knowledge. Instead of banishing her equerry to some foreign parts, as was done with Group Captain Peter Townsend some thirty-four years earlier because he had fallen in love with Princess Margaret, she invited Laurence to Balmoral during the family holidays that year of 1989. Anne turned up with Tim at church, and made no secret of their picnic together on the banks of a Highland loch.

Far from banishment, Commander Laurence received one of the Queen's personal honours, membership of the Royal Victorian Order, when he left her service. And where once an officer who had the audacity to write personal letters to the daughter of the Sovereign would have been drummed out of the service with his career ruined, as was Townsend's, the young Commander Laurence was given his own command, the £150 million frigate *Boxer*, one of the navy's most powerful modern ships.

It almost seemed as if the royal family were going out of their way to apologise to Laurence for his having become involved in Anne and Mark's marital scrap; at the very least it was giving signals that all of this furore over Anne's separation was not Laurence's fault. I was told by one close to them as early as 1986, 'Theirs is now a marriage of convenience. If Anne wasn't the Queen's daughter, they'd have ended it by now. They have their flirtations but seem to think that it's not hurting anyone – and especially they don't want to hurt their children.' Even then, the possibility of a separation or divorce seemed out of the question.

Another mystery was perhaps also explained by the knowledge of Miss Tonkin. In March 1988 – a couple of weeks before Commander Laurence's abrupt appearance in the headlines – various newspapers quoted one Miss Pamella

Bordes who claimed that she had enjoyed some rather special moments with Princess Anne's husband while she was attending one of his courses. 'We were drawn to each other,' she gushed, 'so we spent the evening drinking and talking.' The innuendo was clear but might have been disregarded since it came from a woman who was said to be nothing more than a social-climbing high-class call girl and the *femme fatale* in a libel action between two opposing Sunday newspaper editors. Yet, Mark Phillips's friends were astonished when a Buckingham Palace spokesman – who could not have been speaking off-the-cuff on such an issue – confirmed their friendship to inquiring journalists. It was left to Mark to take the unusual step of publicly denying any involvement with her.

Clearly, Mark had been thrown to the wolves.

In May 1989, soon after Laurence's letters were revealed, Anne made a further request to the Queen for a separation. This time, she was going to get her way. Noticeably, an element of bitterness entered the aftermath in Mark's dealings with the royal family. The Queen's solicitor Sir Matthew Farrer acted for Princess Anne and Lord Goodman for Mark Phillips. Between them, the ill-starred couple had two of the toughest legal brains to sort out their affairs and extract the commoner, finally, from his 16-year entanglement with royalty.

In consideration of a cash sum, he gave up all claims against his wife's or the Queen's property, gave her custody of the children and signed a bond of confidentiality. Barbara Cartland once classed Anne and Mark's wedding as an 'historical experiment', a rare marriage of one so close to the throne and a commoner. Perhaps it provided a message, in that the other famous union of Princess Margaret to plain Tony Armstrong-Jones ended in the same way and with just as much black type. One of the few who survived such a marriage was the Duchess of Windsor – but she spent her entire married life ostracised from the duke's family. Alas, it is a fact of life that divorce strikes every family and the royal family's record remains incredibly low. But for those who preferred to view the British monarchy as a high-class soap opera, the ammunition continued to spill forth aplenty. No one in the circle of individuals drawn around the seemingly never-ending series of family difficulties that were exposed in this so brief a timespan, was untouched by sadness, and none more so than the Queen.

At the Commonwealth Conference in October 1989, the Queen's own family problems merged with those of her international family, where some were making no bones about their desire to seek a legal separation from Mrs Margaret Thatcher. 'Like all the best families,' said the Queen, 'we have our share of eccentricities, of impetuous wayward youngsters and of family disagreements.' There was speculation as to whether she was talking about the Commonwealth or her own family – the latest commotion having been recently caused by Marina, daughter of Princess Alexandra and Sir Angus Ogilvy, who revealed she was expecting a baby by her photographer boyfriend and had sold the story to *Today* newspaper for a large fee. No, said a spokesman for the Queen, Marina's story was irrelevant tittle-tattle. The Commonwealth was a most significant and serious issue. The Queen spoke of wise uncles and aunts and the solid dependable family members on whom everyone relies and 'we have shown how to close ranks when neighbours turn unfriendly'. It was this unity which had ensured the survival of the Commonwealth, she told the summit meeting, and she made her point emphatically by saying that the world needed the Commonwealth more than it had ever done in the past. 'I have visited every one of the now forty-nine member-countries,' she said, 'and I know that each, however small, has its contribution to make to the Commonwealth partnership.'[10]

The Queen's speech, perhaps unintentionally, held a message for whoever cared to see . . .

Chapter Twenty
A Matter of Money (1990–91)

The Queen's personal wealth and the state contribution to the workings of the monarchy have become one of the most controversial areas of her reign, and never more so than as she headed towards the fortieth anniversary of her succession, when the two issues merged to provide ammunition for those who continue to express disquiet about the cost of the royal family to the nation. The two areas of her income – personal and state-provided – are often lumped together; rightly so, say the protesters, because much of the Queen's personal fortune derives originally from gifts, property and state money provided for the Queen's ancestors with which they purchased their assets. Furthermore, whether state or privately provided, the Queen and her family enjoy the considerable benefits of all the trappings of monarchy that go with the job. The Queen is as adamant now as she has ever been that the issues are separate, and that the annual allowances she and other members of her family receive from the Civil List and other government departmental grants are used only to cover the expense of running the vast royal empire of people, property, planes, boats and trains, to which she says she is already making an indirect contribution. The two *are* quite distinct and a whole body of people is employed on not merely keeping the books, but keeping the two aspects of her financial well-being entirely separate. Nothing makes her more angry than exaggerated claims about her personal wealth, or the inaccurate references to a 'pay rise for the

Queen' when increases in the Civil List are announced. She regards the former as her private business and the latter as money received from the government to cover her running expenses, none of which can be used for personal items, though the reality is blurred when items such as transport are considered; but perhaps it would be churlish to query, for example, the amount of overseas travelling Prince Philip does on behalf of his various causes. That item, costly though it may be, is a mere flea bite. The question of the morass of royal wealth is complicated first by secrecy and the inherent difficulty in separating out what belongs to the Queen personally and what is actually in her stewardship on behalf of the nation, and secondly because her wealth makes it more difficult to explain away the need for increases in the Civil List budget and contributions from other government departments when elsewhere cuts are constantly being demanded. What is a virtual certainty for the Queen is that the value of her personal fortune has only one way to go: Up. Because she is not required to pay either income tax or death duties, her estate flourishes by the day, and the more she accrues, the greater the speculation over her wealth – especially apparent in 1990 – when the latest surveys on the world's wealthiest people were published coincidentally as Mrs Thatcher's Conservative government was drawing up new proposals for reviewing the Civil List at intervals of ten years instead of annually.

It is perhaps in the area of double benefit – by way of tax-free income and a Civil List allowance for herself and key members of the family – that the Queen is essentially liable to criticism. There is a growing body of opinion which says she ought either to pay taxes in the same way as the rest of the nation, or make a greater contribution from her own resources in financing some of the activities of members of the family. Critics point to the fact that the monarch's personal wealth – as opposed to the assets of heritage, the huge collections of art, porcelain, precious metals, jewels and property over which she has custody – was largely created in the last century.

In fact, when Queen Victoria succeeded her uncle King William IV, she inherited an overdraft of £50,000 and it fell to her husband Prince Albert to begin putting the royal house on an even keel after the years of financial extravagance. The new young Queen did not have many jewels, either; hers was a minuscule collection compared with that owned by her great-great-granddaughter. The comparison is best illustrated by the state of affairs which existed in 1857 when, after a protracted legal argument, Victoria was forced to hand over to the Hanoverian ambassador the main part of her collection which was known as the Hanoverian Crown Jewels, bought by George III for Queen Charlotte. As well as being King of Great Britain and Ireland, George was also King of Hanover. Victoria had frequently worn pieces from the collection because after the Civil War and other crises in subsequent reigns, the Crown of England 'was not very well furnished in this respect'.[1] The government of the day refused point blank to replace them – 'The Queen's popularity was in great measure owing to her own judicious conduct and abstinence from extravagance which had marked the reign of George IV, that nobody cared whether she was attired in fine pearls or diamonds.'[2] And so the new collection which has been gathered over the years to fill today's abundantly stocked royal vault started almost from scratch in that year. Similarly, as the British Empire and the nation's wealth flourished during Victoria's reign, so did the monarchy's own assets, and Albert's shrewd investments and property acquisitions formed the basis of the present Queen's much-discussed wealth that has been amassed in a period of little more than a hundred years.

Although Queen Victoria had no cash reserves, there were an abundance of other assets, though the bulk of her ancestor's properties formed part of the extensive Crown Estates which George III surrendered to the government in 1760 in exchange for the parliamentary grant, which became known as the Civil List and was traditionally fixed at the start of each reign. The palaces were, however, well stocked with fine furniture, art and precious metals, solid gold cutlery, huge Georgian silver soup tureens, so heavy that they require two men to lift them. In 1846, for example, Victoria decided to dispose of Brighton Pavilion, built by George IV. She never liked it, nor Brighton – 'the crowds behaved worse than I have ever seen them . . . we were mobbed by all the shopboys in the town who ran and looked under my bonnet treating us as they do the Band.'[3] Prince Albert supervised the removal of 143 vanloads of furniture, decorations, porcelain, clocks and carpets from the pavilion which were taken to Buckingham Palace and Windsor Castle. Of those items which she did not like, Queen Victoria held a sale on the lawns of Windsor Castle. The proceeds went towards the rebuilding of Osborne House on the Isle of Wight in 1845 which became her first royal retreat. Seven years later, with money Prince Albert had saved by careful management of her £365,000 a year Civil List allowance, the Queen purchased their Scottish retreat, a 17,000 acre Balmoral estate where she built a new castle. These were the foundations for the quite astonishing rise and rise in the fortunes of the present House of Windsor, to the point where today the present Queen has been listed as the world's richest woman with an estimated fortune of £6.6 billion, earning her £2 million a day. The Queen was quick to react to this estimate, published in the magazine *Harpers and Queen* in their annual review of top people's wealth at the end of 1990. She instructed her deputy private secretary Sir Kenneth Scott to write to one of her subjects who had written to her asking why she did not pay poll tax; the response clearly showed the Queen's anguish and took the opportunity of attempting to quell speculation over her wealth by denying recent press estimates as 'wild guesses which bear no relation to the true position'. The letter went on to explain, 'In fact, most of this "wealth" consists of palaces, castles and art treasures which are part of the national heritage and belong essentially to the nation. Her Majesty and members of her family are not free to dispose of this as they please.'[4] The Queen's aide pointed out, once again, that the palaces 'go with the job', in the same way that the Prime Minister had No. 10 Downing Street and Chequers; he denied that the Queen owned property in Europe and America – as had been claimed in a magazine article – and went on to say that though she paid no tax, this was reflected by the amount voted to her by Parliament. Sir Kenneth also made the point that all income from the Crown Estates went to the government.

However, it is a matter of public record that although she receives no income from the now multi-million pound revenues of the Crown Estates, the Queen and her heir retain the income from two other substantial estates, the Duchy of Lancaster and the Duchy of Cornwall. The Duchy of Lancaster is the one from which the Queen derives her own personal cashflow. It consists of 52,000 acres of farmland and some highly valuable real estate in London. In 1989, it yielded £2.7 million which goes into the Queen's private bank account, tax free. The Duchy of Cornwall belongs to the Prince of Wales; it has 125,000 acres ranging from the Isles of Scilly to Surrey County cricket ground at the Oval in London and in the same year it yielded £2.5 million, of which Prince Charles voluntarily pays 25 per cent to the Treasury. The Queen's Sandringham and Balmoral estates provide additional income. Meanwhile, the revenues from the Crown Estates prove that the worst thing George III ever did was to surrender them to Parliament in exchange for a guaranteed income. At the time of the surrender, the gross revenue from the estates was £89,000 a year, from which George III received a net income of £11,000, which was insufficient for his requirements. In the year ending 31 March 1990, the Crown Estates had a gross revenue of £101 million and after tax and expenses £55 million was paid to the Exchequer. Not unnaturally, Prince Charles has said, 'Give us back the Crown Estates, and we'll pay our own way'.

Clearly, it is a touchy subject to the Queen, shown by the attempts to put it into perspective whenever her wealth is widely discussed; but the denials by her advisers of the current estimates of her wealth are meaningless while the secrecy remains. And no one, not even a Commons Select Committee, has been able to penetrate the truth. The Queen's advisers shield her from providing this evidence by stating there is no point in attempting to put a value on her wealth because most of her assets are not only incalculable, but 'inalienable' in the sense that she cannot sell any of them and they have to be passed on to her heir. This is a convenient way of dispensing with agitated inquirers but not an entirely accurate one, because the fact that they live over the shop, in a series of houses that are comparable with national museums, provides a vast and almost indeterminable problem – as to exactly what the Queen and her family can regard as their own and what should truly be regarded as part of the breathtaking collection of national heritage in her care.

When these questions were first examined by the Commons Select Committee in 1971 – and no one has since challenged the findings – the then Lord Chamberlain, Lord Cobbold, said: 'In no practical sense does the Queen regard these items [the Crown Jewels, etc.] as being at her free personal disposal.'[5] There was, however, a considerable amount of property – furniture, art, jewellery – obtained by inheritance, gift, or purchase which the Queen and Prince Philip considered to be their own private property; the issue is so complex that if the monarchy was abolished tomorrow – which it would be if Tony Benn had his way – there is no one on earth who could say with any certainty what she would be allowed to take with her into exile. Two parliamentary investigations and the Queen's own Lord Chamberlain have failed to show just how it could or would be decided that the royal family actually owned one particular item but not another, except to state ambiguously that the description 'not alienable' covered all property and works of art in the Royal Collection purchased by all sovereigns up to the death of Queen Victoria and also including certain property acquired by sovereigns and their consorts since then.

The difference between ownership and custodianship of treasures like the Crown Jewels and a huge number of the works of art is clear-cut; they are national treasures. Equally, the Queen's ownership of much of the exquisite and substantial collection of jewellery amassed and bequeathed by Queen Alexandra and Queen Mary, for instance, can be established. Alexandra collected jewel-encrusted trinkets, bought with her own money, which today are worth a few millions. Queen Mary was a shrewd, if not ruthless, collector. One of her favourite ploys when visiting a household or staying with a foreign host was to say how very much she admired a certain object, and invariably it was gift-wrapped and presented to her on her departure, free of charge; in those houses she visited regularly hostesses were said to cry 'Hide the silver' before she arrived. She also purchased many fine pieces, including a large number of the Romanoff treasures brought to England after the massacre of the Russian imperial family, acquired by Queen Mary at knock-down prices from the penniless Romanoff cousins and now worth millions.

They became her own property, which she eventually bequeathed to her granddaughter. But who owns the jewellery which came flooding in as public wedding gifts to the future George V and Queen Mary in 1893 from the boroughs and shires of England? There was a diamond tiara from the county of Surrey, a diamond and platinum bow with a tremulous pendant pearl from the inhabitants of Kensington, a diamond bow from the county of Dorset, a diamond ring from the people of Windsor. These were all displayed alongside the family presents such as a diamond necklace from the Duke of Westminster, a sapphire and diamond bracelet from Tsar Nicholas of Russia, a sapphire and diamond brooch from the Tsarina Alexandra.

Also debatable is the ownership of 'gifts' made personally to the monarchy, such as those legendary handfuls of priceless emeralds, diamonds and rubies bestowed upon them by Indian princes and maharajahs. At the Delhi durbar for the Coronation of the King Emperor, 135 ruling princes all came bearing gifts. First was a prince who gave the king a ruby necklace in which each ruby was the size of a pigeon's egg. His Highness of Panna brought an umbrella for his throne which was at least 12 inches in diameter and was carved out of a single piece of emerald from his emerald mine. The Duke of Windsor, when he was King, clearly believed they were his own because he gave a large number of the Indian stones to Wallis Simpson; some were found scattered on Sunningdale golf course in 1946, dropped by a thief who had just stolen her jewellery pouch from the country house she was visiting.

This ambivalent attitude towards royal gems is perhaps no better seen than in their ownership of the famous Cullinan diamond. The stone, named after the owner of the mine from which it came, was an unimaginable 3,025 carats when it was found and weighed 1½ pounds. It was presented to Edward VII by the government of South Africa as a peace offering at the end of the Boer War and 'proudly accepted on behalf of myself and my successors' in spite of Lord Esher's advice to the King not to take the gift. It was cut into two principal stones: the first part, Cullinan One, was named the Greater Star of Africa, and was set in the head of the Sceptre and the Cross; the second part, Cullinan Two, was set in the

Imperial State Crown and both form part of the Crown Jewels displayed in the Tower of London.

Nine 'chips' from the Cullinan diamond remained in the hands of the Dutch firm of jewellers as their fee for cutting the original stone in the first place. Edward VII bought one of the chips, the Marquise stone, and presented it to his wife Queen Alexandra the year before he died, and this stone was subsequently inherited by Queen Mary. The Transvaal government purchased the remainder and presented them to Queen Mary in 1910. Thus the entire Cullinan diamond came into the possession of the British royal family and they would doubtless claim direct ownership of all but the first two parts which form part of the Crown Jewels. The fourth and fifth cleavings were formed into a brooch and this single item of jewellery, made from just two of the chips, is now conservatively valued at between £8 million and £10 million, not counting royal prestige value. And of course all the remaining stones are also still in their possession.

Valuations are virtually impossible because no one can really assess the historical worth or appeal. The Duchess of Windsor's jewels were, for instance, expected by the experts to make £5 million at the most – and ended up fetching almost £32 million; and hers was a tiny, paltry collection compared with those of the real House of Windsor. Buckingham Palace vaults are filled with tiaras, necklaces, brooches, rings and pendants; some have not been taken out for years.

While the two parts of the Cullinan diamond in the Crown Jewels cannot, as Lord Cobbold pointed out to the Civil List inquirers, be alienated, the Queen would claim ownership of the remainder. Thus royal stewardship of the collections of national treasure hides the family's own personal mountain of trinkets whose value, on the basis of Wallis's sale, must run into a figure in excess of £250 million. When the assessment is extended to art, porcelain, furniture and precious metal treasures both in their personal ownership and in their custodianship, the result is a mind-boggling confusion. The complete list of their collections of antique furniture runs to seventy-five leather-bound volumes stored at Windsor Castle.

Their art collections run side by side with the inherited

paintings of centuries of British monarchy. The Queen Mother has built up a small collection of French Impressionists. The Queen's own art collection is substantial and includes many fine works which individually value at millions of pounds. Between them they possess well in excess of 35,000 paintings and drawings representing works by virtually all the masters.

In addition to the inherited wealth and treasures, the Queen and Prince Philip have been given literally thousands of gifts since their engagement. One of the finest was the Williamson 23 carat pink diamond brooch, given to the Queen by a Tanzanian diamond mine owner in 1947. And as in the days of the Indian princes, the Arabs have been exceedingly generous to British royalty. When the Queen and Philip last went to the Gulf, they brought back over £1 million worth of gifted jewellery including an 18 inch gold palm tree decorated with rubies, a golden horse encrusted with diamonds, a pearl and diamond necklace from the Emir of Qatar and a golden sword with mother-of-pearl scabbard for Philip. Importantly, what these gifts do show is that royal wealth is not just a matter of property and landed estates and investment portfolios. It is based on personal and public gifts received as a mark of esteem and respect for monarchy – plus more than a touch of sycophancy – built up in less than 150 years, gifts which if accepted by an American President or his First Lady would be taxable.

As far as bricks and mortar are concerned, the Select Committee of 1971 accepted that 'the Sandringham and Balmoral estates are the personal property of the Queen' even though it is known from public records that both properties were bought with money saved from the Civil List. The committee also accepted that some contribution towards staffing should be made since when in residence the Queen continued her official duties, with her necessary staff around her.

So, while the Queen's wealth alone is always sufficient to generate a fair degree of comment and examination whenever the subject is mentioned, which seems to be annually in that popular pastime of financial voyeurism, the nation is entitled to be given some idea, inasmuch as the taxpayers are themselves being asked to contribute something like £160 million a year towards the upkeep of the royal family. Inevitably, the question is asked, 'What do they do for their money?' and the second question is, 'Are they worth it?'

The questions are invariably posed in the collective, because only the most ardent republican would try to argue in Britain today that the monarchy serves no useful purpose and should be scrapped in favour of a presidential constitution or some other form of democracy which does not include a crowned head. Tony Benn has been writing a bill to this effect for some time, but realistically knows that it does not stand the earthliest hope of getting anywhere near a vote in the foreseeable future, and certainly not whilst the present Queen is alive. Opinion polls, regularly held over the past two decades, have never shown any great swing towards it, apart from the occasional blip in the royal popularity ratings. Even the republican movements in Australia and Canada, which came to the fore in the early eighties, have faded in their ardour and the general consensus seems to agree that the monarchy will survive there, too, well into the next century.

However, while the Queen's personal position, and the monarchy itself, seems safe for the time being, there has been, everywhere, a definite trend towards public disquiet about the wealth and privilege afforded to members of the Queen's family. It is here that a case against the broad-based system of monarchy that now exists through the multi-stranded royal family begins to show signs of reasoned argument. It comes back once again to the numbers of them in the public eye, doing what they do at such high profile, even down to the houses they live in. Are they earning their keep? Do we really need them? These questions are being asked with increasing frequency, especially on the campuses and among the young people, not necessarily of a leftish disposition.

Once there were few royal houses known to the public, apart from the Queen's. Today everyone knows that Prince Charles's house in Gloucestershire is worth £4 or £5 million and has a very large double bed in which, if the tabloids are to be believed, he sleeps alone, and that Princess Anne's Gatcombe Park, bought for her by the Queen for £750,000 (with the additional acreage), is now worth £2.5 million and in exchange for an undisclosed sum Captain Mark Phillips has signed away any rights to it.

The Duke and Duchess of York have built, on land provided by the Queen and with her financial assistance, their modern palace of varieties which has been nicknamed 'South York', a £5 million Berkshire adobe filled with chintz, mahogany and marble. We have even seen inside the duchess's boudoir, courtesy of a newspaper which published some dubiously obtained photographs, and the place was warmed with a £20,000 champagne party with a notable guest list which betrays their personal taste, including Elton John, Billy Connolly and Pamela Stephenson. The Yorks even allowed *Hello!* magazine the courtesy of a sickeningly sycophantic exclusive interview, accompanied by forty-eight pages of photographs for which any payment to themselves was denied. Later, the *Daily Telegraph*'s Peterborough column, not renowned for spreading idle gossip, claimed that much of the £240,000 fee for this exclusive found its way to the duchess's recently widowed mother. Further trouble arose when it was revealed that the task of providing a round-the-clock guard on the Yorks' home was costing Thames Valley police an extra £1 million a year – in spite of the fact that they were hardly ever there!

It is the collective impact that causes the wonderment, that perhaps the Queen's family is enjoying too much fat of the land, and there would be no harm in curbing it, especially when most of the nation's housebuyers are struggling to pay their own mortgages.

This criticism was especially inspired – that is, 'Are they earning their keep?' – in July 1990 when Mrs Margaret Thatcher announced that the government was changing the system under which the Civil List allowances were paid. Instead of the annual review in line with inflation, payment was reverting to that recommended by the Select Committee in 1971, whereby an annual figure would be fixed for the next ten years. The immediate effect was to increase the Queen's own Civil List payment from £5.09 million a year to £7.9 million. The rest of the payments were fixed at £640,000 a year for the Queen Mother (compared with £439,500); £360,000 for Prince Philip (£245,000); £250,000 for Prince Andrew (£169,000); £100,000 for Prince Edward (£20,000); £230,000 for the Princess Royal (£154,000); £220,000 for Princess Margaret (£148,500); £90,000 for Princess Alice,

Duchess of Gloucester; £630,000 to be shared between the Duke of Gloucester, the Duke of Kent and Princess Alexandra.

The new allowances came into effect on 1 January 1991 and had a built-in efficiency clause which sought to commit Buckingham Palace to annual savings through better management, although it had already been judged that the organisation of the monarchy – from a purely business point of view – had been keenly costed and professionally operated. If at the end of the decade, there was a surplus, the money would be offset against the level set for the following ten years.

It was actually a common-sense solution to the annual problem of 'giving the Queen a rise'. Yet it was not without its critics and there is some justification in the most popular squeals: 'What does Princess Margaret do for a living?', 'How do the Duke and Duchess of York justify £250,000?', 'Prince Edward's Really Useful £100,000?', which prompts the temptation to examine the workloads as a method of justifying the expenses for the Queen and her family. For this, we must turn to the log-book of Mr Tim O'Donovan, a London insurance broker, who spends his spare time each week analysing the Court Circular published daily in *The Times* and drawing up his own league table of performance. He has been keeping his records since 1979, and the number of engagements undertaken by the royal family has increased substantially, in some cases almost double. For the last available year's log,[6] the Princess Royal was by far the busiest; she accepts a huge diary commitment – workaholic status – undertaking 768 engagements during 1990, 319 of which were made in the course of overseas visits. The Queen had another busy year, with 570 engagements, including 94 abroad, while the Duke of Edinburgh carried out 554 jobs, 260 abroad. The Prince of Wales performed 389 engagements (144), the Princess of Wales, 323 (89), while the Duke and Duchess of York had a fairly unimpressive total of 137 between them which was even fewer than Prince Edward's 219 and Princess Margaret's 152.

In the lower ranks, the tasks the royal family perform are not especially onerous and many of the listed engagements may last only a matter of minutes in length – a hello, a goodbye and a handshake for a palace audience. Most are hidebound by protocol which only the Princess Royal seems capable of casting aside. This caused a particular problem in recent incidents of national disaster and international emergencies, and it highlighted once again the problems the Queen had in dealing with a Prime Minister who was doing many of the things normally expected of the monarch or senior members of the family.

No one in Mrs Thatcher's Cabinet would have expected her to take a backseat in such matters; it had always been her style to be there, at the forefront of national grief or tragedy in which multiple deaths occurred, offering her condolences and talking to the survivors. In the latter half of the eighties, there were twelve major disasters which attracted international attention. Among them were the Bradford football stadium fire in which 56 people died in May 1985, the Manchester air crash also in that year which claimed 55 lives, the *Herald of Free Enterprise* sinking in which 188 lost their lives, the Enniskillen poppy day massacre by the IRA (11 dead), the Kings Cross underground fire (31), the Piper Alpha oil rig fire (167), the Clapham rail crash (33) and the Lockerbie air crash (270). In all twelve of the disasters, Mrs Thatcher was either on the scene or at the hospitals within hours, sometimes already in her car before news had even reached Buckingham Palace.

Historically, members of the royal family have always been the link between the people and the government in expressing concern and sympathy, while the politicians spoke their words of condolence in parliament and made their promises of action and inquiry. While Buckingham Palace was going through the motions of protocol, finding gaps in schedules, arranging transport, informing Scotland Yard for security cover and notifying the Lord Lieutenant of each county through which the royals would pass, Mrs Thatcher was already on her way. She was in attendance within hours at all twelve instances surveyed, while members of the royal family went to only nine. On occasions, the palace has short-circuited protocol to get a member of the family to the scene as quickly as possible; they beat Mrs Thatcher to only two, the Enniskillen bomb attack and the Lockerbie air disaster, although in the latter case only because Prince Andrew happened to be on a ship close to the scene. One courtier said:

> There was no point in trying to explain the Queen's position to Mrs Thatcher or even requesting her to hold back. She seemed to make a point of it, being there and also being seen to be there. She was doing the job of royalty; it was up to them to come and offer comfort, sympathy and soothing words, not a politician. I'm sure she did it for no other motive than caring, but too often it looked as if she was there on a self-promotional exercise, scoring party political points in front of the television cameras.[7]

But could Mrs Thatcher really be blamed? She clearly wanted to make an immediate personal show of sympathy. The royal family could hardly complain if their advisers had not alerted them quickly enough to be there; in this day and age, when the symbol of monarchy is one of the few poignant aspects of it to survive, their performance through these events could only be described as lacklustre. The Lockerbie disaster was especially disappointing. First, to allow Prince Andrew anywhere near the scene was a mistake. His bluff and blustering character and youthful zest was not the kind of royal presence so patently required for a small community in shock. It needed a naturally sensitive person, calm and soft, preferably a husband and wife team, offering the kind of attention Prince Andrew is incapable of providing. Secondly, not a single member of the royal family went to the memorial service, unwilling, we were told, to break off prior engagements – though most were on their sacrosanct holidays.

And so, through these incidents of unfortunate backwardness, the Queen has seen her family criticised for not attending to matters which cried out for royalty, and at the end of the day there was no answer to the complaint that Mrs Thatcher was stealing their thunder. It is in this area of performing their public duties that the Queen's advisers might rescue her from further criticism by ensuring that all the royal family's engagements, from the Queen downwards, are given a positive and frank vetting. If the calls upon their time are such that they are prevented from undertaking work of a more caring, productive nature – very much on the lines of the Princess Royal's approach – then some drastic pruning might well be necessary to allow for a substantive re-think on the kind of work they all undertake. The issue was raised again, in strikingly similar vein, at the beginning of 1991, when the family's organisers were incredibly slow on the uptake to rearrange diaries and cancel frivolous engagements in the run-up to the inevitable outbreak of hostilities against Iraq; once again, a collection of royal incidents came together to provide cause for comment. As the nation's armed forces stood on the brink of combat, the Duchess of York was widely photographed on continental ski slopes, returned only after hostilities had commenced, and even then was seen attending her woman-about-town functions with her friends; the Duke of York, who is colonel-in-chief of the Staffordshire Regiment, was aboard ship in the Mediterranean and just before war broke out was to be found full of high spirits, enjoying two or three days' golf in sunny Spain. Princess Margaret's son Lord Linley appeared on the front page of the *Sun* after attending a fancy dress party wearing strange clothes and red lipstick and then flew off to his mother's holiday home on the isle of Mustique, while Prince Philip and Prince Charles attended to the urgent annual business of culling the Sandringham pheasant population. Added to that was the confession of Lord Althorp, the Queen's godson and brother of the Princess of Wales, to Nigel Dempster that he'd had a brief but adulterous encounter with a model not many months after his marriage, a disclosure which naturally ran and ran in the papers. The royal follies encouraged Andrew Neil, editor of the *Sunday Times*, to once more take the royal family to task. 'The Queen needs urgently to summon the royals to Windsor for a chapel meeting,' he wrote in an editorial on 10 February.

> This country is at war, though you would never believe it from the shenanigans of some members of Her Majesty's clan. As usual, it is not the most important members of the royal family whose behaviour has been less than we have a right to expect, though the performance of even the inner circle since hostilities broke out has hardly been faultless . . . Britain's armed forces stand on the brink of the biggest land battle since the second world war, a battle in which some of the

> nation's finest young men and women are expected to risk their lives. Yet on the home front, too many young royals and their entourages carry on regardless with their peacetime lifestyles, parading a mixture of upper-class decadence and insensitivity . . . the Queen should put a stop to it.

Neil, having set the ball rolling, was himself attacked by his colleagues at the *Sun* who put the spotlight on his own nocturnal activities, which produced an amusing reversal of roles to show that this was no stage-managed attack on the royals by Rupert Murdoch. In fact Neil said on television that Murdoch did not know anything about it when challenged by the Queen's staunch defender, Lord St John of Fawsley (the former Norman St John Stevas), on *Newsnight*.[8]

Neil was attacked from several quarters, but eventually others fell in line behind him as the opinion polls which followed tended to show that the public agreed with him. And it all became a sort of link-up of poll gripes: the *Independent on Sunday*, which normally hates even mentioning royalty, discovered from a NMR poll that 80 per cent felt the royal family should pay income tax; a Mori poll in the *Daily Mail* showed 47 per cent were unhappy with the behaviour of the Duchess of York and 53 per cent said they were dissatisfied with Prince Edward's performance; a Mori poll for the *Sunday Times* found that 42 per cent thought the royals were an expensive luxury the nation could ill afford, compared with 24 per cent the previous year.

The figures confirmed that there was disquiet abroad in the nation; freak times produce a healthy upsurge of republicanism which would never stick when it came to the crunch. It has always been there, latent and below the surface. Young people have seldom agreed with the sentimentalism of their parents over royalty – and then, before long the young are parents themselves and they too get caught up in the nostalgia and go for the survival of the monarchy. Each generation warms to them and at the turn of the 1990s more than half the population of Great Britain cannot remember a time when the Queen has not been there – the great mother of the nation, as Lech Walesa described her. Mrs Margaret

Thatcher, towards the end of her own reign, swept aside any past differences, unadmitted though they were, and confirmed with characteristic insistence, 'The vast majority of people in this country regard the royal family as the greatest asset that the United Kingdom possesses and greatly admire everything the Queen does.'[9]

Mrs Thatcher knew from the statistics that the monarchy, in spite of the rising costs, probably still comes out to the good when invisible earnings from tourism and trade encouragement are added to the revenue from the Crown Estates. The fact that Mrs Thatcher relentlessly used the family as super salespersons is, in the final analysis, a sign that overseas there is now not a lot more that they can do, except continue their ambassadorial roles, promoting trade and political goodwill. The monarch's journeys through the empire have been replaced by the Queen's jetting to the Commonwealth, and this is becoming increasingly difficult to sustain other than for the purely internal reasons of the Commonwealth administration. The view from Buckingham Palace rejects the theory that all that is left abroad are the trade missions, even though they have had to arrange countless seminars on board the royal yacht. The press office has defined their work as follows,

> The royal household does not primarily undertake its duties with an eye on publicity or public relations spin-off. The royal family certainly attracts a great deal of publicity domestically and internationally. The household's role is to support the monarch in her duties and responsibilities. Those duties are to serve the nation's interests in public life, socially, commercially and culturally at home and overseas.[10]

To admit to deliberate promotional work, or to agree that the Queen's ceremonial spectaculars are primarily an excellent draw for tourists, would devalue the cause. The monarchy must retain its dignity, and its mystery.

And there has been a further development. The Queen began her fortieth year under the new regime of John Major, her ninth Prime Minister and the eleventh administration of her reign. The son of a circus performer, Major maintained that his goal was a classless Britain and, should he not stay in office long enough to achieve it, the Labour leader Neil Kinnock promised much the same thing. In either case, the monarchy would remain an integral part of their plans, the epitome of a democratic and constantly changing society. The Queen has been assured of this by both leaders.

Change has been the keynote of her reign. It had to be over a 40 year period and while change arrived incessantly, there is surprisingly little new in life's challenges. The monotonous repetition of all that she does, even says, is recalled only by casting an eye back through the years. Even the criticism is the same. In the thirties, it was the sex scandals of Dickie and Edwina Mountbatten, the Duke of Kent and the Prince of Wales that kept society agog. In the fifties and sixties, the Queen became the unprecedented focus for the adulatory worship as Diana did in the eighties, while Prince Philip, Princess Margaret, Lord Snowdon and the Windsors provided the spicy headlines in between. The mixture is simply as before, but more of it, and appears to have done no lasting harm. The performing monarchy continues, trivialised, brutalised and thoroughly sensationalised, but as long as the sovereign retains the traditions and the respect, does it matter that some of the lesser royals have a comportment problem? It does. There are too many of them, getting into too many publicity scrapes. They ought to be slimmed down in terms of media exposure. What they need is a strong press office and a constant jab from public relations advisers to curb their own excesses, if only to ward off the trivialisation and the prurient.

Life would be dull without them, but the royal juggernaut has rolled so far now that it is by and large out of control; its destiny is already decided and we, the subjects and the audience, wait to see its fate. What will it be? Continuation, more of the same *ad infinitum*, following the cyclical behaviourial patterns which have occurred like clockwork since George III? Or a sad farewell when the public finally tires of them in the next reign or the one after that?

With the exception of the Queen and Princess Anne, the rest of the family often look and act more like showbusiness people, and mix with them, too. But some may argue that

that is what is required in this day and age; that the prophets of doom who say that familiarity breeds contempt and that eventually the monarchy will drift off into a sea of obscurity, are overlooking the fact that this has been threatened for several decades now.

The Princess of Wales is likely to remain what she has become since she married into the royal family – a decorous superstar and the royal family's second greatest asset after the Queen and its best hope for the future. The world is her stage, yet she need not speak a word. She works very hard and is taking up worthwhile causes, much in the Anne mould but more as a figurehead than an involved worker. The Duchess of York required reining in because she, especially, had yet to learn the meaning of the word dignity or to show compassion. Princess Michael had already been calmed. The men remain a problem as the Queen reaches her fortieth anniversary. Prince Andrew best serves the nation aboard ship and there are those who feel it would be nicer still if he handed back some of the unwanted £250,000 he receives from the Civil List. Prince Edward is not a rebel, but he desperately needs a cause of supreme worthiness to occupy his mind, or a proper job in the outside world. Charles can do little else than wait for his mother to retire or die. From his point of view, the signs point to a long wait for his coronation. The Windsor women make a habit of longevity and her retirement is unlikely. Those who have speculated on the Queen's abdication in favour of Charles wasted their words. They reckoned she might do it when she was 55, and they reckoned she might do it when she was 60 and again when she was 65. No one knows; but there are two clues. First she hates the word 'abdication' and knows that it could not be masked even by 'retirement'; secondly, it will be recalled that on the twenty-fifth anniversary of her accession, she reiterated the pledge she made to the nation and the Commonwealth in the broadcast she made from South Africa on her twenty-first birthday – that she would serve them all her days. That, as Prince Philip once pointed out to an over-enthusiastic reporter, means until death.

Attitudes change and have changed dramatically in the Queen's lifetime and reign. It could well be that she will consider her position after completing 50 years, by which time

Charles would be 54 and the Queen would still be only 75, but the more likely scenario is the age-old one: 'The Queen is Dead, Long Live the King' and for that Charles may have to wait quite a while longer, perhaps until his late sixties. This prospect was confirmed on Christmas Day 1991, when the Queen made reference to her future intent in her speech to the Commonwealth. In a single sentence she reaffirmed her dedication to serve her people for 'years to come' and once again the spotlight was thrown on this deeply significant aspect of the monarchy for the nineties and beyond.

There was immediate reaction to her speech, with the popular newspapers speculating on what role Prince Charles would assume beyond middle age. For a man already bursting with the frustration of being his mother's son, her Christmas message merely emphasised what he already knew too well, that he must remain in her shadow and in his wilderness of good works and fancy dress, enlivening the boredom of undemanding tasks with occasional self-created controversies.

The problem is that as heir to the constitutional monarchy he must stay on the periphery of the real world, facing endless lines of hands to shake and people to meet, putting on a brave face and making the best of a difficult job which, as we have seen, was the ruination of some of his predecessors. Perhaps the most loaded question in some establishment quarters is whether he will stay the course. There are so many imponderables, not least of which has been his private life. But it goes much deeper than just *his* position. It may well be that the Queen feels that she herself must remain on the throne, solid as a rock as her family confronts some of the challenges of the changing world that she also referred to in her Christmas Day message.

Not least of them is her nation's declining influence in Commonwealth affairs, and indeed this whole question flared up with totally unexpected fervour when the Queen travelled to Australia for her fortieth anniversary tour in February 1992. She walked straight into a veritable hornets' nest and had to take the brunt of a situation which did not really concern her directly. She knew, of course, that the Australian Labour Party is pledged to taking the country towards independence by the year 2000, though the previous Prime Minister, Bob Hawke, once a fairly committed republican, mellowed during his years of contact with the Queen. But by the time she arrived for the tour, Hawke had been ousted and Paul Keating, aggressively republican, had taken over. More than that, he was looking for votes and support to sustain him in office and his speech to the Australian parliament made it all too plain that he was going to use the Queen's visit to sharpen his grip on his new job. The scene was set when his wife did not curtsy to the Queen on her arrival. Keating himself was noted to breach protocal by putting his arm around the Queen as he introduced her to a line of dignitaries.

Then came the broadside. The time had come, he said, when Australia should stop 'doffing our lid or tugging our forelock to anyone'. He criticised Britain for turning its back on its staunchest ally by its trade agreements in Europe, leaving its long-time Commonwealth partner with the task of re-establishing its world trading position. This it had done, with 75 per cent of the nation's trade now concentrated in the Asia–Pacific region. 'We have to be aggressively Australian and proud of it,' he said.

Worse, Keating raised the controversial issue of whether Britain had left Australia to fend for itself in the face of a possible Japanese invasion during the war. The whole row flared for days, and the Queen was left looking positively put out. Even before the row, an opinion poll showed that 57 per cent of Australians would prefer to live in a republic. Only four years earlier, it was 45 per cent – and now the writing is clearly on the wall.

Back home, there was also a withering of respect as the Queen headed towards the anniversary. It is barely possible to imagine the uproar that would have been caused not many years ago by the Channel Four television series called 'Pallas' which consisted of a series of real film footage of the royal family, to which fictitious dialogue had been added. The technique showed how easy it was to poke fun at the sheer banality of Prince Charles's curious life and times.

To give him his due, he has tackled his job as best he could. He works hard, has given patronage to many worthwhile causes and launched fine charitable causes such as the Prince's Trust. He travels the world as ambassador for Britain. These tasks are unending but not especially demanding for a man of his ability and experience in affairs of state. He sought the help of panels of experts and think-tanks and risked heavy criticism when he commented upon the likes of architecture and education. Yet very quickly he faced the same fate that his father met when he went down the same road of trying to liven up proceedings with controversy – not many people listen to him any more. His credibility will diminish as the years pass.

Therein lies his key problem – public image. It may be recalled that the old and dour servant of the Queen, Commander Richard Colville said on his retirement in 1968, 'If there comes a time when the British monarchy ever needs a real public relations officer, the institution of monarchy in this country will be in very serious danger'. But the PR age is upon them and not long before the Queen's anniversary, Prince Charles appointed the young whizz kid PR executive Belinda Harley to his staff. Eyebrows were raised. Questions were asked among royal observers whether this had any significance.

This in a way confirms what I learned in May 1991 that Buckingham Palace – meaning the Queen – was anxious about her son's public image, especially following a further bout of damaging headlines about the state of his marriage and some uncomplimentary words about his qualifications to speak on subjects such as education. It was hoped that in the months ahead, Prince Charles could be shown in a good and fair light by the media, to reflect the work he does for his various causes and to demonstrate that he has an ability which is greater than some have given him credit for; indeed it was the author's information that two newspaper executives had been called to the palace to discuss this very topic, and to secretly glean their advice on the future.

Soon afterwards, the favoured journalist, Sir Peregrine Worsthorne, former editor of the *Sunday Telegraph*, also made the remarkable suggestion in his diary column in the *Daily Telegraph* in May 1991 that Prince Charles might consider renouncing his right to the succession as a 'way out' of his dilemma – thus releasing him from the constraints of protocol and allowing him to take up more meaningful tasks in life. This is a very valid solution to a good many problems confronting Prince Charles and the only way that he could involve himself in politically dangerous areas. By renouncing the throne, Charles could devote his working days to demanding causes, leaving the nation to look forward in due course to the succession of a fresh young monarch, William, rather than the familiar – and by then, possibly tired and aged – face of Prince Charles himself.

Whether as the continuing heir apparent or as Regent to his son, there is already plenty that Charles could get stuck into. He could start by taking a fresh look at the palace and the Queen's household, which is still clogged by protocol, stiff with snobbery and awash with inherited arrogance; in that direction not a lot has changed and it needs knocking into shape for the next century. Though the Queen cleared a lot of the cobwebs away years ago, the underlying problem is that attitudes within the palace are so strictly bound by conformity to tradition, that apart from computerisation and such modernising techniques, little has progressed these past two decades. They are still living in the past and, in some respects, so is the Queen. The last years of her own reign could be bolstered by some clever thinking by her son to replace the *modus operandi* thought out by Prince Philip and Mountbatten, which is now both dated and dangerous. She needs a few sparkling years to give her reign a true ring of glory.

The Queen needs this kind of new thinking to save the monarchy from slumping to its lowest ebb, overburdened by a constant need to compensate against over-exposure and showbiz-style trivia, and it should start among those around her. She alone, scandal free, unstinting and selflessly devoted, has carried her family and the nation on her shoulders for forty years and has often succeeded in spite of them. She has deserved better support, even from those closest to her, and to use her own analogy of casting a stone into a pond and watching the ripples, it is from this inner circle that some of the ripples have grown. The strength of the Queen and the reliance that is placed upon her from so many quarters of private and public life was never so evident than in a new film about her, screened by the BBC as part of the fortieth anniversary celebrations. It came twenty-four years after Richard Cawston's 'Royal Family' was shown and this time director Edward Mirzoeff's 105-minute documentary made no less impact. The Queen allowed a six-man BBC film crew to follow her around for almost a year for what Mirzoeff described as classic fly-on-the-wall television. The film was another royal milestone, taking viewers into areas never previously seen, such as the audiences with her prime minister. Bearing in mind what happened after the last programme, when the intrusion into private royal lives increased, the Queen had shown a degree of courage in allowing herself to be 'brought up to date'.

But perhaps that sums her up. She can only be admired for her iron will that pervades throughout the House of Windsor, the nation and the Commonwealth. There is no point in a valediction; it would sound immensely sycophantic. What has gone before in the forty incredible years of her reign, packaged together with her mercurial family, speaks for itself. They were tumultuous years; she came to the throne a young, shy, inexperienced slip of a girl when Britain was impoverished by war and its great days were said to be over. Her years have been littered with gloomy forecasts, indifferent politicians and a dozen national plans which never worked. She alone has held the Commonwealth together, in spite of itself and some of the alleged national leaders whom she has encountered on the way. She has seen international statesmen come and go, some in spectacular fashion through assassination, scandal, lying and sheer incompetence.

The Queen is still there and at the point of this interim report, there is every sign that her reign will eventually be recognised as a New Elizabethan Age comparable with the first.

Elizabeth II will go down in history as a great Queen of England – and perhaps the last.

Appendix 1
Royal Income and Expenditure

Royal Income

More than ninety per cent of the cost of official duties of the royal family is met by individual government departments, including, for example, the running of the royal yacht *Britannia*, the Queen's Flight, travel by train, security services, the upkeep of the royal palaces and state visits overseas. The remainder is financed through the grant the Queen and her family receive through the annual Civil List payment.

The Queen's finances are derived from three main sources. First, the Queen's Civil List, a payment from public funds approved by Parliament, finances the costs of running the Royal Household and other expenses incurred in the course of her official duties as head of state. Secondly, the Privy Purse, financed from the revenues of the Duchy of Lancaster, which in 1990 were around £2.75 million a year, which goes to meet the cost of private expenditure including the maintenance of the Queen's private residences at Sandringham in Norfolk and Balmoral in Scotland, charitable subscriptions and donations, and staff welfare and amenities. The Privy Purse has also met Civil List deficits in the past, and contributes to the official expenses of other members of the royal family. Finally, the Queen's personal expenditure as a private individual is met from her own personal resources obtained from her inherited wealth, savings and investments.

The Duchy of Lancaster comprises some 52,000 acres,

mostly of farmland and moorland. The royal palaces, together with the Crown Jewels and the royal collections of art, stamps and books, are vested in the Queen as Sovereign but cannot be alienated; they must be passed on to her successor. They are therefore not her personal property. There are also many other items – for example, some of the jewellery and personal collections – which the Queen regards as heirlooms and are at her free personal disposal.

The Crown Estate, comprising properties throughout Great Britain, traditionally belongs to the Sovereign 'in right of the Crown', and is quite separate from her personal property. Under the Crown Estate Act 1961 management of the estate is the responsibility of commissioners appointed by the Sovereign on the advice of the Prime Minister. An annual report on the estate is submitted to Parliament. The land revenues from the Crown Estates Commissioners for the year ended 31 March 1990 totalled £101 million, of which £57 million went to the Exchequer after expenses and salaries.

The basic Civil List is paid automatically by the Treasury under an Act of Parliament. In exchange, the Sovereign surrenders to the Exchequer the revenue from the Crown Estate and certain other revenues. Over the centuries there has been a continuous process of change in the arrangement of the finances of the monarchy. Until 1760 the Sovereign had to provide for the payment of all expenses of government, including the salaries of judges, ambassadors, civil servants, and the expenses of the royal palaces and households. For this purpose the Sovereign had available hereditary revenues comprising income from Crown lands and from other sources such as prerogative rights of treasure trove, of royal mines, of royal fish and swans and from certain ecclesiastical sources such as tithes or the income of bishoprics during a vacancy. In addition, Parliament granted the Sovereign the income from some customs duties, from certain assigned taxes (for example, those on beer and cider), and the Post Office revenues.

The income from these sources eventually proved inadequate and, when King George III acceded to the throne, he turned over to the government most of his revenues and received in return an annual grant (Civil List) from which he continued to pay royal expenditure of a personal character and also the salaries of the Civil Service, judges and ambassadors, and certain pensions. This in turn proved insufficient, and in 1830 these extra costs were removed and the Civil List grant was reduced. Present arrangements for the payment of the Civil List derive from the Civil Lists Acts 1972 and 1975, and the Civil List (Increase of Financial Provision) Order 1975.

The Queen's Civil List covers expenditure on the salaries and expenses of the Royal Household (staff of the Royal Household are almost entirely paid and pensioned on a basis analogous to that in the Civil Service), and the royal bounty, alms and special services. About three-quarters of the Civil List provision is required to meet the salaries of the staff who deal among other things with state papers and correspondence, the organisation of state occasions, visits and other public engagements in the United Kingdom and overseas, and arrangements for the interviews and investitures undertaken by the Queen.

The Civil List Act 1972 fixed the Queen's Civil List at a figure thought sufficient to cover expenditure for a period of about five years, but because of inflation Parliament increased the Queen's Civil List to £1.4 million in 1975 and the Queen contributed a sum of £150,000 from her own resources. The amount payable to some members of the royal family was increased at the same time.

In view of these developments and the continuing pressure of inflation, settling the amount of the Civil List by legislation at relatively infrequent intervals was no longer practical, so the Civil List Act 1975 established a system whereby payments were adjusted annually. This system remained until 1990. The payment of pensions to retired staff of the Royal Household was also taken over by the Treasury. The current payments, originally set to last ten years, may be adjusted if they are deemed to be insufficient.

The Queen receives	£7,900,000
The Queen Elizabeth the Queen Mother	£640,000
The Duke of Edinburgh	£360,000
The Duke of York	£250,000
The Princess Anne	£230,000
The Princess Margaret	£220,000

The Prince Edward	£100,000
Princess Alice, Duchess of Gloucester	£90,000
The Duke of Gloucester (share) The Duke of Kent (share) The Princess Alexandra (share)	£630,000

The Prince and Princess of Wales draw their income from the Duchy of Cornwall – about 125,000 acres in south-west England and London. At the age of twenty-one the present Prince of Wales became entitled to the whole of the net revenues but he undertook voluntarily to surrender one-half to the Exchequer; this was reduced to a quarter upon his marriage. In 1991, he received an income of around £3 million from the duchy's funds.

Taxation

As part of the royal prerogative the Queen is not liable to pay tax – either on her private wealth and income, or on the Queen's Civil List – unless Parliament decides otherwise. This immunity extends to income from the Duchy of Lancaster which goes untouched into the Queen's personal accounts.

The income and property of the Duchy of Cornwall are similarly exempt from income tax, capital gains tax and capital transfer tax. The Prince of Wales's estate, valued in 1990 at around £275 million, remains unthreatened by taxation. He had a substantial share portfolio, said to be worth £20 million. Any other income or property of the Prince of Wales is liable to taxation in the ordinary way as though it were his total income or property. Annual annuities payable under the Civil List Act 1972 to named members of the royal family are exempt from income tax either wholly or in part, to the extent that they are used to meet official expenses incurred in carrying out public duties, but their private income is taxed.

Payments made by the Royal Trustees to cover the official expenses of other members of the royal family, in accordance with normal taxation practice, do not rank as income for tax purposes.

Departmental Votes

Other expenditure arising from the official duties of the royal family is borne by departmental votes. The costs of the royal yacht *Britannia* and of the Queen's Flight of aircraft are met by the Ministry of Defence. Travel by train on official business by the royal family and staff of the Royal Household is paid for by the Department of the Environment. Other items of expenditure met by government departments include the cost of official travel overseas, stationery and office equipment, and the provision of service equerries. Postal services are provided free of charge by the Post Office, but the cost of telecommunications is met by the Department of the Environment.

The Department of the Environment also has responsibility for the upkeep of the royal palaces: Buckingham Palace, Windsor Castle, St James's Palace, Hampton Court Palace, Kensington Palace, Kew Palace and the Palace of Holyroodhouse in Edinburgh. Of these, Buckingham Palace, Windsor Castle and the Palace of Holyroodhouse are state residences of the Sovereign. The cost of upkeep of the royal palaces in 1990 was £20 million.

At the Queen's private residences, Balmoral and Sandringham, however, the only costs met by the department are those for the fuel and electricity required when the court is in residence.

Buckingham Palace has been the London residence of the Sovereign since 1837. The present building was originally erected in the eighteenth century and was redesigned in 1825; it was refronted in Portland stone in 1913.

Windsor Castle has been a principal residence of the Sovereign for nearly 900 years. Built by William the Conqueror (reigned 1066–87) and extended in the fourteenth and fifteenth centuries, it was extensively restored by George IV (1820–30). Notable features are St George's Chapel (fifteenth and sixteenth centuries) and the State Apartments, containing many historic and artistic treasures.

The Sovereign's state residence in Scotland is the Palace of Holyroodhouse, built on the site of an abbey founded in 1128. The original early sixteenth-century royal palace was largely destroyed by Cromwell's soldiers in 1650 and the present building dates from the seventeenth century.

The importance in former times of St James's Palace in London is reflected in the fact that ambassadors of foreign states are still accredited to the Court of St James's.

Balmoral Castle was built by Queen Victoria and Prince Albert and first used as a royal residence in 1855.

The Sandringham estate was bought by Edward VII (then Prince of Wales) in 1863, and in 1871 the existing house was pulled down and replaced by one in red brick. Substantial alterations, considerably reducing the size of the house, were completed in the early 1970s.

Other departmental costs estimated for 1991 include: the royal yacht *Britannia* run by the Royal Navy, at an annual cost of £10 million, excluding refits every two to three years costing between £5 million and £10 million. The Queen's Flight, funded by the Ministry of Defence, has 180 officers and men on permanent attachment to operate the Queen's aircraft and helicopters, at an annual cost of around £12 million excluding replacement costs and other capital items. The royal train, financed by the Ministry of Transport, costs £1.2 million a year. Security and protection plus the royal bodyguards from the military, which now accounts for the largest slice of royal expenditure, is shared by the Home Office, the Defence Ministry and the Department of Environment, and is almost incalculable; a recent estimate put the figure at £100 million a year.

The Royal Household

Great Officers of State

The royal household was originally the centre of the system of government. The leading dignitaries of the palace – the Sovereign's closest advisers – were, by the nature of the executive power directly exercised by the monarch, also the principal administrators of the state. With the development of ministerial responsibility for executive acts, many of the leading members of the original royal household of England – the Lord Chancellor, the Lord President of the Council, the Lord Privy Seal and the Secretary of State (an office now divided between a number of ministers) – became members of the political administration and entirely divorced from household duties. The ancient office of Lord High Treasurer has been put in commission, while two other offices – those of the Lord High Steward and Lord High Constable – are now granted only for the single day of a coronation. While none of the Great Officers of State retains household functions, two (the Lord Great Chamberlain and the Earl Marshal) have continuous duties in connection with royal ceremonial.

The Lord Great Chamberlain

The office of Lord Great Chamberlain dates back to the reign of King Henry I (1100–35), when it was invested in the father of the first Earl of Oxford and his heirs. After that date it was held by his descendants up to the eighteenth century and has continued through the female line. At present, the Cholmondeley family holds the office every alternate reign, and the Ancaster and Carrington families each hold it every fourth reign. The Lord Great Chamberlain was originally head of the Sovereign's personal household and all royal palaces. Few of these duties are nowadays attached to the office, but the holder is responsible for the arrangements when the Sovereign attends Parliament, and at the coronation ceremony, when he stands on the left of the Sovereign in Westminster Abbey, fastens the clasp of the imperial mantle after investiture, and arrays the Sovereign in purple robes before the procession out of the Abbey.

Since each Lord Great Chamberlain enters upon his duties immediately a new reign begins, it falls upon him to make arrangements, in conjunction with the Department of the Environment, for the lying-in-state of the dead monarch at Westminster Hall.

The Earl Marshal

The office of Earl Marshal of England originated in the reign of King Henry I, and has been hereditary in the family of the Duke of Norfolk since 1672. The Earl Marshal is head of the College of Arms and has a supervisory status in relation to the Heralds in matters of ceremonial, titles, precedence and heraldry. He is also responsible for the arrangement of coronations, royal funerals and other state functions.

Officers of the Royal Household

Some offices of the household have become obsolete with the passage of time, and a few have been created comparatively recently to meet the requirements of the modern age. A number of them have, however, been retained in title since Plantagenet and Tudor times, although the duties attached to them now differ very greatly from those that had to be performed in the days of the peripatetic courts.

Although the ministerial holders of Great Offices of State (such as the Lord Chancellor and the Lord President of the Council) are no longer members of the royal household, certain officers in the present household have governmental, as well as household, duties to perform. Thus the Treasurer, Comptroller and Vice-Chamberlain of the Household all act as Government Whips in the House of Commons, and the Captain of the Gentlemen-at-Arms, the Captain of the Yeomen of the Guard and three of the five non-permanent Lords-in-Waiting act as Government Whips in the House of Lords. Although the Lord Chamberlain, Lord Steward, Master of the Horse and the non-political Lords-in-Waiting have, since 1924, been appointed by the personal choice of the Sovereign, they are appointed on condition that they do not vote against the government of the day in the House of Lords (of which they are all members).

The royal household consists of a number of departments and offices, each under a principal household officer.

The Lord Steward

For several centuries the Lord Steward was responsible for the management of the palace belowstairs, which covered the control of the catering arrangements for state banquets, courts and all other forms of royal entertaining, the appointment and supervision of those employed in the service of the Sovereign, and the payment of all household expenses. Nowadays, his functions in this respect are carried out by the department of the Master of the Household, who is a permanent officer. The Lord Steward, who receives his appointment from the Sovereign, still retains the titular authority and, on ceremonial occasions, he bears a white staff as emblem and warrant of his position.

The offices of Treasurer of the Household and the Comptroller of the Household, which are political appointments changing with a change of government, are by tradition under the Lord Steward.

The Coroner of the Household, who exercises jurisdiction

in the royal palaces and in any other places where the Sovereign may be staying, is appointed by the Lord Steward.

Lord Chamberlain

The Lord Chamberlain was originally a deputy of the Lord Great Chamberlain, but he later acquired independence of his superior and took over all ceremonial duties relating to the household as such. He is the senior officer of the household, and carries a white staff and wears a golden key on ceremonial occasions as a symbol of his office. The Lord Chamberlain is in charge of all court ceremonial, including all arrangements for royal weddings, for royal garden parties, for ceremonial connected with state visits to the United Kingdom and for communication with Commonwealth countries about ceremonial matters. He acts as the Queen's emissary to the House of Lords.

The other functions of the Lord Chamberlain include: carrying out the wishes of the Sovereign in the appointment of royal chaplains, royal physicians and surgeons, and other household officers; superintending the royal collection of works of art; and supervising the internal administration of certain of the royal residences. By tradition, the Vice-Chamberlain is the deputy of the Lord Chamberlain. Nowadays his appointment, like that of the Treasurer and the Comptroller, is a political one and he takes no part in the work of the Lord Chamberlain's office. During parliamentary sessions the Vice-Chamberlain sends to the Queen a daily confidential report on parliamentary proceedings.

The Lord Chamberlain's office consists of: the Comptroller and his staff, who assist the Lord Chamberlain in the supervision of the household and the preparation of the ceremonies for which he is responsible; the Gentleman Usher of the Black Rod, who is the Principal Usher in the kingdom, and has the duty of summoning the Commons and their Speaker to the House of Lords (where he is responsible for the maintenance of order) when they are required to hear a speech from the throne, for example; other Gentlemen Ushers in attendance upon the Sovereign; the Constable and Deputy Constable of Windsor Castle; the Ecclesiastical Household (see below); the Marshal of the Diplomatic Corps (assisted by a Vice-Marshal), who is responsible for the ceremonial involved in the reception of foreign ambassadors; Lords in Waiting, who are called upon to carry out duties as occasion demands; the Serjeants-at-Arms; the Pages of Honour, who are youths who wait upon the Sovereign on state occasions; the Keeper of the Jewel House, Tower of London; the Master of the Queen's Music; the Poet Laureate; the Art Surveyors; the Bargemaster; and the Keeper of the Queen's Swans.

The Ecclesiastical Household consists of the Clerk of the Closet, usually a bishop, whose traditional duty it was 'to attend at the right hand of the Sovereign in the Royal Closet during Divine Service to resolve doubts concerning spiritual matters; the Deputy Clerk to the Closet; the Dean and Sub-Dean of the Chapels Royal; and a number of domestic chaplains and chaplains-in-ordinary. The chaplains-in-ordinary are not concerned solely with the court; they have a rota of attendance to conduct divine service and preach at royal chapels.

A chapel royal is a chapel attached to the court (historically it moved from place to place with the court), and is subject, not to the jurisdiction of a bishop but (in England) to that of the Dean of the Chapels Royal. There are chapels royal at St James's Palace, Hampton Court Palace and the Tower of London.

The Master of the Horse

The Master of the Horse is the third dignitary at Court. Formerly the holder of a powerful office, he now has charge of the Sovereign's stables, and is responsible for the provision of horses, carriages and motor cars required for processions and for the daily needs of the royal family. His duties are carried out day by day by his deputy – the Chief or Crown Equerry. The Master of the Horse rides immediately behind the Sovereign in state processions.

All equerries of the household – regular, extra, or honorary – are officers seconded from the armed services. There are usually two regular equerries, who have a continuing role of attendance, as one of them is always in waiting upon the Sovereign.

The Keeper of the Privy Purse and Treasurer to the Sovereign
The Keeper of the Privy Purse and Treasurer to the Sovereign deals with personal payments made from the Sovereign's private resources and with the payments of salaries and wages to the officers and servants of the Sovereign. His department consists of the Privy Purse Office.

The Private Secretary
The post of Private Secretary, which lapsed in 1688, was revived by King George III in 1805, and has been held continuously ever since. As a rule each Sovereign appoints his own secretary. The Private Secretary, helped by a Deputy and an Assistant Private Secretary, deals with all the correspondence between the Queen and her ministers, whether of the British or other Commonwealth governments. Government appointments for which the Queen's approval is required go to the Queen through her private Secretary. The Secretary is also concerned with the Queen's speeches, messages and private papers, and is responsible for her engagements, both in the United Kingdom and overseas, for the office of the Press Secretary and for the royal archives.

Other Appointments
The Mistress of the Robes is the senior lady of the Queen's Household, and is usually a duchess. She is responsible for arranging the rota for the Ladies in Waiting. She is in attendance on the Queen on state occasions, and sometimes accompanies her on important state visits abroad. Through many reigns the appointment was entirely political, and at one time the Mistress of the Robes was an important person in national politics. Nowadays the appointment is of no political significance, and the Queen names whom she pleases. The Ladies in Waiting, who are on duty daily in rotation, attend upon the Queen when she goes out in public, deal with her private correspondence and undertake personal services.

The two Ladies of the Bedchamber are usually the wives of earls. They attend the Queen on the more important public occasions, but they do not go into waiting regularly. There is also an extra Lady of the Bedchamber who occasionally attends upon the Queen.

The four Women of the Bedchamber, who take turns for

a fortnight at a time, attend the Queen on all public and semi-private engagements, make arrangements of the more personal kind, do shopping and make inquiries about people who are ill. They also deal with the Queen's private correspondence and reply to letters about her children and all letters written to her by children. There are also three extra Women of the Bedchamber who are in waiting occasionally.

The Palace Steward is the head servant in the Royal Household and is responsible for the work of all the male servants. Others associated with the Royal Household are the Sovereign's Aides-de-Camp, who are appointed from the naval, military and air forces, and Her Majesty's Representative at Ascot, who has a number of duties in respect of Royal Ascot, including the supervision of the issue of tickets for the Royal Enclosure.

Kings, Heralds and Pursuivants of Arms

The Corporation of the College of Arms in England and Wales is a corporation of thirteen members – three Kings of Arms, six Heralds and four Pursuivants. All these are members of the royal household, appointed by the Crown, by letters patent under the Great Seal, on the nomination of the Earl Marshal. The history of the heralds as members of the household goes back to the thirteenth century, but they were not constituted into a corporation until 1484, and the present corporation dates from 1555.

Royal Bodyguards and Household Troops

The practice of maintaining bodyguards round the person of the Sovereign is of great antiquity. It is said to have been introduced into England by King Canute (1016–35), and it is certain that for many centuries reigning monarchs were surrounded by specially chosen bands of noblemen and retainers whose duty it was to protect the royal person and to see that the royal will was obeyed.

The passage of time has brought about many changes in the status and organisation of the royal bodyguards as well as in their duties. At present they are divided into two groups. To the first belong the non-combatants-at-Arms; the Yeomen of the Guard; and, in Scotland, the Royal Company of Archers. To the second belong those regiments of the Regular

Army which have the special duty of guarding the Sovereign and the metropolis of London: the Household Cavalry and the Foot Guards.

The Gentlemen-at-Arms

The Honourable Corps of Gentlemen-at-Arms is termed the 'nearest guard' since it is (and from its inception always has been) the guard in the closest personal attendance upon the Sovereigns of England. It was created in 1509, and was composed of 'young nobles gorgeously attired'. It was reorganised in 1539, but did not acquire its present designation until the reign of King William IV (1830–37).

In its early days the guard took part in a number of battles and won honour on the field, notably at the Battle of the Spurs (1513). Its principal function, however, was to attend the person of the Sovereign both within the precincts of the Court and on all occasions of state ceremonial, and it has continued to discharge this duty ever since. Today, the corps is under the administrative control of the Lord Chamberlain; it attends the Sovereign on all state occasions, and is present at many palace functions.

The present strength of the Honourable Corps of Gentlemen-at-Arms is 28 Gentlemen, and four officers. The Gentlemen have all been officers of the Army or Royal Marines. All appointments to the Honourable Corps are made by the Sovereign, from whom the officers receive their sticks, the Captain's appointment being upon ministerial advice, those of the others by the Sovereign's prerogative.

The Yeomen of the Guard

The Yeomen of the Guard form a permanent military corps which has been in attendance on the Sovereign for more than 450 years. While the corps is the oldest established royal bodyguard and military corps in the world, some remnants of an even older corps exist in the persons of the Serjeants-at-Arms – royal household officials on duty in the Houses of Parliament, and on ceremonial occasions in attendance on the Sovereign. The present duties of the guard are for the most part purely ceremonial. They include attendance on guard at the reception of foreign dignitaries and heads of state; at state banquets; at state balls and gala operas; at the ceremony of the distribution of Maundy money on Maundy Thursday in Westminster Abbey (a ceremony first attended by the Yeomen of the Guard in 1486); at the Epiphany offerings of gold, frankincense and myrrh in the Chapel Royal, St James's Palace; at Westminster Hall during a royal lying-in-state; and at the searching of the vaults of the Houses of Parliament at the opening of each session – a duty dating from the Gunpowder Plot of 1605, when Yeomen of the Guard seized Guy Fawkes and others of his fellow-conspirators and conveyed them to the Tower of London.

The nickname 'Beef-Eaters', which is sometimes associated with the Yeomen of the Guard, had its origin in 1669, when Count Cosimo, Grand Duke of Tuscany, was in England and, writing of the size and stature of 'this magnificent body of men', said: 'They are great eaters of beef, of which a very large ration is given them daily at the Court, and they might be called beef-eaters'.

The Royal Company of Archers

The earliest written records of the Royal Company of Archers date from 1676, when it was called His Majesty's Company of Archers. Towards the end of 1704 a charter was granted to the Company by Queen Anne and the Royal Company still exists under that charter. During the royal visit to Edinburgh of King George IV in 1822, the Royal Company was granted the honour of becoming the King's Body Guard for Scotland.

The Household Cavalry

The Household Cavalry comprises the Life Guards and the Blues and Royals (the latter regiment was created in 1969 by the amalgamation of the Royal Horse Guards (the Blues) and the Royal Dragoons). It provides a tank regiment and an armoured car regiment, with one mounted squadron from each regiment for state duties in London.

Their state duties – the daily mounting of the Queen's Life Guard at Horse Guards, Whitehall, and escorts for the Queen on ceremonial occasions – are carried out by the two mounted squadrons stationed at Hyde Park Barracks. These squadrons are part of (and known as) the Household Cavalry Regiment (Mounted).

On state occasions the Colonels of both the Life Guards

and the Blues and Royals carry out the office of Goldstick, created in 1678 because of public concern for the safety of King Charles II. It was ordered that one of the King's captains should attend on foot near him carrying an ebony staff or truncheon with a gold head engraved with the royal cipher and crown, and that another principal officer carrying an ebony staff with a silver head should wait near the captain and relieve him when necessary. Nowadays on ceremonial occasions the latter office, known as Silverstick, is performed by the Lieutenant-Colonel commanding the Household Cavalry.

The Foot Guards

The Foot Guards, like the Household Cavalry, are Household Troops and consist of five regiments: the Grenadier Guards, raised in 1656 from officers and men who had remained loyal to the royalist cause; the Coldstream Guards, originally formed by Cromwell from companies of the New Model Army, but later taking up arms in the service of the royalist cause and helping to restore the monarchy; the Scots Guards, re-formed in 1660 from a regiment raised in 1642 by the Marquis of Argyll; the Irish Guards, raised in 1900 at the instigation of Queen Victoria; and the Welsh Guards, raised by order of King George V in 1915.

Appendix 2
The Queen's Travels

Overseas visits made by the Queen since her accession, with the Duke of Edinburgh (omitting private visits)

1953–4 *Commonwealth* tour to *Bermuda, Jamaica, Fiji, Tonga, New Zealand, Australia, Ceylon, Uganda, Malta, Gibraltar.*

1955 State visit to *Norway* (June).

1956 Three-week tour of *Nigeria* January/February.

State visit, with the Duke of Edinburgh, to *Sweden* from 8 to 10 June. After the state visit they were joined by Princess Margaret and the Duke of Gloucester and stayed privately for a further week to attend the equestrian events of the Olympic Games.

1957 State visit to *Portugal* in February.

State visit to *France* in April.

State visit to *Denmark* in May.

Visit to *Canada* and the *United States* in October.

On 14 October the Queen opened the 23rd Canadian Parliament, the first Sovereign to open the Canadian Parliament in person. From 16 to 21 October the Queen and the Duke visited the *United States*, during which the Queen addressed a special meeting of the United Nations General Assembly in New York.

1958 State visit to the *Netherlands* in March.

1959 Six-week tour of *Canada* and visit to the *United States* June/July, during which the Queen opened the new St Lawrence Seaway and carried out a tour of *Canada*, visiting many outlying districts never seen by a reigning monarch.

1961 Six-week state visit January/March including visits to *Cyprus, India, Pakistan, Nepal, Iran* and *Turkey*.

State visit to *Italy* and the *Vatican* in May.

Visit in November/December to *Ghana, Sierra Leone, the Gambia* and *Liberia*.

1962 Visit to the *Netherlands* to attend celebrations of silver wedding anniversary of Queen Juliana and Prince Bernhard of the Netherlands.

1963 Tour of *New Zealand* and *Australia*, visiting *Fiji* en route, February/March.

1964 Visit to *Canada* for centennial celebrations in October commemorating visits of the Fathers of Confederation to Charlottetown and Quebec City.

1965 State visits to *Ethiopia* and *Sudan* in February.

State visit to the *Federal Republic of Germany* in May, including a visit to Berlin.

1966 *Caribbean* tour February/March.

State visit to *Belgium* in May.

1967 State visit to *Canada* for 100th anniversary of Confederation and visit to Expo 67.

Visited *Malta* in November – first state visit as sovereign to an independent Malta.

1968 State visits to *Chile* and *Brazil* in November, calling at Dakar, *Senegal*, on return journey.

1969 State visit to *Austria* in May.

1970 Tour of *Australia* and *New Zealand*, visiting *Fiji* and *Tonga* en route, in March/May, with Princess Anne, and accompanied by the Prince of Wales for part of the time.

Visit to *Canada* in July (to mark centenaries of North West Territories and Manitoba) with the Prince of Wales and Princess Anne.

1971 Visit in May to *Canada* with Princess Anne to attend the centennial celebrations of the province of British Columbia.

A state visit to *Turkey* in October, when the Queen, the Duke and Princess Anne were the guests of President and Mme Cevdet Sunay.

1972 Tour in February/March (with Princess Anne for part of the tour), to *Thailand, Singapore, Malaysia, Brunei*, the *Maldive Islands*, the *Seychelles, Mauritius* and *Kenya*.

State visit to *France* in May.

State visit to *Yugoslavia* in October.

1973 In July a visit to *Canada* (Ontario, Prince Edward Island, Saskatchewan and Alberta).

Visited *Canada* 30 July–4 August to attend meeting of the Commonwealth heads of Government in Ottawa.

Went to *Australia* in October to open Sydney Opera House.

1974 In January and February, after visiting the *Cook Islands* en route, tour of *New Zealand*, in the course of which the Queen and the Duke attended the Commonwealth Games. Subsequently in February to *Norfolk Island*, *New Hebrides*, *British Solomon Islands* and *Papua New Guinea*, and then tour of *Australia* where Her Majesty opened Parliament. (The Queen returned to London for the general election, while the Duke continued the tour into March.)

State visit to *Indonesia* in March, returning to Britain via *Singapore*.
Visit to *France* on 16 June to watch her filly Highclere run in the Prix de Diane at Chantilly.

1975 In February visited *Bermuda*, *Barbados* and *Bahamas*.

State visit to *Mexico* in February/March.

Visit to *Jamaica* in April during meeting of Commonwealth heads of Government.

State visit to *Japan* in May, also visiting *Hawaii*, *Guam* and *Hong Kong* en route.

1976 State visit to *Finland* in May.

One-day visit to *Bermuda* in July en route to the United States.

1976 State visit to the *United States* in July in connection with the bicentennial celebrations.

Went to *Canada* (Nova Scotia and New Brunswick) before opening and attending the Olympic Games in Montreal. Accompanied by Prince Andrew and, briefly, the Prince of Wales and Prince Edward (Princess Anne competed with the British team in the equestrian event).

State visit to *Luxembourg* in November.

1977 In February and March made Silver Jubilee tours of *Western Samoa, Fiji, Tonga, Papua New Guinea, Australia* and *New Zealand*.

In July made a one-day visit to the *Federal Republic of Germany* for the Silver Jubilee review of the British Army at Sennelager.

In October made Silver Jubilee tours of *Canada* (Ottawa area only), *Bahamas, Antigua, British Virgin Islands* and *Barbados*.

1978 In May made a state visit to the *Federal Republic of Germany*, including visits to Bonn, Mainz, Berlin, Bremerhaven and Bremen.

Visited *Canada* (including Newfoundland, Saskatchewan and Alberta), from 26 July to 6 August, and attended the Commonwealth Games.

1979 In February visited *Saudia Arabia, Kuwait, Bahrain, Qatar*, the *United Arab Emirates* and *Oman*.

In May made a visit to *Denmark*, including visits to Copenhagen, Fredensborg, Aarhus and Helsingör.

In July and August made state visits to *Tanzania, Malawi, Botswana* and *Zambia*.

In October was present at a dinner party at the

Elysée palace given for Her Majesty by the President of *France*, after a private visit to Beaune and the châteaux of the Loire.

1980 In April and May made a state visit to *Switzerland*.

In May visited *Australia* (Canberra, Sydney and Melbourne).

In October made state visits to *Italy*, the *Vatican*, *Tunisia*, *Algeria* and *Morocco*.

In November visited the European Commission in *Belgium* and the North Atlantic Treaty Organisation.

In December visited the *Federal Republic of Germany* to inspect the 1st Battalion of the Royal Welsh Fusiliers.

1981 In May made a state visit to *Norway*.

In September and October visited *Australia* (Melbourne, at the time of the Commonwealth heads of Government meeting, Sydney, Hobart, Perth and Adelaide) and *New Zealand* (Christchurch, Wellington and Auckland).

In October made a state visit to *Sri Lanka*.

1982 In April visited *Canada* for the Patriation Ceremony in Ottawa.

In October visited *Australia* (attending the Commonwealth Games at Brisbane), *Papua New Guinea*, *Solomon Islands*, *Nauru*, *Kiribati*, *Tuvalu* and *Fiji*.

1983 In February and March visited *Jamaica*, *Cayman Islands*, *Mexico*, the *United States* (the West Coast) and *Canada* (British Columbia).

In May made a state visit to *Sweden*.

In November made state visits to *Kenya, Bangladesh* and *India* (New Delhi, at the time of the Commonwealth heads of Government meeting, Hyderabad and Pune).

1984 In March made a state visit to *Jordan*.

On 6 June visited *France* to attend ceremonies in Normandy to mark the fortieth anniversary of the Allied Landings (D-Day).

Visited *Canada* from 24 September to 7 October (New Brunswick, Ontario and, after the return of the Duke of Edinburgh on 4 October, Manitoba).

1985 In March made a state visit to *Portugal*.

In July made a one-day visit to the *Federal Republic of Germany* to visit the Royal Tank Regiment at Sennelager.

Visited *Belize* from 9 to 11 October without the Duke of Edinburgh; from 11 to 18 October visited the *Bahamas* at the time of the Commonwealth heads of Government meeting and was joined by the Duke on 16 October. From 23 to 27 October made one-day visits to *Saint Christopher and Nevis, Antigua, Dominica, Saint Lucia* and *Saint Vincent and the Grenadines*. Visited *Barbados* from 28 to 29 October, *Grenada* on 31 October and *Trinidad and Tobago* from 1 to 3 November.

1986 Made a state visit to *Nepal* from 17 to 21 February.

Visited *New Zealand* from 22 February to 2 March.

Visited *Australia* from 2 to 13 March (Australian Capital Territory, New South Wales, Victoria and

South Australia on the occasion of its 150th anniversary).

Made a state visit to the *People's Republic of China* from 12 to 18 October and visited *Hong Kong* from 21 to 23 October.

1987 Visited the *Federal Republic of Germany* from 26 to 27 May in connection with the 750th anniversary celebrations of Berlin.

Visited *Canada* from 9 to 24 October (British Columbia at the time of the Commonwealth heads of Government meeting, Saskatchewan and Quebec).

1988 Visited *Australia* from 19 April to 10 May (Western Australia, Tasmania, Victoria, Queensland, New South Wales and Australian Capital Territory) in connection with the country's bicentenary celebrations.

Visited the *Netherlands* from 4 to 6 July in connection with the William and Mary tercentenary celebrations.

Made a state visit to *Spain* from 17 to 21 October.

1989 In March visited *Barbados* in connection with the 350th anniversary of the Barbados Parliament.

In October made state visits to *Singapore* and *Malaysia* (Kuala Lumpur, at the time of the Commonwealth heads of Government meeting).

1990 Visited *New Zealand* (including Auckland, Wellington and Christchurch) in connection with the Commonwealth Games and the celebration of the 150th anniversary of the Treaty of Waitangi.

Bibliographical and Source Notes

'That which I know which is interesting, I can't tell,' said Dr David Owen to the author, 'and that which I know and can tell is either boring or will sound sycophantic.' Like all government ministers Dr Owen, a former Foreign Secretary and by virtue of that appointment a lifelong member of the Privy Council, is bound by the code of confidentiality which surrounds government business, and especially matters relating to the Crown. Matters relating to the government and the monarchy are immediately covered by the 30 year rule, which means that documents relating to the royal family which have come before the Cabinet or any other government department will not be revealed for thirty years. Even then, there are times – many times – when the subject matter is considered so sensitive or delicate that the government of the day slaps a further secrecy order on the file. The author, for example, discovered that there at least twenty-seven 'closed' files at the Public Records Office at Kew relating to the royal family which came before the Cabinet or government offices between 1952 and 1960; some are to remain secret for fifty, but most are marked 'Closed for 100 years'. I have been able to glean an insight into some of these matters with research elsewhere and putting together the pieces of the jigsaw gleaned from memoirs and other writings. Apart from the 'official' secrecy surrounding the Crown, and the fact that ministers and members of the household are bound 'not to tell', the Queen has always been surrounded by a loyal band of courtiers who quite rightly keep her secrets, too. Thus, this work is largely devoid of gossip and trivia. For research for this and previous works on which I have now gathered substantial files, I have drawn from numerous interviews, searches of archives and collections of papers and diaries and published works in Britain, America, Australia and European centres over a period of several years.

At the Public Records Office at Kew, I have drawn on the papers of the following: Clement (later Lord) Attlee under the Prem 4 and Prem 8 series; Sir Winston Churchill, prem 8 and prem 11; Sir Anthony Eden (later Lord Avon), Prem 4, 8, 11, Foreign Office 371 and 954 series, the Avon papers, FO 954; Harold Macmillan (later Lord Stockton), Prem 11, Foreign Office, Dominions Office, plus consultation of his memoirs and biographical works. General Cabinet papers, letters and conclusions to 1960, under the PRO reference CAB 65, 128 and 129 series; general Foreign Office under 115 series, Dominions Office; Colonial Office and War Office files where applicable; the Bevin Papers, FO 800 series; Halifax Papers, FO 800; Captured Documents on German Foreign Policy, Series 'C' and Series 'D', selected volumes; the Lord Beaverbrook Papers, House of Lords; papers of the Duke de Grantmesnil (at Hoover Institute and handed to me personally); Sir Robert Menzies, papers and Cabinet reports, Canberra and memoirs; John G. Diefenbaker, papers, Public Archives, Canada, plus memoirs; the Federal Bureau of Investigation, Washington DC, Duke of Windsor General File, released to me on request under Freedom of Information Act, in August 1990, and FBI 'Blunt, Anthony', two files; National Archives, Washington DC, 800 code; Roosevelt Library, New York; President Eisenhower (papers and letters), Dwight D. Eisenhower Library, Abilene.

General published diaries and memoirs consulted include those of Sir Robert Bruce Lockhart, Sir Harold Nicolson, Sir Noël Coward, Cecil Beaton, Lord Stockton, Lord Avon, the Earl of Harewood, Cecil King, Tony Benn, Hugh Dalton, Richard Crossman, Lord Callaghan, Group Captain Peter Townsend, Lord Wilson, Lord Hailsham, Sir John Colville and others covered by specific mention in source notes and bibliography.

Bibliography

Acland, Eric, *The Princess Elizabeth*, Winston, Canada, 1937.
Airlie, Mabel, Countess of, *Thatched with Gold*, Hutchinson, London, 1962.
Alexandra of Yugoslavia, ex-Queen, *Prince Philip: A Family Portrait*, Hodder & Stoughton, London, 1969.
Allen, Robert and Frost, John, *The Daily Mirror*, World Press, London, 1981.
Asquith, Lady Cynthia, *The King's Daughters*, Hutchinson, London, 1937.
Avon, Lord, *The Memoirs of the Rt Hon. Anthony Eden*, 3 vols, Vol. 1, *Full Circle*, Vol. 2, *Facing the Dictators*, Vol. 3, *The Reckoning*, Cassell, London, 1960, 1962 and 1965.
Bagehot, Walter, *The English Constitution*, 1st edn, London, 1867.
Benn, Tony, 4 vols, Vol. 1, *Out of the Wilderness 1963–67*, Vol. 2, *Office Without Power 1968–72*, Vol. 3, *Against the Tide 1973–76*, Vol. 4, *Conflicts of Interest 1977–80*, Hutchinson, London, 1986–90.
Bloch, Michael, *Operation Willi*, Weidenfeld & Nicolson, London, 1984; *The Secret File of the Duke of Windsor*, Bantam, London, 1989.
Boothroyd, Basil, *Philip: an informal biography*, Longman, London, 1971.
Bryan, J. and Murphy, Charles J. V., *The Windsor Story*, Granada, London, 1979.
Callaghan, James, memoirs, *Time and Chance*, Collins, London, 1987.
Carrington, Lord, memoirs, *Reflect on Things Past*, Collins, London, 1988.
Cathcart, Helen, *The Queen Herself*, W. H. Allen, London, 1975.
Churchill, Sarah, *Keep on Dancing*, Weidenfeld & Nicolson, London, 1981.
Clark, Brigadier Stanley, *Palace Diary*, Harrap, London, 1958.
Colville, John, *The Fringes of Power: Downing Street Diaries*, Vol. 1, *1939–55*, Vol. 2, *1941–1955*, Hodder & Stoughton, London, 1985 and 1987.
Cordet, Helene, *Born Bewildered*, Peter Davies, London, 1988.

Costello, John, *Mask of Treachery*, Collins, London, 1988.
Coward, Noël, *Noël Coward Diaries*, ed. Sheridan Morley and Graham Payn, Weidenfeld & Nicolson, London, 1982.
Crosland, Susan, *Tony Crosland*, Sphere edn, London, 1983.
Crossman, Richard, *Diaries of a Cabinet Minister*, Jonathan Cape and Hamish Hamilton, London, 1975.
Dalton, Hugh, *The Political Diaries of Hugh Dalton*, ed. Ben Pimlott, Jonathan Cape, London, 1986.
Dempster, Nigel, *HRH the Princess Margaret: A Life Unfulfilled*, Quartet Books, London, 1981.
Diefenbaker, John G., *One Canada, Memoirs of the Rt Hon. John G. Diefenbaker*, Macmillan, Toronto, 1977.
Dimbleby, Jonathan, *Richard Dimbleby: a Biography*, Hodder & Stoughton, London, 1975.
Eden, Anthony, *see* Avon, Lord.
Edinburgh, HRH Duke of, *Down to Earth*, Collins, London, 1989.
Evans, Harold, *Good Times Bad Times*, Weidenfeld & Nicolson, London, 1983.
Everingham, Barry, *Marie-Christine, Maverick Princess*, Bantam Press, London, 1985.
Fisher, Graham and Fisher, Heather, *The Queen's Travels*, Robert Hale, London, 1987.
Foot, Michael, *Aneurin Bevan*, Vol. 2, Paladin, London, 1975.
Gilbert, Martin, *Never Despair*, Heinemann, London, 1988.
Grigg, John, *Lloyd George, the People's Champion*, Methuen, London, 1978.
Hailsham, Lord, *A Sparrow's Flight*, Collins, London, 1990.
Harewood, Earl of, *The Tongs and the Bones*, Weidenfeld & Nicolson, London, 1981.
Hastings, Selina, *Nancy Mitford*, Hamish Hamilton, London, 1985.
Hatch, Alden, *The Mountbattens*, W. H. Allen, London, 1966.
Hibbert, Christopher, *The Court at Windsor*, Longman, London, 1964.
Horne, Alistair, *Macmillan 1894–1956*, Macmillan, London, 1988.
Hough, Richard, *Edwina, Countess Mountbatten of Burma*, Weidenfeld & Nicolson, London, 1980.

Howard, Anthony, *RAB, the Life of R. A. Butler*, Jonathan Cape, London, 1987.
Knightley, Philip and Kennedy, Caroline, *An Affair of State*, Jonathan Cape, London, 1987.
Lockhart, Sir Robert Bruce, *The Diaries of Sir Robert Bruce Lockhart*, ed. Kenneth Young, Macmillan, London, 1959.
Longford, Elizabeth, *The Queen: The Life of Elizabeth II*, Alfred Knopf, New York, 1983.
Macmillan, Harold, memoirs, 4 vols, Vol.1, *Tides of Rising Fortune 1945–55, Vol.2* , *Riding the Storm 1956–59*, Vol. 3, *Pointing the Way 1959–61*, Vol. 4, *At the End of the Day 1961–63*, Macmillan, London, 1969, 1971, 1972 and 1973.
Martin, Kingsley, *The Crown and the Establishment*, Hutchinson, London, 1962.
Martin, Ralph G., *Charles and Diana*, Grafton Books, London, 1986.
Menkes, Suzy, *The Royal Jewels*, Grafton Books, London, 1986.
Menzies, Sir Robert, memoirs, *Afternoon Light*, Cassell, London, 1967.
Moran, Lord, *Winston Churchill: The Struggle for Survival*, Constable, London, 1966.
Morrah, Dermot, *To Be a King*, Hutchinson, London, 1968.
Mortimer, Penelope, *Queen Elizabeth: A Life of the Queen Mother*, Viking, London, 1986.
Morton, Andrew, *Theirs Is The Kingdom*, Michael Joseph, London, 1989.
Nicolson, Harold, *Diaries and Letters 1930–64*, Collins, London, 1980.
Nicolson, Harold, *King George V*, Constable, London, 1952.
Parker, Eileen, *Step Aside for Royalty*, Bachman & Turner, London, 1982.
Parker, John, *Prince Philip*, Sidgwick & Jackson, London, 1990.
Pearson, John, *The Ultimate Family*, Michael Joseph, London, 1986.
Pope-Hennessy, James, *Queen Mary*, Allen & Unwin, London, 1959.
Reagan, Nancy, *My Turn*, Weidenfeld & Nicolson, London, 1989.

Rhodes James, Robert, *Anthony Eden*, Weidenfeld & Nicolson, London 1989.
Ribbentrop, Joachim von, *Memoirs*, trans. Oliver Watson, Weidenfeld & Nicolson, London, 1954.
Sampson, Anthony, *The Changing Anatomy of Britain*, Hodder & Stoughton, London, 1982.
Schellenberg, Walter, *Memoirs*, André Deutsch, London, 1956.
Soames, Mary, *Clementine Churchill*, Cassell, London, 1979.
Sunday Times, *Book of Jubilee Year*, Michael Joseph, London, 1978.
Thornton, Michael, *Royal Feud*, Michael Joseph, London, 1985.
Thorpe, D. R., *Selwyn Lloyd*, Jonathan Cape, London, 1989.
Townsend, Peter, *Time and Chance: an autobiography*, Collins, London, 1978.
Vickers, Hugo, *Cecil Beaton, the Authorised Biography*, Weidenfeld & Nicolson, London, 1985.
Wheeler-Bennett, Sir John W., *King George VI: His Life and Reign*, Macmillan, London, 1958.
Wilson, Harold, *The Governance of Britain*, Weidenfeld & Nicolson and Michael Joseph, London, 1976.
Windsor, Duke of, *A King's Story*, Cassell, London, 1951.
Woodham-Smith, Cecil, *Queen Victoria*, Vol. 1, Hamish Hamilton, London, 1972.
Woolton, the Earl of, *The Memoirs of the Rt Hon. Earl of Woolton*, Cassell, London, 1959.
Young, Hugo, *One of Us*, Macmillan, London, 1989; References taken from Pan edn, London, 1990.
Ziegler, Philip, *Mountbatten*, Collins, London, 1985; *Edward VIII*, Collins, London, 1990.

Notes

Chapter 1

1 Brigadier Stanley Clark, *Palace Diary*, page 70.
2 PRO, Cabinet Conclusions, nos. 11/12, 'Secret', 6 February 1952, CAB 128/24.
3 PRO, Prem 11, general papers and letters, 51–64.
4 Mary Soames, *Clementine Churchill*, page 432.
5 Michael Foot, *Aneurin Bevan*, Vol. 2, page 349, note 2.

6 Lord Avon, *Full Circle*, page 40.
7 Philip Ziegler, *Mountbatten*, page 302.
8 Lord Beaverbrook Papers, Box 13, House of Lords.
9 James Pope-Hennessy, *Queen Mary*, page 619.
10 Sarah Churchill, *Keep on Dancing*, page 142.
11 Winston Churchill, speech to House of Commons, *Hansard*, 11 February 1952.
12 PRO, HO 486.
13 Ziegler, *Mountbatten*, page 509.
14 Michael Bloch, *The Secret File of the Duke of Windsor*, page 265.
15 *New York Times*, 8 February 1952.
16 *Southern Daily Echo*, 13 February 1952.
17 Bloch, *The Secret File*, page 265.
18 D. R. Thorpe, *Selwyn Lloyd*, page 162.
19 Writing in the *Daily Herald*, 7 February 1952.
20 PRO, Prem 11, papers and letters.
21 PRO, Cabinet Conclusions, 'Secret', 7 April 1952, C52.114. CAB 128.
22 Quoted from 'The Mountbatten Lineage: the Direct Descent of the Family of Mountbatten from the House of Brabant and the Rulers of Hesse, prepared for private circulation by Admiral of the Fleet, the Earl Mountbatten of Burma, KG, PC, GCB, GCSI, GCIE, GCVO, DSO, LLD, DCL, BSc', deposited at the British Museum.
23 *News Chronicle*, 18 February 1952.
24 Penelope Mortimer, *Queen Elizabeth: A Life of the Queen Mother*, page 237.
25 The Queen Mother, speech to the nation, 17 February 1952.
26 Description to author, recorded in *Prince Philip*, pages 142–3.
27 Helen Cathcart, *The Queen Herself*, page 146.
28 PRO, FO 371.
29 Clark, *Palace Diary*, page 79.
30 Hugo Vickers, *Cecil Beaton, the Authorised Biography*, page 359.
31 *Lancet*, June 1952.
32 The Queen, BBC radio broadcast, 15 December 1952.

Chapter 2

1 Robert Allen and John Frost, *The Daily Mirror*, page 59.
2 Lord Ardwick (John Beavan) writing in the *Manchester Guardian*, 30 May 1963.
3 Jennie Lee, MP, *Evening News*, 21 July 1953.
4 From *The Times*, 2 January 1953.
5 PRO, Cabinet Conclusions, 'Secret', 19 January 1953, CAB 128/24.
6 Basil Boothroyd, *Philip: an informal biography*, page 79.
7 Quoting from *London Evening News*, 10 February 1952.
8 Sir Alan Lascelles Papers, PRO, Prem 11.
9 Ardwick, *Manchester Guardian*, 30 May 1953.
10 Robert Rhodes James, *Anthony Eden*, page 358.
11 James Pope-Hennessy, *Queen Mary*, page 261.
12 Extracts from speech, 12 March 1953.
13 Extract from speech, 27 March 1953.
14 Quoting from *Sunday Express*, 4 February 1953.
15 PRO, Prem 11/2045.
16 *Daily Express*, 12 October 1952.
17 Group Captain Peter Townsend, *Time and Chance: an autobiography*, page 193.
18 ibid., page 198.
19 Lady Longford, *The Queen: the Life of Elizabeth II*, page 164.
20 Privately supplied information.
21 PRO, Cabinet Conclusions, 'Secret', 2 April 1953, CAB 128/26-7-(8).
22 Quoting Richard Dimbleby, from contemporary broadcast.
23 From *The Times*, 6 June 1953.
24 *Sunday People*, 14 June 1953.
25 Peter Townsend, *Time and Chance*, page 201.
26 Rhodes James, *Anthony Eden*, page 362.
27 Mary Soames, *Clementine Churchill*, page 432.
28 John Colville, *The Fringes of Power: Downing Street Diaries*, Vol. 2, page 669.
29 Letter from the Queen, 26 June 1952, quoted by Lord Moran, Churchill's doctor.
30 Sarah Churchill, *Keep on Dancing*, page 146.
31 Rhodes James, *Anthony Eden*, page 368.

32 PRO, Cabinet Conclusions, 'Secret', 11 November 1953, CAB 128/26-C183.

Chapter 3

1 Walter Bagehot, *The English Constitution*, page 108.
2 Noël Coward, *Noël Coward Diaries*, page 223.
3 PRO, Prem 11/244.
4 Duke of Windsor, *A King's Story*, page 133.
5 ibid.
6 Philip Ziegler, *Mountbatten*, page 515.
7 FBI, Windsor, Duke of, General File, released to author August 1990 from Office of FoI, Washington.
8 Hugh Dalton, *The Political Diaries of High Dalton*, page 602.
9 Lady Longford, *The Queen: The Life of Elizabeth II*, page 187.
10 John Colville, *The Fringes of Power: Downing Street Diaries*, page 706.
11 Robert Rhodes James, *Anthony Eden*, page 385.
12 Colville, *Fringes of Power*, page 706.
13 Longford, *Elizabeth II*, page 187.
14 PRO, Prem 11/2065.
15 ibid.
16 Longford, *Elizabeth II*, page 191.
17 Harold Nicolson, diaries, page 290.
18 ibid.
19 Coward, *Diaries*, page 244.
20 PRO, Cabinet Conclusions, 'Secret', CAB 128/27 C334-74-4.

Chapter 4

1 PRO. CO 1023.
2 Quoting from the Queen's speech.
3 Speech to nation, 17 February 1954.
4 Ralphe White, unpublished memoirs.
5 Malcolm Muggeridge, *New Statesman*, 20 July 1956.
6 John Pearson, *The Ultimate Family*, page 121.
7 Reader's questionnaire, *Reynolds News*, 12 November 1959.
8 Duke of Windsor, *A King's Story*, page 132.
9 Lord Avon, *Full Circle*, page 422.

10 *The Times*, 1 August 1956.
11 Avon, *Full Circle*, page 420.
12 PRO, SUEZ Files, plus Sir Anthony Nutting, quoted by Alistair Horne, *Macmillan*, page 428.
13 ibid., page 434
14 Lord Hailsham, *A Sparrow's Flight*, page 41.
15 Philip Ziegler, *Mountbatten*, page 546.
16 Noël Coward, *Noël Coward Diaries*, page 349.
17 Avon, *Full Circle*, page 539.
18 Quoting from an article, *Star Weekly*, January 1959.
19 Robert Rhodes James, *Anthony Eden*, page 600.
20 Anthony Howard, *RAB, the Life of R. A. Butler*, page 249.
21 *Sunday Pictorial*, 13 January 1957.
22 Horne, *Macmillan*, page 341.
23 Documents, 'Closed for 100 years', PRO, Prem 11, 1955–6, including File Nos. 1565, 1566, 1569–71.

Chapter 5

1 Interview, 5 February 1959.
2 John Parker, *Prince Philip*, page 185.
3 *Baltimore Sun*, 13 February 1957.
4 Ralphe White, unpublished memoirs.
5 Alexandra of Yugoslavia, *Prince Philip. A Family Portrait*, page 159.
6 White, unpublished memoirs.
7 *National and English Review*, August 1957.
8 Prince Philip, in Foreword to *Down to Earth*.
9 Philip Ziegler, *Mountbatten*, page 498.
10 Taped interview with Georges Sanegre, the Windsors' butler, June 1986.
11 Selina Hastings, *Nancy Mitford*, page 207.
12 Beaverbrook Papers, Box 13, House of Lords archives.
13 Sir Robert Bruce Lockhart, *The Diaries of Sir Robert Bruce Lockhart*, Vol. 11, page 755.
14 Duke of Windsor, 29 June 1957.
15 Noël Coward, *Noël Coward Diaries*, page 256.
16 Philip Ziegler, *Edward VIII*, page 553.
17 Michael Bloch, *The Secret File of the Duke of Windsor*, page 296.
18 Churchill Papers, quoted by Martin Gilbert, *Never Despair*, page 1227.

19 *National and English Review*, August 1957.
20 John Osborne, writing in *Encounter*, September 1957.
21 PRO, Prem 11, File No. 2067.

Chapter 6

1 Alexandra of Yugoslavia, *Prince Philip: A Family Portrait*, page 200.
2 Duke of Windsor, *A King's Story*, page 267.
3 Basil Boothroyd, *Philip*, page 48.
4 Tony Benn, diaries, *Conflicts of Interest 1977–80*, page 185.
5 Harold Nicholson, *Diaries*, page 342.
6 PRO, Prem 11, File No. 2064 (Board of Trade).
7 PRO, Prem 11, File No. 2067 (Board of Trade).
8 Helen Cathcart, writing in *Star Weekly*, 23 April 1961.
9 Hugo Vickers, *Cecil Beaton, the Authorised Biography*, page 437.
10 Alexandra, *Prince Philip*, page 210.
11 Beaverbrook Papers, Box 13, House of Lords archives.
12 R. A. Butler, memo to Macmillan; Macmillan Papers.
13 Anthony Howard, *RAB, the Life of R. A. Butler*, page 276.
14 Harold Macmillan memoirs, *Pointing the Way 1959–61*, page 161.
15 Howard, *RAB*, page 277.

Chapter 7

1 Philip Ziegler, *Mountbatten*, page 573.
2 Richard Hough, *Edwina, Countess Mountbatten of Burma*, page 119.
3 Quoting from *The Times*, leader, 27 February 1960.
4 Godfrey Smith, *Sunday Times*, 6 March 1960.
5 Hugo Vickers, *Cecil Beaton, the Authorised Biography*, page 436.
6 Noël Coward, *Noël Coward Diaries*, page 431.
7 Vickers, *Cecil Beaton*, page 438.
8 Harold Macmillan, memoirs, *Pointing the Way 1959–61*, page 30.
9 PRO, Prem 11, File No. 2035.
10 Statement authorised by the Queen, 11 April 1955.
11 PRO, Prem 11.

12 Hugh Gaitskell, Labour Party Conference, 3 October 1960.
13 Macmillan, *Pointing the Way*, page 457.
14 PRO, Prem 11.
15 Macmillan, *Pointing the Way*, page 464.
16 'Private and Confidential', Winston Churchill, letter to Macmillan, 19 October 1961.
17 PRO, CO 1023.
18 *London Review*, 1948, page 48.
19 *Hansard*, 13 November 1961.

Chapter 8

1 Ralphe White, unpublished memoirs.
2 Larry Adler, interview for the author, October 1989.
3 Lord Mountbatten, taped interview for Donald Zec, page 238.
4 Leonard Mosley, 25 February 1957 (*Daily Express*).
5 Quoting from *Observer* magazine, 14 November 1967.
6 Speech, 16 February 1963.
7 *Hansard*, 3 March 1963.
8 Noël Coward, *Noël Coward Diaries*, page 539.
9 *Hansard*, 5 June 1963.
10 *Hansard*, 30 June 1963.
11 As explained by Buckingham Palace press office, 17 June 1963.
12 Philip Knightley and Caroline Kennedy, *An Affair of State*, page 65.
13 Lord Hailsham, *A Sparrow's Flight*, page 438.
14 Harold Macmillan, memoirs, *At the End of the Day 1961–63*, page 503.
15 Hailsham, *A Sparrow's Flight*, page 356.
16 Alistair Horne, *Macmillan*, pages 4–5.
17 Quoted from Knox Cunningham's unpublished memoirs.
18 Anthony Howard, *RAB, the Life of R. A. Butler*, page 319.
19 D. R. Thorpe, *Selwyn Lloyd*, pages 378–9.
20 ibid.
21 Quoted by Lady Longford, *The Queen: The Life of Elizabeth II*, page 254.
22 Interview, *Panorama*, 14 November 1966.

23 ibid.
24 John Costello, *Mask of Treachery*, page 585.
25 Professor John Loftus, to the author.
26 Interview, October 1990.
27 Richard Crossman, *Diaries of a Cabinet Minister*, page 29.
28 ibid.

Chapter 9

1 Mary Soames, *Clementine Churchill*, page 505.
2 Noël Coward, *Noël Coward Diaries*, page 553 and author's visit to Firefly, Jamaica.
3 J. Bryan and Charles J. V. Murphy, *The Windsor Story*, page 528.
4 Duke de Grantmesnil to author.
5 Bryan and Murphy, *Windsor Story*, page 528.
6 Supreme Headquarters Allied Expeditionary Forces, April 1945, docs SHAEF entries, 254–80.
7 Frankfurt, 1947; Allied Denazification Tribunal; reports and papers for 19 December, sentence of Philip of Hesse.
8 'I'm glad I'm not German', Mountbatten to Prince Louis of Hesse, quoted by Philip Ziegler, *Mountbatten*, page 102.
9 Helen Cathcart, *The Queen Herself*, page 207.
10 ibid., page 209.
11 Hesse Castle plunderers, Military Court, Frankfurt, papers June 1946 to May 1947.
12 Privately supplied information.
13 Richard Crossman, *Diaries of a Cabinet Minister*, page 257.
14 ibid., page 593.
15 Interview, 20 April 1986.
16 Crossman, *Diaries*, page 368.
17 Alden Hatch, *The Mountbattens*, page 136.

Chapter 10

1 Description to author.
2 Earl of Harewood, *The Tongs and the Bones*, page 218.
3 The *Sunday Telegraph*, 15 January 1967.
4 The Queen to Lord Mountbatten, quoted in J. Bryan and Charles J. V. Murphy, *The Windsor Story*, page 531.

5 Taped interview with Georges Sanegre, the Windsors' butler, June 1986.
6 ibid.
7 *Daily Sketch*, 7 June 1967.
8 Speech by General de Gaulle, news tapes, 31 July 1967.
9 Tony Benn, Diaries, *Office Without Power 1968–72*, pages 38–9.
10 John Grigg, *Lloyd George, the People's Champion*, pages 303–4.
11 Dermot Morrah, *To Be a King*, jacket notes.
12 Neilson to Checketts; information supplied to author.
13 Richard Colville, interview, 13 December 1967.
14 Quoting the *Sunday Times*, 29 March 1981.
15 Cecil King to author, 29 March 1981.
16 Interview, 16 April 1981.
17 Cecil King's *Daily Mirror* leading article, 19 May 1968.
18 Philip Ziegler, *Edward VIII*, page 555.
19 ibid.
20 Privately supplied information.
21 *Hansard*, 11 November 1969.

Chapter 11

1 Lord Mountbatten, taped interview for Donald Zec.
2 John Pearson, *The Ultimate Family*, page 199.
3 Tony Benn, diaries, *Office Without Power 1968–72*, page 215.
4 William Heseltine, statement to press correspondents, 30 March 1970.
5 *Sydney Sunday Telegraph*, 6 April 1970.
6 Benn, diaries, *Office Without Power*, page 271.
7 ibid.
8 Quoting published extracts from diaries of Lady Alexandra Metcalf.
9 *New Statesman*, 28 May 1971.
10 Philip Ziegler, *Mountbatten*, page 684.
11 ibid.
12 Letter from John Colville, *The Times*, 9 June 1971.
13 Taped interview with Georges Sanegre, the Windsors' butler, June 1986.
14 ibid.
15 Benn, diaries, *Office Without Power*, pages 430–1.

16 The *Guardian*, 29 May 1971.
17 J. Bryan and Charles J. V. Murphy, *The Windsor Story*, page 555.
18 ibid.
19 Countess Romanones, interview, September 1987.

Chapter 12

1 Lady Longford, *The Queen: The Life of Elizabeth II*, page 291.
2 Queen's speech, 25 December 1972.
3 *Toronto Star* leader article, 23 July 1973.
4 Pierre Trudeau, speaking on Canadian radio, 23 July 1973.
5 Editorial, *Le Devoir*, Montreal, 7 August 1973.
6 *The Times*, London, 30 May 1973.
7 Interview for Press Association, 31 May 1973.
8 Interview, August 1980.
9 Interview for ITN/BBC, 10 November 1973.
10 Tony Benn, diaries, *Against the Tide 1973–76*, page 94.
11 11 January 1974.
12 Interview, 21 April 1986.
13 Benn, diaries, *Against the Tide*, page 74.
14 Privately supplied information.
15 Taped interview with Georges Sanegre, the Windsors' butler, June 1986.
16 Philip Ziegler, *Mountbatten*, page 681.
17 ibid.
18 From Duke de Grantmesnil to author, July 1987.

Chapter 13

1 British Information Services, Pamphlet R5526/77, page 14.
2 *Hansard*, 27 February 1975.
3 Quoting article, *New Yorker*, 4 April 1977.
4 H. G. Wells, letter to *The Times*, 17 April 1917.
5 Lord Wilson, in a special article for the *Sunday Express*, 5 June 1977.
6 Joe Haines, recollections to author.
7 ibid.
8 Recalled by Lord Wilson in interview, 21 April 1986.

9 Claim by William Hamilton, MP apprearing on *Hot Seat* television programme, 4 July 1980.
10 Nigel Dempster, *HRH the Princess Margaret: A Life Unfulfilled*, page 109.
11 Privately supplied information.
12 ibid.
13 Tony Benn, diaries, *Against the Tide 1973–76*, page 549.
14 Buckingham Palace press office statement, 19 March 1976.
15 To author, April 1991.
16 Description to author by one present, privately supplied information.
17 Vincent Mulchrone, reporting, *Daily Mail*, 21 April 1976.
18 Editorial, *Daily Mirror*, 21 April 1976.
19 Susan Crosland, *Tony Crosland*, pages 344–5.
20 ibid, page 351.

Chapter 14

1 Published extracts from the diary of King George V, 6 May 1935.
2 Signed article by Prince Philip, published in the *Director*, 18 January 1977.
3 ibid.
4 *Hansard*, 19 January 1977.
5 Keith Waterhouse column, *Daily Mirror*, 20 January 1977.
6 Editorial, *Sunday Telegraph*, 6 February 1977.
7 Tony Benn, diaries, *Conflicts of Interest 1977–80*, page 31.
8 Susan Crosland, *Tony Crosland*, page 344.
9 Interview, 12 February 1977.
10 Audrey Whiting, special article in *Sunday Mirror*, 5 December 1975.
11 Extract from Queen's speech, 7 June 1977.

Chapter 15

1 Dr Mervyn Stockwood, in special article entitled 'The Queen and her Church', *Evening Standard*, 28 October 1972.

2 Barry Everingham, *Marie-Christine, Maverick Princess*, page 24.
3 Privately supplied information.
4 Taped interview with Georges Sanegre, the Windsors' butler, June 1986.
5 Tony Benn, diaries, *Conflicts of Interest 1977–80*, page 187.
6 *Zambian Daily Mail*, 2 August 1979.
7 *The Times of Zambia*, 1 August 1979.
8 Hugo Young, *One of Us*, page 179.
9 *The Republican*, on Mountbatten's murder, 19 July 1979.
10 Philip Ziegler, *Mountbatten*, page 701.

Chapter 16

1 PRO: under the single Prem 11 reference alone at the Public Records Office, relating to Cabinet discussion concerning the royal family between 1952 and 1960, the author discovered there are at least 27 separate files which have been closed for 50 or 100 years.
2 Attorney John Loftus to author, October 1990.
3 ibid.
4 John Costello, *Mask of Treachery*, page 466.
5 FBI Files, 'Blunt' 65-5648, Washington.
6 FBI, 'Blunt' 100-73-37183-653, 31 July 1953.
7 FBI, 'Blunt', 16 March 1953, file no. and details blacked out.
8 Philip Ziegler, *Edward VIII*, page 550.
9 Historian A. J. P. Taylor in a special article for the *Sunday Express*, 2 February 1979.
10 Anthony Sampson, *The Changing Anatomy of Britain*, page 10.
11 Hugo Young, *One of Us*, page 239.
12 Quoted in Sampson, *Changing Anatomy*, page 47.
13 From information supplied to the author by two of those present.

Chapter 17

1 From John Nott's Defence Review, published 1981.
2 Hugo Young, *One of Us*, page 565.
3 *Hansard*, 9 February 1982.
4 From published evidence to the Franks Committee, set

up by Mrs Thatcher to look into the events leading up to the Falklands War.
5 Interview, August 1982.
6 Extracts from the Queen's speech, 27 May 1982.
7 Nancy Reagan, *My Turn*, page 251.
8 From published police reports.
9 Bow Street Magistrates Court, London, 19 July 1982.
10 Old Bailey, 23 September 1982.
11 *Hansard*, 12 July 1982.
12 The Kenneth Harris interviews, *Observer*, August 1980.
13 John Grigg, special article for the *Evening Standard*, 4 February 1982.
14 Edward Heath to author, May 1989.
15 Reagan, *My Turn*, page 262.
16 ibid.
17 Description by John Edwards who was on the tour for the *Daily Mail*.
18 Jan Harwood, 3 December 1983.
19 Description supplied by Christopher Buckland who was covering the conference for *Today* newspaper.

Chapter 18

1 Author present on Maxwell's arrival on executive floor of *Daily Mirror*, and wrote the headline, in the issue of 13 July 1984.
2 From Stephen Lynas, reporting from Malaysia for the *Daily Mail*, 31 March 1984.
3 Audrey Whiting, to author April 1991, and article, *Sunday Mirror*, 8 April 1984.
4 Recalled by Lord Wilson, 5 June 1977.
5 *Hansard*, 29 October 1985.
6 George Gale column, *Daily Express*, 30 December 1983.
7 Letter from Queen's secretary Sir William Heseltine, to pensioner John Holmes, 29 June 1984.
8 James Naughtie, writing in the *Guardian*, 22 July 1986.
9 Sir William Heseltine 'commanded to write' to *The Times*, letters page, 28 July 1986.
10 Dr Thomas Hewes, quoted in Paris, August 1982.
11 Taped interview with Georges Sanegre, the Windsors' butler, June 1986.

Chapter 19

1 Edward Heath to author, May 1989.
2 Princess Anne's speech to media gathering, 17 September 1986.
3 Joe Haines, special article for the *Sunday Mirror*, published 29 October 1986.
4 Interviewed by UK *Press Gazette*, 15 March 1987.
5 Prince Edward's interview with *Woman's Own*, 16 June 1987.
6 Interview, 24 October 1987.
7 *Hansard*, 29 October 1987.
8 Editorial in *Daily Telegraph*, 7 November 1987.
9 Mori Poll, 8 November 1987, published in the *Sunday Times*.
10 Extracts from Queen's speech, Malaysia, 18 October 1989.

Chapter 20

1 Cecil Woodham-Smith, *Queen Victoria*, Vol. 1, page 387.
2 Lord Lyndhurst memo, October 1984, Royal Archives, quoted by Woodham-Smith.
3 Queen Victoria's journal for 8 February 1845, quoted by Woodham-Smith.
4 Letter from the Queen's deputy private secretary, published in the *Daily Express*, 1 March 1991.
5 Report of the Commons Select Committee on the Civil List, 1971 on the Queen's finances. See also Appendix 1.
6 Tim O'Donovan, annual log of the royal family's engagements for the year, published in a letter to *The Times*, 4 January 1991.
7 Privately supplied information.
8 BBC *Newsnight* debate, Andrew Neil and Lord St John, 11 February 1991.
9 Interview, 18 September 1990.
10 Statement from Buckingham Palace in response to inquiry, 21 October 1990.

Acknowledgements

The publishers are grateful for permission to reproduce extracts from the following copyright sources:

Diaries of a Cabinet Minister by Richard Crossman, Hamish Hamilton;
Tony Crosland by Susan Crosland, Jonathan Cape;
Cecil Beaton: The authorised biography by Hugo Vickers, Weidenfeld and Nicolson;
The Noel Coward Diaries by Graham Payn and Sheridan Morley, Weidenfeld and Nicolson;
Tony Benn Diaries, Tony Benn, Jonathan Cape.

Index